RENEWALS 458-4574

DATE DUE

GAYLORD			PRINTED IN U.S.A.

Trustworthy Systems
Through Quantitative
Software Engineering

Trustworthy Systems Through Quantitative Software Engineering

Lawrence Bernstein
C. M. Yuhas

A John Wiley & Sons, Inc., Publication

Published by John Wiley & Sons, Inc., Hoboken, New Jersey
Published simultaneously in Canada

For general information on our other products and services or for technical support, please contact our Customer Care Department within the United States at (800) 762-2974, outside the United States at (317) 572-3993 or fax (317) 572-4002.

Wiley also publishes its books in a variety of electronic formats. Some content that appears in print may not be available in electronic formats. For more information about Wiley products, visit our web site at www.wiley.com.

Library of Congress Cataloging-in-Publication Data:

Bernstein, Lawrence, 1940–
    Trustworthy systems through quantitative software engineering /
Lawrence Bernstein, Christine M. Yuhas.
        p. cm.
    Includes bibliographical references and index.
    ISBN-13 978-0-471-69691-9 (cloth)
    ISBN-10 0-471-69691-9 (cloth)
    1. Software engineering. 2. Computer software—Reliability. I. Yuhas, C. M.
II. Title.
    QA76.758.B466 2005
    005.1—dc22

                                                                2005007007

Printed in the United States of America

10 9 8 7 6 5 4 3 2 1

To our sons, daughters-in-law, and grandson

Contents

12. The Final Project: By Students, For Students   **404**

INDEX   **429**

Preface

This book advances the idea that standard principles of good engineering, which have been honed through meticulous application, examination, revision, and refinement, should be practiced in creating trustworthy software. It provides the student/practitioner with structured experiences that teach the critical engineering skills needed to build reliable software products. Good practices are illustrated with case studies and elicited through practical projects that apply stresses common in the business world after which student responses and their logical consequences are examined. Quantitative analysis is applied to software engineering principles. The course based on this book is managed in a style modeled on industrial software development.

Lawrence Bernstein teaches in the Computer Science Department at Stevens Institute of Technology in Hoboken, NJ. For more than 30 years, until his retirement in 1996, he was a leading software executive and software project manager at Bell Laboratories. He has more than 40 years of experience in developing, managing, and teaching software. He saw that developers too often do not want to think about the downstream consequences of what they do. To the extent that we can teach a code of ethics, we can raise the quality of practice and reduce risks. This book confronts both new and experienced developers with the need for critical thinking during software development and for making those engineering tradeoffs that will make systems safe, secure, and reliable.

I HEAR AND I FORGET; I SEE AND I REMEMBER; I DO AND I UNDERSTAND (CONFUCIUS)

The aim is to give the student/practitioner the intellectual and teamwork skills needed to make practical engineering tradeoffs during product realization.

Too often, novice computer scientists jump into software development ignorant of proven tools, processes, and theory. Passing mention in a distant course lecture hardly suffices to impress how critical to project success are such practical tradeoffs. They learn from harsh on-the-job experience just how important it is to plan, measure, and assess each stage of development. This book captures these experiences and describes them in the context of real-life examples. Rather than preaching how important software engineering is and dwelling on the "Best Current Practices," the emphasis is instead on problem analysis, fitting the software engineering structure to the problem, and producing products that are on schedule, within budget, and satisfactory to the customer. The concepts of simplification, trustworthiness, risk assessment, and architecture are stressed.

Software engineering, as opposed to hacking, is a key feature of this text. Software engineering is the ability to make judgments based on measurements to structure and monitor the development of a software product. Engineering implies that limitations face the developer. In software, the issue of balancing feature content, schedule time, system performance, and cost face the project manager every day.

PERSPECTIVE STUDY

Two Stevens Institute of Technology professors examined the effects of the course described in this book. They conducted a perspective study of 150 students who took the course over a period of 3 years. Before beginning the course, naïve students were questioned concerning the use of software engineering methods and the acceptance of constraints. Approximately 60% voiced acceptance, which might have been colored by lack of experience and malleability, but 40% vigorously opposed the constraints of the process, perhaps dazzled by the glories of hacking. By the completion of the two-semester course, most students were competent to function in design teams of eight to ten people and to consistently apply the rigorous standards of engineering to software. Of those students initially opposed, only 10% remained opposed and opted to work in fields requiring small projects that would suit their solitary natures. A significant measure of the teaching technique's success was the ability of the students to find jobs in large companies during difficult economic times because of successful interviews. The students had mature answers to situations posed by interviewers and reported that the course gave them a differential advantage.

PREREQUISITES

The idea of project-based development drives the course. Assignments are structured so that fundamental software engineering practices are provided exactly when the need arises. The student begins to appreciate the need to go beyond the boundary of the small one-, two-, or three-person assignments that were used to teach programming. This book expects the reader to know programming and expands that perspective to include the real-world problems facing projects requiring 10 to 25 people a year. Larger projects exist, but they are not emphasized in this text.

It is important that software project teams consist of eight to ten students working together for one, one and a half, or two semesters. Some students and faculty object to this large size and long duration, but smaller projects do not help students learn to deal with the problems of communication, priority setting, risk assessment, and dealing with different personalities. On smaller projects, students tend to self-select people who are like themselves and thereby avoid conflicts.

METHOD

Students attempt a short initial project to experience the real-world environment. Then they work on a second project, longer in duration, that produces a useful software product employing the best current software practices. The practices show how the problems faced on the first project can be handled in a systematic way.

Many computer science, information technology, computer engineering, and software engineering courses require students to build a software product, but building a system out of individual little products is brushed by in theoretical steps only, with little emphasis on how to manage the product realization process. The complexity of project interactions is not emphasized. In this course, it is actively experienced.

Regrettably, students often are taught how to use tools but not how to make critical judgments about the appropriateness of when and where to use them. There are many software engineering tools. Projects can fail by running after the latest fad and therefore having no stability in their development environment. At the other extreme, projects become obsolete or too expensive when new tools are fearfully shunned. How a software engineer decides whether to adopt a tool is an important part of a software engineering education. UNIX and Linux operating systems, the C, C++ and JAVA languages, software tools that find memory leaks, fault tolerance, stress testing, regression testing, configuration management, change control, informal project meetings, prototyping, visual programming, and the Spiral Model constitute a brief litany of some that are successes. This book explains these and other tools and then provides the criteria for deciding whether to use them. Students are then competent to solve the inevitable problems they face developing a software product.

Supplemental materials are used in this course such as videotapes and current news summaries. These materials can be accessed through the publisher's website associated with this book.

AUDIENCE

Software professionals will refer to this book as a guide during their real-life projects. Experienced project mangers share the common experience of failure but do not often have the luxury of examining the causes that are common to failures. The novice does not yet have this experience. This book follows a logical path of increasing software engineering appreciation by the developer in contrast to the common style of following a prescribed theoretical software development process. It is not a complete compendium of all development theories, but it serves as the foundation to the entire quantitative software engineering series.

The emphasis of this book is on quantitative software engineering decision making. It is geared toward the student who wants to know the "why" as well as the "how." Successful completion of the course described in this book makes a software engineer valuable to a company both as a team member and as a manager of outsourced developments.

Overall, it is shocking how few of the available tools or software engineering practices are actually used in software project development. With marketing people currently in ascendance and controlling development budgets, there is no comprehension of the need to invest in tools and skills development. Software professionals under marketing pressures have neither the resources to grow nor to argue their cases effectively. Hope lies in the freshly educated engineers emerging from colleges and universities who are fluent in mathematics and programming and convinced by their own experience of the utility of new methods and tools. The systematic adoption of software engineering practices in industry requires that an appreciation of its importance be conveyed to computer science students.

THE SOFTWARE CRISIS

In the fall of 1968, NATO convened a meeting to confront a crisis that did not make the headlines—"the software crisis." Experts from a dozen countries, representing industrial laboratories as well as universities, met in Garmisch, Germany, to grapple with two basic questions that are still with us: Why is it so hard to produce functionally correct and reliable software that meets both users' needs and performance requirements and still comes in on time and within a projected budget? Where should software producers be looking for solutions? The answers revolved around "software engineering," a term coined by the organizers of the Garmisch conference—somewhat controversial at the time, and wholly inspirational—to focus on a missing discipline with the potential to resolve the crisis. Software production should be "industrialized." Systems should be built from reusable components. Development processes should be more systematic and predictable. The people who design, produce, and maintain software should be better equipped to do what engineers do: Make things that work to meet someone else's needs.

There have been significant advances. Programmers are better now, most code is written in high-level languages, better tools exist, development is done online, better design models exist, and standards have been established in some key areas. Several recently developed or recently successful innovations include object-oriented programming, client/server and thin client applications, application programming interfaces, graphical user interfaces and development tools, prototyping, and source-level debugging. Components exist and are widely used, which belies the common wisdom that software components are rare. The C libraries with all their richness of fundamental or atomic functions provide 20% reuse in most industrial strength UNIX-based applications. Software that makes a library of graphical elements, or a text-processing tool, available to multiple applications, with a major reservation, is also in wide use. IBM and others are using software libraries providing generic fault avoidance and recovery.

The industry has been much less successful in creating larger reusable components or "bricks" than in reusing some kinds of "mortar" to hold programs together—such as UNIX pipes and filters or object-oriented programming techniques. There have been significant advances in software process—in areas such as incremental development, inspection, change control, and testing—and in software tools such as test drivers, profilers, and configuration management.

These process advances have helped software producers gain ground on the elusive goal: timely, cost-effective development of reliable, user-friendly software. Yet as far as software research and development have come since 1968, there is still a long way to go, in part because progress in the field tends to have an amplified effect on rising expectations. The central problems discussed in Garmisch persist. Software design and production still do not resemble engineered industrial processes. Maybe they never will. Reuse is still an issue, more promise than practice. Complexity has been compounded by networking and distributed applications.

Like the problems, some of the most promising ideas and techniques have been around for a while. The idea of cleanly separating design intent from the method of implementation is a powerful one with a lot of mileage left in it. Modularity based on the Parnas concept of information hiding has been a key to progress in software and will continue to be applied broadly and on many levels. The idea of layered architectures—with software on one layer connecting to software on another—is a proven aid to interoperability in network systems and is working its way through all sorts of applications. Browsers are a familiar kind of layer that users see; platforms and middleware are typical uses of layered software behind the scenes. Domain engineering embodies key insights for large-scale software reuse: Think in terms of families of software components within a domain, and determine what common elements can be reused in several generations; develop reusable components and establish a process for using them to build new applications—new product line members—rapidly, efficiently, and with confidence in their reliability and performance. Experiences with domain engineering indicate that it could help software producers realize the promise of reuse.

All approaches to problems in software continue to benefit from program notation and formal methods, remedies that come from software's mathematical roots. Programming languages have long provided precise notations for specifying computations. There is movement toward the use of specifications to capture inter-relationships as well, which makes it easier to reason about the behavior of complex software such as distributed systems.

Complementary work emphasizes the human side of software engineering. An early insight repeatedly confirmed by experience is that development problems have as much to do with people as with technology. In programming languages, a trend exists toward more intuitive notations. Discovery tools such as data visualization can make it easier for members of a development team to get their heads around millions of lines of code. Another prime example of the human focus is the patterns discipline (sometimes called the patterns "movement" to distinguish it as an idea taking hold in a community). Developers are recording design insights and experience in "patterns"—more a literary form than a kind of documentation—each pattern capturing "a solution to a problem in a context." Collections of patterns that work together are said to form a "pattern language." The patterns discipline assumes that most knowledge needed to build and maintain a reliable system already resides in the development community. But people tend to move around, taking expertise with them, and projects can go on for a long time. Many developers must work with code that has been around longer than they have. That fact produces questions: What was the software architect's original intent? What lessons did the developers learn? How can I get inside the experts' minds?

It will be important to experiment with various software tools and practices to see how much better the technical solutions fare in concert with approaches that focus on the people who build the software systems.

WHO CAN PROFIT FROM THIS BOOK

This book presents the basic skills needed to apply these software technologies to the realization of software products on time, within budget, and with known quality. It is especially useful for those who must produce trustworthy software systems. It is geared toward several kinds of readers:

- The formally educated computer professional who aspires to a managerial career and wants comprehensive hands-on knowledge in the skills needed to identify customer requirements, develop software designs, manage a software development team, and evaluate the resulting software product relative to customer specifications.
- The formally educated computer professional who wants to remain an individual contributor, yet wants a solid foundation in the practical application of computer science technology to the realization of software products.

- The computer professional whose educational background is not in computer science or computer engineering, but who has learned software skills on the job and who now wants to begin to understand software engineering.
- The systems engineer and software project manager who wants to understand software engineering technology.
- The venture capitalist who wants to assess the likelihood of a software company's success.
- The CEO who finds software fundamental to the company's products and services.

The book may be used for a one- or two-semester undergraduate course in software engineering. The one-semester course should meet 3 hours/week for 14 weeks with weekly project meetings outside of class. Class meetings are for project presentations, presentation of case histories and technologies, and discussions. Each project presents a requirements review, an architecture and design review, a code and test review, and a final product demonstration. Weekly progress reports are suggested. Monthly updates to the development plans are helpful. If the instructor wishes to have the project meetings during scheduled class time and to provide time for a larger, more realistic and richer project experience, then a two semester sequence such as that used at Stevens is recommended. Intensive 6-day professional short courses can be tailored to specific needs.

THE ISSUE OF TRUSTWORTHINESS

Software trustworthiness, which refers to the attributes of reliability, security, and safety, is the next major area in which academia and industry must focus. Software trustworthiness is critical for medical devices, plant control systems, and weapon systems; for management of sensitive records; for critical infrastructure; for new accounting requirements; and for dependable cybersecurity. As practitioners of such a pervasive part of so many lives, we have a serious ethical responsibility. This course will help make you ready to assume your responsibility for trustworthiness in our young profession. Additional information is available on the publisher's website at ftp://ftp.wiley.com/public/sci_tech_med/trustworthy_systems.

LAWRENCE BERNSTEIN
Industry Research Professor
Stevens Institute of Technology
Hoboken, New Jersey

C. M. YUHAS
Freelance Writer
Short Hills, New Jersey

Acknowledgment

There is an Italian saying, "All roads lead to Rome." In writing this textbook, we became acutely aware that for much of the innovation in our field, all mental roads lead to Barry Boehm. We are grateful for his inspiration, his advice, and his friendship.

Part 1

Getting Started

1

Think Like an Engineer—Especially for Software

Software engineering as a discipline needs a sturdy underpinning of classic engineering principles and discipline. Societies depend on engineers to keep bridges from falling down, factories from exploding, and generally to protect us from our carelessness and ignorance. Software now drives much of our lives, so computer scientists need to accept the engineer's responsibility to produce something that will work reliably and protect human life and work. Engineers do pretty well now with the nuts and bolts of daily life, but that wisdom did not come cheaply. It was built up from thousands of individual experiences of success and analyses of failures, codified, and passed on to new people in the profession. Computer scientists can learn to be engineers in the same way, although our materials are less tangible and our constructs and stresses are measured in different ways.

It is possible to experience the principles and theories of quantitative software engineering in a controlled environment before applying them in a live business project. "Quantitative" is the operative word. Software engineering practices are designed to make the development of software less chaotic, reliably repeatable, and more humane, but unless there are specific measurements to apply, volumes of good practices would make better doorstops. Extraordinary people who are highly motivated can make any process work, but dream teams are rare and burning out talent is shortsighted, cruel, and expensive. Heroics in software development are an indication of process failure that leads to dysfunctional behavior in both organizations and

Trustworthy Systems Through Quantitative Software Engineering,
by Lawrence Bernstein and C. M. Yuhas
Copyright © 2005 IEEE Computer Society

individuals.[1] Worst of all, the resulting projects are difficult to maintain, difficult to upgrade, and the developers have little learning to bring to the next project.

We will use a model-based approach to software development. Models will be used to calibrate, bound, and validate your estimates. There will be cost-estimation tools, risk definition and analysis, and prototyping. System models and scenarios will produce test results with actual system performance. You will find problems and solutions, case studies, and "magic numbers" in each chapter. The latter are easy-to-remember rules gleaned from the experiences of people who have earned the right to call themselves engineers of software or from explanations of folklore whose meanings are buried in the mists of early computing.

1.1 MAKING A JUDGMENT

Engineering is a balancing act. When applied to software, the spinning plates are functions provided, time to produce, cost, and complexity. The fundamental software reliability equation is as follows:

$$\text{Reliability} = e^{-k\lambda t},$$

where k is a normalizing constant, λ is complexity/ effectiveness × staffing, and t is the time the software executes from its launch.

This model equation only approximates reality, but it is useful for making engineering tradeoffs if it is stipulated that software fails at a constant rate. It is reasonable, if unorthodox, to model the software engineering *process* based on this model. Field failure rates for IBM and Microsoft products show a constant failure rate 10 months after product release.[2]

The complexity factor incorporates the elements the software project manager controls through the development process. The software engineer might alter effectiveness by providing better software tools, such as higher level languages, to designers and thereby increase the reliability of the final product. By reusing reliable components, the software engineer reduces the complexity of the system, which again makes it more reliable. By adding staff beyond the minimum predicted by staffing models, more effort can be placed on such activities as diabolic testing and system audits in the interests of improving reliability.

---

[1] Yourdon, Edward. *Death March: The Complete Software Developer's Guide to Surviving "Mission Impossible" Projects*, Prentice Hall, Englewood Cliffs, NJ, 1997.
[2] Chillarege, Ram, et al. "Reflections on Industry Trends and Experimental Research in Dependability," *IEEE Transactions on Dependable and Secure Computing*, IEEE Computer Society, Vol. 1, No. 2, April–June 2004, Figure 5, www.computer.org.

The reliability equation is the framework for quantitative analysis and making tradeoffs. The software project manager must invest in these ongoing activities: measuring complexity, measuring effectiveness through investments in tools and technology, and measuring staffing requirements.

On your way through several approaches to software design, you will acquire a background in why systems fail and how to avoid failure with risk containment techniques. Topics include risk identification and analysis, designing for reliability, design simplification, and testability. The merits of top-down and bottom-up design are compared. Code reviews and inspections are used with static quality assessment techniques. Testing approaches include unit, integration, stress, reliability, and diabolic testing. Rapid prototyping, top-down, bottom-up, successive refinement, extreme programming, design constraints, and data abstraction are presented. You, the quantitative software engineer, are responsible for producing studies for each activity.

Optional organizational structures can help with ways to manage suppliers, determine span of control, identify key employees and retain them, examine staff churn, and conduct performance evaluations. The economic drivers of diminished defect leakage, earned value, and economic value-added can help to evaluate project viability. The capability maturity model for software (SW-CMM) was created in the early 1990s by the Software Engineering Institute at Carnegie Mellon University to gauge the sophistication and reliability of software products coming out of any given organization. When applied to an organization's methods of developing software, SW-CMM assigned a level of sophistication and reliability to the process and product ranging from a low of 1, initial; through 2, repeatable; 3, defined; 4, managed; to a high achieved at the time only by NASA of 5, optimized. Most organizations were rated only a 1. For most, level 3 was a sufficient goal.

In 2000, SW-CMM was upgraded to the capability maturity model integration (CMMI). CMMI is now being adopted worldwide, including North America, Europe, India, Australia, Asia Pacific, and the Far East to provide models for process improvement.

The CMMI best practices help organizations to more explicitly link management and engineering activities to business objectives. The product or service is the center of engineering activities to make sure it meets customer expectations. CMMI also encourages robust, high-maturity practices in areas such as measurement, risk management, and supplier management. Businesses are helped to comply more fully with relevant International Standards Organization (ISO) standards.

Because this is a quantitative book, occasionally there will be examples with solutions in addition to problems at the end of each chapter. Keeping in mind that, as Hamming remarked, "The purpose of computing is insight, not numbers,"[3] consider the ramifications of the following example.

[3] Hamming, Richard. *Numerical Methods for Scientists and Engineers*, McGraw-Hill, New York, 1962.

EXAMPLE:

A software system is designed so that after every hour of normal operation, it stops and relaunches from its initial state. This process is called software rejuvenation. Assume that the mean time to failure for the software is 10 hours and the mean time to repair is 5 minutes. Repair means restoring the software to an operating condition by relaunching it from its initial state.

What is the probability that the system fails within 30 minutes of operation? Note that e^x is approximately $(1 + x)$ for small x.

SOLUTION:

$R(30) = 1/e^{\{30/(10 \times 60)\}} = e^{-0.05}$ using the approximation, $e^x \cong 1 + x$ for small x, we get $R(30) = 0.95$, probability of failure $= 1 - R(30) = 0.05$. This means that there is a 5% chance that the software system will fail in its first 30 minutes of operation. Without doing the quantitative analysis, the software engineer would not understand the risks of releasing such buggy software.

1.2   THE SOFTWARE ENGINEER'S RESPONSIBILITIES

The software engineer uses critical judgment and analysis to make informed decisions. These decisions typically involve making engineering tradeoffs, but this analysis is meaningful only when supported by project data. You will learn a framework for exercising informed engineering on software products. Skilled software project managers produce systems that meet customers' needs within budget and on schedule. This framework captures, in a quantitative way, the thought processes of skilled managers. This approach uniquely weaves software engineering theory and case histories, quantitative analysis, and technology into the project effort.

This textbook models industrial software development. Teamwork and cooperation are encouraged. Teamwork is one of the hardest lessons for students because they have been schooled in competing for so long. Quantitative analysis is required. Knowledge of, and sensitivity to, software engineering ethics are stressed.

1.3   ETHICS

The ethical software engineer makes sure that a product solves the customer's problem, that it is tested, that good software engineering practices are used in its development, and that any limitations of the product are clearly stated.

Professions are defined by the willingness of their practioners to establish and abide by a code of ethics. Human nature being variable as it is, meaningful disciplinary action is necessary to make ethics stick. There is currently no penalty for software engineers who are unethical, but new laws may change this. What follows is the ratified ACM/IEEE-CS Joint Task Force on Software Engineering Ethics and Professional Practices (Reprinted by permission). It defines the minimum behavior one must exhibit to be truly professional.

ACM/IEEE Software Engineering Code of Ethics and Professional Practice (Short Version)

PREAMBLE

The short version of the code summarizes aspirations at a high level of the abstraction; the clauses that are included in the full version give examples and details of how these aspirations change the way we act as software engineering professionals. Without the aspirations, the details can become legalistic and tedious; without the details, the aspirations can become high sounding but empty; together, the aspirations and the details form a cohesive code.

Software engineers shall commit themselves to making the analysis, specification, design, development, testing and maintenance of software a beneficial and respected profession. In accordance with their commitment to the health, safety and welfare of the public, software engineers shall adhere to the following Eight Principles:

1. PUBLIC—Software engineers shall act consistently with the public interest.

2. CLIENT AND EMPLOYER—Software engineers shall act in a manner that is in the best interests of their client and employer consistent with the public interest.

3. PRODUCT—Software engineers shall ensure that their products and related modifications meet the highest professional standards possible.

4. JUDGMENT—Software engineers shall maintain integrity and independence in their professional judgment.

5. MANAGEMENT—Software engineering managers and leaders shall subscribe to and promote an ethical approach to the management of software development and maintenance.

6. PROFESSION—Software engineers shall advance the integrity and reputation of the profession consistent with the public interest.

7. COLLEAGUES—Software engineers shall be fair to and supportive of their colleagues.

8. SELF—Software engineers shall participate in lifelong learning regarding the practice of their profession and shall promote an ethical approach to the practice of the profession.

These goals are exemplary, but in the rough and tumble of business, they can be overruled in the interests of expediency. Customers, as half of the partnership, must insist that every product have a named software architect and software project manager to assign responsibility specifically and to have a firm point of control. The same person may perform both roles.

The software architect affirms that the software product solves the customer's problem; affirms that the software product is suitably reliable, easy-to-use, extendible, not harmful, and robust; and affirms that the requirements are valid.

The software project manager affirms that the software was successfully tested against the requirements; affirms and identifies that good software engineering processes were used in the software development and integration; and affirms that the project is within budget, on time, and performs satisfactorily.

Case Study[4]: The Case of the Sacrosanct Date

You are a successful project manager. The boss of the boss of your boss wants you to assume the management of a project in deep trouble. It is a mission-critical, complicated store-and-forward message switching system requiring a large database and significant communication software for computer-to-computer interfaces. The following issues have confounded the current project manager:

- The software is fragile. Its mean-time-to-failure is 2 hours, measured by field-reported crashes.
- This is a large project with 100 people. There are 30 developers and 10 testers. There are five human factors designers helping the users cope with the system deficiencies. They cannot alter the design, to which they had little input.
- The next release of the software is scheduled next week. This schedule has been in place for 1 year, and the customer purchased the system with the assurance that the feature package in this upgrade would not be delayed. The schedule is now in jeopardy.
- Release testing is going poorly; developers and testers are often diverted to find and fix field problems.

Question: Do you accept the position?

Answer: Only if you have the authority to fix the situation. The best time to have a clear understanding of job expectations is when you agree to take on new responsibilities. You need to understand your authority, the resources available, and the consequences of failure. Responsibility without authority leads to frustrations.

Question: You cannot resist a challenge and take the job. Now what do you do?

---

[4] Thanks to Associate Professor A. David Klappholz of the Stevens Institute of Technology for helping to write several of these case studies.

Answer: Delay the release and stabilize the software (debug it!). Talk directly to the customer and say you need time to make the system stable because you will not ship faulty software just to meet a schedule.

Question: The customer wants a special utility that recovers the system after a crash. To implement such a utility, you need 4 months and two of your best developers. So what do you do?

Answer: Explain that it is better to fix the system so that it does not crash in the first place. Tell the customer that he will get his recovery utility, maybe in 8 months, after you do a quantitative analysis of the resources required for all the tasks facing you.

Question: The customer is angry. At a follow-on meeting with you and your boss, the customer says, "I do not want to do business with your company if you can't see that that recovery utility is my highest priority." Your boss wants to keep the customer happy. What is the ethical thing to do?

Answer: Explain the situation to your team. Focus the team on fixing the stability problems, plan for the utility, and keep your boss, the customer, and the customer's people aware of the steps you are taking.

Question: The crisis is under control so far; however, the pressure from the customer continues. The customer uses the progress data you supplied against you. Your reputation is at stake. What do you do?

Answer: Continue sending progress data to the customer and your boss. Review the situation with your boss's boss to make sure you still have internal support. Work to establish your credibility with your team; otherwise, they might attempt heroics to placate the customer. If that happens, they will not be working to stabilize the software, and you will lose control of the project.

Question: How do you get the team's compliance?

Answer: IT professionals already have high salaries and benefits, so these things will not motivate them. Fear of job loss will keep some loyal, but not necessarily the best. You must keep the team well informed of the steps you are taking and your reasons for taking them. You might invest in a small study for new technology. Giving the team the chance to advance their skills excites them and builds loyalty to your stabilize-then-add-features plan.

Question: Some developers on the team are happy with the current situation. They like the thrill of solving problems and being a hero. But every time they put in a fix, several other things go wrong. How do you deal with them?

Answer: Explain the reality of this magic number at your next group meeting. Post copies of it everywhere. Stop rewarding "heroic" behavior by turning to these people in a crisis.

MAGIC NUMBER!

It takes ten times the effort and money to find and fix a problem in the test and integration laboratory than it would have taken the developer to fix it during the unit test. If the bug gets out the door and the customer has to report it, the fix costs 30 times what it would have taken the developer to fix it originally. Field fix:developer fix::30:1!

Then give the testers the "right of rejection." Explain that their job is to assure stability and quality and that it is the developers' job to fix problems on time. Insist that testers reject software that testers judge to be unreliable.

Question: Before you took charge, your team shipped blank tapes on the previous release date to buy time. They reasoned that the customer would take a week to install the software in their test site and that integration testing could continue. The entire release would then be sent as a large fix. Based on this unethical behavior, the customer, quite rightly, does not believe that you will deliver on your schedule commitments. How do you restore that confidence?

Answer: Establish regular meetings with the customer to show progress. Make it clear that the persistent addition of features creates an atmosphere that breeds desperate measures. Therefore, the only person who can commit to additional features is you.

Question: People are afraid of talking about the problems in the software because they fear that, as the bearer of bad news, they will get into trouble. How do you get these people to speak?

Answer: Celebrate the courage and perceptiveness of people who find problems. Each discovered problem is a problem that the customer will not have to face.

Conclusion: Make sure you stabilize the software, deliver it on the revised schedule, and deliver the utility as promised. Divide and conquer by forming a crisis team and a next-release team. Commit based on this two-team approach. Set goals that exceed the commitments, leaving the difference between the customer commitments and your team goals as slack that you, as project manger, can use to handle unforeseen situations.

1.4 SOFTWARE DEVELOPMENT PROCESSES

There is no best approach to software development. As is true for all engineering disciplines, the approach used and the tools chosen depend on the problem, the skill of the engineer, and the money available. What is the best choice? **It depends!** Quantitative software engineering is aimed at gathering data so that each choice can be insightful.

New development processes evolve as problems become more complex and engineers become more adept at handling software. One of the first development processes defined was the Waterfall Model. Current processes are the agile method, including commercial off-the-shelf (COTS) based and open source-based development, but new and better methods are always being created to adapt to new developments.

Bitter experience with building software that did not do what the client wanted inspired the creation of methods for requirements development. These methods examine ways to distinguish vital requirements from the merely important and to tease out hidden requirements. Descriptively stated requirements must be translated into firm specifications that include an expected operating point and the expected range of performance.

EXAMPLE:

A descriptive requirement might be, "The Customer Resource Management System must respond to online customer Web inquiries for account status." What can a designer do with this requirement?

SOLUTION:

It must become a specification before it can be a design objective. Let us take just one element of this descriptive requirement—respond. In what way? If there are errors, how shall they be described? Suppose the customer needs help? How much of the account should be shown? How fast must something appear after the customer presses ENTER?

Consider only the issue of speed of response. Jones remarks that, "The meanings of various lengths of elapsed time do not vary widely from one person to another: Less than 1/3 sec is 'instantaneous', Less than 1 sec is 'fast'. Less than 5 sec is a 'pause' and Greater than 10 sec is a 'wait.' Transaction interactions should be without 'wait.' "[5] Today, human factors research describes three levels of human cognitive experience.[6] "Perceptual processing time (about 0.1 second) is the time the human perceptual system spends integrating and processing signals. Two stimuli within this time seem fused, and responses feel instantaneous. . . . Immediate response time (about 1 second) is the smallest time needed to react to a new situation—for example, the appearance of a new form on a screen. Unit task time (about 10 seconds) is the time scale of simple tasks."[7]

This bit of data gathering has often been translated into a 3-second response time specification. Other studies show that variability of the response time dissatisfies users more than an average response time. A good designer seeks to relax the 3-second operational specification to 6 seconds with a 1-second bound. Most companies would accept this compromise. This discussion is just one part of one simple requirement.

"Respond" to the mind of the software developer means the execution time needed to retrieve and format the information inside the computer. A hidden requirement is that the communications link to the data server must support the speeds of data transfer needed. A hardware engineer would check to make sure that the data links have enough capacity. But whose responsibility is it to make sure that the communications software within the data server is configured properly and that the software communication drivers can support the transmission links, the protocols, and provide any needed buffering?

Too many developers are unaware of the need to perform this engineering function. Without a good job here, exhausting buffer pools could lead to intermittent delays in the response time to the customer. A prototype is the best way to validate specifications and to let the customer understand the interface before major investments are made in implementation.

1.5   CHOOSING A PROCESS

The software project manager must choose the process the team will follow to produce the software product. The choices range from the top-down, document-driven Waterfall Model and similar planned methods to flexible and responsive agile methods. Each process evolved out of whatever process was in use at the time in response to a core element that was deemed critical, but missing. At various times, those core elements have been documentation, schedule, functions, risk analysis, or hierarchical control, but no one process was meant to totally replace what came before. As each process evolved, layers

---

[5] Jones, T. Capers. *Four Principles of Man Computer Dialog Computer Aided Design*, Vol. 10, No. 3, May 1978, p. 197.

[6] Newell, A. *Unified Theories of Cognition*, Harvard University Press, Cambridge, MA, 1990.

[7] Obrenovic, Zeljko and Stancevic, Duse. "Modeling Multimodal Human-Computer Interaction," *IEEE Computer*, Vol. 37, No. 9, Sept. 2004, p. 67.

have been added, emphases have shifted, and the result is a continually improving, responsive mixture of tools. Sometimes the business constraints will direct the choice of method and sometimes the project manager's personal style will dictate the most comfortable choice. There have been analyses of management styles that favor structure, control, and authority versus those that favor team-building, collaboration, and flexibility, variously called Types A and B or Theories X, Y, and Z[8], but ultimately each process will emphasize one core element and include the others to a lesser extent. Proponents tend to argue for their own (most comfortable) approach, but it is best to fit the solution to the problem.

The only true failure is to create a software product without any method at all. Novices will want to restrict the size of the product to what three or four people can do, create a set of features as they go along, and then deliver a working system to a customer. Typically they have special domain knowledge that is built into the product and delights the customer. They have found what they think is the silver bullet of software development (Fred Brooks to the contrary!). When they try to build a follow-on system, they find that it is bigger than the tight-knit team can handle, key members of the team have moved on, or their tool base changes. Then they must adapt. Unfortunately, the more technically competent a team is, the more resistance they have to new technology. The organizational device of an "Office of Technology Planning" helps organizations adopt technology and keep current.

When teams are successful, they are asked to build other systems or to extend the first system. As the number of customers grows, they are asked to add customer-peculiar features. These features may be incompatible with other features of the original system, so the number of system versions grows. There are no economies of scale. To handle a growing business, the only thing most entrepreneurs can think to do is hire more people like themselves who also have no knowledge of process, configuration control, or release control. When a customer calls with a serious problem, like total system failure, there is a mad scramble to reproduce the problem. First the developers must reproduce the configuration the customer is using. If they do not know it, a designer is quickly dispatched to the customer site to fix the problem. Without change control, the problem is not recorded and other customers may report similar problems. This Keystone Cops routine was true in the 1960s and still occurs today.

There are too many design and development methodologies to discuss them all. The particular method a project adopts should provide some structure and discipline while being compatible with the abilities of the designers and developers. The best methods tighten the structure and discipline as the project proceeds through the development cycle. Loose control at first encourages several cycles of design synthesis and analysis before the developers commit to

---

[8] Leavitt, Nancy and Bahrami, Homa. *Managerial Psychology*, University of Chicago Press, Chicago, IL, 1988. Peters and Waterman. *A Passion for Excellence*, Random House, New York, 1985. Ouchi. *Theory Z*, McGraw-Hill, New York, 1981.

production code. Table 1.1 shows some methods. Simplicity in design is an important element of successful systems development, whatever the process.

TABLE 1.1. Popular Software Development Processes

Method	Description
Evolutionary	Software requirements and design will change and grow throughout the development process. Often associated with user-oriented systems or systems not yet fully understood—high volatility.
Incremental	A linear model of the software development process that allows the software developer to iterate among the activities within each life-cycle phase for each increment defined for the system.
Object Oriented	The use of all object-oriented techniques for requirements analysis, design, coding, and testing by a development team that is experienced and motivated to use object-oriented approaches.
Prototype	Informal development process applicable for prototypes, proof of concept, or demonstration software. Development is iterative, with minimal up-front requirements effort.
Spiral	A cyclical model of the software development process in which a repeating set of activities is performed on an increasingly more detailed representation of the product. A risk assessment must be performed at the end of each cycle and before starting a new cycle.
Waterfall	A linear model of the software development process in which the activities of each phase of the life cycle must be completed before continuing to the next phase.

With highly skilled and experienced developers on a small team, subjective evaluation criteria can be used, but for everyone else, the following advice applies: "Manage critical goals by defining **direct measures and specific targets**, assure accuracy and quality with **systematic project document inspections**, and control major risks by **limiting the size** of each testable delivery."[9]

Large projects with several teams, each having a mixture of inexperienced and skilled people, need more structure and metrics. Boehm and Turner[10] define five project dimensions that affect method and metric selection:

Size: Agile methods do not scale well. These work for projects with ten or fewer team members. Management structures, however, can incorporate teams into a large project.

Dynamism: Measured as the rate of recruitments change per month.

People Skills: The ration of highly skilled to journeyman developers.

---

[9] Christensen, Mark J. and Thayer, Richard H. *The Project Manager's Guide to Software Engineering's Best Practices*, IEEE Computer Society, New York, 2001.

[10] Boehm, Barry and Turner, Richard. *Balancing Agility and Discipline: A Guide for the Perplexed*, Addison-Wesley, Reading, MA, 2004.

Culture: The ratio of people that thrive on chaos to those people who need order to work productively.

Criticality: The potential loss of life or money because of failure.

The primary responsibility for a manager is to regularly review metrics and take action based on them. If the manager is unwilling or unable to interpret the metrics, it would be better to never require them. Forcing people to accumulate data from which there will never result analysis and action leads to low morale and problematic accuracy. Figure 1.1 shows the degree of software engineering needed under various circumstances, and it can be assumed that the degree of metrics would be comparable.

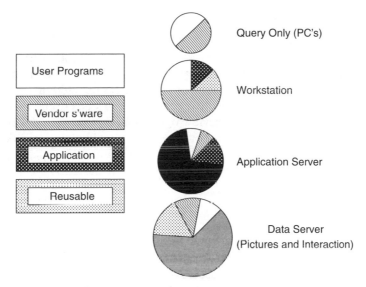

Figure 1.1. *Degree of software engineering needed under various circumstances.*

Another way of thinking about choosing a process is to look at the results that can be expected from any given process. Six processes follow, each with an explanation of the core element that caused their creation, along with a rationale of when each might be feasible.

1.5.1 No-Method "Code and Fix" Approach

Programmers sketch an idea in their heads or on a napkin and then immediately code and test at their workstations. Once they have a program that satisfies them, they give it to the customer. The customer is left to integrate the solution. There is no overhead, so the programmer can respond quickly. This approach is undisciplined, although many programmers have used it. It was the way they learned to program in their earliest classes, or it was the way they experimented with their hobby systems. This is not to be confused with agile methods, which are disciplined. This no-method process is simply Code → Use → Debug → Fix.

This approach results in unstable systems. It can work in the short term but is not sustainable as projects grow. Although it may satisfy immediate user needs, it does not keep up with evolving user requirements. Other methods and processes are in reaction against this approach. The reason it is dignified with a name and listed first is that it is still used in crises when the chosen process breaks down. It is important to recognize this process for what it is— the bankrupt choice born of desperation.

1.5.2   Waterfall Model

In the early days of software development, computing resources were scarce, so the Waterfall Model was formalized to reduce the computer time needed to develop and test a program (Figure 1.2). The scarcity of computer time forced reliance on documents—lots of them, all subjected to meticulous review—to organize thinking and chart progress. The steps of the method are separated by the production and review of documents. Software development can proceed through these steps; other steps may be added or deleted. Extensive literature exists on the Waterfall Model that will not be repeated here.

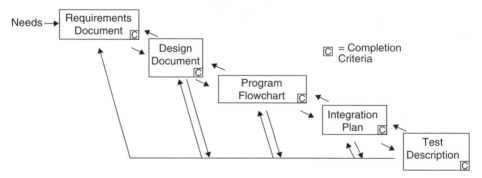

Figure 1.2. *Stages of the Waterfall Model.*

The Waterfall Model proved to be too document-intensive. The time needed to update documents often exceeded the time needed to update the code, which caused documents to be out of date and negated their value. This careful systematic approach led to long development cycles. Companies that needed short time-to-market cycles abandoned the dogmatic Waterfall Model even as they kept elements of it deep within their development methods. Last, the need for elaborate documentation tends to discourage the use of COTS, which increases development costs, slows development, and lengthens delivery time. On the other hand, high license fees of COTS components can drive up the cost of systems. This concern encourages the use of internally developed components or open-source modules.

MAGIC NUMBER!

A good practice is to have no more than 20% of the ultimate staff participate in the requirements and architecture steps of the Waterfall Model.

A key assumption in the Waterfall Model is that requirements can be defined and carefully controlled. Unfortunately, in real life, requirements emerge as the project proceeds. That realization forced further evolution, as Barry Boehm, the prophet of the Waterfall Model, quickly realized.

Case Study: The Case of the Mandatory Requirement

Let us return to the modest store-and-forward message switching system from the *Case of the Sacrosanct Date*. We have now chosen to use the Waterfall Model. The customer's requirements (remember that a key assumption of this process is that requirements can be defined and carefully controlled) are as follows:

Requirement 1: Do not lose a message.
Requirement 2: 10-second response time is critical.

Concerning Requirement 1, the software designers were told that if they were uncertain about losing a message, they should cause the system to stop. But in a mission-critical system, there is an implied requirement that the system should not stop. High availability is needed. Availability is calculated as Mean-Time-to-Failure/(Mean-time-to-Failure + Mean-time-to-Repair).

Here the mean time to repair is the time to recover any messages that might be lost, save them, and relaunch the software. The design choice that preserved every message caused a system availability requirement to emerge.

Question: How do you resolve this contradiction?

Answer: Implicit requirements like availability are often forgotten during the writing of requirements and the implementation of a system. Sometimes to avoid a complicated design flaw, it is necessary to relax what at first seems to be a firm requirement.

Question: To satisfy Requirement 2 and reduce system costs, the architects decide to have a common buffer pool for those messages coming into the system and those going out. The input buffer requests are given higher priority to preserve the 10-second response time, which allowed users to always input messages. This solution worked and gave the required response time until more output buffers were needed than were available. The system then hung as the input process captured all the buffers. Now what can you do?

Answer: The right solution is to invert the priorities of the system. Instead of "Accept input—Drain output" change to "Drain output—Accept input." The customer was only convinced that this change was wise after seeing the new buffer request strategy demonstrated in a controlled prototype environment where that was the single change made and the system was driven with high traffic loads.

 ***MAGIC NUMBER!***

Only 40–60% of the system requirements are known at the start of the project. The rest emerge from studies of system use. Barry Boehm coined the phrase "emergent requirements" to describe them.

1.5.3 Planned Incremental Development Process

Staff and resources are never infinite. To compensate for less than ideal, i.e., normal, conditions, this process evolved to allow the separate packaging of individual functions. Here time is not necessarily critical. The idea is to divide the project into parts and apply the Waterfall Model to each part, which is sometimes called the incremental development method or the parallel development process. Each increment becomes a project unto itself, the ultimate system emerging when all the individual projects are in place.

1.5.4 Spiral Model: Planned Risk Assessment-Driven Process

The Spiral Model grew out of the incremental model, its advantage being that at each point, we have a partial view of the product. Each cycle in the Spiral could be one stage of the project processes described in the Waterfall Model. The focus is on continuous risk assessment. At each cycle, project risks are reassessed and plans are modified to contain them. The Spiral Model reduces risk, allows feedback, and is not derailed by failure because individual failures are small and constrained by the method (Figure 1.3).

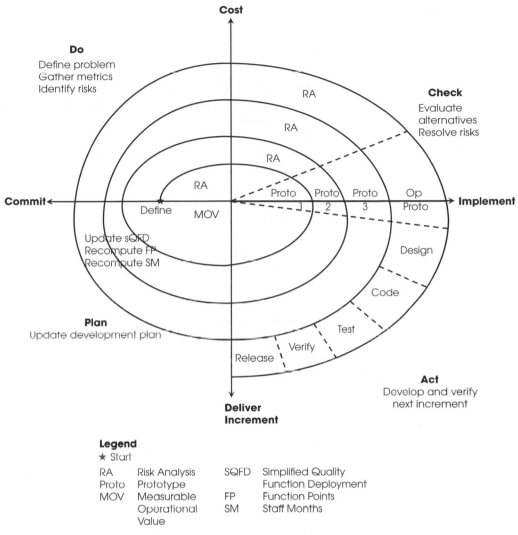

Figure 1.3. Boehm's Spiral Model of the software process.

Case Study: The Case of the Threatened Bottom Line

You are the project manager of a 20-person team. Your customers love your product. Suddenly, a competitor offers a product with similar features but for half your price. You do an analysis and determine that the only way to meet the price point is to reduce the team to ten people (which can be accomplished by moving ten people to another exciting project).

Question: How do you maintain quality with only half the staff?

Answer: Run your problem through several spins of Boehm's Spiral Model.

Spiral Round 1

Objective:	Identify cost reduction items
Constraints:	Meet annual profit estimates
	Meet customer commitments
Alternatives:	1. Object-oriented libraries → increased productivity
	2. Object-oriented database → increased productivity
	3. Find an existing product and tweak it
	4. Improve organization/communication issues
Risks:	1. Object-oriented database is not widely used
	2. Difficult to quantify improvements
	3. Customers may not accept the change
Risk resolution:	1. Have a pilot or prototype
	2. Do a cost analysis
	3. Hire a consultant
	4. Benchmarking
Result:	We discover that alternative 1 is the best
Discoveries:	It takes 6 months for programmers to learn the object-oriented approach
	Investment: $10,000 (software tools) + $10,000 (hardware) object-oriented databases (alternative 2) are not mature
Plan for next phase:	Introduce object-oriented technologies

Spiral Round 2

Objective:	Double to triple maintenance productivity
Constraints:	Payback or profitability has to happen within 1 year
	Results must be scalable to other projects
	Feature deployment has to be reduced from 2 years to 3 months
Alternatives:	1. Variety of compilers, debug tools, test tools
	2. Workstations
Risk:	1. Investment costs
	2. Finding an expert may be difficult
	3. One team resists object-oriented approach
Risk Resolution:	1. Jump-start with an object-oriented expert in the team
	2. Adopt older, more stable tools
	3. Drop object-oriented databases
	4. Develop features in parallel in C
Plan for next phase:	Build the next version of the software using object-oriented techniques
	Have monthly progress reviews

Spiral Round 3

Objective:	Calibrate productivity achieved
	Deploy first object-oriented team
Constraints:	Schedule
	Features and requirements
Alternatives:	1. Procedural programming
	2. Object-oriented approach
Risk:	1. Compiler may produce unreliable code
	2. Six-month learning curve
Risk resolution:	1. Develop critical features in C
	2. Train team
	3. Add object-oriented experts
	4. Reduce reporting
Plan for next phase:	Integrate into development plan
Results:	You attracted better staff.
	Customer got desired quality and price.
	Less documentation, more comments.
	Code reuse doubled.
	30% less code to write.

Interestingly, even though change costs are a third of what they were, there was only a 50% overall cost reduction because code changes accounted for 70% of the costs: $0.3 + (0.7 \times 0.33) = 0.53$.

The Spiral Model demands knowledge of project objectives, constraints, and preferred architectures. The customer knows only the features required to do a subset of the job—the subset the customer thinks is most important. Special aspects of the problem, well known to problem domain experts, are frequently unstated. Ideally, the developer would simply ask the customer what was required and the customer would provide sufficient detail to proceed; the customer would be totally familiar with the expert's unstated constraints. This expectation is unreasonable, and significant negotiations between both parties are required to balance functionality, performance, and reliability with cost and schedule considerations.

Boehm's WinWin Spiral Model, shown in Figure 1.4, derives its name from the objective of these negotiations. The client wins the product that satisfies most needs, and the developer wins by working to realistic and achievable budgets and deadlines. To achieve this objective, the model defines a set of negotiation activities at the beginning of each pass around the spiral. The following activities define the customer communication:

Identification of the system stakeholders—those in the organization that have a direct business interest in the product to be built and will be

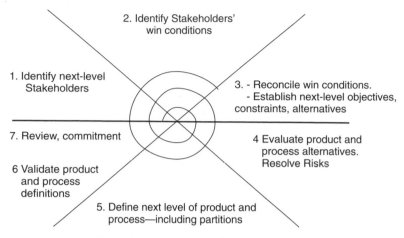

Figure 1.4. Boehm's WinWin Spiral Model.

rewarded for a successful outcome or criticized if the effort fails (e.g., user, customer, developer, maintainer, interfacer, etc.).

Determinations of the stakeholders' "win conditions."

Negotiations of the stakeholders' win conditions to reconcile them into a set of win–win conditions for all concerned (including the software project team).

In addition to the early emphasis placed on the win–win condition, the model also introduces three points that help establish the completion of one cycle around the spiral and provide the decision milestones before the software project proceeds:

Life-Cycle Objectives (LCO): Defines a set of objectives for each major software activity (e.g., a set of objectives associated with the definition of top-level product requirements).

Life-Cycle Architecture (LCA): Establishes the objectives that must be met as the software architecture is defined.

Initial Operational Capability (IOC): Represents a set of objectives associated with the preparation of the software for installation/distribution, site preparations before installations, and assistance required by all parties that will use or support the software.

The WinWin process is a framework for distributed asynchronous decision making when there are many stakeholders. It provides a model useful for negotiation. It allows architecture constraints to override a particular requirement once the stakeholder understands its cost or schedule impact. This approach is similar to the agile method of intimate customer interaction in the same workplace. WinWin provides a structured model for capturing all stakeholder concerns. WinWin speeds software development by eliminating rework that occurs from misunderstandings and results in better products by exposing architecture options early in the development.

1.5.5 Development Plan Approach

An effective process for large projects requiring more than 10 people is to write a development plan that answers these questions and is updated at the end of each step:

What will you do?

How will you do it?

What do you depend on?

When will you be done?

Who will do what?

All disciplined methods recognize the need for these steps, if not in this order or with the same mandatory documents. Therefore, all tasks needed to deliver the software product should be identifiable. It is most useful to transform your task list into a table similar to the one shown in Table 1.2 that will reflect the project schedule.

TABLE 1.2. Development Plan Chart

Task	Who	When	Current Estimate

Task: A description of what is to be done with a measurable output
Who: The person in charge of the task
When: Planned completion date that can be modified only by the project manager
Current Estimate: Estimated completion date by the "Who" person.
This unique feature makes this more useful than any PERT or Gantt chart.[11]

The use of the "current estimate" date permits task owners to report trouble in a way the rest of the project can understand without upsetting the entire project plan. Without the current estimate feature, a late task could cause total project replanning when the manager might have been able, with early warning, to resolve the problem without delaying project completion. The early warning of the current estimate feature allows developers to be honest about where they stand while giving the project manager time to expedite or replan incrementally.

The core element of the development plan is hierarchical control via the itemization of concrete signposts that indicate to every project member the health and condition of the project (Figure 1.5). This nonjudgmental

---

[11] L. Bernstein developed this approach while working for Victor Vyssotsky at Bell Laboratories. Mr. Vyssotsky described it to Fred Brooks, who was pleased to use it in his book, *The Mythical Man-Month.*

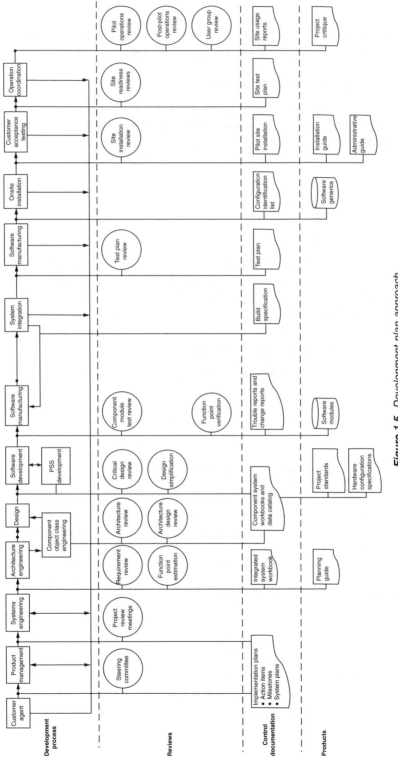

Figure 1.5. Development plan approach.

reporting tends to focus all team members on the person's responsibility to the larger objective of project completion. The hazards of this method are that it may lead to functional boundaries that are too sharply defined, that task divisions may lead to suboptimization, or that it may discourage risk management. Figure 1.5 is an elaborate schematic, used to manage a project with 500 people. Select only those elements that fit your project.

1.5.6 Agile Process: an Apparent Oxymoron

Agile advocates are not antimethodology. They embrace modeling, but not merely to file some diagram in a dusty corporate repository. They embrace documentation, but not to waste reams of paper in never-maintained and rarely used tomes. They insist on planning, but recognize the limits of planning in a turbulent environment. The core element that agile process proponents emphasize is the schedule. It is the most important criterion of success. Agile methods drive organizations to schedule containment.

Those who brand proponents of XP, SCRUM, or any of the other agile methodologies as hackers are ignorant of both the methodologies and the original definition of the term (a "hacker" was first defined as a programmer who enjoys solving complex programming problems, rather than someone who practices ad hoc development or destruction).[12]

Early proponents of agile methods felt sufficiently beleaguered by the rigid enforcement of oppressive process that they actually voiced a "manifesto" declaring their values. These were as follows:

Individuals and interactions over processes and tools

Working software over comprehensive documentation

Customer collaboration over contract negotiation

Responding to change over following a plan

If we look at one agile process, extreme programming (XP), we find that it is highly disciplined. It is not chaotic, even though some slipshod programmers hide behind the term and slovenly software shops describe their approach as XP. On the contrary, it involves considerable emphasis on disciplined planning:

Close and teaming customer interactions

Documented user stories and use cases

Paired programmers working closely together

Testing before coding

Simplicity in design

Relatively frequent small releases

Iteration planning

---

[12] www.agilemanifesto.org/hisoty.html.

XP demands devotion to agreed-on standards, frequent integration, deferred optimization, and unit tests before integration release and for every bug. Acceptance tests are run often, and the results are published and made available to all project team members, including the customer.

1.6 REEMERGENCE OF MODEL-BASED SOFTWARE DEVELOPMENT

This approach is from the early days of large system development when computer resources were limited and expensive. With the need to use components to speed software development, the use of architecture patterns, frameworks, and models became popular. Components could be evaluated in terms of how well they fit into an integrated software system.

The Model-Driven Software Development (MDSD) paradigm supports development teams with 20 or more developers. It evolved from software product line engineering where families of applications for a specific market segment are built. Emphasis on agile software development sets MDSD apart from the earlier Waterfall Model, planned incremental development, and the Spiral Model. MDSD, like prototyping, produces working software early in the development cycle, but MDSD also provides the scalability that is not inherent in popular agile methodologies.

The Safeguard Anti-missile Missile System in 1968 is an example. Developing its software was a major challenge. No configuration control guidelines or standard software processes existed. The National Academy of Sciences opined that such software could not work. Only NASA faced similar complexity and performance demands. Although Safeguard borrowed many techniques from NASA's Apollo project, a unique approach to software development evolved spontaneously. Many projects modeled and simulated system performance, but Safeguard was the first to use the models and simulations to drive its software development. After some early false starts, the entire software effort fell into lockstep with the model and simulation program.

Once the decision was made to develop a tactical anti ballistic missile (ABM) system, a system evaluation department was formed to provide quality assurance. Its objective was to ensure that the design met the system objectives and that the implementation met the system requirements.[13] To carry out that objective, the department designed field tests. This effort emerged as so important that it became the driving force for the software development effort. Typical mission scenarios measured software progress throughout the entire development cycle. These scenarios are now called use cases.

[13] Bernstein, L., Burke, E. H., and Bauer W. F. "Simulation- and Modeling-Driven Software Development," *Crosstalk: The Journal of Defense Software Engineering*, Vol. 9, No. 7, July 1996, pp. 25–27.

The system evaluation team took the approach of developing a family of simulations to predict and confirm system performance. The highest-level simulation predicted the performance of the entire system to a full-scale attack. To facilitate the design of the simulation, the models of subsystems (missiles and radars) were only as detailed as was required to enable the system simulation to model overall system performance. Detailed simulations of all major subsystems validated the high-level models. In some cases, the phenomena modeled in those subsystem simulations were based on even more detailed simulations accounting for the fundamental physics involved.

Being able to produce several models simultaneously for different subsystems is fundamental to model-based development. The appropriate model iterates and validates each small increment of the system. There is no attempt to create a single, all encompassing model for the entire scope of the desired system. Models are merely abstract representations of software and therefore may not be completely accurate. They must be validated with realistic data, but the focus should remain on only the uncertain aspects of the subsystem. Attempts to create a highly detailed model should be avoided; good engineering judgment and problem domain expertise are essential for deciding just how detailed the model needs to be. Test cases evolve from the modeling efforts. The major benefit of model-based development is that discrepancies between the model and the test results efficiently point to specific areas to correct.

During the 1980s and 1990s, projects became schedule-driven to the exclusion of other needs. Faster time-to-market became the way to success, and models were seen as delaying product deployment. As the need for trustworthy systems captured the imagination of the public, model-based development gave developers a way to understand safety, reliability, schedule, and performance concerns while meeting their schedule commitments.

1.7 PROCESS EVOLUTION

Suppose one or another of the processes described appeals to a design team, or a new technology bursts on the scene, but middle management seems to stonewall any suggestions to adopt new ways. Software developers and company executives are favorably disposed toward anything that speeds development and reduces bugs, but there is no incentive for middle managers to risk using a new approach. This position is astonishing initially, especially if those middle managers were themselves software developers in recent memory, but, on examination, it is perfectly rational. Training and staffing are cost items in their budget against a method with which they have no experience. If their organization does not deliver, they are to blame. If they are successful, the executives take the credit for having the vision to move to a new technology. So how can an organization ever evolve to using more sophisticated processes?

The answer is to invest in corporate-funded investigations of technology, training, and shared risk. Companies can move to new technologies by making informed decisions. An organization with more than 250 technical people needs a well-defined "someone" to encourage the adoption of new software processes.

An office of technology planning (OOTP) could encourage the adoption of new technology. Table 1.3 shows how such an office might work. The Chief Technology Officer (CTO) leads the office and has some discretionary funds for evaluating, trialing, and deploying technology throughout the organization, which plugs the drain on middle managers' profits as their people's skills are improved. The CEO determines how much the company can and should invest and the CTO makes the investment pay off.

TABLE 1.3. Technology Deployment Processes

Market Input →
Ideas →
Technology →
Assessment

| Technology Initiatives |
| Metric: percent of new product revenue for the last three years and royalties |

→ Processes &
Products with
Embedded New
Technology

Technology Initiatives Subprocesses

Technology Plan Development	Acquire Technology (Make/Buy)	Prioritize Applied Research	Contract Applied Research Initiatives	Deploy Technology

FUNCTIONS

CEO	— Review technology plan for consistency with strategic plan
CHIEF TECHNOLOGY OFFICER	— Provide technology vision — Facilitate and accelerate technology transfer/diffusion — Lead the Office of Technology Planning — Recommend technology initiatives — Integrate 2- to 5-year product line initiatives — Ensure consistency with personnel policies — Chair Intellectual Property Study team
OFFICE OF TECHNOLOGY PLANNING	— Drive to asset-based business — Professional societies — Recommend technology priorities — Manage and implement the technology plan — Assess R&D capability and technology for benchmarking
Tool Providers	— Provide technology base and roadmap technologies

Bernstein was the CTO from 1991 to 1994 for the Bell Laboratories network management development organization comprising 2000 people. The technology transfer process was aimed at creating new products and services for the customer base and for making software development more effective and cheaper. Input came from customers, sales teams, internal and external researchers, developers, and formal, chartered technology assessment efforts.

The OOTP held monthly meetings that the CTO chaired to determine technology priorities. For example, a study of object-oriented database technology in 1992 showed it to be too immature for wide use. Two projects stopped using it before they reached the point of firm commitment to the method. On the other hand, tools to find and fix memory leaks were found to be effective and were deployed to every project within 4 months of completion of the technology assessment report. The OOTP managed the technology budget for the organization, funded initiatives, and produced a technology plan. It also managed the adoption of the technology project by project, providing experts as needed to expedite adoption of the new tool, process, or component. The ratio of revenue from new products doubled in the interval, while productivity increased fourfold.

1.8 ORGANIZATION STRUCTURE

There are two possibilities for deploying the staff talent that any company engaged in software products must confront. Each has its benefits and drawbacks. The functional organization is efficient because each functional group does only its job for every product produced. For example, people expert at writing requirements will do only that for every product produced. The drawback to this style is that communication problems can develop among functional groups. Also, a sense of the whole product, and the concomitant sense of satisfaction in its ultimate success, is lacking. Project organization is less efficient but generally more effective in encouraging personal growth and reducing professional burnout. This style does foster a commitment to the success of the project as a whole and a sense of broad responsibility to the customer.

No right answer exists. Functional organization is efficient for manufacturing an established product. Project organization tends to be successful for software, especially when either the problem or the technology is not well understood. Firm commitment to one or the other style of organization is best made after a working prototype is achieved and risks are assessed (Table 1.4).

TABLE 1.4. Functional vs. Project Organization

Functional	Project
Requirements	Customer interface
Design	Program design
Code	Integration
Test	Validation and verification

Project organizations form teams more easily because their members are focused on a common goal. In functional organizations, most people are assigned to several teams to take advantage of their special skills. As a result, they can be distracted when there are unexpected problems and some of their teams are necessarily shortchanged.

What is the difference between a mediocre and a championship team? Is it train-train-train, secure the best talent available, or devise innovative strategy?

These are important, but the most important factor is commitment to quality. Members of a championship team, whatever the game, share similar qualities:

Want to be in the game. They are not content to sit on the sidelines and watch the action; they want to participate in the effort and share in the victories.

Are highly and visibly enthusiastic. It is contagious. Contributions are recognized and rewarded, resulting in increased confidence.

Desire to be top performers and realize that open and honest feedback among coaches and other team members is critical to individual and group success. Asking, "How am I doing?" or "How can I do my job better?" ensures that opportunities are available to always improve knowledge and skills.

Use the word "we" rather than "I," realizing that strategies are developed for group action.

Respect the talents and abilities of fellow teammates, while analyzing the strengths and weaknesses of rivals.

Understand the value of communication—that it is important to know where the team is going and how individual action can attain the goal.

Anticipate change and react quickly while continuing to drive toward the goal.

Have confidence in their team, their managers, and themselves.

Another dimension of organization structure is hierarchical versus network. Hierarchical organizations reduce the number of communication paths among people. Pair-wise communication requires $n(n-1)/2$ between n people. A small shop of 7 people requires 21 paths, so everybody tends to know what is going on. A shop of 50 people would require 1225 paths, a much more difficult situation for maintaining a fully informed team.

A hierarchical organization might group together everyone defining requirements in one group, those creating the architecture in another, software developers, human/computer interface experts, testers, and integrators in yet other discrete groups. Each group would have a supervisor reporting to next-level managers, and so on to the highest corporate executive. If everyone was focused on a single product, it would be both a project and a functional organization of the hierarchy. More likely, specialized skills would be shared by more than one product line. To understand how an organization really works, a network view is necessary. Software manufacturers are the common communication point that pulls together each product line and reduces the number of communication paths. Figure 1.6 illustrates this.

Software manufacturing is a systematic approach to system building, deliverable documentation production, configuration identification, change control, and packaging for delivery. Software manufacturing is in-line, not overhead. Software developers do not do the job of system building; people with pro-

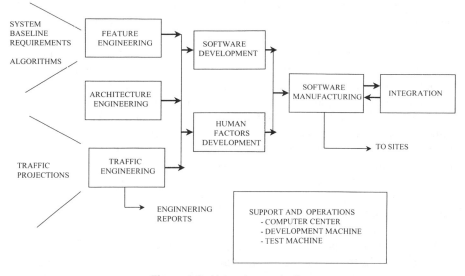

Figure 1.6. Network organization.

duction skills and specially trained expediters, in numbers amounting to approximately 5% of the programming staff, build systems.

The software manufacturing group runs the computers for the project. All releases to system integration and the field must go through software manufacturing. When schedules get tight and the resident wunderkind is sure that running to the customer with a fix or two will save the day, the discipline of software manufacturing stands between fiscal sanity and chaos.

1.9 PRINCIPLES OF SOUND ORGANIZATIONS

People make the difference. Hire good people and respect their individual talents. People are not interchangeable. Software people thrive on challenge and new technology. Some experts can produce ten times more than journeyman programmers. Because customer service and innovations are increasingly important competitive weapons, it does not pay to create a sullen, dispirited, or burned out workforce.

Here are some ways to "turn down the heat:"

Work is NOT an endurance contest.

Be flexible in work hours.

Ask your people how to restructure the work.

Reserve overtime hours for true crises, not part of the standard day.[14]

---

[14] O'Reilly, Brian. *Fortune Magazine*, March 12, 1990.

Make the customer and your supplier your teammates and you can halve the development time by reducing confusion and misunderstanding. Before the first release, customers want lower prices, more features, and shorter schedules. When the system becomes operational, they want better reliability, throughput, and response time. Your suppliers can ruin your hard-won teaming relationship. To make sure that your suppliers understand the importance of your customer, it is vital that you let them participate in all phases of the project.

Understand the requirements: Validate, prototype, and make sure there are numeric operating and bounds specifications for every requirement. Customers **need** some features and **want** others. A successful project manager distills the needs from the wants and satisfies the needs while delivering a reliable system at reasonable cost. Firm commitments are best made after a prototype works.

Configuration management, the control of changes to the software, is essential in all projects, large and small. Quality and simplification in the earliest steps save time and money.

Finally, none of these will work unless our profession recognizes the next core element in the evolution of software processes as a fundamental principle. Software trustworthiness is the next major area in which academia and industry must focus—both for national security reasons as well as to ensure that the U.S. software industry maintains its leadership. The three attributes of software reliability, security, and safety comprise trustworthiness. Fostering these attributes can spark another round of American software innovation that will stem the wholesale outsourcing of our industry.

Companies and people will act to assure trustworthiness only if there are economic consequences to not doing so. Evaluation and liability, both corporate and individual, are the only means to bring awareness to the impact of negligence. Software trustworthiness is critical for medical devices, plant control systems, and weapon systems; for management of sensitive records; and for critical infrastructure. Dependability is fundamental to cybersecurity.

Doctors and lawyers are members of old professions and as such recognize that being an important part of many peoples' lives carries with it ethical responsibility and liability. This course will help make you ready to assume your responsibility for trustworthiness in our young profession.

Case Study: The Case of the Dissed Discount

Once upon a time, a computer manufacturer offered 10% price discounts for a volume purchase. The cost of the computers was 25% of the cost of the system.

Question: The value of the system to the customer was 50 times the cost of the system if it could be available by a critical date. Would you accept the discounts and run the risk of having no leverage over your supplier's scheduling? If not, what else might you do?

Answer: In this case, the best strategy was to let the manufacturer charge list price, but to insist on premium service, delivery without a contract in hand, and a guarantee to have spare parts on-site.

The manufacturer shipped the computer to the operational site while the customer's purchasing organization processed the paperwork. Insurance concerns prevented them from installing the computer, but they could leave it on their moving van, and they did. They left the van containing the computer sitting at the loading dock for 2 days, and the installers were kept on immediate call. Within 15 minutes of getting the signed contract, the waiting installers set to work and had the computer operational in record time. This saved the normally scheduled 2-week installation time and helped make up for other schedule slips.

The moral of the story is that you must be a world-class customer before you can be a world-class supplier!

1.10 SHORT PROJECTS—4 TO 6 WEEKS

1.10.1 Project 1: Automating Library Overdue Book Notices

An elementary school of 500 students is using a manual method for tracking books on loan. As books are taken from the library, the book card is taken from the book jacket and filed by date. Books may be borrowed for 2 weeks. As books are returned, the card is put back into the book jacket. Books that are not returned in 2 weeks are considered overdue, and an Overdue Book Notice is sent to the students. Students who do not return a book within 3 weeks are given a second notice. Books not returned in 4 weeks have a third notice and are reported on a special "Critical Overdue" librarian's report. This report is sent to the student's teacher and to the principal. The book card is given to the librarian.

Clerks write overdue book notices on half-sheets of paper for about 200 books each week. These are distributed weekly. This form has been used for many years:

Glenwood School Overdue Book Notice

Book Title:

Student Name:

Teacher Name:

Date of Notice:

Notice   1   2   3   (circle one)

This book is overdue. Please return it promptly.

PROBLEM:

Automate the overdue book notice process with a computer borrowed from the computer class. The computer room is next to the library. This is the first computer automation project in the school. Data may not be left on the computer from week to week. The computer is not networked.

1.10.2 Project 2: Ajax Transporters, Inc. Maintenance Project

Ajax Transporters, Inc. manufactures exactly one size of one model of one product, the Ajax Personal Transporter, which they sell directly to customers. Ajax's computer system consists of an order entry (sub-)system and an inventory/order fulfillment (sub-)system ("inventory system," for short).

Orders arrive by phone or by mail and are entered into the order entry system by clerks. The order entry system's main, although not its only function is to check the validity of each incoming order, retain a copy of each valid order in its database, and send valid orders to the inventory system.

The inventory system checks whether there are enough personal transporters to satisfy an incoming order. If there are, the warehouse workers remove the required number of personal transporters from inventory and bring them over to Schlepper Shipping, Inc., which ships the order to the customer. The inventory system also sends a message to the order entry system indicating that the order has been filled. If there are not enough personal transporters to fulfill the order, the inventory system puts the order into its database as a "back order." Warehouse workers check back orders each day and fill as many as possible, given inventory on hand, which is increased whenever Ajax's Manufacturing Division manufactures more personal transporters and delivers them to the warehouse.

Ajax currently uses a COTS software package for its order entry/inventory system. It is manufactured by So-So Software, Inc. Because it is a proprietary product, it is distributed only as an executable; nobody outside of So-So gets to see the source code.

The following transactions are recognized, from terminals or the website, by the order entry/inventory system:

Place New Order
View All Orders
Cancel Order by Order Number

You have access to the system's main customer/order file. Many pages detail the transactions and access to the file.

PROBLEM:

The system is working well, and Ajax's sales are increasing when they are told that Schlepper Shipping, Inc. is going out of business because of the economic downturn. The U.S. Post Office agrees to contract for the shipping, but So-So Software, Inc. has accidentally forgotten to include the customer name with other customer information in the file and the Post Office will do the shipping only if the customer name is added to the address. Ajax has asked So-So Software to make this change in the system, but So-So wants far more money than Ajax feels is reasonable to make so small a change.

You work for Amber Consulting, Inc., and your group at Amber has just been given the job of making the change to Ajax's system, but without changing the COTS product currently in use. (You will do this work by building one or more new modules that interact with the COTS system.) Ajax is getting one of their in-house groups to completely rewrite their system, but it needs the upgrade that you have been contracted to do well before the rewritten system can be delivered because they need to continue doing business or they will go bankrupt. Your task is to upgrade the system in 5 weeks.

1.11 PROBLEMS

1.11.1 You have two releases of the system in the hands of four customers. Each customer wants their changes but does not want to be burdened with the changes of the other customers. Your budget is tight.

  a. You insist that there is one release for all and that the customers must upgrade and accept all changes.
  b. You adopt a versioning configuration management system.
  c. You break the system into four systems and customize each.
  d. You refer the problem to the product manager for a business analysis of the best strategy.

1.11.2 You are eager to improve the long-term productivity of the group of developers you are managing, so you

  a. ask them to work overtime.
  b. measure their work.
  c. manage them more closely.
  d. provide them with new tools.

1.11.3 Your program has worked for several months and all users are pleased with it. Suddenly it crashes, so you

  a. blame the user for not being properly trained.
  b. seek program dumps and begin debugging.
  c. determine what changed in the run that crashed.
  d. quit and find a new job.

1.11.4 You find it helpful to discuss your program with a colleague; you review each other's code. This process is called

  a. code inspections.
  b. code reviews.
  c. extreme programming.
  d. a waste of time impacting productivity.

1.11.5   You are asked to produce a program on a tight schedule. Your boss tells you what is needed. To meet the schedule you

a. begin coding immediately.

b. research other solutions.

c. discuss the program with the software architects.

d. design the interfaces.

1.11.6   You see that you need a new tool, so you

a. ask your boss to get one.

b. build it yourself because it would take too long to purchase one.

c. borrow one from a colleague by copying a CD.

d. work around getting it and stick to your development schedule.

1.11.7   When developers use the incremental model to organize their releases in into products, they

a. deliver a full set of modules with limited functionality, and then gradually change the functions of the modules with each new release.

b. deliver a subset of the modules that perform a limited set of functions, and then deliver more modules with each new release.

c. deliver the full set of functions and modules with the first release.

d. deliver a limited set of functions and wait for customer input to add functions.

1.11.8   This problem continues the first example in this chapter. A software system is designed so that after every hour of normal operation, it stops and relaunches from its initial state. This process is called software rejuvenation. Assume that the mean time to failure for the software is measured to be 10 hours and the mean time to repair is 5 minutes. Repair means restoring the software to an operating condition by relaunching it from its initial state.

a. What is the reliability of the system after 4 successful hours of execution and four successful rejuvenations?

b. What is the probability of failure of the system for any 4 hours of operation?

c. What is the availability of the system where $R(t) = e^{-\lambda t}$, where R is reliability, c is the reciprocal of the mean time to failure, and t is the execution time. Note that e^x is approximately $(1 + x)$ for small x.

1.11.9   You are asked to be the architect for the development of a customer resource management transaction system. The system must be fast so that there are no bottlenecks when the system is executing. The agents using the system are trading millions of dollars an hour so transaction speed and system availability are paramount. System cost is of secondary importance. The customer agrees to a margin of three times the required transaction speed. Once you have a first version of the system in your integration laboratory, you run expected use case scenarios and trace transaction execution time. You find that average transaction execution uses 1 million processor instructions with a 100-instruction standard deviation. You have a balanced design in your system. The computer chosen for the production system executes an average instruction in 500 ns.

    a. Assess the risks in the system architecture for the first version.

    b. What design changes are needed to conform to the system performance constraints?

    c. What alternatives to software redesign are possible?

1.11.10   You are the project manager for a client/server system. Your responsibility is for the server. The server software has successfully completed system test and is certified to support 100 clients. The software architect has designed a safety margin of two into the client support requirement. You know that the system will reliably support 200 clients with satisfactory performance, but because of the safety margin, the server software is rated at 100 clients. Your customer calls in a panic. A merger has occurred, and his job is on the line. His server must support 175 clients, or the company will convert to a similar server acquired in the merger. What will you do?

1.11.11   You own a software company that has several projects underway. You need to deliver a system so that you can bill your customers and meet your payroll. Your project manager for one system reports an outstanding problem list of 200 unrelated and uniformly distributed critical problems. Each critical problem is estimated to take 1 week for a tester and a developer working together to resolve. Software developers can fix problems in 2 days if they can resubmit their modules instead of submitting problem fixes. There are five modules that make up the system, and the five system testers working as a test team can fully test a module in 1 day when no critical problems are found. There are five testers and 20 developers on this project. After all problems are fixed, a 2-week regression test period is needed before product ship. Customers are willing to accept software with noncritical problems outstanding. Because the other systems are just entering system test, you need to obtain a loan to cover the time needed to get this system in shape to cover your payroll. What is the shortest time before you can ship the software and therefore the time you need to have the loan? What risks are you taking? Assume no other critical problems are found once these 200 are fixed.

BIBLIOGRAPHY

Bernstein, Larry. "Software in the Large," *AT&T Technical Journal*, Vol. 75, No. 1, Jan./Feb. 1996, pp. 5–14.

Binder, Robert V. *Testing Object-Oriented Systems—Models, Patterns, Tools*, Addison-Wesley, Reading, MA, March 2003.

Boehm, Barry W., et al. *Software Cost Estimation with COCOMO II*, Prentice Hall, Englewood Cliffs, NJ, 2000.

Crowley, Thomas. "Safeguard Data—Processing Subsystem," *The Bell System Technical Journal*, Special Supplement, 1975.

Carnegie Mellon University Software Engineering Institute. *The Capability Maturity Model: Guidelines for Improving the Software Process*, Addison-Wesley, Reading, MA, 1995.

Fowler, Martin. *Refactoring Improving the Design of Existing Code*, Addison-Wesley, Reading, MA, 2000.

Hatton, Les. *Safer C-Developing Software for High-Integrity and Safety-Critical Systems*, McGraw-Hill, New York, 1997.

Hoffman, Daniel M. and Weiss, David M. *Software Fundamentals Collected Papers by David L. Parnas*, Addison-Wesley, Reading, MA, 2002.

Jones, T. Capers. *Estimating Software Costs*, McGraw-Hill, New York, 1998.

Leavitt, Harold J. and Bahrami, Homa. *Managerial Psychology: Managing Behavior in Organizations*, 5th ed. University of Chicago Press, Chicago, IL, 1988.

Martin, Robert C. *Agile Software Development*, Prentice Hall, Englewood Cliffs, NJ, 2003.

Maxwell, Katrina D. *Applied Statistics for Software Mangers*, Prentice Hall, Englewood Cliffs, NJ, 2002.

McConnell, Steve. *Software Project-Survival Guide*, Microsoft Press, Redmond, WA, 1998.

Peters, James F. and Pedrycz, Witold. *Software Engineering—An Engineering Approach*, John Wiley and Sons, New York, 2000.

Pressman, Roger S. *Software Engineering: A Practioner's Approach*, McGraw-Hill, New York, 2002.

Van Vliet, Hans. *Software Engineering—Principles and Practices*, 2nd ed. John Wiley and Sons, New York, 2000.

Voas, Jeffrey and McGraw, Gary. *Software Fault Injection: Inoculating Programs Against Errors*, John Wiley and Sons, New York, 1998.

Wallnau, Kurt, et al., *Building Systems from Commercial Components*, Addison-Wesley, Reading, MA, 2001.

2

People, Product, Process, Project—The Big Four

The Council on National Software Studies warns that the United States continues to have major problems developing large and complex software systems.[1] Part of the problem is knowing where to put money to be most effective in creating the desired product. Each case needs assessment. The software project manager must examine the productivity factors that experience has shown to make a difference. One would not get the most return on the salary of a world-class designer except on cutting-edge projects. The investment in the process to produce real-time, safety-critical systems is higher than that needed for simple systems because if the schedule for an order entry system slips there is potential economic loss, but if a medical or defense system slips there is potential for injury or death.

When the city of Denver was refurbishing its airport, errors in the software that controlled the automatic baggage system persisted for 9 months. The airport's planners watched their bond rating fall to junk status because the project hemorrhaged red ink at the rate of $1.1 million a day in interest and operating costs. The impact of similar stories repeated over time is that poor software causes major cost overruns, exposes companies to potential liability for defects, and jeopardizes economic opportunity.

The wise project manager knows that four factors correlate to productivity in sophisticated systems: **people**, **product**, **process**, and **project**. In this chapter,

[1] http://www.cnsoftware.org/issues/trustworthy/.

Trustworthy Systems Through Quantitative Software Engineering,
by Lawrence Bernstein and C. M. Yuhas
Copyright © 2005 IEEE Computer Society

we will examine each to be able to weigh its value for a given product, and thereby give you the basis to develop a rationale for the apportionment of available money.

2.1   PEOPLE: CULTIVATE THE GURU AND SUPPORT THE MAJORITY

The skill and dedication of software developers continues to be the most critical factor in reducing schedule and quality risks. The long-term survival of a software business depends on the productivity of its best designers, because people endure across projects and can uplift the entire organization. On a single project, the investment in this skill can reduce cost by factors of 10 to as much as 20, but the ongoing benefit can be much greater. The landmark book, *Peopleware*,[2] by DeMarco and Lister explains how to manage software people. We begin where DeMarco and Lister leave off. Everyone can spot the person with uncanny ability, insight to problems, and the easy grace to teach others. Their peers refer to them as gurus, and we will too.

The best programmers can be as much as 20 times more productive than average ones. A simple example will illustrate the cost effectiveness of a guru programmer. Assume a group of 100 programmers, 99 who are average and competent, but that last one being a guru. If the average programmer's weighted cost is $100k, the guru should be paid twice as much, $200k, and have whatever special tools and technology he or she needs, at a one-time cost of $50k. The cost of the group is (99 × $100k) + $200k + $50k = $10,150k, or $150k more than a group of 100 ordinary people. The effectiveness of the group, however, is conservatively that of 119 average programmers or $11,900k (conservatively because gurus tend to teach others by example and bring up the work of others). The presence of a guru produces the equivalent of $1750k or almost $2 million more work than an organization of 100 competent programmers.

MAGIC NUMBER!

1 guru = 10 average programmers, in addition to bringing up the quality of the entire organization.

[2] DeMarco, Tom and Lister, Timothy. *Peopleware: Productive Projects and Teams*, 2nd ed., Dorset House Publishing Co., New York, 1999.

But there is a problem with the notion of gurus. When asked to rank themselves, over 50% of programmers consider themselves to be in the "best" category. In fact, only 1% is actually in this class. What do real gurus, not just want-to-be gurus, look like, so that all managers can have a way to spot them, attract them, and keep them working?

2.1.1 How to Recognize a Guru

Gurus have unusually broad competency. They have usually worked across the board, in hardware and software, in applications and systems. They are not just generalists, however. This broad range is coupled with depth and profound innovation in at least one area.

Gurus are often, but not primarily, engaged in teaching on the job. Their colleagues recognize their ability to simplify and illuminate problems and so go to them as sounding boards.

Gurus can do bottom-up design. They can do the textbook top-down design that is important for broad system layout, but they also have the higher skill, insight, and experience it takes to do bottom-up design. The ultimate use of a system can rarely be foreseen, so the best programmer is one who builds the best platform for growth. They build systems that are robust for a wide range of input types and loads. They are sensitive to the wide variability in traffic their software may be asked to handle.

Gurus have a mental spatial map of the system and an uncanny nose for bugs. They will go almost straight from symptom to cause, using debuggers as tools for quick critical verification rather than as instruments for aimless poking around. Their fixes rarely hang or crash the system.

Gurus can iterate the design, both during the design phase and during restructuring of deployed systems, to make it "as simple as possible, but no simpler," as Einstein once remarked. They can cite quantitative measures of the "goodness" of the system. They assume individual responsibility for maintaining their code.

Gurus have lively, flexible, independent intellects. They are intensely focused on problem solving. They tend to insist on doing the right thing, regardless of other business concerns. They do not suffer fools gladly. They can be hard to manage, especially by the nontechnical bottom-line focused boss.

The secret for attaining guru status: mastery as a mindset. Masters tend to work intensely at the start of a project or introduction of new technology to reap the long-term rewards of greatest result with the least total amount of energy and time expended. They display deep intellectual curiosity. However, a master knows that it is always possible to make things better and tries several approaches for accomplishing any task. The master is savvy about judging which approaches are likely to be the more "elegant" and then experiments with those finalists to get the best result. A master of any tool has usually invented new purposes and techniques that even its creators had not envisioned.

2.1.2   How to Attract a Guru to Your Project

The culture of the organization can attract master programmers. The manager can lay bait to attract a guru. An organizational reputation for high-quality software arrests their attention. A good manager knows that system stability and reliability during design and coding produce a 30 to 1 advantage in efficiency (remember that Magic Number from Chapter 1) as compared with the chaos and crises typical of finding and fixing bugs exposed by customers. Good design and code go further to meeting schedules and budgets than any harangues or draconian methods possibly could. Additional bait could be provision for discretionary work and the tools to explore where the guru's intellect leads.

Sometimes good managers can stimulate latent gurus to bloom by preparing the ground properly. Managers can use prototyping to delay code optimization and iterative development to encourage orderly development. Managers can insist on maximal change, rather than on minimal change. Replacing whole modules instead of a few lines here and a few lines there reduces paperwork and bureaucracy. Managers can make humane schedules by using graveyard shifts only for automated test, reliability, and stability runs. Managers can support effective code inspections, so that a budding guru is not driven to distraction. Selective code inspections tend to work best; few object to having their code inspected when first joining a software shop. If the inspection shows guru potential, then removing the requirement for code inspections is reasonable as long as the code submitted to the test team is of the highest caliber. Another way to choose the modules that will be inspected is to use a program that computes a complexity metric on the source code, and then select for inspection the modules having results that are ten times worse than the average.

One might object that such pampering and protection would surely cause jealousy and dissension in a group because the manager is not even-handed. On the contrary, those programmers who are good clearly recognize the guru's talent and aspire to excellence when it is obviously recognized and rewarded. The manager's job is to protect the company assets, and the guru is a major asset. The Software Engineering Institute has done work in codifying levels of achieving organizational technical competence and has created models to identify and encourage the spread of excellence.

What separates the entry-level developer from the guru? Certainly experience, but hours logged do not necessarily track with level of proficiency. Some developers spend 10 years on a job and have only 1 year of experience, repeated ten times. Someone with an inquisitive nature who is willing to challenge the status quo with questions such as "Sure, it's tradition but remind me, why do we do it this way?" may well hold a key to mastery over software. However, a true master may go further than mere "What if . . . ?" questions and attempt to answer them with innovative solutions. With software, you will find a wide range of proficiency from one practitioner to the next.

The skilled project manager has software groups with gurus having specific skills that contribute directly to the success of the project. Developers, testers, and architects are handpicked by the project manager provide the project with key guru-level technical people. The gurus must have previous large-scale development expertise and/or extensive functional expertise within the problem domain. This combination of experience and knowledge provide the technical expertise to implement things properly and the assurance that the proper things were being implemented. The gurus train those new to software development and provide a foundation for reasoned technical decisions.

2.1.3 How to Keep Your Gurus Working

One pays a guru more in job satisfaction and collegial esteem than in dollars, although dollars can help. The manager must move the guru with the new work to keep the challenge high. Many must be protected from an unfortunate promotion to a management position, because this rarely suits such a temperament.

Disciplined and motivated people develop quality software. The common mistake that drives gurus away is an attempt by a boss to micromanage their work. The problem is that the guru's discipline seems like no discipline at all to the document-focused manager. Gurus meet regularly with others to discuss the project, and they ask others to review their work. They are intolerant of poor quality work. They know that meeting a short-term milestone with poor quality software too often leads to crises. Gurus focus on the *substance* of meetings and artifacts, whereas many managers are occupied with procedural *form*. The software guru must be allowed to hold the sort of meetings and reviews that are appropriate to the state of the project. The status of the project needs to be derived from the natural progression of the development cycle. The manager lucky enough to be blessed with a guru should humbly recognize that the managerial function is one of stewardship and respect *substance* over *form*.

2.1.4 How to Support the Majority

Most computer science degrees require intensive individual work. When a graduate moves to an industrial project, the most difficult challenge is shifting from working alone to working on a project with ten or more people. The previous premium on individuality has cultivated an attitude that it is easier to do tasks alone rather than work with others. This attitude is both so ingrained and so unexamined that new programmers automatically tend to break a project into isolated modules. This is especially true in startup companies. Each member takes a distinct module to design and develop that will later be integrated with the others' modules. This approach results in each group member having knowledge of only one aspect of the project. The ability to identify and resolve risks, to integrate the components into one working project, and to assist members in need of help is severely limited. When the size of the team exceeds three, this human tendency leads to chaos. The need to avoid this situation is a fundamental driver for the capability maturity model (CMM)[3] and for agile programming methods.

Once programmers are assembled for a project, a structure must be created to truly form a team. A deliberately structured communication network keeps everyone aware of the project progress as a whole and their part in it; regularly scheduled review meetings, e-mail progress reports, and instant messaging can all be used. If programmers or designers are newly appointed to supervise groups, they must be taught first how to manage people and, only after learning that, how to manage projects. By using a simple queuing analysis study, it can be shown that if a team leader wanted to spend an hour per week with each person in the group, six is the maximum number of employees that the supervisor could coach, manage, and still get the job done.

The following table assumes that the team leader works in a matrix organization. The team leader reports to a functional manager and is assigned to several project mangers. Table 2.1 shows probable allotments of time.

TABLE 2.1. Typical Week in the Life of a Team Manager

Team Manager interacts with:	Importance of Interaction	Requests per Week	Time per Request (hours)
Functional Manager	1	1	4
Project Managers	2	4	1
Technical Direction for Team of 6	3	4	2
Career Development for Team of 6	2	1	0.5
Administrative	2	1	0.25

Assume all service times are exponentially distributed. The queuing analysis (Table 2.2) will answer this question: How many software developers can the technical leader supervise?

TABLE 2.2. Results of Queuing Analysis

Employees Reporting to a Team Leader	Hours/Week used for Technical Direction	Number of employees awaiting technical direction at any time	Average number of hours/employee awaiting career development
6	8	1.1	10
8	12	2.2	35
10	14	3	332
12	15	5	Absurdly high

This analysis shows that if the team leader is expected to provide career development to every software developer, eight is the maximum that the team leader can supervise. When eight people report to the technical leader, two developers are idle awaiting technical direction.

---

[3] CMM is a product of the Software Engineering Institute of Carnegie Mellon University.

One solution to the time crunch is having subteams of three or fewer, so supervisors can grow their teams to 10 to 12 people. Technical subteam leaders have no administrative responsibility but are the project interface with the supervisor. Another alternative is to use matrix organizations with project managers focused on getting the job done and functional managers focused on developing their people and sharpening their skills. There is no best approach; the structure depends on the nature of the people and the project. Executives of productive companies understand that any organization is imperfect and that reorganizations help to invigorate teams by trying new combinations of personalities and perhaps methodologies.

> ### MAGIC NUMBER!
>
> When the size of a group, or the number of groups, exceeds three, consciously structure communication methods.

Once a project requires the work of more than three supervisory groups, formal project meetings and a project newsletter must be put in place. Everyone on the project needs to know how things are going. The "power of the press" can be applied to project communications by reporting the minutes of project meetings, including customer letters of plans, praise, and complaint. Usually this is a written newsletter, but Bernstein, as CTO for a 2000-developer organization, effectively broadcasted voice mail announcements. It is easy and efficient to compose a message weekly and distribute it Sunday night so that the people could hear a 4-minute summary of successes, problems, new technology directions, and changes first thing on Monday morning. To be effective, these communications in whatever form must be scrupulously honest in containing "the good, the bad and the ugly." The communication must discuss project problems and troubles to convey the management belief that such things must be brought to light promptly and dealt with rationally. All projects have problems; those that do not (because people are afraid to reveal them) are in deep trouble.

2.2 PRODUCT: "BUY ME!"

A customer presents a business problem and your corresponding marketing colleague feels sure we have just the thing to suit their needs—or we can build it in short order. What shall this product do and how, exactly, shall it do it? Let us hold for a moment the whole question of determining the validity of the customer's view of the objectives and the vendor's input concerning the practicality of the enterprise. What characteristics can we reasonably expect of a finished product? Fred Brooks defines a programming product as "a program that can be run, tested, repaired, and extended by anybody [and further describes a programming system as] a collection of interacting programs, coordinated in function and disciplined in format, so that the assemblage constitutes an entire facility for large tasks."[4] The software product is both a programming product and a programming system.

MAGIC NUMBER!

Fred Brooks points out that it takes nine times the effort that was required to get a program working to make it into a supportable software product, because problems are hard to find and hard to fix.

Software products are packages of systems designed and integrated to work together in a particular architecture to perform a set of tasks. Software products have become increasingly more complicated. With a higher level of complexity and functionality comes a higher risk of failure. To handle complexity, product developers have resorted to a system of systems that can be scaled to meet the demand of a given task set.

Functional and structural partitioning is fundamental to this way of creating software products. The necessary corollary to partitioning is some way to achieve software component integration. When we partition to manage complexity, there is an implied need to integrate. There is a tendency to brush off the product integration as no more than the purchasing of commercial off-the-shelf (COTS) products and binding them together, but integrating a software product so that it will be reliable, useful, and provide a good user experience is the not-so-easy task of the manager and each designer.

2.2.1   Reliable Software Products

How can we guarantee that a software product does not contain any bugs and will not malfunction? Thorough testing is only part of the answer. Careful design and honoring design standards is another.

---

[4] Brooks, Frederick P., Jr. *The Mythical Man-Month*, Addison-Wesley, Reading, MA, 1995, p. 6.

MAGIC NUMBER!

More than 60% of the errors in a software product are committed during the design and less than 40% during coding.

Errors in early design phases are contained in the basic building blocks of the software. Programmers can spend more time testing a few lines of code than in writing them, although the error detection work is most efficiently done at this point. Consider two lines of code dealing with one IF–THEN–ELSE statement, processing an array of 100 elements. There are 2100 different outcomes. Even on a fast machine, testing all combinations would take far too long. One modern way of dealing with this problem is to consider what would be required to prove the system before any code is written. There is an idea in hardware methodology of designing against testability requirements. Extreme programming has elaborated on this idea to create the technique of "pair" programming. One programmer writes the tests while the partner programmer writes the code.

No matter the technique, however, we cannot guarantee that a software product is fault-free under every circumstance and for all time. We can test, keep a record, and fix faults that are found, but we cannot guarantee that there are no more faults beyond the boundaries of those tests. The aim then becomes to eliminate as many faults as possible, given time limits, effort costs, and how critical certain needs are to the customer.[5] Testing is expensive, budgets are tight, time is limited, and most attention is given to the design and product implementation. Testing must be smart and thoughtful to resist shortchanging this ethical requirement in the face of great pressure to deliver the product at the end of the system production cycle.

2.2.2 Useful Software Products

The existence of many software product development companies, small and large, ensures a healthy competition as those companies strive to outdo one another. Clients want to choose the provider who offers the best deal in terms of maximum benefit, minimum cost, and shortest time to delivery to ensure the profitability of their companies.

---

[5] The authors advocate a technique called software rejuvenation to keep critical systems operating only within an exhaustively tested range. NASA uses this technique for space missions.

The nature and use of the software product influence the need for trust-worthiness, and the degree of trustworthiness required increases the time and effort needed to build the software product. As the size of the project grows, time and effort grow exponentially unless the product is partitioned into component subproducts. To estimate the effort required, estimate the effort for each subproduct and then add a 10% planning and integration effort. If COTS products are used, then there is a 5% integration effort required.

A product must be on time, within budget, and adequate to the problem domain to be useful.

MAGIC NUMBER!

Software for controlling operating systems, communications, or drivers to fit the peculiarities of a hardware device is twice as hard to write as software for online transactions products. Online transaction software is five times more difficult to write than data processing or report generation software.

2.2.3 Good User Experience

In a fast-paced environment where technological advantage can be a deciding factor in the life of a company, time to delivery is as important as cost and benefit. Often, however, the initial estimates of cost and time to delivery of software products are underestimated with the pressure of competition. The result is that after a couple of extensions of the deadline for delivery, the client gets frustrated, the developers get pressured to complete the project, and there is little time left for proving the system against the requirements. There is a tradeoff between exhaustive testing and letting the customer find out the bad news in real time. Customer testing is not a new approach. In fact, the customer may accept "good enough" because the push to early market presence seems to reward this low-quality approach. The customer is frustrated by failures but can be willing to continue if sufficiently impressed with the attention the developers give to finding and fixing faults. Some projects have been nimble at staying one step ahead of massive failure. But eventually, low quality equals low satisfaction and a crisis occurs that, in the absence of a history of good faith and performance, results in a lawsuit.

The responsible software developer engages the customer in a partnership to solve a problem. This requires some human factors analysis to ensure that the problem being solved is the problem that exists and that the elements of the solution fit the customer's environment.

2.3 PROCESS: "OK, HOW WILL WE BUILD THIS?"

Processes describe *how* a project will be produced; they do not deal with *what* the ultimate software product will do. Agile processes and object-oriented design are efficient processes that can adjust to the current state of a project. Processes provide a framework for control, the degree of which can vary as the project evolves.

2.3.1 Agile Processes

Agile processes change rapidly to meet project needs. They are characterized by dynamic changes in the amount of control as the project matures. In the early inventive stages, control is loose, but as the product takes form, more formal control is enforced. No process should rigidly insist on the same level of control through the entire life cycle.

Until the mid-1990s, most software processes were rigidly planned because software organizations wanted to mimic traditional product manufacturing and gain legitimacy by increasing process predictability. The most significant problems were deployment delays or cancellations, which led to excessive reliance on questionable software metrics. The result was bureaucratic software development without any corresponding increase in software quality. A major issue was metrics that gave no insight to the real progress of software development.[6]

2.3.1.1 Great processes can never be a substitute for incompetent managers. The principle cause of project failures is poor management. Martin Fowler and Jim Highsmith, gurus of the agile method philosophy, said, "Facilitating change is more effective than attempting to prevent it. Learn to trust in your ability to respond to unpredictable events; it's more important than trusting in your ability to plan for disaster."

New approaches to software development (extreme programming, crystal methodologies, SCRUM, adaptive software development, feature-driven development, and dynamic systems development methodology, among them) are the current stage of process evolution. Agile methods recognize the importance of process and tools, with the additional recognition that the interaction of skilled persons is of even greater importance. Similarly, comprehensive documentation is not necessarily bad, but the primary focus must remain on the final product—delivering working software. Therefore, every project team

---

[6] This cavil is neither new nor unique to software. Scott expressed it in 1911 in his book, *Increasing Human Efficiency in Business*: "The service in more than one company has been made intolerable for people of spirit and creative ability by the arrogant and dominating spirit of the management. Those who continue to sacrifice their individuality to the whim or the arbitrary rule of their superiors, in time lose their ambition and initiative; and the organization declines to a level of routine, mechanical efficiency only once removed from dry rot."

needs to determine what documentation is essential. Contract negotiation, whether through an internal project charter or external legal contract, is not a bad practice, just an insufficient one. Contracts and project charters may provide some boundary conditions within which the parties can work, but only through ongoing collaboration can a development team hope to understand and deliver what the client wants.

The highest priority is to satisfy the customer through early and continuous delivery of valuable software. A software development manager once questioned the feature or story approach to iterative cycle planning. "But aren't requirements specifications and architecture documents important?" he asked. "Yes," Jim Highsmith replied, "They *are* important, but we need to understand that customers don't care about documents, diagrams or legacy integration. Customers care about whether or not you're delivering working software to them every development cycle—some piece of business functionality that proves to them that the evolving software application serves their business needs."

2.3.1.2 So welcome changing requirements, even late in development. Agile processes harness change for the customer's competitive advantage. Rather than resist change, the agile approach strives to accommodate it as easily and efficiently as possible, while maintaining an awareness of its consequences. Although most people agree that feedback is important, they often ignore the fact that the result of accepted feedback is change. Agile methodologies harness this result, because their proponents understand that facilitating change is more effective than attempting to prevent it.

Deliver working software frequently, every couple of weeks or months, with a preference for short timescales. For many years, process experts have stressed the use of the incremental or iterative style of software development, with multiple deliveries of ever-growing functionality. Although the practice has grown in use, it is still not predominant; however, it is essential for agile projects. Furthermore, business realities push hard to reduce delivery cycle time. *Deliver* is not the same as *release*. Your customer may have valid business reasons for not putting code into production every few weeks. Some projects do not achieve releasable functionality for a year or more, but that does not exempt them from the rapid cycle of internal deliveries that allows everyone to evaluate and learn from the growing product.

Customer and developer work together daily throughout the project. Many customers want to buy software the way they buy a car. They have a list of features in mind, they negotiate a price, and they pay for what they asked for. This simple buying model is appealing, but for most software projects, it does not work. Agile developers use a radical change to the requirements process. For a start, they do not expect a detailed set of requirements to be signed off at the beginning of the project; rather, they see a high-level view of requirements that is subject to frequent change. Clearly, this is not enough to allow design and coding, so the gap is closed with frequent interaction between the customer and developers. The frequency of this contact often surprises people. Prototyping is a wonderful tool that expedites this approach.

2.3.1.3   Agile processes respect the power of human interaction by building projects around motivated persons, giving them the environment and support they need, and trusting them to get the job done. Managers must still deploy the tools, technologies, and processes, even in agile processes, but people make the difference between success and failure.

The most efficient and effective method of conveying information with and within a development team is face-to-face conversation. Inevitably, when discussing agile methodologies, the topic of documentation arises. The issue is *not* documentation—the issue is *understanding*. Physical documentation has heft and substance, but the real measure of success is abstract: Will the people involved gain the understanding they need? Project teams can and should use the most effective communication techniques. "Tacit knowledge cannot be transferred by getting it out of people's heads and onto paper," writes Nancy Dixon. "Tacit knowledge can be transferred by moving the people who have the knowledge around. The reason is that tacit knowledge is not only the facts but the relationships among the facts—that is, how people might combine certain facts to deal with a specific situation."[7] So the distinction between agile and document centric methodologies is not one of extensive documentation versus no documentation, but a differing concept of the blend of documentation and conversation required to elicit understanding.

2.3.1.4   Working software is the primary measure of progress. Project teams cannot afford to realize they are in trouble just before delivery. It can be a nasty surprise to see that even though they did the requirements on time, the design on time, maybe even the code on time, the testing and integration took much longer than expected. Iterative development provides milestones that cannot be fudged, which imparts an accurate measure of the progress and a deeper understanding of the risks involved in any given project.

Continuous attention to technical excellence and good design enhances agility. When many people look at agile development, they see reminders of the "quick and dirty" rapid application development (RAD) efforts of the 1990s. But although agile development is similar to RAD in terms of speed and flexibility, there is a big difference when it comes to technical discipline. Agile approaches emphasize quality of design, because design quality is essential to maintaining agility. One tricky aspect, however, is the fact that agile processes assume and encourage the alteration of requirements while the code is being written. As such, design cannot be a purely up-front activity to be completed before construction. Instead, design is a continuous activity that is performed throughout the project. Every iteration has design work.

---

[7] Dixon, Nancy. *Common Knowledge*, Harvard Business School Press, Cambridge, MA, 2000.

Simplicity—the art of maximizing the amount of work *not* done—is essential. Any software development task can be approached with a host of methods. In an agile project, it is particularly important to use simple approaches, because they are easier to change. It is easier to add something to a process that is too simple than it is to remove steps from a complicated one. Hence, there is a strong taste of minimalism in all agile methods. Include only what *every*body needs rather than what *any*body needs. The same principle applies to the product. "Simple, clear purpose and principles give rise to complex, intelligent behavior," says Dee Hock, former CEO of Visa International. "Complex rules and regulations give rise to simple, stupid behavior." No methodology can ever address the complexity of a modern software project. Giving people a simple set of rules and encouraging their creativity will produce far better outcomes than imposing complex, rigid regulations.

The best architectures, requirements, and designs emerge from self-organizing teams. The best designs emerge from iterative development and product use rather than from early plans. The second point of the principle is that emergent properties (*emergence*, a key property of complex systems, roughly translates to innovation and creativity in human organizations) are best generated from self-organizing teams in which the interactions are high and the process rules are few.

Case Study: The Case of the Late (but Great!) Operating System

In the 1980s, there was a service crisis in the U.S. telephone industry. To resolve it, a high-risk, high-payoff, large-scale telecommunications business system, which affected all Regional Bell Operating Companies, was designed using a supplier-provided operating system (SOS). It saved $1 billion a year in reduced operating costs from the mid-1980s to the present, at a development cost of $500 million, 5 years, and 300 to 400 team members, including 40 persons dedicated to systems planning and testing.

It arrived pretty much on schedule with functionality that exceeded the original requirements, despite late delivery of the communications subsystem by the vendor and early architecture problems. How was this feat accomplished?

Solution: Processes and organizational structures to cope with uncertainty were put in place from the start. The design consisted of five major subsystems, each of which could be deployed alone as well as integrated with the others. Architectural problems emerged immediately. New technology was needed to create databases, integrate the systems, and track customer orders. The system architect shifted the project from COBOL to C language to attract the best designers and to take advantage of the extensive C run time libraries. The libraries were an early example of software reuse and reduced the design effort by 15%.

Then it became apparent that although most of SOS was world-class, efficient, and reliable, the communications subsystem was obsolete. SOS agreed to provide an upgrade, but because of the difficulty of the task, it delivered it 18 months behind schedule. Because of the delay from SOS, the project team was inspired to create an environment that allowed testing the core application logic without the underlying operating system. Gurus developed an "adaptive layer" to run the application on a temporary UNIX OS, which allowed testing logical code performance. The five major subsystems were built so that the data structures and relations were independent of the operating system.

The project schedule became a dynamic tool for project management. The variables that counted were **resources**, **time allocation**, and **dependencies**. To meet the final deliverable dates, the project team implemented a new, cooperative testing process. As each module was completed, it would be tested in the UNIX environment. The integration team, idled by the wait for SOS, helped to do subsystem functional testing. They tossed out defect tracking with all its attendant overhead and paperwork. Instead, a buggy module would be entirely replaced with a new one. These actions applied Boehm's precept of "Start with loose controls and tighten as the project evolves."

Conclusion: When timelines and cost are not greatly affected, new and innovative solutions to project goals can be entertained. This was especially useful in the project when development teams were stuck at some roadblock. When traditional methods failed, the freedom to "try anything" allowed new methods to be explored without condemnation. Therefore, **allow experimentation when there is little to lose.**

Foster an atmosphere of cooperation. Cooperation is empowerment. This is not only stated to the team members explicitly, but it is encouraged through the actions of management. The recognition of their value to the project and their trustworthiness to make appropriate decisions gives team members a sense of ownership and control. Through this support, the team participates more actively and works together to achieve results.

Learn that success breeds success. Never change a development plan until a significant milestone is achieved. Continual redefinition not only destroys morale and self-confidence, but it leads to sloppy work habits. Everyone needs closure to see that something has been accomplished.

2.3.2 Object-Oriented Opportunities

When was the first time a computerized system really got it right and changed a company for the better? And how have we been doing since? Let us begin with the answer to the first question and then spend some time on the second question.

Case Study: The Case of the "Lion's Share" at Tea Time

The Lyons catering company in England supplied small teashops with cakes and sandwiches in the 1950s. They ran their business with fleets of women who would call each retail shop every day to calculate their needs. The far-sighted management became convinced that the power of computers could be harnessed to increase their profits and serve their customers better. They actually built a computer and succeeded in deploying an enterprise-wide automation system. The changes ranged from anticipating orders based on past patterns to defining the order of loading the trucks for maximum efficiency in delivery. They came to dominate the take-home cake and sandwich business in the United Kingdom. Everyone ate Lyons cakes and sandwiches! This heady success led to the spinoff of a computer company that eventually became ICL.

Conclusion: The history of Lyons is noteworthy because it is the exception. Most software projects fail to live up to expectations. Often developers understand neither the business practices they are automating nor the business changes they will cause. The developers have also been known to do a poor job of producing the software. Lyons' developers started from scratch. They controlled the requirements, and they worked closely with the hardware developers to build a system suitable for them. Force-fitting this system to others proved problematic.[8]

2.3.2.1   Thomas Landauer points out that, in the telephone industry, computers have led to measurable productivity gains.[9] The telephone companies achieved a 2% per year productivity gain with the introduction of computer technology, a gain not seen in other industries. Telephone companies have spent 50% of their annual capital investments in information technology products and services since the mid-1960s. This long-term commitment has paid off. Today, information technology is at the core of the telephone business. The telephone companies took a giant step to assure success of their overall program when they invested in standardizing their businesses processes. They produced the Bell System Standards that defined how telephone companies would operate. As the business changed, these practices were updated. After the 1984 breakup of the Bell System, Bellcore maintained them. These business practices became the basis for the subsequent automation. Of course, not every system worked. Some missed the mark, but many served to increase the productivity of the telephone worker. Because there was a carefully maintained set of practices, there were many opportunities to redo the systems that

[8] ACM, *Computer Pioneers and Pioneer Computers Dawn of Electronic Computing 1948–1950*, The Computer Museum, 1996, www.acm.org.
[9] Landauer, Thomas, K. *The Trouble with Computers Usefulness, Usability and Productivity*, MIT Press, Cambridge, MA, 1995, p. 24.

failed. With this habit of designing business practices first, it was natural for the telephone industry to quickly adopt object-oriented technology. Enterprise-wide object classes were derived from the practices. These object classes speeded the introduction of object-oriented technology.

2.3.2.2 One modern telephone software system is enlightening. The system supports the use of new, very fast broadband networks in the telephone company plant. Because this was clearly a large-scale development effort, the designers adopted the use of objects early. The size of the project in its first release was 12,600 function points contained in 22 software modules with 47 interfaces and 12 databases. This complexity was organized into 278 object classes and 1200 objects. The developers adhered to four overarching principles in making their design decisions. **System synthesis** melds methods and business objects from the customer's, not the developers', viewpoint. **Modular architecture** separates data from applications and enforces strong data stewards. **Object-oriented analysis** includes extensive domain analysis, rigorous requirements, business usage scenarios worked out with the user, formal external and internal interface agreements, and an integrated data model. **Object-oriented design** uses client/server architecture and industry-wide telecommunications management standards.

The most serious problem on this project, which may be extrapolated to most projects, is the need to keep data consistent. Older design methods used convoluted error paths to do this; error paths often use more code and time than building new systems, adding features to existing systems, or building bridges to vintage systems. Object oriented technology can lead to predictable system developments with fast time-to-market and solid performance. It allows system updates in a timely manner without waiting 9 to 12 months for the next big release. It lets developers make frequent and important changes to the human interface and to accommodate changes in business processes. It makes reuse easy and drives system designs to better reflect the problem than older procedural methods.

Until object-oriented design becomes a habit, an enforced object encapsulation strategy with centralized object libraries is vital. Skilled project managers must insist that all subsystems and modules use the same operation, administration, and management software, which achieves meaningful reuse and results in huge savings, as much as $5000 per client.

With object-oriented approaches, the developers delivered in 18 months what would have taken 36 to 42 months by other means. A record level of reuse among customers was achieved; the most tailored system required 15% custom code, and the least customized required none. The time to market for new customers is now 90 days, and productivity, measured in terms of function points per staff, continues to increase 25% with each release.[10]

---

[10] Bernstein, Lawrence and Yuhas, C. M. *Basic Concepts for Managing Telecommunication Networks*, Plenum Press, New York, 1999, Chapter 7.

2.3.2.3   That these wonderful results can be attributed to a disciplined use of object-oriented technology is supported by other experiences. The Swiss Bank Corporation saw a 50% productivity improvement during its reengineering that started in 1991.

In 1994, at a conference in Japan, engineers described installing their new object-oriented system. Reuse was the key to their success. The benefits of prototyping and adherence to clean object class definitions exceeded expectations. They managed risks by adhering to standard enterprise object classes and gluing them together. They anticipated some performance problems, and these did occur. The cost/performance improvement of new computer servers more than compensated for the 10% performance overrun they saw.

Foster Wheeler reports that using objects with their business rules drives the applications development. A decision-making process is modeled and then iteratively modified. Rule bases are made part of the object methods so that the rules can be applied dynamically. This approach allows the inheritance and distribution of intelligence among objects at various levels. As changes are made to the rules, they naturally migrate to the affected objects. By using this approach, they reduced the time for projects from 12 months to 8 weeks, which may herald the reawakening of the expert system technology that held so much promise in the 1980s.

AT&T developed more than 50 object-oriented systems using a unique "objects in memory" approach. The objects are locked in memory while the system runs. One such system may be biggest and fastest object-oriented network management system in the world. It uses 1 GB of memory for its 15 million objects and thousands of transactions per second on a high-end work-station. It has been in production for several years with no significant problems. It replaced a vintage host-centric provisioning system. This exciting new approach will become widely used as computer memory is extended to 64-bit addresses and added to the natural structure of object-oriented databases. This will open virtual memory machines to objects and regain the freedom from memory constraints enjoyed by application developers in earlier transaction systems. Objects tend to drive designers to single-threaded solutions, so execution platforms that encourage multithreading are the next step in decision making for reliable components.

2.3.2.4   The MCI Data Warehouse Project relied on off-the-shelf relational databases rather than object-oriented bases. It is a textbook example of the use of a gateway and client/server relational databases to gather information from many databases to produce reports. The multiplatform distributed set of databases consisted of IBM DB/2 as well as others. It has the look and feel of a single SQL server. This project was not trivial. The challenge was to analyze, organize, normalize, link, and migrate data onto a database that end users could easily access without having to formulate complex SQL queries or write code. This is wholly different from developing databases that meet the stringent performance needs of network management systems. They routinely download data from network management systems to populate their data-mining server. Here is a situation where object-oriented databases can live in harmony with relational ones. The performance needs are met with the object-oriented ones, whereas the flexibility for inquiries is met with a relational database.

In the MCI case, data analysts were called on to model data in a way that maximized usefulness to service planners, which meant rethinking the data model so that data availability and flexibility were maximized while retaining sensitivity to long inquiries. This data modeling job was hard because of the several layers of indirection required to use the relational database management systems in the source systems. Direct use of object modeling and object-oriented databases, instead of relying on relational databases in most source systems, could have simplified this task and made the data models more flexible for unanticipated use. Without MCI's earlier and large investment in data management, this project could have easily failed because research into a complex web of poorly modeled and documented databases is nearly impossible.

2.3.2.5 Large-scale evolving software presents a special challenge to object architects. Typically, an application consists of a network of objects connected through compatible interfaces. The need to meet new requirements or fix defects often results in new interfaces and object versions. In this dynamic environment, there is a premium in keeping all modules consistent. Often this is left to the test teams, where, as we recall from the Magic Number in Chapter 1, it is an expensive activity. Object oriented technology opens the door to dynamic checking of interface states and internal consistency. Projects can effectively use libraries of interface object classes to do this job.

When a new version of an object is created, it must be dynamically installed without causing disruption to existing software. Objects must be intelligent enough to handle the problems of dynamic reconfiguration, coordinate inter-module communication, and track the internal states of both the objects and the links. This process increases the complexity of objects and can prevent them from being reused in different contexts. One solution is to not allow interface changes. This harsh rule often makes the application difficult to build. Often application-level interfaces are imprecise because of timeouts and repeated transmissions triggered by buffer losses in asynchronous communication. The interface specifications are vague and not amenable to analysis. Creating a design that allows for easy testing is difficult to achieve. It leads to a loss of confidence in the system. Developer productivity falls rapidly because so much time is spent resolving interface problems. Object-oriented technology within modern platforms can solve this problem.

2.3.2.6   The Common Object Request Broker Architecture (CORBA) object standard is becoming one way to do distributed computing. CORBA is the object middleware standard, but CORBA has not yet provided the tools and methods needed for large applications. It locks the sender until the receiver gets and acknowledges the message, which makes concurrency difficult to achieve for distributed applications. CORBA does not support multicycle transactions. CORBA's object module is evolving and may become the standard of choice. *Network Computing* magazine reported in 1997 that Object Request Brokers are ready to use for development, but they lack sufficient services and ties to existing networks to deploy them. Meanwhile, the DCOM object standard sponsored by Microsoft for Windows offers an object approach to communications. Another group, the Message Oriented Middleware Association, extends CORBA by using message-oriented middleware (MOM). They add asynchronous communication, scalability, and quality-of-service features to CORBA through MOM. Most organizations are using CORBA or DCOM in combination with uniquely developed interfaces.

2.3.2.7   Getting started in object-oriented design cannot be done by simply saying so or by selecting a demonstration project in the hope that its success will spill over to the rest of the organization. Resistance is most strong among middle managers because they see the need to retrain themselves and their people while they try to meet tight schedules and cost goals. Managing unfamiliar new technology is difficult.

A successful approach is to reinvent business practices using object-oriented design techniques. It demands that object-oriented technology be at the heart of the enterprise architecture. With middleware being widely adopted for building robust enterprise-wide applications and with companies moving to thin clients, or at least thick ones controlled from a central systems' management organization, the time is ripe to embrace objects. Object technology ties the desktop, the Web, legacy, and client/server applications into a coherent whole.

With the spread of JAVA and the adoption of component technologies, applications can be developed rapidly. By coupling an object approach with rapid prototyping, development is reduced from years to months. The formal adoption of Boehm's spiral approach with its focus on getting the requirements right early in the development cycle adds another tool for rolling out applications quickly.

MAGIC NUMBER!

Transparent computing using JAVA interpretive programming gives a three-fold increase in productivity and regularly achieves 80% reuse.

Jump-starts have proven remarkably effective. Two people experienced in object-oriented design are assigned to a development group for 3 months. They answer the questions developers struggle with in the transition from procedural programming to object programming.

All parts of a system do not need to be simultaneously converted to object technology. A good approach is to start with the system administration and human interface functions, then move on to the core objects that model the enterprise. A gradual evolutionary approach is best.

2.3.2.8 Here is a typical pattern of the transition experience.

- The first object-oriented release has no increase in productivity. Extensions are two to four times cheaper and faster than before. Defect-free code is produced.
- Software build times grow exponentially until object classes are nested.
- A software process team is essential throughout the development cycle.
- C++/OO experts are critical during the move from procedural programming. Keeping the architecture team small is important. A throw-away prototype is important.
- Software middle managers are appointed once the architecture exists and the first development iteration begins.
- Design rules constrain the use of memory, language constructs, object classes, and communications.
- Engineers staff the complex real-time embedded portions of the system.
- Incremental development and phased releases work well with object-oriented technology.
- Templates for object classes work well.
- Limiting the number of objects works to produce a manageable number of global objects.
- Staff accepts object-oriented technology.

A rich integration of object and relational databases with a strong focus on module interactions is a good technical practice. Organizations adopting object-oriented technology eventually gain a three-fold productivity advantage over those that stay with procedural methods.

2.3.3   Meaningful Metrics

Remember, projects that have no problems are in deep trouble. If there are no problems, either the staff is afraid to speak for fear of their jobs or the metrics are defective. In the first case, the project manager is a fool and should be fired. In the second case, meaningful metrics help bridge the gap between perception and reality. If the metrics are rosy but the customers complain, something is wrong with what is being measured or how it is measured.

When the metrics warn of a serious problem, the first step is to make sure you understand what the numbers are telling you. Then you can decide on a plan of action. The problem with meaningful metrics is that they are not always measurable. The metric "percent of code completed" cannot be measured. The metric "module delivered to test team" is measurable. However, the *measurable* metric could mean that a module is under change control, the code has been reviewed, or the code follows commenting conventions and has been unit tested. To make this metric *meaningful*, acceptance criteria must be defined for both the test team and the developers.

Meaningful metrics drive the development process to reduced time, lower cost, and better quality testing. Analysis of metrics can show the current state and trends in the software development process and whether a project is following its plan. But for metrics to be effective, management must use them, analyze the reasons behind the numbers, and understand their context.

MAGIC NUMBER!

Things to measure:

Defects found during development versus 1 year of deployment.
Testing hours required to find a defect.
Percent of tests showing no defects.

The skill of the tester and the form of the test affect the results as much as the objective quality of the software. Consistently high- or low-pass rates and the subsequent performance of the passed modules can suggest actions to management. Table 2.3 shows actions that can be effected before it is too late to change the course of testing.

TABLE 2.3. Actions in Response to Challenging Test Results

	Unreliable Modules Passed	Reliable Modules Only Passed
High-Pass Rate	Alter and strengthen the testing program because: 1. Tester does not recognize problems or 2. Tester does not test correctly.	See if good methods can be further automated. If yes, redeploy resources as needed.
Low-Pass Rate	Refocus testing and testers. 1. If multiple symptoms of the same problem, STOP until root cause is fixed. 2. If unintended uses tested, STOP for clarification.	Continue in the same direction and keep improving the software.

The continuing challenge of software metrics will yield a more cost-effective process by optimizing resource utilization. In other words, the job will be continually refocused toward efficiency. The necessary condition for optimal operations is the positioning of evaluation checkpoints inside the phases of the current process. The need to challenge applies not only to testing but also to reviews, code walkthroughs, and simulations.

Given limited resources, it is important to focus these resources on the most important tasks. For instance, if we know that a particular requirement modifies a fragile set of modules, the activity in all phases for this set of modules should be given high priority, from system requirements to field delivery. Conversely, a reasonably sound area in the hands of experienced developers can be given lower priority. This prioritization should occur dynamically so resources freed from low-priority tasks can be moved to high-priority ones.

2.4 PROJECT: MAKING IT WORK

Finally a customer comes through the door with a business need for you to meet and you must start THE PROJECT with your background, experience, tools, and essentially a blank slate. You know the broad objectives and realize that building a prototype is often the best way to get started.

As you assemble the design team, be aware that people do not bring the same level of commitment, reliability, or competency to a job. In many organizations, the top performers usually are tapped for several important projects. To recruit these people to your project team requires defining the benefits of being on the team, such as recognition, uniquely challenging work and professional development, as well as reallocating their time from ongoing job responsibilities and other projects. An All-Star team may not necessarily guarantee smooth functioning. People with other talents, such as group communications, problem mediation, or patience for working through gritty details are also needed.

Projects are plagued with developing the wrong functions, designing poor user interfaces, overengineering, and shifting requirements. Prototyping is an excellent technique for getting the design right, as long as we do not get so caught up in the prototype that we think it is the product. If the customer finds the prototype exciting, the temptation is to package it for sale without any redesign. The redesign phase takes into account the needs of more than one market, scaling for different sizes, and the peculiarities of local conditions. The prototype can also be too good at showing the system concept. Customers who love the concept but hate the price might develop a system themselves if the design cannot be protected with patents.

With these caveats in mind, put the prototype into the customer's business situation (or a mock-up of the conditions) and allow the team and the customer to play with it. From this experience, you can judge the accuracy of your understanding of the objectives and estimate the size of the job by using function points and an estimation tool such as COCOMO.

After an analysis of the prototype, the organization can be enlarged based on the size estimate. Large projects often require bringing together a multidisciplinary group of people with varied skills, areas of expertise, and roles in the organization. As you assemble these people, keep the following questions in mind: What expertise will be needed—technological, operational, financial, legal? Which affiliated departments will be needed? What information will be needed and who has access to it? In addition to the obvious technical skills, are human relations skills, including persuasion, negotiation, research, and written and verbal communication identified?

Using top-down design, partition the project into modules, define and control interfaces, and appoint module owners. Use modern software interface conventions such as object classes, pipes, and tag value data.

Reduce complexity in the design with a formal "design simplification" effort. Establish a simplification target by maximizing reuse, eliminating redundancy, and simplifying algorithms. Specific approaches useful for this effort include

(1) Refactoring
(2) Validating requirements with prototypes
(3) Relaxing design constraints
(4) Eliminating generality
(5) Finding COTS to eliminate development effort
(6) Firm interface contacts or standards that normalize data and control exchanges.

Implement designs, using structured programming techniques, only after they have been inspected. Submit tested software and work practices through an independent manufacturer (or builder) to the quality assurance and integration organization.

Test incrementally. Create a simple working system, and then add sets of changes to gradually increase capability. Do regression tests on each new increment using test cases developed for the previous increment.

Using the good relationship you have developed with your customer through the prototyping experience, together identify a friendly operational site where workers are willing to try out new features before they are formally released. This may also be the soak site for new product releases.

Do not juggle too many areas at once. Avoid developing a new application on new hardware and/or new operating system software. Have maintainers share some of the continuing development responsibility.

Case Study: The Case of Stabilizing the Aegean Stables

You, Hercules, are a successful project manager. Mr. Eurystheus, the boss of the boss of your boss, asks you to manage a troubled project. This is a career enhancement opportunity for you. You will gain the experience to balance short- and long-term customer needs, project goals, and the changing focus of work, but only if you are clever and strong.

The project is a customer resource management system, which handles all customer purchase orders. The current project team consists of 50 people who are torn apart by destructive internal politics and favoritism. The existing managers are unskilled in software, and as a result, the software is very buggy. The current measure of system performance is the time between crashes. Planning amounts to daily 8:00 AM "stand up" meetings to assign firefighters for the day. The date for the next release of the software is in 1 week.

Question: What do you do?

Answer: Delay the release and stabilize the software (debug it!). Talk to the customer and say that you need time to make the system stable.

Conclusion: You get the crisis under control. Your team is allowed to focus on the critical bugs without customer interference. When your management asks why you ignore customer requests for a technical meeting, you reply, "The customer will not let the technical people make the technical decisions." Now your career and the reputation of your company with this important customer are on the line. There is tremendous tension between the customer's staff and your staff.

Problem: You must first establish your credibility with your development team; otherwise each person will decide alone what the best course is and pursue it alone. If that happens, you will lose control of the project and the system will continue to crash. The developers have been working long, hard hours under a "forced march" project philosophy and have learned this way to survive.

Question: How do you win developers' acceptance?

Answer: More pay will not work; software developers already have high salaries and benefits. You do know, however, that by allowing the developers to choose their technology and tools, they will be committed. They want to work on a time-sharing system, so you decide to risk all by allowing the project to jump from a batch development environment to a time-sharing system.

Problem: Many developers on the project like to be heroes. They enjoy the excitement of crises. They do not like to plan or design. You know that people whose values do not match those of the organization become malcontents, but you need their talents and would rather not confront them head-on.

Question: How do you deal with them?

Answer: Empower the testers to reject code that they judge to be not reliable enough or that does not conform to standards you define. An ancillary benefit is that the testers, who had neither power nor respect previously, suddenly have both and search for bugs with a vengeance.

Question: How do you restore confidence between you and the customer?

Answer: Establish regular meetings between your people and the customer's staff charged with installing and operating the system to discuss *only* the contents of the next release and not any changes or improvements or "while you're there" extras. You must prevent "creeping featurism." Too much was being attempted without a configuration system. Make it clear to all that you and you alone have the authority to commit to features and schedules.

Problem: People are afraid to talk about software problems because they fear that, as the bearer of bad news, they will get into trouble.

Question: How do you get people to speak up about legitimate problems?

Answer: Celebrate each problem found in house as being one less found by the customer. Praise the diligence of those who find problems. People need lots of stroking with just a little poking.

Lessons Learned: Employ project managers skilled in software. Choose the right people and nurture them; treat them with respect. Create an open environment. Encourage problem identification.

For a troubled project, stabilize the organization, fix the problems, and then grow. The long-term strategy is to mortgage sales for management discipline, because *without a today, there is no tomorrow; without a tomorrow, why bother?* Quality is vital: Set and enforce high standards for software delivered to the test team.

Create a good relationship with the customer. Control commitments. Honor the four P's of project management: People, Product, Process, and Project.

2.5 PROBLEMS

2.5.1 You are developing a system in which code will be written in C++ and Perl; mySQL will be used for the system's database. All three people in your group are skilled in C++ and in Perl, but not in mySQL. You estimate that there is enough work for the three to do 2 months each of C++ work, 1 month each of Perl work and possibly 2 months each of mySQL work. You cannot hire any additional software developers, and you have decided there is ongoing benefit to sending all three to mySQL training. Which is the safest plan to start with?

a. Do the C++ and Perl coding first, and then send the three people for mySQL training.
b. Send the three to mySQL training after they have done about half of the C++ and Perl coding.
c. Send the three to mySQL training before doing any C++ or Perl work.
d. Send one or two people to mySQL training while the remaining person/people start the C++ and Perl coding. Send the other(s) to mySQL training at a later point.

2.5.2 Your team is developing a system for a small company that sells one-of-a-kind antiques on the Web. The system will contain modules for creating and editing descriptions of items for sale, uploading descriptions to the website's database, taking orders over the Web, validating and processing credit card payments, maintaining the status—for sale, ordered, or shipped—for each item, creating records of ordered items for mailing by the shipping department, and performing accounting activities for tax and other purposes. Completion on the various modules is as follows:

• Creating and editing descriptions of items for sale: 80%
• Uploading descriptions to website's database: 90%
• Taking orders over Web: 75%
• Validating and processing credit card payments: 65%
• Maintaining the status for each item: 95%
• Creating records of ordered items shipping: 80%
• Performing accounting activities: 60%.

This process puts you about 2 months behind schedule. You will have to tell that to the client, but the client understands that scheduling software is not a precise science and will probably agree to a 2-month extension if you have something to show. You are meeting with the client soon. You estimate that you can accomplish one of the following by the time of the meeting. Which one do you do?

a. Work on all the modules to get them all, with any luck, to 90% completion.
b. Get the editing and uploading functions 100% complete and working. Leave five modules at the current completion levels.
c. Get status maintenance, shipping order, and accounting functions 100% complete. Leave four modules at the current completion levels.
d. It does not matter as none of the above three alternatives is any better than the others.

2.5.3 A software shop is concerned with the productivity of its developers, so they do a time study. They survey 22 software people for a typical 40-hour workweek. The results are shown in Table 2.4.

TABLE 2.4. How Developers Keep Busy

Activity	Hours Spent
Nonproject meetings	3.0
Field problems	3.0
Meetings	3.0
Administrative chores	0.5
Equipment problems	0.25
Junk mail	1.0
Customer interaction	0.0
Training	0.0
Testing	8
Documenting	5
Analysis	4
Design	4
Coding	7.25
Idle	1.0

The 22 people surveyed work on transaction-based systems. They use the document-focused Waterfall Model for development. The organization averages 200 NCSLOC per staff month and wants to increase productivity to 250 NCSLOC per staff month.

a. What technical changes would you try?

b. What organizational changes would you try?

c. What management changes would you try?

2.5.4   You are developing a transaction processing software system for a large international bank. The system will receive transactions 24 hours a day, 7 days a week. Research has indicated that the average daily transaction rate, with 95% probability, will be about 240,000 transactions per day. You are constructing a test plan for the system. You should be safe if you test the system for performance at up to 40,000 transactions per hour, i.e., for four times the expected transaction rate.

a. Agree strongly

b. Agree

c. Disagree

d. Disagree strongly

2.5.5   You are project manager for a safety-critical software system. Your test team finds two test cases out of 1000 producing some unexpected results in areas of the system not critical to its prime functions. In fact, the customer does not plan to use the features that are problematical for a year. The customer is demanding delivery as promised, a competitor company has offered an equivalent system to your customer at a significant price reduction, and your management questions your judgment in wanting to reveal the flaws. What do you do?

a. Explain the problem to the customer and recommend that they let you find and fix the problem before you ship it.

b. Explain the problem to your management and recommend that they let you find and fix the problem before you ship it.

c. Hold up shipment to isolate and understand the extent of the problem before you ship the software.

d. Label the system "provisional" and include a description of the problem in the release letter.

e. Ship the system on-time and continue testing because you know the customer will not use the faulty functions for a year.

2.6   ADDITIONAL PROBLEMS BASED ON CASE STUDIES

Case Study: The Case of Putting the Application before the Middleware

A project team needs to develop a system using tools and components that were delivered late and were still being changed by the supplier. The supplier happens to be the customer. The team needs to build the system on top of a moving foundation. They need to identify the problem, assess the risk, and develop a way to cope with shortcomings in their supplier turned customer.

The customer has a highly intensive database transaction system to track customers and the computers they buy. An earlier attempt failed because the software technology chosen proved unable to convert and track all the information and replace paper systems and records.

Design is the primary concern of the project. The project team wanted a system that was scalable and robust. They required that it accept and share data with any of the customer's legacy systems. To this end, the project manager decided against a traditional mainframe system and opted for the newer UNIX system, using C for the development language. It was thought that by using UNIX, the system would be more flexible and implementation would be cheaper.

One aspect of the development environment was homogeneity. The entire environment was UNIX with C, which greatly reduced integration issues, and the flexibility of C allowed any to be corrected quickly when they develop. Constant communication across the project team led to a reduction in integration issues, as plans and tactics were discussed openly and early enough for all to adapt.

The subsystems were to run on new middleware tuned to database performance. However, it slipped and was projected to be 10 months behind schedule. Despite this delay, system development moved forward because of the flexibility that was built into the system. With the delay in the operating system, the project team constructed a workaround that would allow for testing the core application logic.

Problem: You are the process design engineer for this team. What four processes might you include to compensate for the delivery problems?

Case Study: The Case of the No-Service Service Request

BU&U is a statewide company with headquarters in Delaware. Part of BU&U's business is to satisfy service requests for equipment installations, repairs, and so on. at customer sites. Each request is handled by dispatching a BU&U technician to the customer site, from the BU&U work center nearest the customer location. BU&U has ten work centers.

The service request system was completely manual until the VP for Customer Service at BU&U telephoned the Director of BU&U's software development team (SDT) to see if the SDT could design and implement a computerized version of the service request system as a potential cost-saving measure. The SDT delivered an automated service request system that operated as follows:

- A clerk enters a service request into BU&U's central service request computer. Each transaction requires some processing by this central computer.

- Customers sometimes call to inquire about the progress made on their as-yet-unsatisfied service requests. Each call requires that an average of two inquiry transactions to the service request computer.
- Each work center has 10 clerks. They process, on average, four service requests and two inquires per hour. Each work center is open daily from 8:00 AM until 10:00 PM.
- At each BU&U work center, a dispatcher is responsible for scheduling service visits to customer sites by BU&U technicians. Each dispatcher has a new computer connected via BU&U's intranet to the BU&U central service request computer from which the Dispatcher periodically requests a service request report that is a list of service requests that must be satisfied within 48 hours by the requesting work center. Two summary service request reports a day are normally wanted.
- The dispatcher uses the service request report to dispatch technicians to customer sites and to determine if overtime is necessary to satisfy all service requests on time.
- At the end of each day, a daily transaction profile (DTP) is sent back to the SDT for analysis. The DTP includes the transaction type, its arrival time, and the time at which its processing was completed.

The system is delivered, and at the end of the first week, acceptance testing goes smoothly. The first center is put online at the start of the second week. The system performs well. The second center is put online at the beginning of the third week.

At the end of the third week, everything has gone smoothly, except that on Wednesday of that week, the Operations Manager, the BU&U employee responsible for all ten work centers, mentions that the inquiry transactions are taking longer to process than during the first and second weeks. As far as the SDT can tell, all transactions are being processed well within the response time specified in the requirements document, but the operations manager is correct. There is no explanation for this subtle increase in response time. Other work distracts the SDT, and they do not pursue this glitch. So the operations manager signs the software acceptance form and thanks them for a job well done. It was on schedule and within budget.

The third work center goes online on the first day of the fourth week. On Tuesday, the Director of the SDT gets an irate call from the operations manager. "The system died yesterday at about 3:00 PM, and nobody at the three work centers has any idea why! When we restarted, it worked, but very sluggishly; transaction response times were sometimes not within specification, but they got better late in the day." The operations manager demands an immediate solution, or she will return to the old manual system. "We can't run a business this way," she says.

Problem: What do you, as director of the SDT, do first?

Problem: At about 3:00 PM the next day, the system hangs again in your presence. What is happening here?

Problem: What short-term actions do you take?

BIBLIOGRAPHY

Barton, John J. and Nackman, Lee. *Scientific and Engineering C++*, Addison-Wesley, Reading, MA, 1995.

Bernstein, Lawrence and Yuhas, C. M. "And the Walls Come Tumblin' Down," *IEEE Communications Magazine*, Dec. 1992.

Boehm, Barry. *Software Engineering Economics*, Prentice Hall, Englewood Cliffs, NJ, 1981, Sections 26.3 and 33.6.

Booch, Grady. *Object Oriented Analysis and Design with Applications*, Benjamin Cummings, Redwood City, CA, 1994.

Coplien, James O. *Advanced C++ Programming Styles and Idioms*, Addison-Wesley, Reading, MA, 1992.

DeMarco, Tom and Lister, Timothy. *Peopleware: Productive Projects and Teams*, 2nd ed. Dorset House Publishing Co., New York, 1999.

Frey, Anthony. "Into ORBit, Object Request Brokers: Servers of the 21st Century," *Network Computing*, Vol. 8, No. 4, March 1, 1997, pp. 51–60.

Gamma, Erich, Helm, Richard, Johnson, Ralph, and Vlissides, John. *Design Patterns: Elements of Reusable Object Oriented Software*, Addison-Wesley, Reading, MA, 1995.

Gaudin, Sharon. "Object Stamp of Approval," *ComputerWorld*, Vol. 31, No. 11, March 17, 1997, p. 1.

Goldberg, Adele and Rubin, Kenneth S. *Succeeding with Objects: Decision Frameworks for Project Management*, Addison-Wesley, Reading, MA, 1995.

Graham, Ian. "Making Progress in Metrics, Task-Point Analysis Can Be Performed at the Requirements Stage," *Object Magazine*, Vol. 6, No. 8, October 1996, pp. 68–73.

Highsmith, James A. III. *Adaptive Software Development*, Dorset House Publishing, New York, NY, 2000.

Korson, Tim and McGregor, John D. "Understanding Object Oriented: a Unifying Paradigm," *Communications of the ACM*, Sept. 1990, pp. 41–60.

Landauer, Thomas, K. *The Trouble with Computers: Usefulness, Usability, and Productivity*, MIT Press, Cambridge, MA, 1996, pp. 13–35.

Levy, Leon. *Taming the Tiger—Software Engineering and Software Economics*, Springer-Verlag, New York, 1987, ch. 4.

Mancl, Dennis and Havanas, William. "A Study of the Impact of C++ on Software Maintenance," *Proceedings IEEE Conference on Software Maintenance*, Nov. 1990, pp. 63–69.

McGregor, John D. and Sykes, David A. *Object Oriented Software Development: Engineering Software for Reuse*, Van Nostrand Reinhold, New York, 1992.

Meyers, Scott. *Effective C++: 50 Specific Ways to Improve Your Programs and Designs*, Addison-Wesley, Reading, MA, 1992.

Murray, Robert B. *C++ Strategies and Tactics*, Addison-Wesley, Reading MA, 1993.

O'Donnell, Debra. "Hello MOM and OOP Shops," *Software Magazine*, April 1997, p. 25.

Shneiderman, Ben. *Software Psychology-Human Factors in Computer and Information Systems*, Winthrop Publications, London, U.K., 1980, Sections 1.3.5 and 3.5.

Software Engineering Institute, Carnegie Mellon University. *The Capability Maturity Model: Guidelines for Improving the Software Process*, Addison-Wesley SEI Series in Software Engineering, Reading, MA, 1995. See www.sei.cmu.edu/cmmi/general for updates on CMMI.

Taylor, David. *Object Oriented Technology: a Manager's Guide*, Addison-Wesley, Reading, MA, 1990.

Van Vliet, Hans. *Software Engineering-Principles and Practices*, 2nd ed., John Wiley and Sons, 2000.

Vaughan-Nichols, S. "Corporate Success Stories: Integrating Objects With Rules," *Object Magazine*, Vol. 7, No. 1, March 1997, p. 66.

Weinberg, Gerald. *The Psychology of Computer Programming*, Van Nostrand Reinhold Company, New York, 1971, pp. 135–136.

Wilkinson, Nancy M. *Using CRC Cards*, SIGS Books, New York, 1995.

Wirfs-Brock, Rebecca J., Wilkerson, Brian, and Wiener, Lauren. *Designing Object Oriented Software*, Prentice-Hall, Englewood Cliffs, NJ, 1990.

Part 2

Ethics and Professionalism

3

Software Requirements

When customers present ideas that need system solutions, developers have an ethical and professional obligation to help customers define their problem. You must build the best solution to the customer's problem, even if the customer does not yet understand how to ask for it. The customer should be encouraged to write a short prospectus that states the purpose of the system, its value, and any constraints essential to making it useful. This prospectus should not be confused with a complete set of requirements, which will emerge only through an iterative process. This chapter will lead you through the steps necessary to arrive at refined requirements and help you resist the eager impulse to plunge ahead and build a system that might not meet the customer's needs. A formal requirements understanding, verification, documentation, and control process is essential for delivering software systems that delight customers.

3.1 WHAT CAN GO WRONG WITH REQUIREMENTS

The requirements and design phases are important steps in a software project. If these steps are not well done, the quality of the final product will almost certainly be low. It is good to perform these steps with paper designs to maintain a fluid, dynamic design methodology. Any production computer investment activity during this interval, including early coding, imposes a psy-

Trustworthy Systems Through Quantitative Software Engineering,
by Lawrence Bernstein and C. M. Yuhas
Copyright © 2005 IEEE Computer Society

chological reluctance to change anything already created. Unrestrained ability to change is necessary to developing a quality design. Investing in prototyping and modeling at this stage is helpful, but both customer and designer must remember that the artifacts produced will not necessarily find their way directly into the product.

Without an iterative plan for approaching the development of requirements, the design organization can find itself, months along on the project, **developing the wrong software functions**. The designer of a stock ordering system for a grocery could not guess that suppliers' invoices would not be directly related to orders because suppliers grouped orders for their delivery convenience. The customer would not mention this because "Mildred always knew how to square things" and nobody ever thought about it.

A formal process has a cutoff point, which prevents the **continuing stream of requirements changes** that can prevent coding and testing from moving along. Changes can be made in an orderly way in future releases after evaluation, but not by altering the requirements document.

The sales team can sometimes infect both the customer and the design organization with the desire to **gold plate** the product and provide what is *desired* rather than what is *required*. The design team needs to be fully aware of this tendency born of enthusiasm and resist it, without being negative or disheartening. The attitude must be to get the core functionality right.

Finally, many design organizations do not have the necessary human factors specialists to analyze the users' tasks. Without specific attention to the people who will use the product, the organization can **develop the wrong user interface**.

3.2   THE FORMAL PROCESSES

The requirements engineering shown in Figure 3.1 provides a foundation for staffing and planning the rest of the project. Explicit synthesis and analysis of the various input elements can prevent these issues from undermining the software project development. The requirements process starts with a system prospectus. Here are steps the design organization can use to help the customer construct a good prospectus:

(1) Elicit feature or functional requirements from the customer's people.

(2) Understand the constraints on the project such as performance, recovery, administration, and availability needs. These *nonfunctional* requirements come from the environment in which the software product will operate.

(3) Analyze the requirements to make sure they mesh and there are no contradictions. This analysis derives the business flows and results in a set of *use cases*. Software architects will use these cases to define the components of the system and their interactions. System testers will also use them to create the system test plan.

(4) Develop a prototype to understand and validate the requirements.

(5) Produce and control a requirements specification. This core document is variously called the **system or software requirements specification** (SRS) or the **functional requirements specification** (FRS).

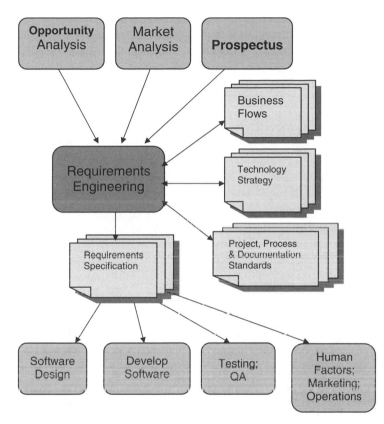

Figure 3.1. Components of requirements engineering.

Boehm and his colleague Farquhar developed a technique that has been highly successful in combining the free discussion advantages of group discussion with the advantages of anonymous estimation. They called the technique Wideband Delphi (wideband because it calls on the expertise of several experts and Delphi from the location of the ancient Greek oracle who was the predictor of future occurrences). A coordinator calls a group meeting to which all are asked to bring written estimates to discuss. The private estimation and group discussion cycles for as many rounds as are necessary.[1]

---

[1] Boehm, Barry. *Software Engineering Economics*, Prentice-Hall, Englewood Cliffs, NJ, 1981, pp. 333–336.

MAGIC NUMBER!

Boehm suggests that as much as 40% of the features that become part of the production system are not in the requirements when development begins. Requirements must be revisited, reviewed, and revised to make the SRS or FRS as complete as possible.

As an ethical professional, you must help the customer understand how his business procedures must change to realize the benefits of the new software. This is the source of *emerging* requirements. Your customer may not fully appreciate the ripple effect the introduction of a new software system may have. Figure 3.2 shows the elicitation-analysis-specification aspects of teasing out accurate specifications.

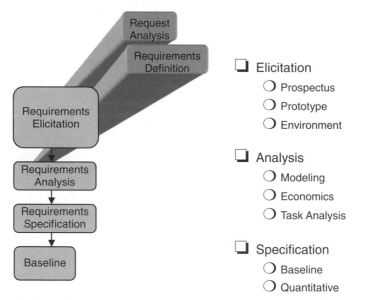

Figure 3.2. *Finding hidden or emerging requirements (with the permission of Rand Edwards).*

Case Study: The Case of Creative Consulting—Automated Customer Service

The prospectus for a new decision support system says to create software that will diagnose problems in real time and provide dynamic solutions to requests or problems. The fundamental architecture employs the concept of an "error tree." Your customer's clients will be asked to answer a series of questions, and based on their responses, the system will provide solutions.

Some commercial off-the-shelf (COTS) products are available, but they are narrowly defined. We would like to create flexible software that could be configured to meet the requirements of all kinds of industries in the hope of having a widely marketable product for ourselves. Our marketing department sees the following possibilities:

(1) Hospitals can use for diagnosis

(2) Technical firms can use to provide troubleshooting help to users

(3) Service firms can solve or appropriately route user problems

The software indicated by the description of the system in the prospectus includes the following:

(1) Front-end Web service using ASP.NET

(2) Middle tier architecture using C#

(3) Backend database system SQL Server 2000

Step 1 Requirements Elicitation: The first thing we need is an adequate description of the problem, which will begin with the prospectus and interviews with both the customer and the users. A business flow or process is a defined sequence of tasks required to perform some function that must be performed frequently across the enterprise. They combine people, systems, and data and are consistent, repeatable, and measurable.

Understanding the business flows, business interactions, and user interactions is essential when creating software requirements. It is also important to heed Fred Brooks' warning, "Don't automate an undisciplined work flow. The computer won't solve what the customer's management can't." The prospectus wants us to *create software that will diagnose problems in real time and provide dynamic solutions to requests or problems.*

The next thing we need is a description of the environment, which includes the legacy systems and this new system that together form the **system of systems** comprising the customer's business. The roles of the operational users and the information technology staff as well as system administration policy and the expectation of customers would be included here. The prospectus describes the environment simply: *The fundamental architecture employs the concept of an "error tree" . . . clients will be asked to answer a series of questions, and, based on their responses, the system will provide solutions.* A prototype may help the transition to the next step in finding all requirements.

Step 2 Analysis: The analysis models the complexity of the solution. Consistency in the "face" the system presents to the user will make it more readily accepted. Mixes of complex and simple features cause user disaffection because it causes the user to become impatient with the simple (Couldn't the software do this?) or flummoxed by the random complex feature (Where's the guru to answer this?). Here is the scope:

> There are some COTS available, but they are narrowly defined. We would like to create flexible software that could be configured to meet the requirements of all kinds of industries in the hope of having a widely marketable product for ourselves. Our marketing department sees the following possibilities:
>
> (1) Hospitals can use for diagnosis,
> (2) Technical firms can use to provide troubleshooting help to users,
> (3) Service firms can solve or appropriately route user problems.

A detailed task analysis for each user of the present method of operation (PMO) is necessary. The requirements engineers then model the environment as the user will see it once the new system is installed. This is the vision of the future method of operation (FMO). Some rough economic predictions may be made at this point.

Step 3 Specification: The customer must be able to quantify the specific set of changes that the system will make to the current baseline. A specific measurable operational value (MOV) needs to be identified that all developers understand. An MOV might be "Reduce the need for human handling of medical payment applications to a maximum of 10%." The project goal for such an MOV would be, "Direct payments for medical payment applications without human intervention."

Specification also includes any constraints on the behavior or structure of the solution. If there were organization standards for the choice of hardware, networks, or software tools, they would be detailed in this step. The prospectus has these technical constraints: *Front-end Web service using ASP.NET, middle tier architecture using C#, backend database system SQL Server 2000.*

Conclusion: So what is missing from the prospectus? The interfaces that are needed for the wide variety of medical databases, adherence to privacy laws, and the user interactions are missing. These will emerge as critical requirements necessary to transform the project from a prototype feasibility model to a commercial product. Implications of legal liability to the development organization and adherence to the new medical privacy laws are missing. Features emerging from these concerns can dwarf the original system concept. When this project was undertaken in a software engineering class, the system produced could not be sold commercially because of the emerging requirements.

3.3   ROBUST REQUIREMENTS

The requirements for a system must be robust and not aim at a narrow point solution. The ideal solution shown in Figure 3.3 provides the performance at the specified load and the same performance over a wide range of input. Typically, software requirements and the systems built based on them work at a point solution and quickly lose performance when unexpected traffic levels occur.

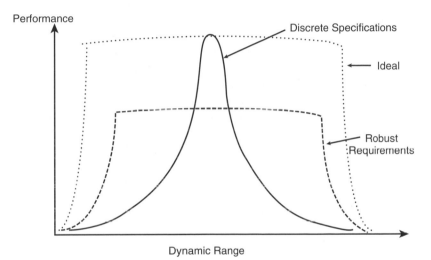

Figure 3.3. *System performance resulting from robust requirements.*

The software requirements engineer must make needed tradeoffs between performance and range so that the system becomes appropriately robust. These tradeoffs require an understanding of the business flows and rules that are incorporated into the environment in which the system will operate. Prototypes are an excellent tool for understanding these tradeoffs. Building and using prototypes are a fundamental part of the requirements analysis process.

High or low loads can cause a system to crash or hang. A test that all systems need to pass is the **no-load** test, that is, bringing the system up and entering no transactions. Many systems fail while in this state. Microsoft Windows 95 could tolerate the absence of activity for only 49.7 days before it hung. A new system used by the FAA to control ground-to-air communication fell victim to this same problem.

Case Study: The Case of the Puzzling Patriot

During the Gulf War, the U.S. Patriot missile defense system was widely hailed as a savior of the war. News reports and government sources alike attributed to it a nearly perfect success rate in destroying Iraqi Scud missiles. Not until the war was over did observers begin to express doubts regarding the success of the Patriot. Although controversy persists concerning the actual effectiveness of the Patriot missile in the Gulf War, one thing is certain: The Patriot failed to intercept a Scud missile that hit an American military barracks in Dhahran, Saudi Arabia, on February 25, 1991. In fact, no Patriot missile was launched to intercept the Scud that day—28 people were killed, and 97 were injured. Why did the Patriot fail to respond to this threat?

Eventually, the Army attributed the Patriot missile failure in Dhahran to "a software failure in the . . . computer" as a result of "long use of the radar system." But, as is the case in any failure of a complex system, many factors may have contributed to the failure of the Patriot missile to reliably perform its duty. The Patriot problems likely stemmed from one fundamental aspect of its design: The Patriot was originally designed as an anti-aircraft, not as an anti-missile, defense system. With this limited purpose in mind, Raytheon designed the system with certain constraints. One such constraint was that the Patriot system was not to operate for more than a few hours at a time. It was designed for use in a mobile unit rather than at a fixed location.

At the time of the Scud attack on Dhahran, the Patriot battery had been running continuously for 4 days—almost 100 hours. This fact alone probably explains why the Patriot failed to intercept the Scud that hit the American barracks, but some more discussion is required to understand why extended operation caused the Patriot to fail.

When the Patriot system is in operation, it must have a way of determining whether "targets" it finds in the air are actually incoming missiles rather than false alarms. The Patriot makes this determination by tracking the target to determine whether it is following the expected path of a ballistic missile. Ballistic missiles travel at extremely high speeds, so that the time interval between radar "sightings" of the target must be very small. The Patriot tracks a target by first noting the location of the original radar sighting and then by using knowledge of the characteristics of a ballistic missile in flight to anticipate where the target should be at the next radar sighting—a fraction of a second later. If, at the second radar sighting, the target does not appear in the "range gate," the calculated zone in which the target will appear if it is a ballistic missile, then it is classified a false alarm and subsequently ignored by the Patriot.

To make this path calculation, the Patriot depends on its internal clock. Because the memory available to the program was limited, the clock value was truncated slightly when stored. Prof. Arnold writes insightfully:

> It turns out that the cause was an inaccurate calculation of the time since boot due to computer arithmetic errors. Specifically, the time in tenths of second as measured by the system's internal clock was multiplied by 1/10 to produce the time in seconds. This calculation was performed using a 24 bit fixed point register. In particular, the value 1/10, which has a non-terminating binary expansion,

was chopped at 24 bits after the radix point. The small chopping error, when multiplied by the large number giving the time in tenths of a second, led to a significant error. Indeed, the Patriot battery had been up around 100 hours, and an easy calculation shows that the resulting time error due to the magnified chopping error was about 0.34 seconds ... A Scud travels at about 1,676 meters per second, and so travels more than half a kilometer in this time. This was far enough that the incoming Scud was outside the "range gate" that the Patriot tracked. Ironically, the fact that the bad time calculation had been improved in some parts of the code, but not all, contributed to the problem, since it meant that the inaccuracies did not cancel.[2]

Therefore, the Patriot classified the incoming Scud as a false alarm and ignored it, with disastrous results.

The Israeli military, analyzing data from Patriot batteries operating in Israel, found the clock drift error. They calculated that after only 8 hours of continuous operation, the Patriot's stored clock value would be off by 0.0275 seconds, causing an error in range gate calculation of approximately 55 m.

On February 11, 1991, after determining the effect of the error over time, the Israelis notified the U.S. Patriot project office of the problem. Once they were notified, the programming team set to work solving the problem. Within a few days, the Patriot project office made a software fix correcting the timing error and sent it out to the troops on February 16, 1991. At the time of the Dhahran attack, the software update had yet to arrive in Dhahran. That update, which arrived in Dhahran the day after the attack, might have saved the lives of those in the barracks. In the meantime, they had sent out a warning that very long run times could affect the targeting accuracy. On the day of the Dhahran attack, two Patriot batteries were deployed to cover the Dhahran area. One battery was having trouble with its radar, a problem unrelated to the clock drift error. For this reason, the other battery had been running continuously for 4 days to provide uninterrupted coverage over Dhahran. Additionally, the phrase "very long run times" was not specific, so the Patriot operators could not know that they were operating under dangerous conditions when the attack occurred.

Conclusion: There are several lessons to be learned from analyzing the Patriot failure. First, testing in computer-controlled systems must be robust, especially when safety is at stake. If the Patriot had been tested under varying conditions, including long periods of continuous operation, the clock drift error would likely have been discovered long before the Patriot was used in the Gulf. Also, special care must be taken when redesigning a system for a new use; when the uses seem similar, as an anti-aircraft versus anti-missile weapon, there can still be unexpected difficulties in adaptation. Software fault tolerance techniques that reset the system periodically could have prevented the

[2] http://www.ima.umn.edu/~arnold/disasters/patriot.html, Douglas A. Arnold, Professor of Mathematics and IMA Director, Institute for Math. and its Applications, University of Minnesota, Minneapolis, MN. E-mail: arnold@ima.umn.edu.

problem.[3] Last, communication among the designers, programmers, and operators of a safety-critical system is imperative. Once the fix was known, expedited change management could have had it installed before it was needed. Even if the other suggestions were not implemented, better communication might have saved lives in Dhahran both by informing users of specific limits (reboot every 8 hours) and by expediting the software upgrade.[4]

3.4   REQUIREMENTS SYNTHESIS

The requirements engineers now must begin to list, evaluate, and bound the features for the new system. The WinWin Spiral Model developed by Boehm is a way to capture features systematically and include the views of all the "stakeholders," who are all those who will be affected by the new system's presence (Figure 3.4). Negotiation techniques are a critical success factor in getting the requirements right and improving the outcome of software projects.

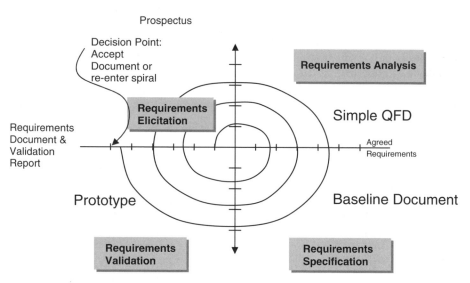

Figure 3.4. *Elements of the WinWin Spiral Model.*

The USC Center for Software Engineering developed a negotiation-based approach to software system requirements engineering.[5] Their approach has three primary elements:

[3] Bernstein, L. "Software Fault Tolerance Forestalls Crashes: To Err is Human; To Forgive Is Fault Tolerant," *Advances in Computers*, Elsevier Sciences, New York, 2003, pp. 239–285.
[4] http://www.fas.org/spp/starwars/gao/im92026.htm.
[5] http://sunset.usc.edu/cse/.

(1) Theory W, a management theory and approach, which says that making winners of the system's key stakeholders is a necessary and sufficient condition for project success

(2) The WinWin Spiral Model, which extends the spiral software development model by adding Theory W activities to the front of each cycle

(3) WinWin, a groupware tool that makes it possible for distributed stakeholders to negotiate mutually satisfactory (win–win) system specifications

The WinWin Spiral Model is likely to be useful for software projects that must deal with rapidly moving technology, little user or developer experience with similar systems, and the need for rapid completion.

The original Spiral Model uses a cyclic approach to develop increasingly detailed elaborations of a software system's definition, culminating in incremental releases of the system's operational capability. Each cycle involves elaborating product and process objectives and constraints, evaluating alternatives, identifying risk, redefining the product and process, and finally planning the next cycle. The life-cycle plan is then updated, including partitioning the system into subsystems to be addressed in parallel cycles. This process can include a plan to terminate the project if it is too risky or infeasible. Management must then commit to proceed as planned. Since its creation, the Spiral Model has been successfully applied in numerous projects. However, determining where the features, constraints, and alternatives come from drove extensions that became the WinWin Spiral. At the front of each cycle, these activities are added:

(1) Identify the system or subsystem's key stakeholders.

(2) Identify each stakeholder's win conditions for the system or subsystem.

(3) Negotiate win–win reconciliations of the stakeholders' win conditions.

The problem statements in a customer's prospectus are much less voluminous than a typical requirements set in a contractual agreement, even though both can be just as obscure. Requirements engineers can range in extremes from short statements to a consistent set of prototypes, plans, and requirements specifications. The WinWin approach fosters trust between developers and the customer, but transitions from WinWin stakeholder agreements to requirements specifications can be difficult. A WinWin groupware tool helps smooth this transition and makes it easy to have frequent contact with the customer. The use of an agreed prospectus with an MOV as a checklist for developing WinWin agreements effectively focuses stakeholder negotiations.

The most important outcome of product definition is not a rigorous specification, but a team of stakeholders with enough trust and shared vision to adapt effectively to unexpected changes. A list of features will be the product of these efforts.

3.5   REQUIREMENTS SPECIFICATION

With a list of features, a specification can be written. Each feature needs to be quantitatively qualified and should state how it contributes to the MOV. Complex projects often need benefits modeling at this stage to assure that the features are well understood. The features deal with explicitly stated customer needs. System "needs" become a structured list of requirements and a set of relevant and measurable product characteristics.

There are many suggestions for the contents of a requirements specification. At minimum, the following elements should be stated:

(1) Project title, revision number, and author
(2) Scope and purpose of the system
(3) Measurable operational value
(4) Description
(5) Feature list
(6) Interfaces
(7) Constraints
(8) Change log and expected changes
(9) Responses to the unexpected
(10) Glossary
(11) References

To do requirements modeling well, the project team needs to be allowed to succeed, and many times this unfortunately is not the case. Requirements modeling efforts are often undermined by less than ideal circumstances. For example, it is the rare stakeholder who has the creative imagination to fully understand the implications of a decision.

Problems common to the effort to synthesize requirements are common to many human endeavors. The demands of their jobs may make your access to project stakeholders limited, or they may be geographically dispersed. On the other hand, there may be too many stakeholders who want to participate and they will either not know what they want or change their minds. Stakeholders are afraid to be pinned down or have conflicting priorities.

The stakeholders are not necessarily disciplined in engineering or creative in design. They may be good at their jobs but woefully unable to see beyond the current situation. They may remain overly focused on one type of requirement to the exclusion of its relationship to the larger system. Some stakeholders cannot describe the problem to be solved, but they jump immediately to prescribing the technology solution.

Stakeholders are not requirements engineers, so expect that they will need significant formality regarding requirements. Do not assume an understanding of modeling artifacts.

Finally, to maintain a certain balance and humility, the requirements engineer should remember that the common fault of the developer is arrogance about the problem domain and the nature of the requirements. You may understand neither.

3.6 QUANTITATIVE SOFTWARE ENGINEERING GATES

At this point, a reasonable set of requirements specifications are available, but the requirements process is not finished. The requirements must be quantified in the context of the development project so that as new requirements emerge and as existing requirements change, the software project manager can make reasoned engineering tradeoffs. Without this quantifying, evolving the features becomes a political rather than an engineering process. This approach can avoid the problem of creeping featurism and misplaced priorities.

For the requirements stage, and every other stage of the project, a quantitative analysis of the feasibility of accomplishing the project on time and within budget is made. The results of this analysis are compared throughout the life of the project to discover trends. So, before any stage of software development is deemed complete, these quantitative techniques should be exercised to manage emerging software requirements:

(1) Perform an ICED-T analysis of the software system represented in the Requirements specification (**i**ntuitive, **c**onsistent, **e**fficient, **d**urable, and **t**houghtful).

(2) Perform a simplified quality function deployment analysis (sQFD).

(3) Compute function points (FPs).

(4) Estimate staff and development time.

(5) Revise the requirements specification to fit the development costs and time into the given budget and schedule. Increases to the budget and longer developments are possible, but not probable.

(6) Recompute function points based on changes made to the Requirements specification.

(7) Replan with a Gantt chart.

(8) Repeat sQFD analysis.

(9) Recompute ICED-T to make sure the system still solves the customer's main problem.

(10) Review the MOV to make sure it is still attainable.

The sQFD analysis (Section 3.7), ICED-T techniques (Section 3.8), and simplified function point (Section 3.9) are explained, followed by an illustrative example.

A critical review meeting of all stakeholders to review the results is recommended and becomes a gate before proceeding to the next stage of development. These gates occur at the end of the requirements, architecture, implementation, and quality assurance stages of the software process, which applies to the first release and, most importantly, to all future releases whatever their size.

3.7   sQFD

Quality function deployment (QFD) is an analysis technique for assigning priorities to requirements. It was developed for use in hardware-intensive and large system projects. It is so extremely complicated that it becomes cumbersome and counterproductive in all but the most highly critical software project situations. A simplified version of the concept, however, can be useful and easy to apply repeatedly to sort out the relative importance of each requirement as the project continues. We will take a quick look at the House of Quality matrix that is the product of the complicated technique and then concentrate on the simplified technique as a more readily useful way to check priorities through the life of a software project.

The **House of Quality** matrix is the most recognized form of QFD. It translates a set of requirements, drawing on market research and benchmarking data, into an appropriate number of prioritized requirements features. It has been used extensively for complex hardware systems. There are many slightly different forms of this matrix, and this ability to be adapted constitutes one of its major strengths. Its most general form is too complex for software projects. The House of Quality matrix has six major components:

1. **Customer requirements** (HOWs): a structured list of requirements features derived from customer statements.
2. **Technical requirements** (WHATs): a structured set of relevant and measurable product characteristics that are called software functions.
3. **Planning matrix** (illustrates customer perceptions observed in market surveys and interviews): includes relative importance of customer requirements, company and competitor performance in meeting these requirements. The matrix is populated with weights based on the mapping of qualitative opinions to quantitative metrics using Wideband Delphi.
4. **Interrelationship matrix:** illustrates the QFD team's perceptions of interrelationships between technical and customer requirements. An appropriate scale is applied, illustrated with symbols or figures. Filling this portion of the matrix involves discussions and consensus building within the team and can be time consuming. Concentrating on key relationships and minimizing the numbers of requirements are useful techniques to reduce the demands on resources. This is skipped in the simplifications for software projects and accounted for explicitly during the architecture phase.
5. **Technical correlation** (Roof): used to identify where technical requirements support or impede each other in the product design; can highlight

innovation opportunities. With dynamic change, this process is too complex to use throughout the software process.

6. **Technical priorities, benchmarks, and targets**: used to record the priorities assigned to technical requirements by the matrix, measures of technical performance achieved by competitive products, and the degree of difficulty involved in developing each requirement. The final output of the matrix is a set of target values for each technical requirement to be met by the new design, which are linked back to the demands of the customer. A simplified approach is to judge the ease of implementation of each feature and map that into a set of numbers from one to nine, one being the hardest to nine being the easiest. The product of the ease of implementation and the requirements feature metric can rank the features. This metric gives the project manager insight to where features can be dropped in the event of projected slippages.

The House of Quality as shown in Figure 3.5 is a feature by requirement matrix.

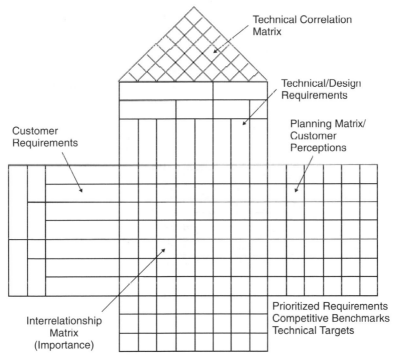

Figure 3.5. *House of quality matrix.*

The **Importance** rating is entered in the Interrelationship cells and is the most salient feature of QFD for software projects. A simplified technique that arrives at this rating is useful for software projects to decide which requirements features to drop. Because 40% of the features of a software product are identified after the requirements specification is baselined, the sQFD analysis needs to be redone at every stage of software development. Software engineers use this, as shown in Figure 3.6, to discover the features most important to the customer and to place them on an ordinal scale. By forcing this quantifying with Wideband Delphi, engineering tradeoffs become possible. Without concrete definition, the opinions of stakeholders get lost in a muddle of subjective emotion. Software engineers can find it impossible then to distill real needs from the wants and desires of the stakeholders, whether they are endusers, purchasing agents, or their own marketing organizations. The example in Figure 3.6 shows a 100-page request for proposal (RFP) for a new military

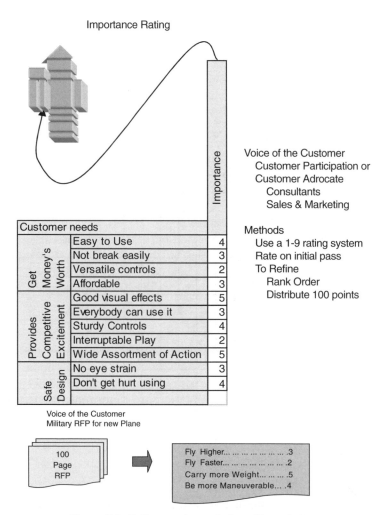

Figure 3.6. *Rating requirements for military airplane.*

airplane reduced to four key features. This scenario is hypothetical but not unrealistic.

Next, an sQFD matrix will compare the importance and ease of implementation for requirements features. Table 3.1 continues the airplane example, mapping the ease of implementing software functions against the four features that resulted from the exercise in Figure 3.6. A generic weighting scale, designed to produce numbers large enough to show clear differences when multiplied, applies these numbers to perceived importance: 1 Weak, 3 Moderate, 5 Strong, 7 Very Strong, and 9 Extremely Strong.

TABLE 3.1. Implementation Ease vs. Feature Importance

Software Function Ease of Implementation		Feature Fly Higher	Feature Fly Faster	Feature Weigh Less	Feature More Maneuverable
Reliability	1	1	1	9	3
Faster Software	3	3	3	1	9
Memory Reduction	5	1	1	9	1

Multiply ease by feature for each cell. Add the products, first across each row (14, 48, and 55) and then down each column (15, 15, 52, and 35). The idea is to drop the lowest scoring elements, but Reliability (14) would then be sacrificed, which is not feasible when a pilot's life is at stake. Therefore, a **judgment override** is applied to the outcome and the Fly Faster feature (15) is dropped. The Memory Reduction function may have to be dropped also if enough function points are not eliminated from the project.[6] The judgment override concept is dangerous because it can be used too frequently and too cavalierly, which undermines the whole point of this exercise. Each judgment override must be carefully and completely documented to prevent abuse.

3.8 ICED-T METRICS

The ICED-T model is a way to measure the quality of a system by mapping its qualitative characteristics on a quantitative scale even before a system is built. The same measures can be taken throughout the development cycle to see how the software improves. Testers can compare their evaluations to the original requirements engineers' evaluations to determine where to stress their testing and suggest improvements. Most importantly, stakeholders can be brought into the process with easy-to-conceive numeric scores to project their assessment of how the software will work at requirements time and then again once the software is operational.

[6] Dalcher, Darren and Tully, Colin. Centre for Systems Forensics and Capability School of Computing Science, Middlesex University, Trent Park, Bramley Road, London N14 4YZ, U.K. d.dalcher@mdx.ac.uk; c.tully@mdx.ac.uk.

ICED-T breaks down the overall subjective measure of the software's quality into five separate groups of related measures. These groups are intuitive, consistent, efficient, durable, and thoughtful. They reflect how a customer would subjectively feel about the software. Categorizing these measures has two main benefits. First, by calling attention to each group separately, it encourages requirements engineers to focus on each aspect of software quality. Second, customers give more worthwhile feedback. Instead of simply saying, "This software design doesn't fit my needs," customers say how the product must be improved for them to deploy it. This process can be done before the software is developed, which allows the requirements engineers and managers to focus their attention more precisely on how to build a better product. The model is also useful during the architecture and test phases of development. Tracking the ICED-T metrics at each stage gives customers and managers insight on how the quality of the software is evolving.

3.8.1   ICED-T Insights

The ICED-T model asks the following questions:

Intuitive: Does the use of this product make sense?
Consistent: Does the product operate in a uniform manner?
Efficient: Is the product quick and agile to use?
Durable: Does the product respond reliably without breaking?
Thoughtful: Does the product anticipate the users' needs?

The first category (I) asks whether all actions produce a logical result, which does not mean only that the application produces the result it is supposed to, but goes beyond that to look at whether that result really makes sense and responds to the user's expectation. For example, a user pressing a button labeled **Back** expects the application to return to the previous screen. If some other screen appears, even if by design, this might not be intuitive. The Microsoft silliness of selecting **Start** to shut down a system would not pass this test. Another aspect that affects an application's intuitiveness is whether the software's design implies its use. In other words, can users look at a screen and understand how they are supposed to use the interface and what actions should result? Such things as the layout of controls and the amount of on-screen information can affect intuitiveness. Intuitiveness of the requirements is best evaluated by a observing a naïve user operate a prototype.

The second category (C) measures how uniformly the software operates. Consistency can be measured though several aspects. If the software is consistent within itself across time, the user can expect that doing an action today and doing the same action tomorrow will get the same results—provided there were no changes to the system or its environment. If the software is consistent throughout its user interface, the same standards for design and function have been followed throughout the product. For example, the same field will always have the same name or abbreviation no matter in which window it appears. If the software is consistent with other applications, the user can expect to transfer learning to this product, which can apply to other software from the same company, as well as to general standards for platforms or operating systems. For example, if the operating system is Windows and the product does not use **Ctrl-X** to mean cut, then the software has a consistency problem.

The third category (E) uses modeling, analyzing, and prototyping to determine whether the application is nimble. Efficiency of the **interface and navigation** would involve, for instance, the number of keystrokes and mouse clicks it takes to accomplish a given task. Are shortcuts and hot-keys used effectively? Can any redundancies be eliminated? Is the application designed so that it requires a minimal amount of action and time to navigate? Efficiency of the **code** deals with response time—how quickly the software responds to the user's input or how long it takes to complete a task. This characteristic should be evaluated in the context of the customer's environment and FMO business flows. Therefore, it is important to have the customer's computing and networking environment in mind when estimating efficiency. The time it takes to accomplish a task within these parameters is what users must judge acceptable.

The fourth category (D) addresses software reliability. Objective measures such as crash rate and mean time to failure (MTTF) can affect this subjective evaluation, but it is the overall feeling of solidity that is of concern to this model. Three aspects of durability are evaluated for a given piece of software. First, how often does the software **crash** under normal use? If a certain function causes a crash one time, most users would probably consider it a fluke. If the function causes a crash regularly, however, users would think the application was poor quality. Second, how **catastrophic** are the crashes? Does the user lose data, or was the program designed to auto-save data? Was the exception trapped? Can the application be restarted without restarting the operating system or rebooting the machine? How well does the software hold up under **extraordinary use**? This is the robustness of the software. Users will innocently attempt things with the software that it was never designed to do. Testers need to imagine what these uses might be, try them out, and see what happens. Even if the product was not conceived for that use, it should not cause undue problems for the user who tries it.

The final category of subjective software qualities (T) is perhaps the most subjective of all. It looks at how thoughtful the software is. This category also has the most overlap with the other categories. When evaluating an application's thoughtfulness, the requirements engineers determine if the product provides users with everything they need. Is anything missing from the program that would make it better? This goes beyond evaluating whether the software meets users' needs and examines whether it is as useful and as friendly as it could be. A great example of a thoughtful addition to software is the **Browse** button on a file access dialog. Without this button, users could still specify the file they wanted and the software would work. By adding this button, programs become much more efficient because it is easier for a human to select a choice from a series than it is to retrieve from one's memory the actual file name, properly spelled. Memory-challenged users everywhere bless the kindness of that engineer. A good way to evaluate an application's thoughtfulness is to adopt a **use case-based** method. A combination of features models a business flow. With this mindset, better ways to help users accomplish their tasks will emerge.

ICED-T metrics are a good way to map the qualitative understanding of the system into a quantitative analysis. After a first draft specification is articulated, the entire projected system needs to be quantitatively evaluated. With the ICED-T metrics, requirements engineers can investigate specific issues before making a heavy investment in producing formal software requirements specifications (SRS) or functional requirements specifications (FRS).

3.8.2 Using the ICED-T Model

To weigh the implications of each metric in the ICED-T model, each category must be assigned a numeric value. This task, by its nature, is somewhat problematic. How exactly is one supposed to assign a number to a subjective feeling? In this situation, professional experience is important. An experienced requirements engineer brings to the task the ability to look at a piece of software and make an informed judgment about the software's quality as it is likely to be perceived by the customer. When the customer disagrees with a numeric value, it signals the need for additional analysis and understanding. This is one of the real values of having professionals evaluate a set of software requirements before the system is built. Software engineers, designers, and testers rate the set of requirements on how intuitive, consistent, efficient, durable, and thoughtful it is, and then they assign a numeric value to these subjective ratings. Then a Wideband Delphi approach converges on a collective judgment. For example, testers should have enough experience using various pieces of software to make an informed judgment about how intuitive the software will be. For these ratings to be meaningful across evaluators and across time, a scale should be set in place that gives guidance on what the numbers mean. A simple continuum from one to five with these meanings has proven useful:

(1) Worst I have ever seen
(2) Worse than average
(3) Same as other applications I have used
(4) Better than average
(5) Best I have ever seen

When all is said and done, the customer's evaluation of software is the only one that counts. When they form their evaluation, they probably will not make a list of the defects they find or time how long it takes to accomplish a task. Instead, they will use the software to accomplish whatever it is they bought the software for in the first place, and through this use, they will form an opinion of how good the software is. This opinion will be subjective. An important part of our job is to do whatever we can to ensure that this opinion is a favorable one. That means that we need to go beyond our objective tests and measures and consider the subjective quality of software. The ICED-T model is a tool that puts subjective responses into a form that can be more easily evaluated and tested and allows us to consider the broader picture of the software's quality. This process gives important feedback to engineers, developers, managers, and testers. By making these subjective qualities an integral part of every stage of our project, starting with the requirements stage, we can improve the software quality. Quality software is the goal.[7]

3.9 DEVELOPMENT SIZING AND SCHEDULING WITH FUNCTION POINTS

Given a refined feature list and an understanding on the parts of both customer and requirements engineer of what this means, the next question is whether there are enough development resources and time to build it.

The name Bell Laboratories is associated with such breakthroughs of modern computing as the UNIX operating system, parallel processing, C and C++ languages, and many others. To keep this focus on software, Bell Laboratories managers, including Bernstein, regularly reevaluated the way software was built into its products and services. Its software initiative strongly emphasized continuous process improvement and effective use of software metrics. AT&T spent several billion dollars in software development and sold billions of dollars of software products every year. Software added value to virtually everything AT&T did. In the 1980s, function point metrics became the foundation of some measurement programs and was used for estimating staffing and development time as well as defect rate in many projects. Measurements such as function points per staff month, cycle time, and defects per delivered function point provide insight into the feasibility of building a system on time and within budget.

3.9.1 Function Point Analysis Experience

AT&T support was crucial to the creation of the International Function Point Users Group (IFPUG). By 1990, AT&T had more than a dozen certified function point specialists.

Even though much was accomplished in AT&T's odyssey through software measurement, function point analysis (FPA) was not easy. It required an

---

[7] Roth, Andy. "Using the ICED-T Model to Test Subjective Software Qualities," *International Conference on Software Testing, Analysis & Review*, November 1–5, 1999, San Jose, CA.

investment in people to establish comprehensive expertise. Experts from outside a project performed function point analysis. Project managers resisted having these outsiders invade their turf and worried that their personal shortcomings would be exposed. With differences in the capability of the software developers, the complexity of the software produced, and the relations with the customer not measured, it was impossible to draw comparisons among projects based on function points. Meaningful FPA should be done by an expert; the introduction of the technology was slowed.

Bell Laboratories defined a set of metrics based on FPA for the entire development process using these principles:

(1) Measurements must be used to measure processes, not people.

(2) The measurement process must have clearly stated objectives and goals.

(3) The measurement process has to be tightly coupled to an overall quality management process.

(4) Data collection must be simple, and automatic tools for extracting data should be used whenever possible.

(5) The measurements must be repeatable and independent of the observer.

(6) The measurement process is an ongoing process and subject to improvement.

(7) The results of the metrics must be shared with the developers.

(8) The measurement process must be integrated into budgets and plans.

Bell Laboratories experts have counted over one million function points in more than 600 projects. These make up more than 20% of all their early 1990s software projects. Analysis shows that productivity as measured by function points per staff month varies as a function of the type of software being built. The complexity of the software alone accounts for a 10:1 difference in software productivity. Operating system or hard real-time software sensitive to the peculiarities of its environment is ten times more difficult to produce than administrative software. Figure 3.7 shows the productivity in function points per staff month for projects that use different database managers or operating systems. The data are drawn from 80 projects in 1990 and 98 projects in 1991. It shows that productivity of the projects based on the UNIX operating system, especially using the fourth-generation INFORMIX database, is four times higher than projects based on mainframe systems, especially those that use IBM's Information Management System database.

3.9.2   NCSLOC vs. Function Points

The culture of many software organizations is more comfortable with ad hoc estimation based on previous experience or with counting new or changed source lines of code (NCSLOC). As in almost every other software organization, the Bell Laboratories metrics program was deeply rooted in a culture

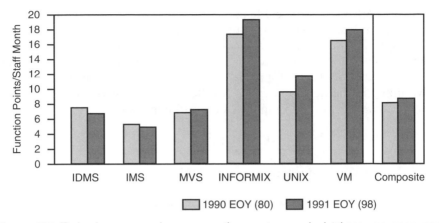

Figure 3.7. Technology comparisons: operating system and database manager new development projects.

that used SLOC. Endless discussions raged as to what SLOC actually meant: physical or logical, with or without comments. Bell Laboratories software engineers developed dozens of tools to count the different kinds of lines of code.

Historical data based on C code became useless with the wide introduction of the C++ language and JAVA languages in the 1990s. Developers now often use sophisticated Wideband Delphi analysis methods to predict the number of SLOC, based mostly on their previous experience. Even with this sophistication, early estimations of size and effort using NCSLOC, especially those that involve a new language or methodology, are inaccurate and often lead to significant cost and time overruns.

Function points are a logical (functional) unit measure of system software functions as seen by the user. They provide the essential value of what the software does with data from a user's point of view. The requirements engineer creates a first-cut understanding of the system structure and counts internal logical files, external interface files, external inputs, external outputs, and external inquires. Counts can be made during the requirements stage because the effort and cost estimation based on adjusted function points does not depend on language and technology. Function points can prevent requirements creep from customers and management because the additional effort to satisfy "just this one little thing" can be quantified.

3.9.3 Computing Simplified Function Points (sFP)

At this point, it is difficult to apply the entire function point technique because so little is known about the software design and architecture. A first-cut architecture is available, and the architect is still evaluating alternative approaches. Nevertheless, it is useful and insightful to compute the number of function points this early in the project life to allow a rough sizing. FPA requires a complexity determination to be affixed to various aspects of the project, but at this early stage, we assume an average complexity for all aspects. In the equation below for determining the value for the unadjusted function points, Albrecht determined the coefficients for average complexity through trial and error and curve fitting in the development of his theory. All projects are also deemed average complexity in the simplified FP (sFP) approach.

$$sFP = (UFP)(VAF),$$

where UFP is the unadjusted FP and VAF is the value adjustment factor.

$$UFP = 4I + 5O + 4E + 10L + 7F,$$

where I is the number of inputs that change data, O is the number of outputs that arise from a data change, E is the number of inquires that do not change data, L the number of logical internal files, and F is the number of interfaces.

VAF $= 0.65 + 0.01(\Sigma c_i)$, where c_i is calculated based on 14 adjustment factors that take into account the nature of the application. These factors measure the difficulty of the development job. For example, communications software is twice as hard to produce as transaction software. We will return to function points in Chapter 6.

3.10   CASE STUDY: THE CASE OF THE EMERGENCY NO-SHOW SERVICE[8]

The story of the London Ambulance Service (LAS) began in the mid-1980s. The background to the story had two key features. First, LAS was falling short of recently established national standards of performance for ambulance mobilization and arrival times. Second, the introduction of the so-called "internal market" to the National Health Service in the United Kingdom, together with chronic shortages from long-term under-investment, led to relentless pressure to squeeze budgets while improving performance.

The LAS is the largest ambulance service in the world. It covers an area of just over 600 square miles and serves a resident population of about 6.8 million, boosted by commuters and visitors to as many as 10 million. In the mid-1980s, the LAS owned over 300 accident and emergency ambulances (two thirds of which might be in use at any one time), operating from 70 ambulance stations, with a central control room at LAS headquarters. It received a daily average of over 2000 calls, resulting in ambulances attending about 1200 incidents. It transported a daily average of over 5000 patients, about 1400 of which were emergency cases.

[8] We thank Darren Dalcher and Colin Tully for these insights.

In the early 1980s, a national standard of 3 minutes was established for ambulance dispatch in response to emergency calls. The LAS decided that a computer-based system was essential to enable them to meet that standard. It was also decided to commission a system to handle not just dispatch but the whole range of control room functions, involving mobile radio (voice and data) transmission. The prospectus called for the following features:

(1) A computer-aided dispatch system, with incident record-keeping
(2) An automatic vehicle location system, with mobile data terminals, that minimizes response time by positioning units optimally and tracks long-term asset performance
(3) A computer map display system

In October 1990, the project was terminated after two peak load tests failed. The project was severely behind schedule and had already overrun its budget by 200%. LAS sought damages from the prime suppliers, claiming the suppliers did not understand the requirements. The vendors replied that specifications were ambiguous, lacked clarity, and were subject to constant change. An out-of-court settlement was eventually reached.

The LAS chief executive sponsored an independent assessment of the failed project to be conducted by Arthur Andersen Consulting. It was based on the original statement of requirements, excluding mobile data capability. Arthur Anderson recommended acquiring a packaged system on a turnkey basis, estimating a cost of $2 million and a 19-month development time. Several packages were evaluated, including some operated by other U.K. ambulance services, but none were judged satisfactory. LAS then embarked on specifying requirements for a new custom system.

The proposed system would automate not only manual tasks but also decision making. Once information from callers was fed into the system, it would take over allocating and mobilizing ambulances, interacting with crews, and monitoring vehicle positions and performance. The control room would no longer communicate with vehicles by radio or with ambulance stations by telephone because the system would handle all communications. Intervention by controllers would be required only in exceptional cases, such as failure to dispatch an ambulance within 11 minutes, failure of an ambulance crew to acknowledge a message, or an ambulance going to the wrong location.

The requirements specification was completed in early February 1991, less than 4 months after abandoning the old system. It now required the system to be operational in 11 months. The requirements specification was detailed and prescriptive, leaving little opportunity for suppliers' judgment. The Present Method of Operation (PMO) included the following functions:

(1) *Call Taking*: Emergency calls are received by ambulance control. Control assistants write the details of incidents on preprinted forms. The location of each incident is identified, and the reference coordi-

nates are recorded on the forms. The forms are then placed on a conveyor belt system that transports all forms to a central collection point.

(2) *Resource Identification*: Other members of ambulance control collect the forms, review the details on the forms, and based on the information provided, decide which dispatcher should deal with each incident. The dispatcher examines the forms for a particular sector, compares the details against information recorded for each vehicle, and decides which unit should be sent. The status information on these forms is updated regularly from information received via the radio operator.

(3) *Resource mobilization*: The dispatcher either telephones the nearest ambulance station or passes instructions to the radio operator if an ambulance is already mobile.

The major rationale expressed for automation was the time-consuming and error-prone nature of current activities such as identification of the precise location of an incident, the physical movement of paper forms, and maintaining up-to-date vehicle status information. Writing was illegible, and forms were sometimes lost. The functions envisioned in the FMO for the computer-aided dispatch system were as follows:

(1) *Call Handling*: British Telecom (BT) operators would route all medical emergency calls to headquarters (HQ). HQ receivers were then expected to enter the name, telephone number, and address of the caller, and the name, destination address, and brief details of the patient. This information would then be transmitted over a local area network to an allocator subsystem.

(2) *Allocator*: The system would pinpoint the patient's location on a map display of areas within London. The system was expected to monitor continuously the location of every ambulance via radio messages transmitted by each vehicle every 13 seconds. The system would then determine the nearest ambulance to the patient.

Experienced ambulance dispatchers were organized into teams based on three zones (south, northwest, and northeast). Ambulance dispatchers would be offered the details of the three nearest ambulances by the system and the estimated time each would need to reach the scene. The dispatcher would choose an ambulance and send patient details to a small terminal screen located on the dashboard of the ambulance. The crew would then be expected to confirm that it was on its way. If the selected ambulance was in an ambulance depot, then the dispatch message would be received on the station printer. The ambulance crew would always be expected to acknowledge a message. The system would automatically alert HQ of any ambulance that made no acknowledgment. A follow-up message would then be sent from HQ. The system would detect each vehicle's location messages and determine whether an ambulance was heading in the wrong direction. The system would then alert controllers. Additional messages would tell HQ when the ambulance crew arrived on the scene, when it was on its way to a hospital, and when it was free again.

Several meetings were held with prospective suppliers covering questions on the specification and resolving other potential technical and contractual issues. It was clear that most suppliers raised concerns over the required deadline. They were all told that this timetable was non-negotiable.

To prepare the requirements specification for the proposed new system, a team was assembled under the leadership of the director of support services with the systems manager, a contract analyst, and the control room services manager. Other persons were also involved representing training, communications, and other areas. There was little involvement with the ambulance crews, although invitations to participate were given to union representatives.

Work progressed on the SRS, which was finally completed in February 1991. The work was done primarily by the contract analyst with direct assistance from the systems manager. The proposed new system would impact significantly the way in which staff carried out their jobs; yet as in the case of the ambulance crews, there was little consultation on this new work.

The SRS was detailed and contained a high degree of precision on how the system was to operate. It provided little scope for additional ideas to be incorporated from prospective suppliers. However, as is usual in any SRS, certain areas were yet not fully defined. In particular, there were few details on the relationship with, and interface to, other LAS systems, including the communications interface.

The system was lightly loaded at startup on October 26, 1992. Staff could effectively manage any problems caused particularly by the communications systems (such as ambulance crews pressing the wrong buttons, or ambulances being radioed in weak signal areas). However, as the number of ambulance incidents increased, the amount of incorrect vehicle information recorded by the system increased. This problem had an avalanche effect, and the system made incorrect allocations based on the information it had. For example, multiple vehicles were sent to the same incident, or the closest vehicle was not chosen for dispatch. Consequently, the system had fewer ambulance resources to allocate. The system also placed calls that had not gone through the appropriate protocol on a waiting list and generated exception messages for those incidents for which it had received incorrect status information. The number of exception messages increased to such an extent the staff could not clear the queue. It became increasingly difficult for staff to attend to messages that scrolled off the screen. The increasing size of the queue slowed the system. As a result, with fewer resources to allocate, and the problems of dealing with the waiting and exceptional queues, it took longer to allocate resources to incidents.

Conclusion: Several nonfunctional feature issues typical of large systems were apparent:

(1) No backup procedure

(2) Haphazard design of user interfaces

(3) No provision made for system overload

At the receiving end, patients became frustrated with the delays in ambulances arriving at incidents, which led to an increase in the number of calls made back to the LAS HQ relating to already recorded incidents. The increased volume of calls, together with a slow system and an insufficient number of call-takers, contributed to significant delays in answering calls that, in turn, caused more delays to patients. At the ambulance end, crews became increasingly frustrated at incorrect allocations. This frustration may have led to an increased number of instances in which crews failed to press the right status buttons or took a different vehicle to an incident than that suggested by the system. Crew frustration also seems to have contributed to a greater volume of voice radio traffic, which in turn contributed to the rising radio communications bottleneck that caused a general slowing in radio communications that, in turn, fed back into increasing crew frustration. A reorganization of sector desks caused loss of local knowledge.

Claims were later made in the press that 20 to 30 people died as a result of ambulances arriving too late on the scene. The LAS chief executive resigned.

This case history shows the importance of the participation of key stakeholders. Senior management (of the enterprise for whom the system is being developed), the system developers/suppliers (either in-house or external), the subcontracting group (where the developers/suppliers are external), and the system users must fully participate. It is essential that those (and other) stakeholder groups are integrated into the system process using a process like WinWin, with each having an effective voice to express both their needs and their knowledge. Poor intergroup communication increases risk, and success relies on establishing stakeholder ownership and commitment. Examples of dysfunctional relationships among groups in this case study are as follows:

(1) Failure of senior management to understand issues, get involved and committed, organize for the systems effort, and undertake properly informed and joined-up decision making

(2) Failure of senior management to relate the systems effort to other concurrent problems/changes within the enterprise (such as restructuring of sectors)

(3) Unreasonable pressure by senior management on development teams and lack of attention by senior management to staff concerns (both developers and users) exacerbated by major overspending of scarce resources on glossy brochures, management consultants, and corporate image.[9]

[9] Dalcher, Darren and Tully, Colin, *Learning from Failures*, Software Forensics Centre, School of Computing Science, Middlesex University, London, U.K., http://www3.interscience.wiley.com/cgi-bin/abstract/102529019/ABSTRACT.

3.11 PROBLEMS

3.11.1 Overdue Book Notices

The librarian of a relatively small elementary school of 500 students is still using a manual method for tracking library books on loan. As a book is taken from the library, its card is taken from the pocket and filed by date. Books may be borrowed for 2 weeks. When a book is returned, its card is put back into the pocket. A book that is not returned in 2 weeks is considered overdue, and an Overdue Book Notice is sent to the student. Volunteer clerks write overdue book notices for about 210 books each week. It is getting hard to attract volunteers, and the librarian proposes the need to hire two full time clerks at $2000 per month ($20 per hour) to track and recover overdue books. The average cost of a book is $25. The school prides itself on the reading skills of its students and expects half the students will take out one book per week. There are 2000 reading books in the library. Assume that any student will take out any reading book. The notices are distributed weekly. The manual system induces a book loss of 5% per week. A book that is out for 4 weeks is deemed lost.

This format has been used for the Overdue Book notice for many years:

```
Glenwood School Overdue Book Notice
Book Title:
Student Name:
Teacher Name:
Date of Notice:
Notice Number 1 2 3 (circle one)
This book is overdue; please return it promptly
```

A student who does not return a book within 3 weeks is sent a second notice. A book not returned in 4 weeks results in a third notice to the student, the entry is purged from the system, and the book is entered on the principal's "Critical Overdue Report"; the book's card is kept by the head librarian. The book is declared lost. Your task is to perform the requirements engineering to automate the overdue book notice process, using a computer in the computer classroom. The computer is only available to the librarian one lunch hour per week. The computer teacher does not commit to providing the same machine to the library, only the same computer configuration. The replacement cost of the computer is $500. This is the first automation project in this school. Data may not be left on the computer from week to week. The computer is not networked. Cost factors for a good business case are as follows:

(1) Assume that each clerk costs $2000/month.
(2) Assume that the computer was not broken so there is no operational cost.
(3) Assume that the paper cost is insignificant.

(4) Assume that the librarian can accomplish the computer tasks, give the school secretary the overdue notices within the current school day, and will not demand a raise to reflect the new skill level.

You need not actually implement the system. Instead, answer the following four questions with all the required tables, charts, and so on:

(1) Identify five project stakeholders and their roles.
(2) Write an MOV in a clear and concise statement, and provide support with quantitative analysis.
(3) List at least two use cases that need to be developed for the requirements analysis.
(4) Identify and explain at least five gaps in the prospectus that will emerge as requirements during development.

3.11.2 Prospectus
Enhance an existing customer relations manager system using distributed client/server and thin client architecture to maintain a record of all customer transactions. Use an accounting style double-posting database, and make sure the system does not lose a message and is fast and nimble. Always be available to accept a user's screen input. The primary access key is a telephone number.

Your Task: Identify at least four gaps in this prospectus.

3.11.3 You are appointed **product** manager and **project** manger for the following prospectus:
Your company is hired by a new bed-and-breakfast (B&B) chain to build a software system. There are four B&Bs in the chain. They each have five bedrooms for guests. They want a system to manage the reservations and the arrival times for guests. Checkout is noon, and check-in is two o'clock, but guests may request later checkout times. The chain wishes to track gross revenues. They accept credit cards. They negotiate room price and 1-night deposit with the customer for guaranteed reservations. They hold reservations without deposits for 1 month.

Your Task: Write five functional and nonfunctional qualitative feature requirements for this system.

3.11.4 List four requirements **risks** that face software requirements engineers.

3.11.5 Compare the characteristics of evolutionary prototypes with those of throwaway prototypes.

BIBLIOGRAPHY

"Best Current Practices: Software Architecture Validation," AT&T, Murray Hill, N.J., 1993.

"Function Points as Asset Reporting to Management," *IFPUG Conference Proceedings*, 1990.

"Process Engineering with the Evolutionary Spiral Process Model: Version 01.00.06," *Tech. Report SPC-93098-CMC, Software Productivity Consortium*, Herndon, VA, 1994.

Bachman/Function Point Analyst, Product Announcement, Bachman, Inc., 1994.

Bernstein, Lawrence. "Where to Invest Your Software Bucks," *IEEE*, Piscataway, NJ Feb. 1995.

Boehm, B. and Bose, P. "A Collaborative Spiral Software Process Model Based on Theory W," *Proceedings of the International Conference of Software Process*, IEEE CS Press, Los Alamitos, CA, 1994, pp. 59–68.

Boehm, Barry et al. "Software Requirements as Negotiated Win Conditions," *Proceedings of the International Conference on Requirements Engineering*, IEEE CS Press, Los Alamitos, CA, 1994, pp. 74–83.

Boehm, Barry, et al. "Prototyping Versus Specifying: A Multiproject Experiment," *IEEE Transactions on Software Engineering*, May 1984.

Boehm, Barry. "Software Risk Management, Principles, and Practices," *IEEE Software*, Jan. 1991.

Boehm, Barry. "A Spiral Model of Software Development and Enhancement," *Computer*, May 1988, pp. 61–72.

Boehm, Barry. *Software Engineering*, IEEE CS Press, Los Alamitos, CA, 1990.

Boehm, Barry. "Anchoring the Software Process," *IEEE Software*, July 1996, pp. 73–82.

Carleton, Anita D., Park, Robert E., and Goethert, Wolfhart B. "The SEI Core Measures: Background Information and Recommendations for Use and Implementation," *CrossTalk*, May 1994.

Fisher, R. and Ury, W. *Getting to Yes*, Penguin Books, New York, 1981.

Flowers, Stephen. "Software Failure: Management Failure," *Report of the Inquiry into the London Ambulance Service*, Feb. 1993.

Frazier, T. and Bailey, J. "The Costs and Benefits of Domain-Oriented Software Reuse: Evidence from the STARS Demonstration Projects," *IDA Paper P-3191*, Institute for Defense Analyses, Alexandria, VA, 1996.

Jones, T. Capers. *Applied Software Measurement*, McGraw-Hill, New York, 1991.

Lusher, Paul W. "Function Point Analysis for Real-Time Weapons Control," *IFPUG Conference Proceedings*, Sept. 1992.

Neumann, Peter G. *Computer-Related Risks*, ACM Press, New York, 1995.

Neumann, Peter G. "Inside Risks," *ACM SIGSOFT Software Engineering Notes*, Vol. 16.3, 1991, pp. 19–20.

Neumann, Peter G. "Inside Risks," *ACM SIGSOFT Software Engineering Notes*, Vol. 16.4, 1991, pp. 17–18.

Neumann, Peter G. "Inside Risks," *ACM SIGSOFT Software Engineering Notes*, Vol. 17.2, 1992, pp. 4–5.

Neumann, Peter G. "Inside Risks," *ACM SIGSOFT Software Engineering Notes*, Vol. 18.1, 1993, p. 25.

Royce, W. E. "TRW's Ada Process Model for Incremental Development of Large Software Systems," *Proceedings of the 12th International Conference of Software*, 1990, pp. 2–11.

Samadani, Hamid, et al. "Army Reuse Center Tackles CASE-Based Reuse," *CrossTalk*, May 1994, Vol. 5, p. 10.

Shneiderman, Ben and Plaisant, Catherine. *Designing the User Interface*, 4th ed. Pearson Addison Wesley, Reading, MA, 2005.

Simpson, Moira. "999!: My computer's stopped breathing!", *The Computer Law and Security Report*, March–April 1994, pp. 76–81.

The National Software Council Charter, April 1995.

4

Prototyping

Software prototyping has become the backbone of most software development. The technique goes a long way toward solving the dual problems of uncertainty in requirements and the early establishment of a close relationship between developer and customer. Prototyping is so important a tool and so useful throughout the development process that we treat it here, early in your learning experience. The prototyping process validates the requirements for a system, which includes finding those requirements that are so obvious the customer did not even think of stating them. Customers have things they want and things they need. Prototyping helps project managers distill customers' *needs* from their *wants* to provide the former and as much of the latter as is consistent with delivering the system on time and at reasonable cost.

4.1 MAKE IT WORK; THEN MAKE IT WORK RIGHT

Very early in the drive to industrialize software development, Royce pointed out the following truths.

> There are four kinds of problems that arise when one fails to do adequate requirements analysis: top-down design is impossible; testing is impossible; the user is frozen out; management is not in control. Although these problems are lumped under various headings to simplify discussion, they are actually all vari-

Trustworthy Systems Through Quantitative Software Engineering,
by Lawrence Bernstein and C. M. Yuhas
Copyright © 2005 IEEE Computer Society

ations of one theme–poor management. Good project management of software procurements is impossible without some form of explicit (validated) and governing requirements.[1]

4.1.1 How to Get at the Governing Requirements

Boehm conducted experiments to compare the efficacy of written specifications to prototyping. His experiments, which are discussed in more detail in Section 4.5, showed that prototyping and specification-driven methods each have valuable advantages that are complementary. For most large projects and many small ones, a mixture of prototyping and specification is preferable to the exclusive use of either. Prototyping became the foundation for Boehm's spiral risk-driven development method because of its efficiency. In addition to clarifying requirements, prototyping is used to simplify software design, to evaluate user interfaces, and to test complex algorithms. Be prepared to expect resistance from management; even though the economics of making the initial high investment in prototyping equipment is still small in comparison with the huge amount spent later to fix unsuitable products in the field, these economics are either not a part of the cultural wisdom or are irrelevant because of the length of many projects. The manager who starts the project and takes the hit for the initial money is not there 3 to 5 years later when the benefits accrue.

MAGIC NUMBER!

For every dollar invested in prototyping, expect a $1.40 return within the life cycle of the system development.

4.1.2 Rapid Application Prototype

A rapid application prototype is a dynamic visual model providing a communication tool for customers and developers. It is more effective than documents or static charts for portraying functionality. It provides users with a physical representation of key parts of the system before implementation, and modifications require small efforts.

Rapid application prototypes do not necessarily represent a complete system. Without prototyping, fully 30–40% of all requirements will change before the system is delivered. Prototyping throughout the development process reduces the requirements churn to no more than 10%. Rapid appli-

---

[1] Royce, Winston. *Practical Strategies for Developing Large Software Systems*, Addison-Wesley, Reading MA, 1975, p. 59.

cation prototyping provides a look at the *dynamic states* of the system before building, whereas most other software engineering focuses on source code. The special problems of reliability, throughput, and response time as well as system features are best addressed in prototypes. The prototype can be used to understand the dynamics of performance under various loads, where bottlenecks might occur, and how design algorithms actually function. This process can be done before the much more costly effort is made to actually build a system.

Luqi at the Naval Postgraduate School in Monterey, California coined the term *computer-aided prototyping*[2] to describe an approach to rapid application prototyping that relied on a specially designed tool—in effect, software to help design software. Luqi is particularly interested in software automation, because it can improve software productivity and reliability. Her work involves automating development tasks currently carried out by engineers. She and her Prototyping Research Group are trying to use specifications and abstractions to make prototypes easier to construct, understand, and analyze. They use advances in software modeling to produce tractable formal models of problems and criteria for evaluating solutions. Computer-aided prototyping systems (CAPS) demonstrate the feasibility of automation in software development. Once domain models are formulated, artificial intelligence technology automates the solution processes in relatively narrow areas of tool development.

In rapid prototyping, interactive prototypes are developed that can be quickly replaced or changed with design feedback. This feedback may be derived from colleagues or users as they work with the prototype to accomplish set tasks. This method is concerned with developing different proposed concepts through software or hardware prototypes and with evaluating them. The development of a simulation or prototype of the future system can be helpful, allowing users to visualize the system and provide feedback on it. Thus, it can be used to clarify user requirements options. Later on in the life cycle, it can also be used to specify details of the user interface to be included in the future system. Here is a procedure for adopting the rapid prototyping method:

(1) Schedule 20–30% of the project development time to create the prototype. If the prototype is to be evaluated with users, then allow additional time to design relevant tasks, recruit the users, evaluate the prototype, and report the results. A good approach is to set up a model of the customer business operation in the software development laboratory where the prototypes can be tried in a simulated business environment.

(2) Assemble the necessary equipment, including the hardware and software tools necessary to create the interactive prototype.

(3) Develop the prototype in a specialized language if the only goal is to rapidly understand the feature's needs and the user interfaces. If the

---

[2] Luqi, Yeh R. "Computer-Aided Software Prototyping," *IEEE Computer*, Sept. 1991, pp. 111–112. Luqi, Yeh R. "Rapid Prototyping in Software Evolution," *Encyclopedia of Software Engineering*, John Wiley and Sons, Inc., New York, 1994, pp. 1–21.

goal includes understanding the technology for the final project, then use the computer language planned for the product.

(4) Select appropriate users to test the prototype, trying to cover the range of users within the target population. Hire a facilitator to instruct the users and run the evaluation.

(5) Prepare realistic tasks to occupy the users as they work with the prototype.

(6) Pilot the evaluation procedure, and ensure the prototype can be used to accomplish the tasks.

(7) Provide recording facilities.

(8) Conduct each session. The facilitator instructs the user to work through the allocated tasks, interacting with, and responding to, the system as appropriate.

(9) Interview users after their use of the prototype. Debrief the users.

(10) Analyze the obtained information, and then summarize the observations and user evaluations. Determine the themes and severity of the problems identified.

(11) Summarize design implications and recommendations for improvements and feedback to design team. Video recordings can support this process.

(12) Refine the prototype, and repeat the above process.

(13) Avoid spending too long on the development of initial prototypes as user evaluation often results in substantial changes.

(14) Avoid making the prototype too polished as this may induce users and their bosses to insist that it is finished.

(15) Do not put in features that will raise the users' expectations but that are unlikely to be achieved with the real system (e.g., too fast response times, too sophisticated graphics), and do not put too much effort into particular features (e.g., animations) that may not be required.

Many tools exist for producing rapid prototypes ranging from a sequence of Microsoft PowerPoint screens to script-based programming systems, such as Visual Basic and Visual C++, that can help to create a software prototype. A cost of prototyping is the level of human expertise required to master the supporting development tools, along with the time necessary to implement a software prototype. Helpful websites include http://www.uidesign.net/2000/papers/evangelize.html and http://www.humanfactors.com/downloads/jul042.htm#susan.

4.1.3 What's Soft Is Hard

Software is hard because it has a weak theoretical foundation. The limited theory that does exist focuses on analysis of static behavior, i.e., the source code. To avoid serious problems, software systems are overengineered with a capacity for two or three times the expected load because designers have no idea what resources will be needed in actual operation. This guesswork is expensive, unlike the known security of overengineering a bridge or a building.

Software has the awful propensity to fail with no warning. Even after we find and fix a bug, how do we restore the software to a known state, one where we have tested its operation? For most systems, this is impossible except with lots of custom design that is error prone. Software prototyping has proven its worth in helping designers avoid these problems in production systems.

Much has been written about the best way to develop software applications, much of it with a bit of truth, but there is no "best way." A requirements-driven approach is successful when the requirements are well known, but it cannot work when the situation makes specifying requirements in advance difficult. This result happens most frequently in human–machine interface systems when users cannot specify what they have never seen.

A prototype may be tossed aside once it has served to provide system insight, or it may evolve to become the foundation of the production system. Both prototyping and requirements are necessary because both synthesis and analysis solve software engineering problems. Bottom-up is synthesis. Top-down is analysis. Bottom-up is creating a prototype. Top-down is developing requirements. Working with a tangible prototype creates an invaluable dynamic experience for both customer and designer. Formal written requirements are needed to establish a clear definition of the job, to control changes, and to communicate the system capabilities between the customer and the developer.

4.2 SO WHAT HAPPENS MONDAY MORNING?

The first step is to capture the customer's and your statement of the problem, written in human language, and to develop a broad outline of its solution. A rough sizing of the job in terms of the ultimate staff required to build the working product follows this. Approximately 30% of the full staff will build one or two prototypes for elements of the problem that are not well understood or for which there is no existing technology.

The running prototype can be analyzed with computer-aided prototyping technology. The results can be synthesized to produce a new solution either by refining the existing prototype or by building a new one.

When you and the customer agree that the prototype addresses the problem, requirements that include features, performance goals, product costs, product quality, development costs, and schedule estimates can be mutually developed.

4.2.1 What Needs to Be Prototyped?

Customers need to see and touch new features that have never existed in their business environment. Multiple windows, for example, need to be tried with the tasks that surround their use. Pilot projects use prototypes to explore new technologies. They focus on letting the development staff gain experience with a new approach while working in the problem domain of the project. Pilot projects using object-oriented programming to build a prototype for transaction customer interface systems have been effective. The prototype is not production code. It may eventually become **pre**production code, or it may be completely discarded. In the prototyping effort, we are not concerned with ease of maintenance or with formal documentation. These concerns are extremely important, however, to a deliverable product. Code resulting from prototyping is often used to train programmers, and this is where the corporate ethic of thoroughness and quality in the final product can be emphasized.

Only after we have written specifications resulting from the experience with the prototype should we start the formal development process. If some of the prototype's code can be carried forward, that is a bonus. If not, there is no loss. A prototype may produce running software, whereas the production development produces reproducible, maintainable, saleable software.

4.2.2 How Do You Build a Prototype?

Only a few developers and system engineers need to work together in an unstructured way to gain the insight of the prototype. This team can be much smaller than the development team. Communication among people in prototyping is less of a problem than it is on a large development effort. Because the development schedule does not rely on the use of the prototype's code, it need not be industrial strength nor require change controls. The prototype will reflect the excitement and freewheeling nature of a small project.

A prototype may be a storyboard to display the user interface expected for a transaction system. Some of these transactions should be programmed to gain an understanding of how the system will work, which may be done in a rapid prototyping environment that provides elaborate tools, but the performance overhead renders the resulting system impractical for production use.

A prototype may be built in the expected production environment as a way to train the developers and familiarize them with a new set of programming tools. This opportunity is best taken when an organization is upgrading its technology.

A prototype may be an analytical model built in a higher level language to gain algorithm understanding, all the while understanding that the exercise will not produce code that will fit in to a production system.

4.2.3 How Is the Prototype Used?

Nimbleness to market drives the development business. This pace is set by the customer's willingness to adopt new technology more readily and by increased expectations from both your customer and your customer's customers. A typical cycle from conception to product delivery requires complete system development and fielding in less than 18 months. Prototyping makes this possible. Faster technology adoption means trying new technology with existing products faster to determine its effectiveness. Increased user expectations require the user to be more involved in the requirements engineering process.

Even this is not sufficient to satisfy some customers. If the demonstration of a prototype results in validation of the requirements for that system, the customer may want to take the prototype as is. Because most prototypes are not tested to critical limits nor integrated with existing systems, this may not be possible, practical, or reasonable. A professional will resist this pressure.

A new software evolution paradigm is needed to accomplish speed, accuracy, and reliability, along with the automated tools. Luqi's CAPS incorporates the goals and opinions of the user from the beginning of the software evolution process, throughout the life cycle, and into retirement. Automated tools like CAPS assist the software developer in building executable prototypes of a software system quickly, involving the user in an iterative build–execute–modify loop until the user is satisfied with the demonstration of the prototype. The prototype is then used to build the final version of the software through the use of the architecture included in the prototype, as well as the validated set of requirements constructed during the prototyping process. The resulting final version is delivered relatively quickly, hopefully before the user's requirements have an opportunity to change (Table 4.1).

TABLE 4.1. Evolutionary vs. Throw-Away Prototypes

Evolutionary when	An initial prototype is produced and refined through several stages resulting in the final system.
	Development starts with those requirements that are best understood.
	Best choice when a specification cannot be developed in advance.
	Based on techniques that allow rapid system iterations.
	Verification is impossible because there is no specification.
	Validation means demonstrating the adequacy of the system.
	Accelerates delivery of the system.
	End users engaged early in design are more likely to use the product.
Throw-away when	A prototype is developed from a prospectus.
	A prototype is produced only to discover requirements problems and then is discarded. The system is developed using another development process.
	The prototyping process starts with those requirements that are poorly understood.
	The process reduces requirements risk.
	Some system characteristics can be been left out, especially long-term operation.
	The prototype is usually poorly structured and therefore difficult to maintain.

Luqi, along with many graduate students and visiting researchers, spent years developing CAPS. Their efforts have resulted in a system that can be used to build executable prototypes of embedded real-time systems. The approach uses prototype demonstrations to determine and update the requirements of a proposed system during both requirements analysis and the evolutionary life cycle. Misunderstandings emerge clearly, allowing developers and customers to arrive at an accurate formulation or a reasonable estimate of the system's goal. Prototyping tools provide decision support for formulating a design and establishing system feasibility. An example might be evaluating hard real-time deadlines for software functions relative to proposed hardware configurations.

These prototypes are useful for validating requirements through demonstrations to customers, but they are not practical for providing deliverable products. CAPS rely on external support for building graphical user interfaces and manual translation of requirements into prototypes. This manual translation is problematic. The possibility of misinterpretation by the designer could lead to wasted effort in the prototype building process. Prototypes generated using CAPS generally lack robustness and portability. It is easy to build prototypes as long as proper inputs are made and use follows the designer's expectations. If messy reality intrudes and the designer has not built sufficient error handling into the prototype, execution can halt unexpectedly. Robustness can be built into CAPS prototypes, but automated methods for testing these qualities are not included. Manual methods are possible, but they would severely increase development time. This classic problem is typical of these tools. The demands of the product far exceed the ability of the support tool to produce software that will meet the constraints of the execution environment for the product.

4.2.4 What Happens to the Prototype?

Current software development methods and tools are insufficient to produce usable code in a reasonable amount of time, but rapid prototyping methods approach the needed capability. An incremental software development methodology, using the rapid prototyping paradigm, reduces development time and puts subsets of usable functions in the hands of the customer quickly. For example, Junction Solutions[3] uses a software prototyping approach called a "conference room pilot" to rapidly configure a system for business. The prototype models exactly how the software will work in the business. This approach manages project risk by evaluating exactly how the software will function when it is implemented.

The only purpose for throw-away prototypes is to help the customer identify requirements for a new system. Only the derived requirements will be maintained. The prototype is destroyed because the tools that created the prototype are unsuitable for use or unacceptable to the customer's IT organization as a production system.

---

[3] http://www.junctionsolutions.com/spc/spfa.html.

Quick and dirty prototypes bring up a version of a system that is modified repeatedly until the customer can grant minimal approval. Care must be taken that something intended to be temporary does not actually become permanent.

Detailed design-driven prototypes are the intellectual children of engineering disciplines in which "prototype" means a preproduction model of a system. Like the concept car at an auto show, the model is "test-driven" to uncover defects.

Nonfunctioning mock-ups provide the customer with visual examples of system process inputs and outputs. No data are actually input, nor are results computed and output. The difference between throw-aways and mock-ups is the presence or absence of real data. Mock-ups are not definitive in identifying functional requirements because of the lack of interactive experimentation.

Evolutionary prototypes are easily modifiable and extensible working models of a proposed system, although not necessarily representative of the complete system, which provides customers with a physical representation of key parts of the system before implementation. They are easily built, readily modifiable, ultimately extensible, partially specified working models of the primary aspects of a proposed system. As a cost-effective means of discovering the true and complete set of system functional requirements that will optimally satisfy the legitimate business needs of the user, given a level of funding acceptable to the customer and software developer, the goal is to evolve the prototype into the final system. Evolutionary prototyping techniques can be applied effectively to all phases of the software development cycle.

Detailed analysis and design do still take place. The techniques of evolutionary prototyping are applied concurrently with structured analysis at the beginning of the project and with structured design during the tuning phase. Evolutionary prototypes are characterized by real-world data used during prototyping, their easy modifiability, and the probability that they should, in most cases, develop into the final system.

The risks of rapid prototyping are that mistaken concepts concerning definitions, objectives, and correct application of the technique can lead to poor design, and those disagreements with customers regarding methodology, standards, and tools can lead to insurmountable conflict. Customers need sensitive and firm management to prevent them from becoming pseudo-engineers who want to iterate and evolve the prototype into a system that does everything for everyone all of the time. Budget slashes and attempts to shortcut appropriate efforts are also some temptations engendered by use of the word "rapid" beyond the group of professional software engineers who acknowledge its limited interpretation. The ethical engineer might be in the position of having to refuse premature delivery of a prototype because only a thoroughly documented and tested final product should be released. The final risk can afflict the customer, the engineer, and the management. That is the lure of the overevolved prototype. Elegance and efficiency, the ultimate specialization, can trump the need for flexibility in real-world environments.

Operational scenarios can be understood by prototyping a proposed system. This approach works well where there are complex interactions among systems and between software and people. A high-fidelity prototype models each user's functions, which includes menus, commands, screen formats, screen and operational navigation sequences, response times, error messages, and help messages. The frequency and use of features are modeled in the prototype.

4.3   IT WORKS, BUT WILL IT CONTINUE TO WORK?

When we finally get a system to work, how do we know it will continue to work? As its load grows, can we be sure that it will respond properly to out-of-range data, that it will handle data that arrives when it should not, and that its performance degrades predictably? The prototype that is used throughout the life cycle affords the opportunity to answer these questions.

Prototyping in more traditional engineering disciplines is the common approach to demonstrating the feasibility of the functionality of a system early in the life cycle. Prototyping is also used for risk assessment and to validate end user requirements. Software engineers began to recognize the benefits of prototyping software systems in the early 1980s. The benefit of establishing a standard against which the end user needs are validated is that it reduces the number of problems manifesting late in the life cycle. In addition, the standard serves as a means of design validation. Executable requirements and specification techniques allow for the dynamic demonstration of functionality of a software system.

On the other hand, prototyping has not been as successful as anticipated in some organizations. Unreasonable expectations, the rush to market, poor training, and costs can each have a negative impact on using software prototyping techniques. A common problem with adopting prototyping technology is high expectations for productivity with insufficient effort. In addition to training for the use of a prototyping technique, there is an often-overlooked need for developing a corporate and a project-specific underlying structure to support the technology. When this underlying support structure is missing, software shops experience low productivity as product developers are distracted by the need to perform the support roles. Nevertheless, the prototyping approach is a good software practice. Its use should become the expected way software development is done. Figure 4.1 shows the savings in terms of developmental time and effort with prototyping.

4.4   CASE STUDY: THE CASE OF THE DRIVEN DEVELOPMENT

Today many projects model and simulate system performance, but the Safeguard antimissile missile system was early to use prototypes and simulations

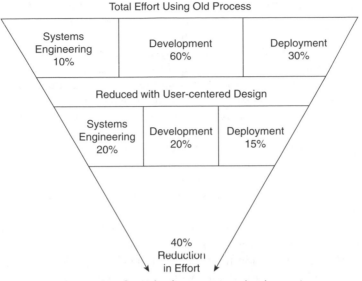

Figure 4.1. Cost of software system development.

to drive its software development. After some false starts, the entire software effort fell into lockstep with the prototype and simulation program. This is the story of the effectiveness of this approach.

Bell Laboratories was responsible for the design and development of the Safeguard System from 1967 to 1977. It was to defend U.S. ICBM silos by intercepting ballistic missile attacks. The intention was to deter enemy ICBMs. The successful development program resulted in the SALT II treaty, which slowed the arms race by halting deployment of ABM systems. It also demonstrated the wisdom of an extensive simulation program calibrated with actual field data.

Safeguard employed long-range and short-range interceptor missiles. The missile site radar (MSR) performed atmospheric target tracking and defensive missile guidance. The radar used phased array technology to form and steer radar beams at electronic speeds under software control. Bell Laboratories designed a computer capable of multiprocessing as many as ten processors in parallel to run the software. A table-driven operating system achieved efficient parallel performance by capitalizing on the predictable sequence of tasks the Safeguard system used to find, track, and intercept enemy reentry vehicles (RVs).

Shortly after the government decided to deploy an ABM system, Bell Laboratories formed a System Evaluation department to provide quality assurance. Its objective was to ensure that the design met the system objectives and that the implementation met the system requirements. To carry out that objective, the department designed field tests to conduct on the Kwajalein test range in the Marshall Islands in the South Pacific, using a prototype of the tactical system. Typical mission scenarios were used to measure software progress throughout the entire development cycle.[4]

The prototype was elaborate, including computers, software, missiles, and radars. This effort became the driving force for the software development effort. An early test showed that the computer design was faulty. There were negative timing margins in some logic chains, which required a redesign of the architecture. The prototype revealed serious support shortfalls in the operating system, the main problem being that it took 5 days to compile the software to get the intermodule references correct and build a working executable software system.

The system evaluation team took the approach of developing a family of simulations to predict and confirm system performance. The highest-level simulation predicted the performance of the entire system in response to a full-scale attack. To facilitate the design of the simulation, the models of subsystems (missiles and radars) were only as detailed as was required to enable the system simulation to model overall system performance. Detailed simulations of all major subsystems validated the high-level models. In some cases, the phenomena modeled in those subsystem simulations were based on even more detailed simulations accounting for the fundamental physics involved.

This approach depended on the validity of the simulations used at all levels of system analysis. Real data taken during subsystem and system tests validated and calibrated the simulations. Extensive simulations were run before the field tests. This approach predicted system performance, found software errors, and eliminated surprises. Before any test, multiple simulations were run to obtain a statistical distribution of predicted performance. Because there were many variables in each test, the precise results could only be predicted statistically. Once the test ran and real data were obtained, the simulation was rerun using the measured data. The simulations reconstructed actual missile flight history and miss distance. Differences were noted, and the models were recalibrated. This method worked well and gave high confidence in simulations of battles against Soviet ballistic missiles.

Each system test cost $5M to $10M. For this reason, the test program design maximized meaningful information obtained per test and minimized the number of tests, which resulted in a program that stressed the entire system and its components in specific areas separately. It validated total system performance. In every case, exhaustive simulations were conducted before the field test so there was high confidence that it would be successful.

---

[4] Bernstein, L, Burke, E. H., and Bauer, W. F. "Simulation- and Modeling-Driven Software Development," *CrossTalk: The Journal of Defense Software Engineering*, Vol. 9, No. 7, July 1996, pp. 25–27.

4.4.1 Significant Results

The radar had to track ballistic missiles at short range, which was a special challenge to the System Evaluation Department. When a warhead reenters the atmosphere, the friction between the ballistic missile and the increasingly dense atmosphere generates tremendous heat as the ballistic missile descends. This heat ionizes the atmosphere, producing a wake of ionized air trailing behind the ballistic missile. The radar pulse is reflected by this ionized wake as well as by the ballistic missile. Consequently, the radar return is a composite of the "clean" reflection from the ballistic missile and an irregular reflection from the extended wake. The task faced by the evaluation team was to model the physics associated with the generation of wake with sufficient fidelity to evaluate the effectiveness of the radar tracking before tests with real ballistic missiles.

The radar used a software closed-loop feedback system to maintain the range gate (a window in time during which the radar would look for the target) and the azimuth and elevation of the radar beam pointing at the target. The design of the range gate assumed a clean target return. As long as a sufficient gap existed between the clean return from the target and the extended irregular return from the wake, the algorithm worked well. However, if there was no gap between the two returns, the range gate would drift back onto the wake and the software would lose track of the target.

This modeling was extremely complex. It had to account for the interaction of the radar pulse that employed a range of frequencies to improve range resolution (known as "chirp") with the reflections from the stationary ionized particles of the wake and the reflections from a fast-moving ballistic missile. The Doppler effect shifts the echo of a chirp pulse from a stationary target away from the echo from a moving target. This shift had a significant impact on the degree of separation, or gap, between the target and the wake reflections and consequently was critical to the evaluation of the tracking software.

After months of painstaking effort to model the effect of wake on the radar tracking scheme, the simulation showed the radar would consistently lose track during the interval of peak wake. This result was unexpected. Had it not been for the simulation, it would have remained obscure until the first system tests on Kwajalien a year later. This analysis prevented a software crisis. The discovery that the tracking algorithm was flawed resulted in a focused effort to redesign it. A threshold scheme insensitive to the gap between target and wake reflections was developed. Simulation results were used to tune and test the new algorithm that would maintain track on a waking target.

The new tracking scheme was not available in time for the initial system tests, which therefore were conducted using the original tracking algorithm. The radar lost track of the target at the altitude that the simulation predicted. Later tests conducted with the revised tracking scheme were successful, again as predicted by the simulation. The new algorithms were implemented in the operational software. The simulation results were then used to check that the algorithms were implemented correctly. The benefit of the evaluation effort was that the development of the revised tracking algorithm began about a year earlier than it would have if the problem had first surfaced during system tests, which advanced the overall system test program by 1 year because low-altitude target tracking was a prerequisite for most system tests. Predicting the problem and having a solution ready before the first system tests preserved the credibility of the System Evaluation Department.

The software development schedules were based on the need to meet the field tests. Each capability was carefully defined, and detailed software verification tests were run to assure that each capability was available in the next software load. After software was assembled for a field test, special software certification tests were run to make sure that the system operated properly for combinations of possible target and interceptor conditions. This approach led to incremental development. Progress in the development of the software modules was tracked by measuring readiness for field tests. The module development plans and tests reflected field test needs as defined by the system simulation engineers.

The newest tracking algorithms for the ballistic missile were validated in the field. The simulations anticipated the failure of the first tracking test because of errors in the software tracking programs. The developers, to their everlasting regret, ignored the simulation results. It took another failure before the software developers took the simulation results seriously.

Computer round-off errors led to a second tracking problem. Early simulations were conducted on a commercial computer, but the computer used in Safeguard was a special-purpose computer. Of particular concern were the algorithms used to track the incoming ballistic missiles. The simulations predicted that the tracking algorithms would work well under the expected tactical situations. However, system evaluation engineers grew suspicious of the difference in the computers and suspected it would affect the validity of the simulations. The commercial computer represented numbers with 36-bit accuracy, whereas the special-purpose computer used in Safeguard had 32-bit accuracy. When the simulation was modified to model the 32-bit accuracy of the Safeguard computer, round-off errors emerged. The tracking algorithms required the inversion of a 9 by 9 matrix. This matrix was characterized by very large diagonal terms and very small off-diagonal terms. At first, it seemed that the algorithms would be adequate, but it was just because the initial target trajectories came directly at the radar. Only after "fly-by" trajectories that were characterized by having high angular velocities relative to the radar were simulated did the discrepancy between the 36-bit and the 32-bit accuracy become apparent. On such trajectories, the off-diagonal terms became important in predicting the target position and, with the 32-bit accuracy, the software would lose track of the ballistic missile target as it began to fly by the radar. The simulations showed the need for double-precision arithmetic in the matrix inversion operation, which was discovered at the same time the field test was conducted. The software lost track of the ballistic missile as predicted. The software was then changed to conform to the model. The model and simulations became the standard for software performance.

After several years of validation with data from live tests, confidence grew in the ability to predict test outcomes. One parameter predicted was target impact. As the difference between predicted and actual target impact was plotted for ten tests, a bias became apparent in one direction. By now the quality of the simulation and the accuracy of the tactical software in all other respects were highly regarded, so other sources of error were suspected. The location of the Kwajalein atoll relative to Vandenberg Air Force Base was in error. A resurvey, treated with great skepticism by the contracting officer, showed that the location was off by precisely the bias detected by the simulations.

In another instance, the quality of the simulations saved a missile test that might otherwise have failed. After intercept, special tests were performed on the interceptor missiles to see how they performed under the greatest stress. An order to the interceptor to turn right as fast as it could was followed after 2 seconds by an order to make a sharp left turn. This maneuver was called the "tail wag" algorithm. The direction of the tail wag was changed to avoid a tight flight safety boundary. Instead of ordering right turn–left turn, the opposite, **left** then **right**, was ordered. If the interceptor chosen for the field test happened to be faster than average, it had room to avoid the range safety boundary.

Whenever an order to self-destruct was sent to an interceptor missile, the missile tracking software continued to track one of its fragments so that the fragment would not fall into an inhabited area. The simulation showed that if the sine of an angle became greater than 1, the software would abort. This would not stop the computer because special code was available to handle recovery from abends, but software checks were added to prevent the abort.

The field test scenarios were run hundreds of times before each live test with only random noise generators changing the details of the scenario. These were Mission Reliability tests designed to stress the computer hardware and software before each field test. There was some controversy about the need for these extensive tests until an operating system race condition was found in the 108th running of one scenario. This latent bug could have stopped data recording during a live field test, which would lead to failure. There was no more discussion about the need for such software testing.

The results of the simulation runs were compared with tests of the tactical software to ensure software correctness. When there was a difference between the simulation and the software tests, comparative tests would be run to isolate the problem, which moved debugging from detective work to analysis. The data reduction approaches invented for the simulations were a model for testing the software loads and eventually led to automated analysis for the software reliability tests. When exceptionally stressful multiple ballistic missile and multiple interceptor scenarios were run, a design error was found in the software scheduler. It did not show up in the simulators, but it caused a system failure when software tasks were improperly dispatched in the Safeguard computer. The simulation data helped to isolate the problem rapidly.

Near the end of the test program, the simulations became so trustworthy that a major catastrophic problem was almost overlooked. Designers would tune the range gates' size in the tracking algorithm for each field test based on the simulation results. Early tests in the program stressed ballistic missile tracking with low-altitude intercepts. Those conducted later stressed interceptor guidance with high-altitude intercepts. As the altitude of the intercepts increased, designers tightened the range gates to decrease miss distance. The software became tuned for high-altitude intercepts, and the software could lose track of the ballistic missile at low altitudes, thereby invalidating all previous tests. When this problem was found, the tracking software was fixed and all the tests were resimulated to validate system operation. Repeating the field tests was avoided because of the quality of the simulation.

In one test, the interceptor actually hit the ballistic missile! The 1970s antimissile system hit a bullet with a bullet.

4.4.2 Lessons Learned

The system evaluation experience validated the overall approach of predicting system performance by extensive analysis and simulation. Validating the simulations with data from live system tests worked. The approach proved effective in four ways:

(1) Exhaustive and detailed simulations revealed requirements flaws and made them easy to fix. There were no schedule slips caused by these flaws.

(2) The number of tests was minimized.

(3) The family of simulations was validated, which modeled the performance of the Safeguard system under full enemy attack.

(4) Scenarios successfully tested the tactical software, found bugs, and tracked software development progress.

This simulation and modeling technique evolved spontaneously during the development of the Safeguard system. It can be used to good effect in the development of any large complex system. It was used successfully in the development of systems used to operate telephone networks. At the University of Florida during the 1980s, Mills[5] showed that scenario-based testing is 30 times better than classic coverage testing.

The technique is to model system components and the entire system in a hierarchy of models. The models are then used to systematically simulate

[5] Mills, Harlan. http.//www.stsc.hill.af.mil/crosstalk/1996/07/simulati.asp.

system performance with typical operational scenarios. The operational software design is based on functional requirements embedded in the models and the operational scenarios run against the production software. The results of the simulation are compared with results from the operational tests, and any differences are resolved.

Validating requirements and providing them to developers unambiguously, moving debugging from detective work to comparative analysis, and measuring software development progress in terms of completing scenario tests led to a successful Safeguard software development program. This approach became known as model-driven software development.

4.4.3 Additional Business Histories

The following case histories are brief summaries of actual problems and their solutions experienced in a business environment.

4.4.3.1 Order Reading and Analysis Software

Purpose: Find a method for order reading and analysis that is applicable to variable formats.

Prototype: The size of the prototype was 12,000 new or changed source lines of code (NCSLOC) written in C, which was 10% of the final system module. This was created and used by four people for 8 months.

Rationale: The software team was being converted from COBOL programming to C programming and had experience in the application domain. They were unfamiliar with finite-state machine design, and the complexity of the control structure was identified as risky. A poor choice would lead to complicated control logic. The modules of the system would be highly coupled and be inflexible. The prototype approach was chosen to get a start on program development ahead of the final definition of the system interfaces and requirements. It was to be an evolutionary prototype. The developers would also become facile in C and its tools and libraries.

Results: Final requirements were written based on prototype results. The experience introduced the possibility of a tunable system to the developers. Early evaluation of functional decomposition and performance was made. The prototype was thrown away because of decomposition and performance problems. The prototype succeeded in the sense that it showed that the finite state machine needed to be based on order activity and not on inventory. Tracking the flow was far more critical than the decomposition of the order. This was not obvious to the developers at the beginning of the project. System designers eliminated usable code alternatives as difficult to change.

4.4.3.2 Store and Forward Message Switch

Purpose: Evaluate a new scheduling algorithm for an existing system.

Prototype: The size of the prototype was 2% of the total system of 500 K NCSLOC. One person used the prototype for 4 months. The production code development required 1 year and 3 staff years.

Results: In a store-and-forward message switching system, the buffer overload strategy was unstable. After the system went into overload and returned to normal processing, it would immediately poll for more traffic. Polling had a higher priority than distributing the messages already queued, in the mistaken belief that polling must be the highest priority task to meet the response time requirement. This exhausted even more buffers, drove the system into overload again, and caused it to stay in overload longer than before. To convince the customer that lowering the priority of polling would solve the problem, a prototype system was created in the test laboratory. It demonstrated stable overload response with an increase in response time that was imperceptible even at ten times the expected load. With the prototype evidence as demonstrable proof, the customer agreed to a system release with improved overload response. Demonstrating with the prototype avoided an emotionally charged battle over response time. The prototype became preproduction code.

4.4.3.3 Evolutionary Prototyping for Order Entry

Purpose: Evaluate human interface, validate economic assumptions, and train software developers before firm requirements are available.

Prototype: The size was 10% of the final project. The prototype took 9 months to build and required seven people for 9 months.

Results: The human interface was changed to put more data on a single screen because the users preferred to see all transactions that could be completed with a single entry. The screens became dense. The table structures were changed for easier maintenance and change. The economics proved in for the system. A high sensitivity of the economics to response time was established. An earlier version had been rushed into production without adequate analysis, which resulted in project termination because of difficulties in operating the system and lack of capacity.

4.4.3.4 Evolutionary Prototyping of an Outside Plant Database System

Purpose: Evaluate database structures for an outside plant database. Experiment with approaches to handling multiple future states of equipment usage.

Prototype: The size of the prototype was 5% of 500 K NCSLOC and required three people for 15 months.

Results: A new database structure using hyper-graph theory was invented,[6] and an algorithm was developed to explain why the heuristic approach being used worked. The prototype became the production code. UNIX was used to model loop plant by way of a directed graph. The prototype was ported to demonstrate the transportability of the code.

4.4.3.5 Estuary Water Flow Models

Purpose: Computer modeling of harbor water tides and currents is now prac-ticed largely by physicists, who are often untrained as programmers and learn to code in FORTRAN as they go. Therefore, the code they produce is not sophisticated, hard to modify, and obscure. The models require large amounts of computer time and long elapsed times to execute because they are largely unoptimized. This project optimizes the processing of the equations, while letting physicists write in the FORTRAN structures that make sense to them. The goals are as follows:

(1) Thirty percent shorter processing time with a dual-processor system.

(2) Fifteen percent less processing time with standard equation rearrange-ment.

(3) Forty percent less elapsed time on a dual-processor system.

Rationale: A requirements analysis resulted in a simplified quality function deployment analysis that showed that the equation rearrangement goal was more important than the multiprocessing goal.

The numbers in Table 4.2 are the mapping of subjective judgments by the customer and developers of the importance of each feature toward reaching

TABLE 4.2. sQFD Analysis Sorts Priorities

Feature/ Function	Ease of Implementation	Correctness	Functionality	Consistency	Reduction in Execution time	Reduction in elasped time	Total Score
Analyze syntax	8	9	9	3	9	8	304
Rearrange equations	3	5	8	8	9	5	105
Insert forks for parallel processing	8	3	8	3	0	9	184

[6] Goldstein, A. J., et al. *Hyperedge Entity-Relationship Data Base*, U.S. Patent 4,479,196, October 23, 1984.

the project goals. A Wideband Delphi approach was used to scale the judgments on a 1 to 9 scale, with 9 being most important. These optimizations became the focus of the design for execution time reduction:

(1) All constants must be grouped together: $(c1)(a)(c2)(b)(c3)$, where a and b are variables and $c1$, $c2$ and $c3$ are constants. Then let:

$$c4 = (c1)(c2)(c3) \rightarrow (c4)(a)(b).$$

(2) Factor all equations:

$$x = (a)(bc) + (a)(ef) \rightarrow x = (a)(bc + ef).$$

(3) Remove zeroes from additions and subtractions:

$$a + b + c1, \text{ where } c1 = 0 \rightarrow a + b.$$

(4) Remove ones from multiplication and division:

$$(a)(b)(c1), \text{ where } c = 1 \rightarrow (a)(b).$$

(5) Remove all values in multiplications and divisions when a zero is present:

$$(a)(b)(c1) + d, \text{ where } c1 = 0 \rightarrow d.$$

The focus on syntax requirements led to the design that the new syntax must capture the information necessary to optimize equations:

(1) Data types should be defined in such a way that indicates some variables change frequently, whereas other variables remain the same.
(2) Syntax must allow definition of high, medium, or low precision for variables.
(3) Variables may be declared as constant (one, zero, or other) or changing.
(4) Syntax should look like FORTRAN.
(5) Compiler must be able to dynamically insert and configure multiprocessing code to satisfy user preferences.

Then an estimate of the size of the system was made based on the requirements using function point algorithms (Table 4.3). The effort was almost the same for the equation rearrangement and the ability to run the code simultaneously in parallel processors. The developers felt that the equation rearrangement was the greater risk and chose to develop it in their first increment. Parallelism was left for the second increment because it was deemed of less importance and might be sacrificed if development schedules were missed because of unforeseen events.

TABLE 4.3. Function Points for Estuary Code Optimizer

	Simple	Medium	Complex	Subtotal
External Inputs	3	2	1	6
Notes: Syntax				
External Outputs	4	1	2	7
Notes: Parallelism				
External Inquiries	0	0	0	0
Internal Logical Files	0	0	0	0
External Logical Files	5	5	0	10
Notes: Code Production				
	SUBTOTAL UNADJUSTED FP			23

FP ADJUSTMENTS

Requires Backup/Recovery	0
Data Communications	0
Distributed Processing Functions	0
Performance Critical	5
Run on existing heavily used environment	4
Requires online data entry	0
Multiple screens for input	0
Master fields updated online	0
Inputs, outputs, inquiries of files complex	5
Internal processing complex	4
Code designed for reuse	5
Conversion and installation included	0
Multiple installation in different organizations	2
Must facilitate change and ease of use by user	0
TOTAL FP ADJUSTMENTS	25

ADJUSTED FP = UNADJUSTED FP × (0.65 + 0.01 TOTAL FP ADJUSTMENTS)
ADJUSTED FP =   23 × (0.65 + 0.01 × 25)
ADJUSTED FP = 20.7

ESTIMATED SIZE OF ESTUARY CODE OPTIMIZER:

Approximate NCSLOC = JAVA SLOC/FP × Adjusted FP
Approximate NCSLOC = 53 × 20.7 = 1000

Prototype: A prototype was built in the JAVA language for both the equation rearrangement and the multiprocessing approach to achieve goals. The choice was made to familiarize the developers with the problem and with the development environment.

Results: The prototype showed that parallelism alone would reduce process-ing time and elapsed time by 60%. This result would exceed project goals by a factor of two. The prototype led the developers to revise their understand-ing of the importance of both approaches and revise their development plan. They made parallelism their first increment, even though they knew that the equation rearrangement would be more fun and let them use their compiler expertise. The prototype became a step toward capturing the final set of formal requirements. It let the system engineer, the developer, and the customer deal with the problem statements and potential solutions in concrete terms and work on the most important part of the project first.

4.5 WHY IS PROTOTYPING SO IMPORTANT?

In the 1980s, advocates of firm specifications argued against the emerging pro-totyping technology. They felt that prototypes led to unstructured projects and a loss of control. Prototype advocates claimed that detailed specifications were no longer needed. Both sides went too far. Prototypes are needed to help understand the technology and to understand the problem. Specifications are needed to manage customer expectations and developer commitments.

In 1984, UCLA wanted to determine if there were any advantages of pro-totyping over a top-down specification process. Barry Boehm conducted these studies.[7] He divided students into seven teams, each to develop a version of the same product. Four used the specifying approach, denoted as teams S1, S2, S3, S4, and three used the prototyping approach, denoted as teams P1, P2 and P3.

A score of 5 was considered satisfactory in the product evaluation. The product was evaluated by a panel of customers, except for the ease of main-tenance category, which was evaluated by the developers sitting as a panel. The factors evaluated for maintenance were design, programming style, size of product, documentation, and product performance at acceptance test.

The overall productivity for all teams was the (sum of NCSLOC)/(sum of staff hours)/7 = 44.04531/7 = 6.2921 NCSLOC/staff hour with a standard devi-ation of 1.8. But the average productivity for the teams that did top-down spec-ifications was 6.25 with a standard deviation of 2.4, whereas the average productivity and standard deviation for the prototyping teams was 6.34 with a standard deviation of 0.21. The average productivity for the prototyping approach is 37.5% higher than the specification approach with an order of magnitude tighter standard deviation. The prototyping approach is more pro-ductive, and the staffing required is more predictable because the prototyping approach led to an average system size of 2064 NCSLOC and the specifica-

[7] Boehm, Barry W., Gray, Terence E., and Seewaldt, Thomas. "Prototyping Versus Specifying: A Multiproject Experiment," *IEEE Transactions on Software Engineering*, Vol. SE-10, No. 3, May 1984, pp. 290–301.

tion approach led to an average system size of 3391 NCSLOC, a difference of 40%. The three prototyping projects were more maintainable than the specification projects. Table 4.4 summarizes the results of the experiment.

TABLE 4.4. Specification vs. Prototyping Experiment Results (with IEEE permission)

Team Name	S1	S2	S3	S4	P1	P2	P3
Team Size	3	3	2	3	2	3	2
NCSLOC	2985	3164	4606	2809	1952	2726	1514
Staff Hours	589	498	459	789	323	422	232
Functionality*	6.33	7	5	6	5.33	5	4
Robustness*	4.67	5.5	6	4.33	4.33	4.33	3
Ease of Use*	2.33	4	2.67	4	6	5.33	2.67
Ease of Learning*	3.67	3.5	4	3.67	5.67	5.33	3.67
Ease of Maintenance*	5.5	4.3	4	4	8	7.3	5.5

*Evaluation of product on a scale from 1, worst, to 10, best. S teams used specifications only, and P teams used prototyping only. A better approach is to use both processes for validating and communicating the requirements specification. NCSLOC was used to measure the size of the product as the experiment was conducted before function points became popular, and in this case, they were counted the same way so they can provide the basis for comparison.

Product size is the driver for determining productivity and maintainability because large projects are hard to design efficiently and maintain effectively. The smaller the product, the easier it is to maintain and the faster it is to develop. We will see that productivity is a nonlinear function that increases with the size of the software developed.

On the other hand, the specification projects had more features and were more robust than those produced with the prototyping approach. Industrial systems need to evolve with business changes and emerging needs, so both approaches are needed. The reasons why prototyping is so important can be summarized as follows:

(1) Provides a vehicle for system engineers to better understand the environment and the requirements of the problem being addressed

(2) Demonstrates what is actually feasible with existing technology and where weaknesses exist

(3) Efficient mechanism for the transfer of design intent from system engineer to developer

(4) Permits developers to meet earlier schedules for the production version

(5) Allows for early customer interaction

(6) Demonstrates to customer what is functionally feasible and challenges imagination, leading to more creative inputs and a forward-looking system

(7) Provides an analysis test-bed and a vehicle to validate and evolve system requirements

4.6 PROTOTYPING DEFICIENCIES

For balance, we now consider prototyping blind spots. If the initial prototype is too far off the mark, we can get some disastrous results, such as souring the customer on the prospect for a responsive system. We could concentrate on short-term needs, tinker with algorithms, or develop suboptimal systems. To avoid these pitfalls, we should write requirements that force us to do a careful analysis of the users' overall problem before plunging into the code. It is difficult to manage and schedule prototyping and hard to get people off the prototype and onto the real system. Specifically, getting them to deal with size, performance, the build constraints, and the practicalities of a production system can be a real management problem.

In one project, we tried to use structured system analysis and failed. Even though it is an excellent analysis tool, it is a painful way to communicate with the customer. The customer sees no need to learn the language of structured system analysis. System engineers, delighted with the tool, tend to jump from the general to the detailed, thereby adding more confusion. Human language feature memos provide a convenient way of communicating across the customer-engineer boundary, but they are hard to keep current and leave too much to the imagination. This is where the power of the Spiral Model comes in. The customer sees what the engineer heard and is in a good position to correct false impressions. With the corrections in mind, the engineer spins anther cycle on the Spiral, getting it right before investing in implementation.

Those who use prototyping see it as highly effective (93%), but it fell off in 2000 during the technological bubble when time-to-market was all that mattered from 50% usage to a mere 20% usage. The fear of widespread downsizing or litigation might also make managers reluctant to challenge unreasonable budgets and schedules and therefore not wish to have the tangible evidence of unreasonableness indicated by a prototype. Prototyping will regain favor when there is more pressure to produce quality software because the enormous costs of postrelease repair and high failure rates of untrustworthy software can no longer be borne.

4.7 ITERATIVE PROTOTYPING

The iterative prototyping process examines the trustworthy behavior of the software architecture.

The process, as shown in Figure 4.2, starts with use case analysis to identify user needs. Based on the use cases, an object-oriented, distributed architecture of the system is augmented with formal specification of timing requirements in terms of a time-series temporal logic. Then the internal structures of the modules are factored until they can be mapped to a prototype. A time-series model executes temporal rules for the target application instrumented with probes used to compare with data from running the prototype.

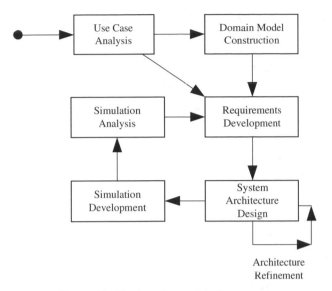

Figure 4.2. *The iterative prototyping process.*

4.8   CASE STUDY: THE CASE OF THE FAMISHED FISH[8]

A Fish Tank Control System controls the fish food dispenser and water quality in a fish tank. The tank has a mechanical feeder that drops pellets of fish food from a feeder tube suspended above the tank. The feeder can be turned on and off by computer software. The tank also has a water inlet pipe and a drain pipe with valves controlled by the computer, and sensors that measure the water level in millimeters from the bottom, the oxygen level in the water measured in parts per million (ppm), and the ammonia level in the water (ppm).

The software must deliver fish food at scheduled feeding times, which are repeated every day. The times when each feeding starts and stops are displayed in a console and can be adjusted from the keyboard.

The software must keep the oxygen level to a minimum of 8 ppm, and the ammonia level below 9 ppm. Fish will die if left in an environment with low oxygen or high ammonia for 1 minute or more. The fish tank is 1 m wide, 2 m long, and 1 m deep (1-mm level = 2-L volume). The software must keep the water level between 60 and 90 cm at all times. The fill/drain valves allow a maximum flow of 0.5 L per second when the valve is fully open. The fresh water coming in the inlet valve contains 30 ppm of oxygen and contains no ammonia. The fish in the tank consume oxygen at a rate of 0.1 mL/s and generates ammonia at a rate of 0.0015 mL/s while resting and at a rate of 0.003 mL/s while

[8] Thanks to Doron Drusinky and Man-Tak Shing of The Naval Postgraduate School. www.time-rover.com/ftp/rsp2003.pdf.

they are eating. The software should minimize water flow subject to the above constraints. Whenever the water level is below 88 cm for at least 3 minutes, the drain valve settings should be at most 10% of the maximum setting per second.

Central to the design is the ***control water flow*** operator, which controls the inlet and drain water flow based on Table 4.5.

TABLE 4.5. Water Flow Decision Table

Water Level	<65 cm	65 to 85 cm		>85 cm	
Oxygen (O₂) & Ammonia (NH₃) Level	Don't care	$O_2 < 8$ ppm or $NH_3 > 9$ ppm	$O_2 > 8$ ppm and $NH_3 < 9$ ppm	$O_2 < 8$ ppm or $NH_3 > 9$ ppm	$O_2 > 8$ ppm or $NH_3 < 9$ ppm
Inlet Valve Setting	open	open	close	open	close
Drain Valve Setting	close	close	close	open	open

What do the requirements mean? Does the software compute an average water level? How precise must the measurements be? Build a prototype to answer these questions and check to make sure that it meets the requirements. The DBRover tools set and system (http://www.time-rover.com) is one way to do this modeling. The prototype implements these temporal rules:

Rule 1: The water level must be between 60 and 90 cm at all times.

Rule 2: The oxygen level cannot be less than 8 ppm for more than 60 seconds.

Rule 3: The ammonia level cannot be more than 9 ppm for more than 60 seconds.

Rule 4: If the water level has been below 88 cm for 180 seconds, then the change of the drain valve setting must be less than or equal to 10% of the maximum setting per second (100).

Now, add four probes to the prototype to verify meeting the timing constraints of these operators. Rapid prototyping and run-time verification methods are usually thought of as two separate phases of the design process. Rapid prototyping has traditionally been used in the early stages of the design process, for the purpose of early system evaluation and demonstration, before implementation and coding. In contrast, formal and run-time verification methods have been used in later stages of the design process to validate and debug code that has already been written. But run-time monitoring and verification can be used as part of rapid prototyping and helps identify errors early in the design and validate the requirements.

Conclusion: Structured system analysis can make sure that our thinking is clear. It is a valuable tool for the system analyst (just do not share the analysis with the customer or the developer). Demonstrating the system concept with a prototype shows that it is possible to build such a system, irons out confusion in the requirements, and makes the discussions fun and effective. The prototype lets developers "fail small" so that they can "succeed big."

4.9 PROBLEMS

4.9.1 You are offered a short-term software development job with tight schedules and loose requirements in a new problem domain requiring technology similar to that you have used successfully on a project nearing completion. You have 20 people in your department who are experienced in the technology. Each person has a fully loaded cost (includes salary, benefits, and overhead) of $144,000 per year. You must negotiate a fixed price for your work. You estimate that the project will take 1 year and 10 staff months using an incremental development process based on specifications. In your experience, it costs one staff week to find and fix problems reported by customers once the system is deployed. If you use prototyping, you will need one support person half time. How much will the prototyping approach cost, if productivity is linear with the size of the system and that because of external dependencies you cannot compress the schedule? Would you use the incremental approach or the prototyping approach? Support you answer with numerical analysis.

4.9.2 Your company's best client employs 1000 agents at a call center to handle customer complaints. Call center managers have the authority to hire and fire agents and can purchase incidental equipment for the operation of the center. Purchases of more than $100,000 require corporate approval, which includes a review by the chief information officer (CIO). The CIO is charged with reducing information technology costs and the number of suppliers.

Typically, an agent uses a predefined script to capture the customer's problem. Once the problem is defined, it is resolved or handed off to a second-tier expert. The agents must follow strictly a script that can resolve 50% of the problems. For example, if a customer claims that he has already paid a bill, the agent asks for the invoice number and checks the accounting database. If the customer's payment has been recorded since the bill was mailed, the agent cancels the bill. If payment has not yet been recorded but this is the first complaint from this customer and the bill is less than $10, the agent forgives the charge.

You prototype the use of new speaker-independent voice-recognition systems and find that customers prefer the clarity and patience of the computer to that of many agents. Reliable and consistently friendly agents that exercise good judgment are hard to find and train at the wages companies are willing to pay. An agent is paid $30,000 yearly, and the overhead is twice the salary.

Desktop computers equipped with voice-recognition equipment, communication hardware, and platform software cost $10,000. These computers can replace one agent. Server computers can share the voice-recognition equipment; communications hardware and platform software cost $120,000. Each server can replace 30 agents.

Your client will buy systems that have a 2-month or less break-even time where the cost of money is not considered because the annual interest rate is 1%. The cost of developing the software is $800,000. This is true for either the server or the desktop solution.

You have a few political problems with this offer:

(1) The CIO does not want to add any new systems in order to stay within the budget.
(2) The CIO is upset about your company's long-term performance.
(3) Local managers are under intense pressure to reduce costs while improving productivity.
(4) Your company just delivered another system late and with bugs.

You are appointed the **product** manager and the **project** manager for this program. Your challenge is to maximize the success of this program.

- Using a flow diagram, show the business flows you would model in your prototype and explain each link.
- Compare the economics of the server and the desktop approach. Do not consider maintenance, operations, and administration costs of either the server or desktop approaches.

4.9.3 It is not useful for a software developer to spend time learning about how to evaluate an algorithm's time and space complexity because memory is cheap these days and chips are very fast. Do you agree or disagree and why?

4.9.4 This is the story of an application that was built before its operating system was ready.

Background: A project needs to use tools and components that were delivered late and were being changed by their suppliers. The suppliers also happen to be the customer. The project needs to build a system on top of a moving foundation. They need to identify the problem, assess the risk, and develop a way to cope with shortcomings in their suppliers.

Project Overview: A highly intensive database transaction system tracks computers purchased and customers. This is the seventh attempt at the project; the previous six attempts failed because of the custom nature of the computer configurations. Earlier software technology proved unable to convert and track the information and replace paper systems and records.

An over-riding concern of the project was design. The project members wanted a system that was scalable and robust. They required that it be able to accept and share data with any of the client's legacy systems. To this end, when initially planning the system design, the project manager decided against a traditional mainframe system and opted for the newer UNIX system, using C for the development. It was thought that by using UNIX, the system would be more flexible and implementation would be cheaper.

Reducing Technical Uncertainty: One aspect of the development environment during the project was homogeneity. The entire environment was UNIX with C, which greatly reduced integration issues because of uncooperative systems. The flexibility of C contributed to integration issues being corrected quickly when they arose. Constant communication among and between project members led to a reduction in integration issues, as plans and tactics were discussed openly and early enough for other teams to adapt.

Operating System Delivery: The subsystems were to run on a new operating system tuned to database performance. However, the operating system slipped and was projected to be 18 months behind schedule. Despite this, system development moved forward because of the flexibility that was built into the system. With the delay in the operating system, the project team constructed a work-around that would allow testing of the core application logic. A team of technical gurus developed an "adaptation layer" that would allow the application to run on a temporary UNIX OS. The inter-subsystem testing used an innovative "Cooperative Testing" approach.

Your task: Assume you are the process design engineer for this team. State four processes that you would include in your innovative "Cooperative Testing" approach.

4.9.5 You are offered a short-term software development job. You must negotiate a fixed price for your work. How would you go about arriving at a reasonably accurate estimate of how long the job should take?

a. Keep track of previous experiences to extrapolate new estimates.

b. Use wideband Delphi estimation with your development team.

c. Use a formal estimation model.

d. Build a prototype.

e. Hire experts with experience.

f. Negotiate a cost-plus-fee contract because of the risks.

g. Refuse the job.

BIBLIOGRAPHY

Andrews, D. C. "JAD: A crucial dimension for rapid applications development," *Journal of Systems Management*, March 1991, pp. 23–31.

Appel, J. J. and Bernstein, L. "Requirements or Prototyping? Yes!," *Proceedings of the Sixth International Conference on Software Engineering for Telecommunications Switching Systems*, Eindhoven, The Netherlands, April 14–18, 1986, pp. 170–175.

Bernstein, L. and Yuhas, C. M. "Software Engineering in Telecommunications Systems," *Encyclopedia of Software Engineering* Volume 2, 2nd ed., John Marciniak, Editor-in-Chief, Wiley-InterScience, New York, 2002, pp. 1497–1507.

Bernstein, L. "Foreword: Importance of Software Prototyping," *Journal of Systems Integration*, Vol. 6, No. 1/2, March 1996, pp. 9–14.

Boehm, B. W. "Spiral Model of Software Development and Enhancement," *Computer*, Vol. 2, No. 5, May 1988, pp. 61–72.

Boehm, B. W. *Software Risk Management*, IEEE CS Press, Los Alamitos, CA, 1989.

Boehm, Barry W. and Sullivan, Kevin J. "Software Economics," University of Southern California and University of Virginia, Dec. 1999, boehm@cs.usc.edu.

Boehm, Barry. *Software Engineering Economics*, Prentice-Hall, Englewood Cliffs, NJ, 1981.

Connell, John L. and Shafer, Linda Brice. *Structured Rapid Prototyping*, Yourdon Press, Prentice-Hall, Englewood Cliffs, NJ, 1989.

Drusinsky, D. and Shing, M. "Verification of Timing Properties in Rapid System Prototyping," *Proceedings of Rapid System Prototyping Conference*, 2003.

Drusinsky, D., Michael, J. B., and Shing, M. "Behavioral Modeling and Run-Time Verification of System-of-Systems Architectural Requirements," *International Conference on Computing, Communications and Control Technologies,* 2004.

Luqi and M. Shing. "Real-Time Scheduling for Software Prototyping," *Journal of Systems Integration, Special Issue on Computer Aided Prototyping*, 1996, pp. 44–72.

Luqi, Berzins, V., Shing, M., and Nada, N. "Evolutionary Computer-Aided Prototyping System (CAPS)," *Proceedings of the TOOLS USA 2000 Conference*, Santa Barbara, CA, July 30–Aug. 3, 2000.

Luqi, Yeh, R. "Rapid Prototyping in Software Evolution," *Encyclopedia of Software Engineering*, John Wiley and Sons, New York, 1994, pp. 1–21.

Luqi. "Computer-Aided Software Prototyping," *IEEE Computer*, Sept. 1991, pp. 111–112.

Rapid Application Development, Center for Software Engineering at the University of Southern California, workshop report.

5

Architecture

Software architecture is the body of instructions, written in a specific coding language, that controls the structure and interactions of software modules. It embodies the structure of a system and provides the framework for the software modules to perform the functions of the system. The design of the interfaces between modules and the constraints on the size and execution of the modules affects the ease with which they can be integrated into a working software system. The architecture of a system enforces constraints on the modules and the properties of capacity, throughput, consistency, and module compatibility are realized at the architectural level.

5.1 ARCHITECTURE IS A SYSTEM'S DNA

Within the system are architectural modules, whether the core operating system, or in the middleware, or custom-designed, that govern how the processing modules work together to do the system functions. Application calls these modules through special interfaces called application programming interfaces (APIs). In the early days of computing, these interfaces were simply the system calls made to operating system functions, like "dispatch a program." The communication architecture is code that governs the interactions of the processing modules with data and with other systems. The data architecture is code that controls how data files are structured, filled with data, and accessed.

Trustworthy Systems Through Quantitative Software Engineering,
by Lawrence Bernstein and C. M. Yuhas
Copyright © 2005 IEEE Computer Society

Once the architecture is established, functions may be assigned to processing modules and the system may be built. Processing modules can vary greatly in size and scope depending on the function each performs, and the same module may differ across installations. In every case, however, the processing architecture, communication architecture, and data architecture constitute the software architecture that is this system's—and this system's only—unique and unchanging "DNA."

When systems share a common architecture, they are as alike as identical twins, regardless of superficial differences in name or in site-peculiar configurations or adjunct functions. When several sites use software systems with a common architecture, they are considered to be using the same software system even though they may do somewhat different things. No two instances of a software system are exactly the same, despite their shared architecture. When a system is installed at two or more sites, localization is always required. Tables are populated with data to configure the software to meet the needs of specific customer sites. The customer may have special needs that require more than minor table adjustments. Customization of some modules may be required. New modules may be added.

Two systems with differing architectures can perform the same function in alternative ways. These systems would be different, even if they were named the same. Function and output do not define a system. Only its architecture can describe and identify a system.

Case Study: The Case of The Double Header Development

In the late 1980s, Bell Laboratories needed to develop a system to control a critical congestion situation. The system was called NEMOS. It used a distributed database with several unique database schemas. Some data overlapped. The schemas were designed to speed processing time. Architecture reviews revealed that this architecture was extremely complex and broke new theoretical ground. Because there was no history of similar development to provide a guideline and the need was urgent, Bell Laboratories decided to develop a second system with a different architecture in parallel to mitigate the architectural risks identified. The insurance system was also called NEMOS but instead used an integrated database architecture, which means a single database for everything. The result was two systems with the same name, performing the same function.

The system with the distributed database architecture could not be scaled to handle network growth and was discarded. The architecture with the integrated database architecture was successfully deployed and demonstrated its robustness when it managed telephone calls during the famous "1989 World Series Earthquake" in California.[1]

---

[1] On October 17, 1989 at 5:04 PM, a major earthquake struck the San Francisco Bay area. The earthquake was nicknamed the World Series Earthquake because it occurred just before a World

5.2 PITY THE POOR SYSTEM ADMINISTRATOR

One of the most common failures of architecture design for software systems is not attending to features needed by system administrators. They have myriad responsibilities:

(1) Training users
(2) Configuring the computer to run the software
(3) Defining network requirements for the network manager
(4) Setting up data files
(5) Maintaining adequate response time
(6) Troubleshooting

System startup is a treacherous time. The system administrator is intimidated by the new system and does not immediately suspect software errors in a freshly tested installation. For example, in the request-response model in Figure 5.1, several host computers are connected to a local area network (LAN) using Ethernet and share the transmission media. Some host computers are servers, and many more are clients. When one server and one client were connected, the system worked well. As several clients were added, the system continued to operate satisfactorily until there was a sudden stop. No messages could be transmitted among any servers and clients. This is an example of a conditionally stable system.

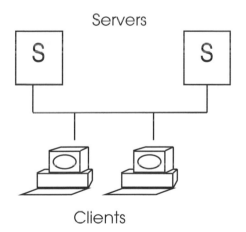

Figure 5.1. *Request-response model.*

Series baseball game was scheduled to begin in Candlestick Park. Millions of people witnessed the motion of the earthquake on television. Sixty-seven people lost their lives, and property damage was estimated at $6 billion, but the telephones worked.

A system is conditionally stable as long as any one of its critical resources is not exhausted. Frequently there are early warning symptoms of slow response time or lost messages before the system halts, but other times there is no warning at all.

In this example, clients were added and the system performed to specifications for a time. Then when the 101st client sent a message, the system stalled. There were so many message clashes on the transmission media that the computers spent all their time resending lost messages. The system administrator had to turn off all hosts, bring up the server, and limit the number of clients until faster transmission media could be installed.

With many computers sending messages, the likelihood of two messages trying to use the transmission media simultaneously increases. When Ethernet LANs detect clashes, Ethernet aborts transmission. When this happens, the applications can timeout. If **n** is the number of clients on a LAN and **p** is the probability a client could be sending a message, with a Poisson probability distribution, the optimal number of clients to minimize clashes is **n = 1/p**. For example, if a client is sending 60 messages an hour or one every minute and the messages contain 1500 characters, then it will take 1500 characters × 8 bits/character/1,000,000 bits/sc = 12 ms to send one message. Allowing ample margin for capturing the transmission line it will take about 15 ms per message. If the probability of a message being on the line from only one client is 0.015, the optimum number of clients is about 60.

Case Study: The Case for Minding Your Mother

A system administrator could not start up the new system. It had been tested successfully, accepted by the company brass, and was fresh off the loading dock. She had two thick handbooks to rifle through and could not find the command that would let her install the database.[2]

The developers believed their software was superior and their system was great. They had documented it fully, and still the system administrator was ungrateful and inept. Hard feelings ensued.

Conclusion: The commands to edit configuration files are considered well-known UNIX library commands. The system administrator was unfamiliar with these commands even though she had been trained in UNIX-based applications. The folklore about the basic steps needed to load the command files is not provided in the user manuals. The commands were listed in a reference book that had no index and was so thick that it was hard to handle and hard to find basic commands.

There is the (possibly apocryphal) story of the mother of one of the original gurus. He tried out his latest and greatest on her, there being no subject more naïve. Mom gave it a try, but when she wanted to shut the computer off at the end, she exclaimed, "It's confusing to have to click START to turn it

---

[2] A video of this situation is on the course website.

off." Her guru son pooh-poohed, saying ***everybody*** knew that's how it worked. And so began a long tradition of counterintuitive confusion.

5.3 SOFTWARE ARCHITECTURE EXPERIENCE

The architect, as the ancient Greek word connotes, is the guardian of the key-stone technology. All else rests on it. It is a pity that brilliant software architects do not get the same fame and glory as architects of more visible structures, because the number of lives affected by their work is probably greater. The architecture is the basis for all technical decisions. It must be documented in a clear and concise way and then communicated to everyone on the project. The process of developing the architecture begins with the prospectus, as shown in Figure 5.2. A first cut is created during the requirements process to see that the system is feasible. Once the requirements are complete, an architecture discovery review makes explicit all non-feature-based requirements. Then the architecture process begins. It is an iterative process that focuses on evaluating design alternatives and simplifying the system. Simplifications are possible when duplicate features are eliminated, when object classes match the problem domain, when existing libraries or components are used, or when algorithms are simplified. An architecture review[3] at the end of the architecture process makes sure that the system can

It encompasses the requirements, architecture and high level design phases of the typical *waterfall diagram. It also continues throughout the life of the project (someone continues to wear the architect's hat).*

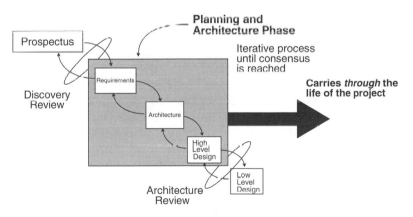

Figure 5.2. *Architecture in a project's life cycle.*

[3] Maranzano, J. F., et al. "Architecture Reviews: Practice and Experience,"*IEEE Software*, March/April 2005, vol. 22, No. 2, pp. 34–43.
[4] Thanks to Joe Maranzano for permitting the use of his insightful diagram.

be built and that it will solve the problem. A specific goal of the review is, again, simplification. One way to measure the degree of simplification achieved in the architecture process is to count the function points at the end of the requirements specification process and again at the end of the architecture process. There should be fewer function points, which is accomplished by simplifying the interpretation of the requirements, eliminating redundancies, simplifying designs, dropping complex features, and employing already working components.

MAGIC NUMBER!

The goal for the architecture process is to reduce the number of function points by 40%.

The architecture process continues throughout the development life of a software system to assure that the integrity of the architecture is preserved as new features and functions are added.

5.4 PROCESS AND MODEL

In 1757, Benjamin Franklin was sailing from New York to London and had lots of time to speculate on the common nautical wisdom that it could never be known how a ship would sail until she was built and could be tested. The trouble was, our philosopher decided, that "one man builds the hull, another rigs her, a third lades her and sails her. No one of these has the advantage of knowing all the ideas and experience of the others, and therefore cannot draw just conclusions from a combination of the whole." Franklin thought that a set of accurate experiments on all such matters, jointly undertaken and carried out to a common end, would be far more efficient than trial and error. He would have made a superb system architect. The industry was just beginning in the decade of the 1990s to act on the understanding that it is important to have structure before jumping into program requirements.

Kruchten[5] describes a "4+1" model of software architecture using five concurrent views, each addressing a specific set of concerns of interest to differ-

---

[5] Kruchten, P. and Thompson, C. "An Object-Oriented, Distributed Architecture for Large Scale Ada Systems," *Proceedings of the Tri-Ada '94 Conference ACM*, Baltimore, MD, November 6–11, 1994, pp. 262–271.

ent stakeholders in the system. The end users embody the first view, the **logical**, which creates the object model for object-oriented design. This view acts as a driver to help system integrators and programmers discover architectural elements during the architecture design. The end user describes the service that must be supplied. The system integrators embody the second view, the **process**, which considers concurrency and synchronization aspects. This view validates and illustrates the architectural design and is the starting point for tests of the prototype and drives the system engineers. How the software will execute on its target machine in terms of throughput, response time, and availability is its concern. System engineers embody the third view, the **extended machine**, which maps software onto hardware and operating system and considers distributed processing implementations, utilities, middleware, and database systems often called the extended machine. Programmers embody the fourth view, the **development**, which is the software's build organization and the tools used to compile, configure, and assemble the components into an executable system. The software is organized into manageable chunks that can be created with well-defined interfaces.

The idea is to organize a description of architectural decisions around these four views and then illustrate the workings of the system with a few use cases, called **scenarios**, which are the "+1" or the fifth view, as shown in Figure 5.3. These scenarios are developed around the functions that are the most important, the most used, and that represent the most significant technical risk. The

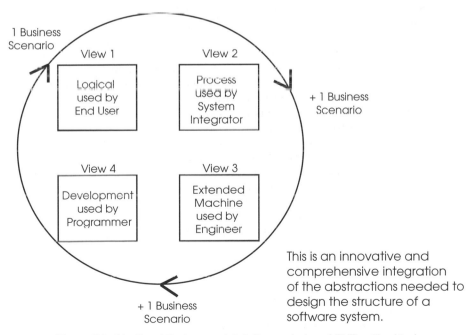

Figure 5.3. "4+1" architecture model. (with permission of Phillipe Kruchten)

experience of running the scenarios from all four views gives the basis for refining requirements.[6]

5.5 COMPONENTS

A software component is a set of formal constraints on a software module. Software component technology builds on prior theories of a software object. An object is a unique, concrete instance of an abstract data type (that is, a conceptual structure including both data and the methods to access it) whose identity is separate from that of other objects, although it can "communicate" with them via messages.

5.5.1 Components as COTS

Doug McIlroy, the Bell Laboratories guru who invented the pipes and filters architecture of UNIX and widely used UNIX tools, such as spell, diff, sort, and join, as long ago as 1968 talked about the need to have software components as well-constructed black boxes, with sizes and robustness ratings and prices all available as easily as nuts and bolts and wrenches. His full white paper is linked on the course website, but the following bits are excerpted from it:

> Software components (routines), to be widely applicable to different machines and users, should be available in families arranged according to precision, robustness, generality and time-space performance. Existing sources of components—manufacturers, software houses, users' groups and algorithm collections—lack the breadth of interest or coherence of purpose to assemble more than one or two members of such families, yet software production in the large would be enormously helped by the availability of spectra of high quality routines, quite as mechanical design is abetted by the existence of families of structural shapes, screws or resistors . . . The market would consist of specialists in system building, who would be able to use tried parts for all the more commonplace parts of their systems. The biggest customers of all would be the manufacturers . . . The ultimate consumer of systems based on components ought to see considerably improved reliability and performance, as it would become possible to expend proportionally more effort on critical parts of systems . . . I would like to see components become a dignified branch of software engineering . . . I want to have confidence in the quality of the routines.[7]

---

[6] Juran, Joseph M. and Godfrey, A. Blanton, Eds. *Jurans Quality Handbook*, 5th ed. McGraw-Hill, New York, 1999, Section 20.7.

[7] McIlroy, M. D. "Mass-Produced Software Components," *NATO Science Committee*, Garmisch, Germany, 7–11 October 1968.

5.5.2   Encapsulation and Abstraction

Parnas et al.[8] explained the need for modularity and the effectiveness of information hiding. He defined a software structure with minimum connections to other modules, called coupling, and a maximum of cohesion within modules, meaning that the subtleties of the software design and data interactions are hidden from other modules. This process is called encapsulation and lays the foundation for object-oriented design. Each view of the 4 + 1 architecture is subdivided into modules with minimum coupling.

It includes the concept of abstraction, which is the ability of a program to ignore some aspects of the information it manipulates. This simplifies programming, because it becomes possible to express a software solution with fewer computer instructions. Each object in the system serves as a model of an abstract "actor" that can perform work, report on and change its state, and "communicate" with other objects in the system, without revealing its structure. It adheres to some interface description language, which is a computer language or simple syntax for describing the interface of a software component. It is essentially a common language for writing the "manual" on how to use a piece of software from another piece of software, in much the same fashion that a user manual describes how to use a piece of software to the user.[9] Functionality is encapsulated in the form of an object, which is a unique conceptual structure including both data and the methods to access it, whose identity is separate from that of other objects although it can "communicate" with them using messages. Some objects can be considered a subprogram that can communicate with others by receiving or giving instructions based on its, or the other's, data or methods. Data can consist of numbers, literal strings, variables, or references. An object also can be thought of as a region of storage. The set of constraints that transforms a module into a component is as follows:

(1) The methods of an object class and procedural programs conform to the principles of structured programming. Namely, each component is a program that can be decomposed into assignment, do_while or if_then_else segments, and a counter having one entry and one exit point.

(2) Interfaces are always through formal structures that normalize data definitions as defined in the Jackson design methodology.

(3) The execution time and space of the component are bounded by rejuvenation technology, and boundary conditions are set limiting the domain of execution of the component. See Sha's pioneering work on bounding software execution on the course website.

---

[8] Parnas, David, et al. "The Modular Structure of Complex Systems," *Software Fundamentals Collected Papers by David L Parnas*, edited by Daniel M. Hoffman and David M. Weiss, Addison-Wesley, London, U. K., 2001, pp. 319–336.

[9] http://ei.cs.vt.edu/~cs2604/Standards/Standards.html. (with permission)

(4) The dynamics of the component are forced to be periodic. On a regular basis, the component states are reinitialized, and upon failure, the states are restored to a well-defined initial state that has the property $R(0) = 1$.

(5) The module is limited in size to reduce defects, as explained by Les Hatton, to the range of 100 to 1000 instructions.

(6) System and reliability testing are performed for ten times the rejuvenation period to reduce the likelihood of executing defect states thereby causing hangs or crashes. Special tests are needed to assure that the component is stable within its constrained execution domain. These tests reduce the liklihood that a small input does not induce a large unbounded output.

(7) A module can only be a component after its third release and 8–10 months of operation when the failure rate becomes constant with time.

(8) A component is documented in the preface of its source listing with a performance worksheet that specifies what the component does, its domain of execution, its inputs and outputs including the data value bounds, and any other special constraints.

Software components provide a common and convenient means for inter-process communication, either within the same computer or over a network. It implies a protocol that guarantees a response to a request. Examples are TCP/IP sockets[10] and Microsoft Windows .NET. There are different forms of software components such as CORBA and .COM.[11] Microsoft paved the way for actual deployment of component software with object linking and embedding (OLE) technology. It was initially used primarily for copying and pasting data between different applications. It later evolved to become architecture for software components. Figure 5.4 shows two schematics for software components. The top is the Unified Modeling Language (UML) diagram, and the bottom is the schematic commonly used by Microsoft .NET objects. The "lollipops" are their interfaces.

5.5.3 Ready or Not, Objects Are Here

Bjarne Stroustrup, the inventor of C++, says that adopting object-oriented programming is not painless, but it is worthwhile. It forces one to think about architecture and design from the beginning, not just as an afterthought. Programs will be modular, hence, easier to maintain and extend. If the system is designed as a collection of classes with clean interfaces, others can use them. And to ease the pain, a new generation of design and implementation tools are becoming available.

---

[10] Donahoo, Michael and Calvert, Kenneth. *The Pocket Guide to TCP/IP Sockets C Version*, Morgan Kaufman, New York 2001.
[11] Tallman, Owen and Kain, J. Branford. ".COM versus CORBA A Decision Framework," *Distributed Computing*, Vol. 1, No. 11, Nov. 1998, pp. 33–36.

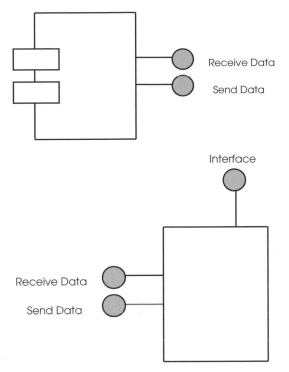

Figure 5.4. *Two component schematics.*

Every significant change carries risk, however. Middle managers will have to learn new techniques to manage object-oriented development well. When a process is not fully mature, it requires education and reworking of legacy systems. There is general agreement, however, that the use of object-oriented design leads to more concise programs and maps the solution domain more easily into the problem domain, which results in a three-fold increase in productivity over time as experience is gained.

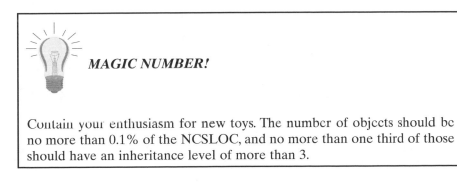

MAGIC NUMBER!

Contain your enthusiasm for new toys. The number of objects should be no more than 0.1% of the NCSLOC, and no more than one third of those should have an inheritance level of more than 3.

5.6   UNIX

The early development of the most influential operating systems in history was unique. Its goal was to demonstrate the portability of software among different hardware architectures. It was successful and was the first demonstration of portable software implementing the operating system as a layer of software separating the application from the unique designs of a supplier's computer. Here was the germ of the idea of the extended machine. It contained the concept of a pipe that signifies that the output of one program feeds directly as input into another program. In contrast, a file in a computer system is a sequence of bits stored as a single unit, typically in a file system on disk or magnetic tape. Although a file is usually presented as a single stream, it most often is stored as multiple fragments of data at different places on a disk (or even multiple disks). One architectural service of operating systems is to organize files in a file system. The pipe is one such service and provides input or holds the output. In the pipe metaphor, a file is a container. A UNIX shell, also called "the command line," provides the traditional user interface for the UNIX operating system and uses the pipe character "|" to join programs. A sequence of commands joined by pipes is known as a pipeline that represents the concept of splitting a job into subprocesses in which the output of one subprocess feeds into the next, much as water flows from one pipe segment to the next. For creating this mechanism, all UNIX tools have access to three distinct special files:

stdin—the standard input file

stdout—the standard output file

stderr—the standard error file

By joining one tool's **stdout** to another tool's **stdin**, a pipeline is formed. Errors are accumulated in **stderr**.

A filter program is a UNIX program that is part of a pipeline between two or more UNIX tools. Generally a filter program will read its standard input, write to its standard output, and do little else. Conventionally a filter program is distinguished by being fairly simple and performing essentially one operation, usually some sort of simple transformation of its input data. An example of a pipeline follows:

$$\text{cat} * | \text{grep "crime"} | \text{grep - v "punishment"} | \text{wc - l}$$

This command will print out the number of lines in all files in the current directory that contain the text "crime," but not the text "punishment."

The pipeline has four parts:

(1) cat * concatenates the text of all files to its **stdout**

(2) grep "crime" reads its **stdin** as lines and prints on its **stdout** only those lines that contain the word "crime"

(3) grep -v "punishment" reads its **stdin** and prints on its **stdout** only those remaining lines that do not contain the word "punishment" (note that -v inverts the selection)

(4) wc -l counts the lines on its **stdin**, and prints a line count on its **stdout**.

The basic idea in object-oriented programming is that software should be written according to a mental model of the actual or imagined objects it represents. Object-oriented programming and the related disciplines of object-oriented design and object-oriented analysis focus on modeling real-world interactions and attempting to create "verbs" and "nouns" that can be used in intuitive ways, ideally by end users as well as by programmers. Software component architecture, by contrast, makes no such assumptions and instead states that software should be developed by gluing prefabricated components together. It accepts that the definitions of useful components, unlike objects, can be counterintuitive and that performance overhead results. This notion has led to many academic debates about the pros and cons of the two approaches. We consider component technology to have evolved from object-oriented technology. It takes significant effort, time, and awareness to write a software component that is effectively reusable, more than twice as much effort. The component needs to be fully documented, undergo more thorough testing, have robust input validity checking, pass back useful error messages, and be flexible for unforeseen uses. There should not be unexpected consequences for using it.

5.7 TL1

At the beginning of any system development, laying out the architecture and defining the way system components will exchange data and work together is critical. These early design decisions lay the foundation for the reliability and the extendibility of the system. In this section, we examine a specific case that influenced the development of the telephone software infrastructure for setting up and managing services. Landauer writes, ". . . the most important factor in the success of telephone operation mechanizations was the way . . . [the systems] were designed and evolved."[12] The decisions described here about designing the interface architecture led to the relatively easy introduction of systems that worked together to save telephone companies billions of dollars annually.

TL1 is the realization of critical system interface structures within an architecture that became the standard for the telecommunications industry.[13] A

---

[12] Landauer, Thomas K. *The Trouble with Computers*, MIT Press, Cambridge, MA, 1996, p. 70.

[13] Man, Fu-Tin. "A Brief History of TL1," *Journal of Network and Systems Management*, Vol. 7, No. 2, June 1999, pp. 143–148. Material here appeared in the Thresholds column and is reprinted with kind permission of Springer Science and Business Media.

feature article in *Telephony*[14] states that, "Most telecom network elements in North America today can be managed using TL1, and no serious telecom management system developer can ignore it."

5.7.1 Mission

Before the 1984 breakup of AT&T, Program Documentation Standards was the predominant operations language used to centrally manage the network equipment in the Bell System. It was used by operation support systems such as the switching control center system to manage the AT&T Electronic Switching Systems and other network equipment.

In early 1985, Bellcore commissioned a task force[15] to recommend a non-proprietary set of network management messages to be exchanged between a network management system and a network element to perform operations, administration, maintenance, and provisioning functions. The members of the task force were subject matter experts in operations requirement, software systems, network management and network elements, and communication protocols.

To help narrow the language candidates under consideration, the task force identified attributes for a viable operations language[16] candidate:

(1) It cannot be owned by any company except Bellcore, who would make it a telecommunications industry standard.

(2) It should be well known in the industry.

(3) It should have good documentation.

(4) It can quickly become public domain.

(5) It can be used by network equipment vendors with little guidance.

(6) It has a good record of accomplishment.

Guided by this list, the task force narrowed the field to two operations language candidates. The first was Bellcore's Flexible Computer Interface Form (FCIF) that was used among Bellcore-developed operations support systems such as between the components of facility assignment and control system (FACS)[17] and between FACS and other systems. It proved so robust that it was extended and used throughout the telecommunications industry. The second one was CCITT[18] Man-Machine Language (MML).

---

[14] Dowling, Connor and Egan, Gerry. "The Story of TL1 provides many lessons about the future of telecom management," *Telephony*, Vol. 233, No. 9, September 1, 1997, pp. 34–36.

[15] Fu-Tin Man was the chair.

[16] Specifically, an operations language is only a language syntax, whereas an operations message contains both language syntax and semantics.

[17] The previous description of the FCIF acronym was the FACS Component Interface Form.

[18] Now renamed the International Telecommunications Union-Telecommunication (ITU-T).

5.7.2 Comparative Analysis

MML was an international standard language adopted for network management in late 1970s. It was documented as a family of Z.300 recommendations in the 1980 CCITT Red Book. Even though FCIF had been a working operations language among Bellcore-developed systems, it lacked documentation.[19]

Both FCIF and MML were character-based and were judged inefficient for communications to network equipment. However, because the command language dialog was a requirement for a local craft interface,[20] the cost of developing two interfaces in network equipment, one for human and one for machine, was considered the greater risk. Inefficient machine-to-machine communication could be solved with faster communication links.

FCIF was less efficient because its parameters were keyword-defined, whereas those in MML could either be keyword-defined or position-defined. Keyword-defined parameters provide flexibility for decoupling software systems and specifying parameter values, whereas position-defined fields use fewer characters.

MML was human-readable as its parameter fields were distinctly separated. FCIF was less human-readable than MML because of its nesting syntax that was designed to capture customer name, address, telephone numbers, and so on.

Both FCIF and MML offered no semantics that could be reused to support a generic set of functions, but MML had several semantic definitions that help specify the semantics. For example, in its input commands, MML reserved the first parameter field for command code (i.e., action to be taken). It also assigned the word "REPORT" (abbreviated as REPT) for network equipment to autonomously report self-detected events and conditions.

Although FCIF had a good record of accomplishment and a wealth of support tools, MML had none (Table 5.1).

TABLE 5.1. Pros and Cons of Operations Language Candidates

Feature	MML	FCIF
Recognition	International	Little known
Documentation	1980 CCITT Red Book	Little
Machine communication efficiency	Poor	Poor
Human communication efficiency	Excellent	Good
Availability of reusable semantics	Little	None
Working track record	None	Excellent
Software support tools	None	Abundant

[19] A Bellcore special report, "FCIF Language Definition," SR-STS-002603, Issue 2, Oct. 1993, was later published.

[20] It is also a current American National Standard as documented in "OAM&P—G Interface Specification for Use with the Telecommunications Management Network (TMN)," ANSI T1.232-1993.

5.7.3 Message Formatting

MML became the operations language, and the task force eliminated its human-oriented features to the extent possible without violating the MML recommendations. Examples of these are white space, line feed, and carriage return. The next task involved formulating the formats for input command, output response, and autonomous message. The formatting task for an input command involved assigning mandatory parameter fields after the command code in an input command. Later, the parameter field after CTAG was designated as a general block, which was reserved for such special bulk transmitted data.

5.7.4 TL1 Message Formulation

Once the language definition was completed, the remaining task was to specify actual TL1 messages (including semantics) that are used to implement functions and publish them in the public domain. The task force selected provisioning, maintenance, and testing functional categories that would be presented in Technical Advisories TA-TSY-00199, TA-TSY-00200, and TA-TSY-00201, respectively.[21] It also named the selected operations language Transaction Language One or TL1, with a view to providing TL2 and subsequent versions, but there was to be no future for TL1.

Bellcore has published hundreds of TL1 messages for different operations domains and network technologies. To provide a roadmap to all of them, GR-811-CORE[22] presents, on an ongoing basis, a listing of, and pointers to, the TL1 messages that have been published in various technical advisories, technical references, and generic requirements documents.

5.7.5 Industry Support of TL1

Most TL1 messages in TA-TSY-00199 are currently used to remotely set cross-connections and channel unit settings as well as to send recent change messages to network elements. Many surveillance and testing systems have also adopted TL1 as their communication language with network elements. They have implemented many TL1 messages documented in TA-TSY-00200 and TA-TSY-00201, respectively. In addition to the Bellcore systems, others use TL1 messages to manage network elements.

Various companies have developed object servers that provide an adaptation between TL1-based and object-oriented technologies. A virtual management information base (MIB) for TL1 exists for translation to the simple network management protocol (SNMP) used in local area networks and to

[21] The bulk of the TL messages in these three TAs have now been migrated to GR-199-CORE, GR-833-CORE, and GR-834-CORE, respectively.
[22] "OTGR: Operations Application Messages—TL1 Messages Index," GR-811-GORE, Issue 3, June 1997.

the common management information protocol (CMIP) used in metropolitan and wide area networks. The virtual TL1 MIB provides an abstraction of managed information compatible with those presented by the SNMP or CMIP MIB. Unification among managed information is crucial to managing a multi-protocol, multivendor network.

The net result of a seemingly simple decision was to tightly couple systems with TL1. As it becomes more difficult to manage network elements, the telecommunication industry is adopting the loosely coupled Internet layered technology. The decision makers in the original task force discounted the architectural advantages of the FCIF software-focused approach and the earlier successful experience of FCIF users. Those who ignored TL1 to continue to use FCIF built robust decoupled systems.

5.8 DOCUMENTING THE ARCHITECTURE

Useful architecture documents are succinct, usually fewer than ten pages. They contain the following items:

(1) One or two paragraphs stating the problem scope, that its requirements are valid, and how the architecture solves the problem.
(2) The major functions that the system will provide and a high-level view of how they will be performed.
(3) Assumptions and constraints that bound the solution including special precedence concerns, the rationale for the choice of solutions, and the interactions with the external environment.
(4) The 4+1 views of the solution with a calculation of function points considering the logical and process view and coupling and cohesion for all the other views.
(5) Performance parameters and analysis relating to critical events that occur in the system.
(6) Documents that the software product is suitably reliable, easy-to-use, extendible, not harmful, and robust, that is, trustworthy.
(7) Current risks are identified with solutions.
(8) Defines the interface language, technology, and conventions among the components.
(9) References to supporting documents or Web pages.

The architecture document describes the selected approach and is used by members of the project to ensure that their activities are consistent with the major direction of the project. It is made available to members of the review team before any architecture review.

The architecture document is an adjunct to the existing documentation (for example, requirements, prospectus, etc.) on the project. For some projects, there will be a hierarchy of documents, comprising a top-level architecture document for the system with separate architecture documents for the subsystems.

5.8.1 Debriefing Report

This document contains a record of architectural decisions, including why a particular alternative was chosen and, more importantly, why an alternative was not chosen. It provides a history of the project and is invaluable to people who join the project later and want to understand the status of the project. The debriefing is not typically done by most projects but should be.

5.8.2 Lessons Learned

When the project is complete, the debriefing report becomes a lessons learned document so other project teams can benefit from the experiences, both positive and negative. The "lessons learned" include the following:

(1) Things that were done especially well that may apply to other projects (for example, design, programming or other techniques that were innovated, refined, or improved on, or simply existing techniques that were used with particular success)
(2) Things that should have been done differently
(3) Problems encountered and recommendations about how future projects might avoid or solve them

5.8.3 Users of Architecture Documentation

The architecture document keeps all stakeholders aware of the system design and system design changes throughout development. It is used for up-front design analysis to validate (or uncover deficiencies in) architectural design decisions and refine or alter those decisions as necessary. This perspective on architecture is, in some sense, inward-looking. It involves making prospective architectural decisions and then projecting the effect of those decisions on the system or systems that the architecture is driving. Where the effect is unacceptable, the relevant decisions are rethought, and the process repeats. This process occurs in tight cycles (most architects project the effect of each of their decisions) and in large cycles (in which large groups of decisions, perhaps even the entire architecture, are subjected to formal validation).

Architecture documentation is both prescriptive and descriptive. That is, it prescribes what should be true, and it describes what is true, about a system's design. The same documentation can serve both purposes. When the "build-as" documents differ from the "as-built" documents, there is a breakdown in the development process.[23]

---

[23] Borrowed with permission from *Software Architecture Documentation in Practice* at the Carnegie Mellon Software Engineering Institute.

5.9 ARCHITECTURE REVIEWS

With the architecture documented, the project is ready for formal architecture reviews. A colleague, Joe Maranzano, provides a checklist for these reviews in Table 5.2.

TABLE 5.2. Maranzano Checklist

Checklist for Architecture Reviews

1. Starting with the "4 + 1" overall architecture diagrams use additional diagrams to describe all components of the system.
2. List major components of the system and the functionality provided by each component.
3. Trace scenarios of how data/information flows through components.
4. Describe and list the special data error handling flows.
5. Describe the user interfaces.
6. List all interfaces with other systems, and for each interface describe:
   a. The IPC mechanism to be used for data and for control
   b. Any expected issues with the IPC mechanism (e.g., performance degradation at some capacity level, problems with overload control, new technology)
   c. Failure modes and error handling for each type of failure
   d. Error recovery to prevent lost data, if needed
   e. Effective bandwidth of the interface mechanism
7. Examine strategies used to keep design simple and avoid unnecessary complexity.
8. Examine robustness of component choices, COTS, or custom-made including:
   a. available support
   b. defect records
   c. Licensing costs
   d. performance under load
   e. extensibility
   f. flexibility
9. Review local databases or data stores used for temporary data storage or reference data storage.
10. Examine performance and capacity budgets by considering the expected traffic and background processing in terms of:
   a. The average load and busy hour of the transaction profile
   b Number of simultaneous users
   c. Expected system response time in terms of its average, variance, and bounds
   d. Peak arrival rates
   e. Overnight processing and calculations
   f. Database sizes
   g. Network demands including congestion strategy
11. Examine the operations, administration, and maintenance approach, including:
   a. Operational environment
   b. Interfaces to external sources and systems
   c. System availability
   d. Failure avoidance and handling
   e. Error handling
   f. Disaster recovery
   g. Security
   h. Data consistency and accuracy

By Joe Maranzano, with permission.

When the checklist is used rigorously, problems tend to fall into typical groupings. Half of all problems are the result of incomplete requirements, which can be undefined usage scenarios, unidentified customers, lack of acceptance criteria, and vague statements. Another 25% can be called performance issues. The customer and/or designers have neglected to provide specified traffic profiles, a model of offered load, data volumes, night or batch processing loads, or a resource budget. The customer may also have an unwarranted expectation of linear scalability.

The final 25% can be divided into four areas. Ten percent is from unspecified operations, administration, maintenance, or provisioning (OAM&P); no analysis of system availability or the recovery system lags the online system so that there is no possibility of database catch-up upon major outage; or database tools are inadequate or conversion tools are missing. Five percent are from no error recovery. Five percent are from using an immature technology. The final 5% are from a lack of analysis of subsystem and module dependencies.

5.10 MIDDLEWARE

Middleware provides a reusable architectural component that solves the distributed application problem. An early 1980s example of middleware was the Tuxedo product used with distributed UNIX applications.[24] Middleware gets its name from being the software component that provides simple access to operating system functions by applications. In an architectural hierarchy, it sits between the low-level operating system and the application software. It helps the programmer easily and quickly build distributed business applications by isolating them from complex design issues, such as working with multiple operating systems, data communication protocols, and transaction recovery across multiple applications and computers. The Open Software Foundation's Distributed Computing Environment (DCE), Object Management Group's Common Object Request Broker Architecture (CORBA), Microsoft's Distributed Component Object Model (DCOM), Enterprise's Java Bean (EJB) and BEA's Tuxedo are widely used middleware products.

Upscale architecture middleware supports the construction of sophisticated systems by assembling a collection of modules with the help of visual tools or programmatic interfaces. These interfaces are called application program interfaces (API) and are the subject of intense design efforts between vendors and customers. Keeping them stable and standard makes it easy to develop some applications but limits growth to new application areas and eliminates the software provider's perceived competitive advantage.

A new concept of a piped dispatch makes it easier to upgrade middleware when necessary. Previously, middleware components were tightly coupled. In piped workflow, a special metadata channel exchanges data among all modules. Whenever the module needs data to continue its operation, it

---

[24] A video showing how it uses two-phase commit technology is linked on the course website.

accesses this data channel. Pipes are one way for data channels to exchange data. The pipe consists of many independent subpipes that interface pair-wise adjacent modules. Each subpipe contains a pair of interface objects that transfer data between the modules and pipes. In one object class, pipes share the same temporary memory, so the intermediate result can be transferred from the nonadjacent modules in an orderly progression of steps. Another approach is to use dynamic dependency to manage components in an already running system. Every component may have a set of hooks to which other components can attach. Some other components (called clients) might depend on server components. Through the communication and event interfaces between hooked components, reconfiguration is possible.

Middleware is intended to mask the problem of building distributed applications among heterogeneous environments, but the complexity of distributed networks and unanticipated requirements make the construction of middleware difficult. There are many standards for overcoming this quandary, but none is perfect.

Case Study: The Case of The Muddled Middleware

You are the architect for a software team developing a customer resource management application. Your architecture review shows that the middleware transaction recovery component is buggy.

A new release of the middleware is scheduled for June. This release is promised to be robust, bug-free, and industrial strength. The new transaction recovery scheme requires minor changes to all application modules. Table 5.3 shows your committed schedule.

You consider the following issues:

(1) Version 3.0 delivery might be later than estimated.
(2) Will Version 3.0 really fix the transaction recovery problem as advertised?
(3) Are the code changes to the application modules needed to interface with the new recovery scheme as simple as advertised?
(4) If people are reassigned from development to test case design, will they look for more satisfying work on other projects or in other companies?

TABLE 5.3. Committed Schedule

	March	April	May	June	July	August
Middleware Version	2.0			3.0		
Application						SHIP DATE
Test		Inventory Retest	Simple Test	Test All Transactions		

You explored these options at the architecture review:

(1) Ship Version 2.0, and upgrade to Version 3.0 later. This field upgrade requires special conversion software and is probably extremely complicated.

(2) Ship Version 3.0. The project manager has conducted a detailed schedule analysis and predicts a 6-week delivery delay with a 1.5-week standard deviation with this option. Your executives will be angry because delayed payments will cause the company to show a profit loss for the year.

(3) Ship Version 3.0, and insist that the middleware supplier provide on-site testing support to avoid project delays. The supplier would have to delay important future middleware features, impacting the supplier's profitability, so the supplier wants premium payments to provide this support. The project manager projects a 50% reduction in profitability, and the company will go from being profitable to breakeven.

Conclusion: This decision is not easy. All options are risky. You, as architect, evaluate the features of Version 2.0 and the risks. Working closely with the project manager and the customer, you decide to ship Version 2.0 and slip future releases while investing in field conversion to Version 3.0.

The architect cannot be distracted by marketing hype such as "Version 3.0 is solid as a rock and has great features!" Risks must be managed carefully and conservatively. The customer must be a participant in the decision.

This seemingly simple decision could have had huge repercussions. The architectural review gave the team the opportunity for thoughtful technical, schedule, and risk analysis. The field conversion took 6 months longer than projected and delayed the next set of features. The customer understood the risks, having participated in the decision, but needed a reliable system and trusted the architect to deliver systems in good order. Business increased as other customers heard about the care and thoughtfulness of the architect in assuring trustworthy products.

5.11   HOW MANY TIMES BEFORE WE LEARN?

Time and again we hear in the news of failures and crises affecting lives or costing fortunes. Natural disaster or human malevolence causes many of these problems, but we, as professional software practitioners, have the ethical responsibility to prevent the ones caused by ignoring basic good practices. Examples taken from Comair, Microsoft, and NASA, all in recent history, are worth studying.

5.11.1   Comair Cancels 1100 Flights on Christmas 2004

Comair, a system for assigning crews to commercial airline flights, was running a 15-year old scheduling software package from SBS International. The software had a hard limit of 32,000 schedule changes per month. Bad weather for a week and the upcoming holiday apparently caused Comair to reach this limit and fail catastrophically. The supposition is that 16-bit integers were being used to identify transactions in the scheduling software. Given that the software was 15 years old, this design decision perhaps was made to save on memory.

Where does the responsibility lie for this failure that affected so many people and cost so much in confusion, irritation, and bad will? Should SBS International have been aware of the use Comair made of its software, realize that the airline industry had changed significantly in 15 years, and upgraded its product? Were the airlines responsible for mission-critical software? Should the hard limit been prominently announced by the developer so that periodic checks could be standard procedure to see if the limit was approached during peak times? Should software rejuvenation have been used?

5.11.2 Air Traffic Shutdown in September 2004

A bug in a Microsoft system, compounded by human error, was ultimately responsible for a 3-hour radio breakdown that left hundreds of aircraft aloft without guidance on September 14, 2004. Nearly all of Southern California's airports were shut down, and five incidents where aircraft broke separation guidelines were reported. In one case, a pilot had to take evasive action.

A Microsoft-based replacement for an older UNIX-based system needed to be reset every 30 days "to prevent data overload," as a result of problems found when the system was first rolled out. However, a technician failed to perform the reset at the right time, and an internal clock within the system subsequently shut it down. A backup system also failed.

Rejuvenation must not depend on human intervention, and the domain within the operating boundaries must be completely bug-free. A mere warning, often at the lowest level of responsibility, relies on human intervention with all its frailties.

The problem could have been avoided if **ANY ONE** of these actions had taken place:

(1) If Microsoft had included rejuvenation in its original solution
(2) If Harris, the supplier of the system to the FAA, had included rejuvenation in its application
(3) If Harris had applied the available Microsoft patch
(4) If the FAA had applied the available Microsoft patch
(5) If the FAA had built a script to periodically restart the system
(6) If software engineers had been taught to design to avoid such problems.

5.11.3 NASA Crashes into Mars, 2004

The $165 million Mars Polar Lander was most likely doomed by a sensor that mistook a spurious signal for landing when the legs deployed, causing the software to stop the descent engines 130 ft above the planet's surface. The problem could have been easily resolved by beaming new software to the lander during its 11-month cruise, if only it had been noticed.

Two reports were released on the Mars fiasco. They found mismanagement, unrealistic expectations, and anemic funding were to blame as much as the mistakes that actually doomed the mission. Too many risks were taken by skipping critical tests or overlooking possible faults. Nobody noticed or mentioned problems until it was too late.

NASA Administrator Dan Goldin took the blame for the botched Mars missions, saying he pushed too hard, cut too much, and made it impossible for spacecraft managers to succeed. But Goldin said he will not abandon NASA's "faster, better, cheaper" approach. "We're going to make sure they have adequate resources, but we're not going to let the pendulum swing all the way back," he told employees of NASA's Jet Propulsion Laboratory, where Mars Polar Lander and the failed Mars Climate Orbiter were managed.

There is a breathtaking management statement: What we are doing does not work, but we will keep on doing it. Unfortunately, when management is irrational, the ethical architect and designer must be even more adamant about not taking risks by skipping critical tests or overlooking faults. The most telling indication of bad management was the fear of mentioning problems. We had said it before: If a project has no list of problems, it is in terrible trouble.

Even the earlier successful Pathfinder mission had a software problem. Unfortunately, NASA did not invest in the good software processes of architectural discovery after that first problem appeared. It was an architectural deadlock problem and is worth examining as a case study.

5.11.4 Case Study: The Case of the Preempted Priorities

The Pathfinder lands successfully, gathers data on Mars, and sends pictures back to Earth (Figure 5.5). Then it occasionally stops sending images, and as times goes on, these stoppages occur more frequently and for longer periods. The mission software engineers note that when this happens, the computers reboot the software.

Three software tasks were involved in the problem. One task rebooted the computer whenever it was idle for a period. A second sent images to Earth,

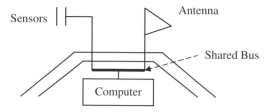

Figure 5.5. *Mars Pathfinder.*

and a third took pictures on Mars. All three tasks used the common shared bus for communication and the computer processor.

A software task dispatch conflict was the cause of the problem. The priorities **should be**:

T1. Reboot

T2. Send images

T3. Gather data

But because of a faulty use of preemptive multithreading, they **were actually**:

T1. Reboot

T2. Gather data

T3. Send images

There was a mismatch in priorities set in the hardware, the software, and the software that controlled the bus. A watchdog counter rebooted the system after it had been inactive for some time, by issuing an interrupt. This is why the probe was rebooting after being silent for too long. This is a **fail-safe** system. The problem is shown in Figure 5.6.

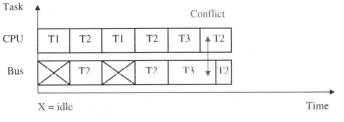

Figure 5.6. *Fail-safe system.*

Conclusion: This problem is a typical deadlock that can happen when access to a resource is not managed. It is similar to the deadlocks studied in database management systems or operating systems courses. Once it was discovered, it could be resolved. The lessons learned were valuable, but the subsequent Mars exploration missions demonstrate how rapidly essential sound practices can deteriorate.[25]

1. **Design defensively**. The Jet Propulsion Laboratory team did this by leaving in the debug code and the fail-safe resets. Build fail-safe systems.

---

[25] March, Steve. "Learning from Pathfinder's Bumpy Start," *Software Testing and Quality Management*, Sept./Oct. 1999, Vol. 1, No. 5, p. 10, www.stqemagazine.com.

2. **Stress test beyond the limits established in the requirements**. It is best to test to the breaking point. The difference between the breaking point and the maximum design load is the system margin. The stress tests for the Mars Explorer were actually thought to be the worst case, but because the data gathering went better than imagined possible on the actual mission, there were more data to process than expected. This resulted in the shared bus not being released. Had testers pushed the system to its breaking point, there is a good chance, although not a guarantee, that they would have found and fixed the fault before it became a failure.

3. **Explain all anomalies that show up during system test**. Sometimes you must release the software for its intended use even though you have not been able to discover the cause of the anomaly. In these cases, treat the release as "provisional" and continue to work on understanding the anomaly. The Mars Explorer anomaly was thought to be a hardware problem even though there were no data supporting this belief. When resets occur, even once, during system test, developers must understand and solve them. Sometimes managers want to classify a problem as a "chance occurrence." These are especially difficult times for the testers. They must insist on having a plan to find and fix the fault before it becomes a failure to avoid sleepless nights, panic, and project bankruptcy.

   Mars is close enough to Earth for the Explorer to have enough fuel to complete the trip once a year. So the testers faced the awesome responsibility of holding the mission for a year or explaining away an anomaly that occurred two or three times. The hardware people were already blaming the software people for schedule delays, and the software people rationalized that if there was a hardware problem, it was not their job to find it.

   In any event, NASA might have chosen to launch on schedule to meet the window of opportunity. They could have called the launch "provisional" because there was a known fault. While the Explorer flew to Mars, the Jet Propulsion Laboratory and NASA engineers might have worked to discover the reset problem in test laboratories well before it occurred on the planet.

   Should the testers have delayed launch until the fault was found and fixed? A management team could have evaluated the risks and decided to "launch or hold" with data about all potential problems.

   This philosophy moves teams from crisis management to problem avoidance. By simply writing off the anomaly, the NASA team shielded their management team from reality. In light of their administrator, it might have been understandable, but it was still inexcusable.

The most difficult step to take in any project is to change the agreed-to plan, but plans are worthless unless they change to meet newly discovered conditions. Beware of both extremes, those who thrive on the thrill of crisis or those who are rigidly committed to "holding the course" despite the data. Architecture reviews with special attention to performance issues are critical. Process-scheduling algorithms need detailed analysis. All shared resources must be understood, and interaction must be analyzed through simulated scenarios. Only data, proof, and the playing out of "what if" scenarios will convince management of the need for an ethical stance because, as the cases in this section all show, to ignore it costs money, reputation, and possibly lives.

5.12   FINANCIAL SYSTEMS ARCHITECTURE[26] (WITH KIND PERMISSION)

Financial systems need to be secure and safe. They usually use a combination of application servers and clients with distributed processing technology.

5.12.1   Typical Business Processes

A bank performs management functions such as asset and liability management (ALM) and commercial management. In addition, there are several innovating functions such as product and market development and support functions. The core of the bank consists of the operational functions, in which financial contracts (such as those for saving, mortgages, etc.) are taken out and managed and where transactions are executed, according to those contracts. Finally there are the business functions, which are responsible for client contact and client management via a range of distribution channels and media. Naturally, communication must be possible between all of these business functions. Figure 5.7 provides a view of the business processes for a typical bank.

Separate systems may be developed for every component of a banking business operation. These systems have to be "fed" by what goes on elsewhere in

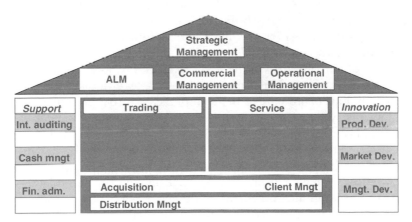

Figure 5.7. Bank business processes.

[26] Arnold, Bertand, Engels, Ariane, and Optland, Martin. "FPS: another way of looking at components and architecture in the financial world: a quest for radical reduction of IT time-to-market," Dutch National Architecture Congress, 2000.

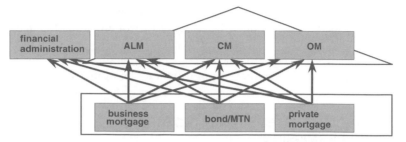

Figure 5.8. *Common application architecture.[27] (with kind permission)*

the bank. A contract system for medium-term notes, for example, must serve to keep other systems up to date about what has been laid down or changed in the contract. In other words, countless links are required, which together form a huge web. This web immediately expands whenever a new product is added or as soon as the organization undergoes change. For example, the bank may decide to identify a "business mortgage system" and a "private mortgage system," as two separate systems for either strategic or administrative reasons, despite the fact that their underlying product, namely the mortgage, is common to both (Figure 5.8).

5.12.2   Product-Related Layer in the Architecture

A product layer will reduce interactions by adding a level of indirection. Each layer represents a virtual machine, that is, a collection of software that together provides a cohesive set of services that other software can use without knowing how those services are implemented. This may cost in performance, but the benefit is in the clarity of the relations between components.

A layer has the properties of cohesion and interface. It provides a cohesive set of services and a set of public interface facilities that may be invoked or accessed by other software. On the other hand, it might add overhead.

Layers are part of the blueprint role that architecture plays for constructing a system. Layers are part of the communication role played by architecture. In a large system, the number of dependencies among modules expands rapidly and layering is an important tool to manage complexity and communicate structure to developers. Layers can be used for analyzing the impact of changes to the design.

In this product-related layer, all knowledge and information relating to the nature of a single product is actually combined. Each banking product therefore can have its own product layer. Refactoring the functions simplifies the architecture and subsequent implementation (Figure 5.9).

---

[27] www.serc.nl/lac/LAC-2001/lac-2000/3-realisatie/fps.doc

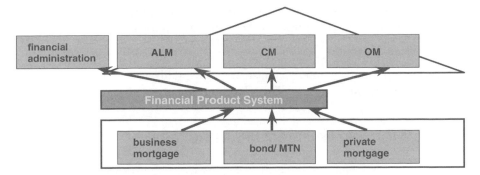

Figure 5.9. *Separate product layer. (with kind permissoin)*[27]

5.12.3 Finding Simple Components

Good architecture has clear product-related layers. The components that reside in this layer reduce coupling and increase cohesion. New components can be rapidly added, and processes made up of these components can implement new features. The trick is to maximize the general nature of the component while minimizing the interactions with other components. Object class refactoring is an important development process that makes this possible.

Components are modules that are limited in size, use single entry and exit points, have an explicit error recovery strategy, and are bounded in time and space and interfaces that normalize data structures between components. Components need to be made linear in the sense that they only interface to other components through well-defined structures. Object classes specially defined for interface support are the most flexible. In practice, three or four iterations at the object class definitions with heavy constraints placed on the number of object classes is vital. The components are easiest to test if they have one entry point and one exit point. The underlying idea is that the speed for adding and altering products can be achieved by composing these products in their specification, using such components.

Now let us consider component size. Should they be small, comprising elementary building blocks such as a simple interest calculation (principal amount times term times percentage)? The product would then consist of many small building blocks. Or should components be larger blocks, such as "complete straight-line repayment lending construction, including variable interest calculations?" The risk is that many similar, but in detail different, constructions might be required. The best size is a mixture of the two in the range of one to ten function points. Hatton points out that this lowers defects; therefore, a vast library of microfeature components does not overwhelm application engineers.

A range of components is needed for the principal amount and interest computation. For example, for principal amounts, the situation may develop in which the principal amount remains the same throughout the term (as is the case in an interest-only mortgage) or the principal amount becomes less throughout the term (as is the case in a linearly amortizing mortgage). This knowledge resulted in the identification of at least two different components for principal amounts. Similarly, there are two different building blocks for interest components, an interest construction for daily-variable interest and an interest construction for a rate-bounded system.

5.13 DESIGN AND ARCHITECTURAL PROCESS

The requirements phase of the project begins with the prospectus. During this phase, prototypes are used to understand and validate the requirements. A first-cut functional and physical architecture is synthesized to determine the feasibility of the project and understand its size. Based on the prospectus and a colloquial language description, a formal product requirements specification is prepared. This specification is readable by financial or other problem domain experts. They therefore determine whether the product specification describes the product as precisely as they intend. This formal specification lays out the components of the system and their interaction. It identifies which components are to be purchases or drawn from a product line library of components and how they will work together.

Some guidelines for synthesis are these:

(1) Use operating system software and hardware familiar to the developers. If this is impossible, invest in extensive training and include extra development iteration.

(2) Partition the software into separate modules. Modularize with well-defined interfaces to simplify testing and feature packaging.

(3) Estimate performance, and then measure it in the prototype. Track module performance during the entire development cycle. Establish performance margins and manage to them.

(4) Maximize the reuse of common modules within and across product lines.

(5) Minimize cross-feature dependencies, and create components from modules.

(6) Isolate hardware and data structure dependencies from the logical functional modules. Understand and allow for levels of indirection that induce performance penalties to reduce development risk.

(7) Simplify the product by refactoring and reusing existing components.

Now the intense architecture and design phase begins. The four views of the 4+1 model are synthesized, and a set of independent use cases are created.

A good architecture readily accommodates changes based on new or modified business functions. Examples are the supervision carried out by banking regulatory bodies, or the change in internal management, or a more detailed

TABLE 5.4. Business Changes vs. System Impact

Change in reality		Typical system changes			
		Kernel object	Reporting system component	Registration system component	Overall impact
Frequency	Reason				
0 ++	external objective	++	++	++	0 ++
	external requirements	0	++	0	
	internal management	(+)	++	+	
	structure	0	+	+	
	Information Technology	(+)	(+)	(+)	

0 = no or little change.
(+) = possible change.
+ = some change.
++ = major change.

method of cost allocation based on market value rather than book value. The result of business changes is new system requirements. Existing kernel objects or components may need to be expanded, and reporting system components will need to be added. New components need to be added to the system configuration through a registration process. Furthermore, changes in technological design can drive changes to the architecture. They usually relate to changes in the information technology operating environment. See Table 5.4. These tools can be divided into the following categories:

(1) Hardware, including network technology
(2) System and network software
(3) Storage technology in a database system or storage area network
(4) System development tools, such as new database systems

A good architecture anticipates these changes so that more frequently occurring changes have lower impact than those occurring less frequently. The frequent changes in hardware and software technology led to layered architectures so that the changes can be shielded from the applications and the users.

Case Study: The Case of The Banker's Benefits

In the 1990s, banks observed that rapid developments in the financial world and within IT necessitated a review of the architecture of their software systems. One bank placed emphasis on the need to correctly register the various financial products according to type of product and to prepare accurate risk and accounting reports.

Implementation was done in phases, by transferring products gradually from existing systems to the new system. While development was underway, a bank merger occurred. The newly formed bank adopted the partially featured system, which was expanded intermittently with a group of new specific applications. This showed that new applications could be quickly added and incorporated into the new architecture.

In subsequent years, treasury front-office systems and reporting systems were connected to the new system. This boosted the quality of information considerably that was available to the financial administration and to the risk management departments. The information was more manageable, verifiable, and reliable. It contained interest-related contracts, derivatives, and bond portfolios. It was linked to front-office systems and other reporting systems. The concept of a system composed of systems that communicated with each other in the form of messages was implemented successfully through the flexible architecture.

When the European Union countries switched to one currency (euro) in 1999, the bank quickly adapted contracts in pre-euro currencies to contracts in euros (allowing the customer to choose the moment of conversion for each contract separately). For each application, a few new methods were added to the specification and the product kernel component was recompiled and loaded.

User departments saw improvement in the quality and consistency of the information in the reporting systems with this architecture in place. Financial product-related calculations were removed from the reporting systems, and specified calculation rules in the kernel calculations are used for the reports. Although front-office staff have dedicated applications, the back-office staff are relieved of many reconciliation problems, thanks to the consistency of the information.

However, the story was different when this architecture was implemented at the savings division of a large retail bank. The initial situation here was entirely different. Within an existing environment that included communication with the network of local branches, the central component containing balance and interest calculations needed to be replaced by a new system. The system had to offer support for the flexible and rapid introduction of new savings products. The environment would need to be adapted further at a later stage. The emphasis was the introduction of the application components within the existing architecture.

The assignment was to link up with many payment-oriented legacy systems for a wide variety of savings applications, with premiums, brackets, and levels, but also for the savings components of mortgage constructions. In parallel, the balance and interest calculations of the current account system such as interest calculation and overdraft identification were centralized into a core kernel. Messages from the applications had to maintain their existing interfaces so that the incoming and outgoing interfaces could maintain their batch character. The account concept remained primary: A withdrawal or deposit is first registered in the account system and then reported to applications. Figure 5.10 shows the required interactions.

The direct benefit is that the kernels contain all rules for the application products in one place. Updates to these calculations now will take place uni-

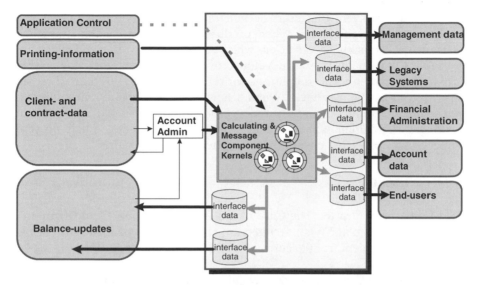

Figure 5.10. *Savings applications of a large retail bank.*

formly. The flexibility introduced could be used in the future to provide online information to front-office staff on the phone with the customer or to Web-based applications. This architecture let the bank introduce new financial products and product variations to the market quickly. The challenge was to handle the more than 1 million accounts and more than 60 million payment transactions a year without degrading performance while changing the applications. These demands were met.

The first phase lasted 20 months. During this time, the new infrastructure was designed, 10 existing applications were upgraded, and two new retail savings applications were added. The architecture's flexibility quickly proved useful. Previously, at the counters of the local branches, calculations of balances and accrued interest were performed manually. Shortly after the implementation, this time-consuming and error-prone procedure was replaced by an application program, which directly used information methods from the kernels, thus guaranteeing the same calculation rules were applied in the front office as in the back office. By doing this, a uniform handling of product rules could be enabled and enforced throughout the bank.

Conclusion: The benefits offered by integrated software architecture go beyond the "sum of the parts." Specifications for new or modified financial products may be specified in financial terms, using financial kernel components as building blocks. Automatic software generation is then possible for quick creation of a prototype. The architecture ensures that the prototype applications created fit into its environment immediately. Applications can be specified, evaluated, developed, and embedded quickly. A formal development phase is needed because generating from a specification language results in software so inefficient that users do not tolerate it. Careful domain analysis ensures realistic scheduling. When products are specified within the same domain, it will quickly become clear which components overlap and which are reusable. Components may be developed or purchased for the money market and capital market business units and for retail front-office offerings of credit, savings, and payment services. When a new domain is entered, new components may be required and their development will slow the development process. Careful domain analysis and component purchases can help prevent unnecessary delays and ensure that the scheduling is realistic.

5.14 PROBLEMS

5.14.1 Let us return to "The Case of the Puzzling Patriot" from Chapter 3. Review the particulars. What architecture changes could be made that would prevent this problem from occurring?

5.14.2 Defensive design means recognizing dangerous coding practices and knowing how to avoid them. Provide an architecture constraint that would help avoid these problems.

5.14.3 Let us return to "The Case of the No-Service Service Request" in Chapter 2. Review the particulars. What possible shortcomings in the requirements specification led to this crisis?

5.14.4 David Parnas teaches that you should encapsulate modules of code with well-defined interfaces. The interior of such a module is the private property of its programmer and must not be discernable from the outside. This is called **module ownership**. Programmers are most effective when they are shielded from, not exposed to, the innards of modules not their own. Indicate true or false for each of the following statements.

  (a) Parnas' teaching is robust to changes in design.
  (b) Parnas' teaching is called "information hiding."
  (c) Parnas' teaching defines object oriented programming.
  (d) Using Parnas' teaching prevents software project disasters.
  (e) Extensive testing of previously built modules is sufficient to permit them to be reused.

BIBLIOGRAPHY

"Krutchen 4+1 Systems," *Proceedings of the TRI-Ada '94 Conference ACM*, Baltimore, MD, November 6–11, 1994.

"Software Architecture Documentation in Practice: Documenting Architectural Layers," The Software Engineering Institute (SEI) Carnegie Mellon University, 2004, http://www.sei.cmu.edu/publications/documents/00.reports/sr004/00sr004chap02.html.

Aho, Alfred V., Kernighan, Brian W., and Weinberger, Peter J. "Awk—A Pattern Scanning and Processing Language," *Software–Practice and Experience*, Vol. IX, No. 4, April 1979, pp. 267–279.

Arnold, B. R. T., van Deursen, A., and Res, M. "An Algebraic Specification of a Language for Describing Financial Products," M. Wirsing (Ed.), *Proceedings of the ICSE-17 Workshop on Formal Methods Applications*, Software Engineering Practice, Seattle, WA, April 1995, pp. 6–13.

Astley, Mark, Sturman, Daniel C., and Agha, Gul A. "Customizable Middleware for Modular Distributed Software," *Communications of the ACM*, Vol. 44, No. 5, May 2001, pp. 99–107.

Bass, Len, Clements, Paul, and Kazman, Rick. *Software Architecture in Practice*, Addison-Wesley, Reading, MA, 1998.

Bernstein, Lawrence. "Software Fault Tolerance Forestalls Crashes: To Err is Human; To Forgive Is Fault Tolerant," *Advances in Computers*, Elsevier Science, New York, 2003, pp. 239–285.

Buschmann, Frank, et al. *A System of Patterns*, John Wiley and Sons, New York, 1996.

Cameron, John. *JSP & JSD: The Jackson Approach To Software Development*, 2nd ed. IEEE Computer Society, New York, 1989, Section 5.

Donahoo, Michael and Calvert, Kenneth. *The Pocket Guide to TCP/IP Sockets C Version*, Morgan Kaufman, New York, 2001.

Gacek, Christina, Abd-allah, Ahmed, Clark, Bradford, and Boehm, Barry. "On the Definition of Software System Architecture," *ICSE 17 Software Architecture Workshop, April 1995*, Center for Software Engineering, University of Southern California, Los Angeles, CA.

Garlan, D. and Shaw, M. "An Introduction to Software Architecture," *Advances in Software Engineering and Knowledge Engineering*, Vol. 1, World Scientific Publishing, Singapore, 1993.

Hall, Jane (Ed.) *Management of Telecommunication Systems and Services*, Springer, New York, 1991.

Hatton, Les. *Safer C: Developing Software for High-integrity and Safety-critical Systems*, McGraw-Hill International, London, 1997.

IEEE Software, Vol. 12, No. 6, Nov. 1995. Entire issue devoted to architectural questions and developments.

IEEE Software, Vol. 22, No. 4, July/August 2005. Entire issue devoted to COTS Integration.

Jackson, M. A. *Principles of Program Design*, Academic Press, New York, 1975.

Kruchten, Philippe B. "The 4+1 View Model of Architecture," *IEEE Software*, Vol. 12, No. 6, Nov. 1995, pp. 42–50.

Landauer, Thomas K. *The Trouble with Computers*, MIT Press, Cambridge, MA, 1996, p. 70.

Leavens, Gary T. and Sitaraman Murali. *Foundations of Component-Based Systems*, Cambridge University Press, Cambridge, U.K., 2000.

Lenzi, Marie. "Conduit and Content," *Object Magazine*, Oct. 1996, pp. 4–6.

Linger, R. C., Mills, H. D. and Witt, B. I. *Structured Programming: Theory and Practice*, Addison-Wesley, Reading, MA, 1979, ch. 4.

Morris, Charles R. and Ferguson, Charles H. "How Architecture Wins Technology Wars," *Harvard Business Review*, March–April 1993, pp. 86–94.

Parnas, David. "Concurrency and Scheduling," *Software Fundamentals Collected Papers by David L Parnas*, edited by Daniel M. Hoffman and David M. Weiss, Addison-Wesley, London, 2001.

Schmidt, D. C. and Cleeland, C. "Applying Patterns to Develop Extensible ORB Middleware," *IEEE Communications Magazine*, IEEE CS Press, Los Alamitos, CA, Vol. 37, No. 4, 1999, pp. 54–63.

Sha, Lui. "Using Simplicity to Control Complexity," *IEEE Software*, Volume 18, No. 4, July/Aug. 2001, p. 27.

Shaw, Mary and Garlan, David. *Software Architecture: Perspectives on an Emerging Discipline*, Simon & Schuster, New York, 1996.

Siewiorek, D. P., Chillarege, R., and Plank J. K. "Reflections on Industry Trends and Experimental Research in Dependability," *IEEE Transaction on Dependable and Secure Computing*, IEEE Computer Society, Vol. 1, No. 2, April–June 2004, p. 120. software@computer.org.

Wallnau, Kurt, et al. *Building Systems from Commercial Components*, Addison-Wesley, Reading, MA, 2002.

Witt, B. I., Baker, F. T., and Merritt, E. W. *Software Architecture and Design–Principles, Models, and Methods*, Van Nostrand Reinhold, New York, 1994.

6

Estimation, Planning, and Investment

With a prototype, a validated set of requirements specifications, and architecture available, the project manager faces the task of estimating what can be done in the time allotted, how many people it will take, and the order of tasks. Staff training, upgrading tools, building test beds, or any other investment needed for project success is best made now. This is also the best time to make feature, schedule, and cost commitments, but usually these are made well before this point. This push for early commitment often leads to project problems and failures. In the United States, the Standish Group reports, "We're losing ground. Only 28% of IT projects succeed these days, down from 34% a year or two ago. Outright failures—IT projects canceled before completion—are up to 18% from 15%. The remaining 51% of IT projects are "challenged"—seriously late, over budget and lacking expected features."[1] In the United Kingdom, canceled government projects plus others that have run over budget—such as tax and child benefit computer systems—cost the United Kingdom £1.5 billion over 6 years, according to a 2003 report from the Office of Government Commerce.[2]

The quantitative approach to software engineering reduces the likelihood of these problems by careful analysis of the requirements and architecture before development begins.

[1] http://www.standishgroup.com. (with kind permission of The Standish Group International, Inc.)
[2] http://www.computing.co.uk/news/1139418.

Trustworthy Systems Through Quantitative Software Engineering,
by Lawrence Bernstein and C. M. Yuhas
Copyright © 2005 IEEE Computer Society

To recap the preceding chapters:

(1) Start with a system prospectus.
(2) Write a set of requirements with quantitative specifications.
(3) Validate the quantitative specifications with a prototype and with the customer.
(4) Use ICED-T metrics to evaluate the proposed system as a whole.
(5) Develop a simple quality function deployment set of metrics showing the importance and ease of implementation for each feature.
(6) Synthesize a first-cut architecture from the prototype and requirements specification using the 4 + 1 model.
(7) Conduct an architecture discovery review to make sure that the project is feasible.
(8) Size the project by computing the function points as explained in this chapter.

Now realistic development planning can begin. This chapter will explain how to estimate the staffing and time required for development. With this information, the project manager can plan tasks and set intermediate mileposts.

6.1   SOFTWARE SIZE ESTIMATION

Intuitively, one might suppose that development effort is proportional to software size, but size of what? Size may be measured by the number of program instructions, the number of function points, the amount of computer memory the program will occupy, the number of interactive screens in an online software system, the number of equations in the computer game physics, or the number of pages in the requirements document. Estimating software size is fundamental to quantitative project planning. A good size estimate leads to good development plans and provides a basis for determining the staff effort and elapsed time needed for software development. With these estimates, project costs can be calculated and projected into a price.

6.1.1   Pitfalls and Pratfalls

The problem with most size estimates is that they are too optimistic. Size estimates are commonly well under the final actual size because they do not consider many nonfunctional requirements, nor do they account for the complexity of the problem. For example, most software people would not imagine that the length of time tomatoes sat on freight cars could impact the quality of tomato soup. If tomatoes sit in open cars in the rain, adding even a small amount of water during cooking yields watery soup, but if there was a dry spell, not adding enough water yields a soup that is too thick. The need for a time and weather module to handle a calculation that is obvious to the chef (but not to the developer) adds several new interfaces and many software modules to the software system hoping to do the chef's job. One chef always parked his car on the far side of the train yard to get some exercise on the walk to the kitchen. Checking the weather was second nature to him, but it is difficult to do automatically. Knowing this business rule for making soup is vital when making computer resource estimates, cost quotations, and schedules. The software effort needed to collect and correlate weather data added significantly to software size estimates.

Software size also becomes an important metric in process measurements. Many metrics like productivity and defect rates are a function of software size. Good managers keep metrics data from previous projects in a software database and use the data for similar elements of new projects. High-level language compliers, fourth-generation languages, software platforms, tools, and software components allow developers to provide more functions with fewer lines of code. The problem is that high-level tools are not always suitable for building performance-sensitive applications. Even though most of any application is not performance sensitive and only 1–2% of the total software needs to be quick, this small percentage must be processed either by the tools used for the entire application or the source code for the application must be divided among different software technologies. This introduces a discontinuity in the architecture view depicting the development process and software tools. The discontinuity presents a serious problem to application maintainers and stresses the configuration control processes. Projects often fail when their source code is split among different languages.

6.1.2 Software Size Metrics

The two most often used size metrics are source lines of code (SLOC) and function points. Counting lines of code has its problems, not the least of which is that you often must build the component before you can count SLOC. Estimators rely on extrapolating from similar components from other projects at the beginning of a new project and then track SLOC to see how good their estimates are. Function point estimation has made great strides and can be used throughout the development cycle to track project schedules and costs. Function point tracking is used to assure design simplicity and the understanding of redesign implications. Function point metrics have problems too, but they are proving to be effective in size estimation. Function points isolate the estimates from the idiosyncrasy of the programming language and allow the estimator to focus on the nature of the problem rather than on the implementation details of the solution. They are not well suited to computation-intensive applications or real-time software development.

SLOC and function points may not be valuable for every project. The number of user screens might more naturally measure a Web-based application or other highly interactive, data-intensive application. The number of different reports or analyses it must produce best gauges analytical software. A computer game can often be the work of a small team of fewer than five people and is best estimated by considering the experience of the developers, the tools and components available, and the complexity of the physics required for the game dynamics. Web application development is difficult to estimate using function points because the tools simplify integration. Function implementation estimators must be careful to include only the work required by the particular application in the estimate, not the efficiency of the tool suite used for implementation.

6.2 FUNCTION POINTS

Function points can be counted from requirements. This alone led to its widespread use. Early on, unsuccessful attempts were made to estimate project-staffing profiles. Today, managers, function point experts, and technical educators strongly emphasize that function point analysis (FPA) is not appropriate for measuring either individual productivity or monitoring day-to-day progress. The following excellent overview can be accessed in its entirety at www.softwaremetrics.com/fpafund.htm. This excerpt is presented with the permission of the author, David Longstreet.[3]

6.2.1 Fundamentals of FPA

Function Point Analysis (FPA) is a structured technique of problem solving. It is a method to break systems into smaller components, so they can be better understood and analyzed. Function points are a unit measure for software much like an hour is to measuring time.

Human beings solve problems by breaking them into smaller understandable pieces. Problems that may seem to be difficult are simple once they are broken into smaller parts. In the world of FPA, systems are divided into five large classes and general system characteristics. The first three classes or components are external inputs (EIs), external outputs (EOs), and external inquires (EQs). Each of these components operates on data in files, and they are called transactions. The next two, internal logical files (ILFs) and external interface files (EIFs), are where data are stored that is combined to form logical information. The general system characteristics assess the general functionality of the system.

6.2.2 Brief History

FPA was developed first by Allan J. Albrecht in the mid-1970s. It was an attempt to overcome difficulties associated with lines of code as a measure of software size and to assist in developing a mechanism to predict effort asso-

---

[3] www.softwaremetrics.com.

ciated with software development. The method was first published in 1979 and then later in 1983. In 1984, Albrecht refined the method, and since 1986, when the International Function Point User Group (IFPUG) was set up, several versions of the *Function Point Counting Practices Manual* have been published by IFPUG. A full function point training manual can be downloaded from these websites: http://www.ifpug.org/ or www.SoftwareMetrics.Com.

6.2.3 Objectives of FPA

Because function points measure systems from a functional perspective, they are independent of technology. Regardless of language, development method, or hardware platform used, the number of function points for a system will remain constant. The only variable is the amount of effort needed to deliver a given set of function points. This becomes the basis for determining if a new tool, a better programming environment, a new software process, or a different language will increase productivity. Comparisons can be done carefully between organizations or the same organization developing different kinds of software applications. This is a critical point and one of the greatest values of FPA.

6.2.4 Characteristics of Quality FPA

FPA requires training and experience. If FPA is attempted without training, it is reasonable to assume the analysis will be poor. An expert in FPA will help the software architect by finding feature duplications, inconsistent use of design rules, poor interface designs, and software modules that need further review. The best FPA experts have the perspective and insight to be excellent system engineers.

6.3 FIVE MAJOR ELEMENTS OF FUNCTION POINT COUNTING

Because it is common for computer systems to interact with other computer systems, a boundary must be established according to the architect's point of view indicating the border between the project or application being measured and the external applications or user domain. Once the border has been established, elements can be classified, ranked, and tallied.

6.3.1 EI

EI is an elementary process in which data cross the boundary from outside to inside from a data input screen or another application. The data may be used to maintain one or more internal logical files. The data can be either control information or business information. Control information does not have to update an internal logical file. Figure 6.1 represents a simple EI that updates two ILFs. In this case, EI = 2.

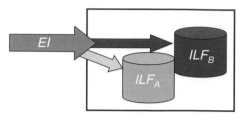

Figure 6.1. EI.

6.3.2 EO

EO is an elementary process that sends derived data across a module boundary. Additionally, an EO may update an ILF. Such data create reports or output files sent to other applications from one or more ILFs and EIFs. Figure 6.2 shows three outputs labeled EO, two are derived from data within an ILF and then passed directly to the EO from their ILFs, but one derives data from each ILF, processes it, and then sends it to EO. In this case, EO = 3.

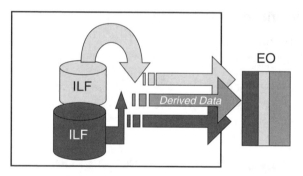

Figure 6.2. Simple and derived EO.

6.3.3 EQ

This is an elementary process with both input and output components that result in data transfer between ILFs and EIFs. In this case, as compared with the previous case, the input process does not update ILFs, and the output side does not contain derived data. Figure 6.3 represents an EQ with two ILFs and no derived data. In this case, EQ = 2.

6.3.4 ILF

This file is an identifiable group of logically related data that reside entirely within the application boundary. In Figure 6.3, ILF = 2.

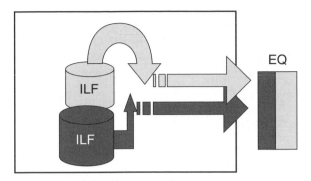

Figure 6.3. *Simple EQ.*

6.3.5 EIF

This file is an identifiable group of logically related data that are used for reference purposes only. The data reside entirely outside the application and are maintained by another application. Note that the EIF is an ILF for another application.

6.4 EACH ELEMENT CAN BE SIMPLE, AVERAGE, OR COMPLEX

The simplified function point equation given in Section 3.9.3 was as follows:

$$FPs = (UFP)(VAF),$$

where UFP is the unadjusted function point and VAF is the value adjustment factor.

Avoid using adjusted function points to compute staff estimates in order to not count complexity twice. For the function points, we assumed an average system complexity, but the complexity of each element need not be average. It may be simple, average, or complex. Here, complexity is a subjective judgment made by the architect and developers. For EI, EO, or EQ transactions, the complexity ranking is based on the number of files updated or referenced and the number of data structures in the files. For both ILF and EIF files, the ranking is based on record classes and data element classes. Other measures of complexity are possible. A record element class is a recognizable, nonrecursive field. The coefficients for the UFP can be taken from the function point complexity table in Table 6.1.

The coefficients represent weights. Theoretically, 15 different possible equations may be used. Each element may have a different degree of complexity and demand a different weight reflected in the coefficient. The VAF coefficients for the equation used in Section 3.9.3 were selected from the average

TABLE 6.1. Coefficients for UFP

Element/ Complexity	EI	EO	EQ	ILF	EIF
Simple	3	4	3	7	5
Average	4	5	4	10	7
Complex	6	7	6	15	10

row. When FPA is first attempted, it is easiest to choose the coefficients corresponding to the overall application complexity. With experience, each element can have its own level of complexity. The counts for each level of complexity for each element can be entered into a worksheet as in Table 6.2.

TABLE 6.2. Element Complexity Counts to Calculate Total Adjusted Function Points

Type of Component	Complexity of Components			
	Low	Average	High	Total
External Inputs	___ × 3 = ___	___ × 4 = ___	___ × 6 = ___	
External Outputs	___ × 4 = ___	___ × 5 = ___	___ × 7 = ___	
External Inquiries	___ × 3 = ___	___ × 4 = ___	___ × 6 = ___	
Internal Logical Files	___ × 7 = ___	___ × 10 = ___	___ × 15 = ___	
External Interface Files	___ × 5 = ___	___ × 7 = ___	___ × 10 = ___	
		Total Number of Unadjusted Function Points		
		Multiplied Value Adjustment Factor		
		Total Adjusted Function Points		

The VAF is based on 14 general system characteristics (GSC) that rate the general functionality of the application being counted. Each characteristic has associated descriptions that help determine the degrees of influence of the characteristics. The degrees of influence range on a scale of zero to five, from no influence to strong influence. The IFPUG *Counting Practices Manual* provides detailed evaluation criteria for each of the GSCs. The value assigned to each characteristic is based on the opinion or the judgment of the architect and the developers. Wideband Delphi is a good technique for doing this value assignment. Table 6.3 is an overview of each GSC.

Then a factor reflecting the complexity of software needed, called either the technical complexity factor (TCF) or the VAF, is computed using the value adjustment equation:

$$TCF = VAF = 0.65 + \sum (C(i))/100,$$

where $i = 1$ to 14 and represents each GSC that can have a value from zero to five.

TABLE 6.3. Weighting GSCs for VAF

General System Characteristic	Description	Value range 0 to 5 (0 = irrelevant; 5 = fundamental)
1. Data communications	How many communication facilities are there to aid in the transfer or exchange of information with the application or system?	
2. Distributed data processing	How are distributed data and processing functions handled?	
3. Performance	Did the user require response time or throughput?	
4. Heavily used configuration	How heavily used is the current hardware platform where the application will be executed?	
5. Transaction rate	How frequently are transactions executed—daily, weekly, monthly, etc.?	
6. Online data entry	What percentage of the information is entered online?	
7. End-user efficiency	Was the application designed for end-user efficiency?	
8. Online update	How many ILFs are updated by online transactions?	
9. Complex processing	Does the application have extensive logical or mathematical processing?	
10. Reusability	Was the application developed to meet one or many users' needs?	
11. Installation ease	How difficult is conversion and installation?	
12. Operational ease	How effective and/or automated are startup, backup, and recovery procedures?	
13. Multiple sites	Was the application specifically designed, developed, and supported for installation at multiple sites for multiple organizations?	
14. Facilitate change	Was the application specifically designed, developed, and supported to facilitate change?	

The final function point count is obtained by multiplying the UFP by the VAF.

$$\text{Function Points } (FP) = (UFP)(VAF)^4.$$

6.5   SIZING AN AUTOMATION PROJECT WITH FPA

Example: A new tool is needed to automate new hire processing. It will be called the employees startup program (ESP) and should reduce the work of the Human Resources Department by 90% and make every step of hiring secure. Audits of the decisions made throughout the process are an essential requirement.

The ESP automates these tasks:

(1) File applications.

(2) Schedule drug tests.

(3) Confirm appointments with new hires.

(4) Access and file results from the medical department computer.

(5) Communicate results to managers.

(6) Negotiate and assign start date.

(7) Enter background check results.

(8) Capture fingerprinting results.

(9) Organize, format, and send new hire data to administrative computer.

(10) Track Human Resources person who decides/commits.

The architecture has been designed, as a first cut, and the function points have been counted for this specific architecture. This is how the first multipliers in the low, average, and high columns in Table 6.4 were determined.

TABLE 6.4. UFP as Calculated from the Requirements and First-Cut Architecture

	Low	Average	High	Results
ILF	3 (×7)	2 (×10)	0 (×15)	41
EIF	0 (×5)	0 (×7)	0 (×10)	0
EI	3 (×3)	2 (×4)	1 (×6)	23
EO	1 (×4)	2 (×5)	1 (×7)	21
EQ	3 (×3)	0 (×4)	0 (×6)	9

UFP = 94.

---

[4] Adapted from an excellent article by David Longstreet, with permission. David@ SoftwareMetrics.Com and www.SoftwareMetrics.Com.

(1) They provide a consistent and abstract measure of size, independent of language and design.

(2) The client more easily understands them than new or changed source lines of code (NCSLOC).

(3) They provide system-wide insight, finding redundant functions and ambiguous requirements.

(4) They avoid the temptation to fudge the number of NCSLOC.

(5) They allow management decisions to be quantitative.

6.5.2 Disadvantages of Function Point Measurement

(1) FP counting is labor intensive; yet it should not be automated.

(2) FP counting requires highly skilled and thoughtful practitioners.

(3) Inexperienced people produce inconsistent counts.

(4) Extensive training in FP counting is required.

(5) FPs are heavily weighted to file manipulation and transaction applications.

(6) The lack of historical data limits the improvement of estimation, but software developers are unwilling to count FP for completed products.

(7) The practice is subject to systematic error peculiar to the person doing the counting. A good practice is to have an FP counting expert assigned to a project for a period of time. Then as misestimates are found, they can be corrected. This helps the project's FP counting expert to improve.

6.5.3 Results Common to FPA

The prediction accuracy for 20 network management systems proved to be better than twice that of the counting NCSLOC approach. Hundreds of function points for redundant functions were discovered and eliminated. These redundancies had crept into the architecture as designers planned an integrated product offering from a library of existing assets (Figure 6.4). By eliminating these redundancies early in the project lifecycle, developers could focus on new feature development.

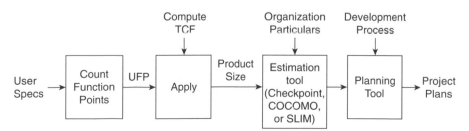

Figure 6.4. FPA process yields project plans.

Now compute the degrees of influence by filling in the values on the chart from Table 6.3 and totaling the 14 values. The values for this example are shown in Table 6.5. The GSC is 23 and is used to modify the function point calculation by accounting for the complexity of the sofeware development.

TABLE 6.5. GSC Chart—Ratings Determined by Wideband Delphi

General System Characteristic	Degree of Influence (scale 0 to 5)
Data communications	0
Distributed data processing	0
Performance	3
Heavily used configuration	0
Transaction rate	1
Online data entry	3
End-user efficiency	4
Online update	2
Complex processing	1
Reusability	1
Installation ease	0
Operational ease	4
Multiple sites	1
Facilitate change	3
Total degrees of influence—GSC	23

$VAF = 0.65 + 23/100 = 0.88.$
$FP = (UFP)(VAF) = 94 \times 0.88 = 82.7.$

Now the project manager for the ESP project must refer to a databas of previous projects to estimate the productivity of the development sta to estimate how long the project will take and how many developers are needed Alternatively, the project manager can use the Constructive Cost Mode (COCOMO) model explained later in this chapter to make this projection.

6.5.1 Advantages of Function Point Analysis

Researchers provided the insight that during the design phase of a project, if function point content should actually decrease. Based on Boehm's prototyping experiments, the goal of 40% reduction was chosen. Another benefit was the elimination of feature creep experienced by most projects. Typically, projects experience 40% average growth in product size because of the user changes in requirement (on average 2% to 3% per month) from original estimation to final release. Using FPA greatly improved communication between developers and product management by giving developers the ability to quantify product size, constrain feature growth, and reduce design complexity. FPA were performed for modern software technology, such as object-oriented client/server, and event/response. They may be computed in early in the lif of the project. The recommendation is to first compute them during th requirements stage and then to compute them at every subsequent develop ment stage. The demonstrated advantages are summarized as follows:

6.5.4 FPA Accuracy

A Bell Laboratories study showed that estimates of project size with FPA are twice as accurate as those obtained from traditional methods. This study was conducted in a controlled environment for three different types of projects; all three types used the same development processes in the same environment, which had a 2.9 SEI rating. Figure 6.5 shows that although estimates for the effort, costs, productivity, and fault removal were reasonably on target, the schedule estimating was poor because the Waterfall Model is built into the

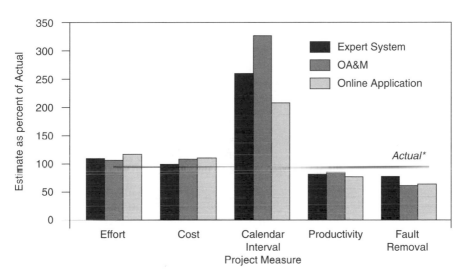

* Accuracy is acceptable, except for Calendar Interval.

Figure 6.5. *How accurate were FP estimates?*

estimation model. New time estimation models incorporating the Spiral Model would produce more accurate results.

Paul W. Lusher of the Navy Dahlgren Division has been using FPA for real-time weapons systems development. He finds that the "backfire" method, which is used to compute function points directly from the source code, must be avoided as it gives poor estimates. He said that "It is more appealing on a philosophical level to measure system functionality vs. source programming language; users, in general, do not care about the source code but do care about the job the system is built to perform." Overall, extensive experience with software metrics shows that no one metric can solve the serious problems of software development. As Capers Jones emphasized, "To become a true engineering discipline, many metrics and measurements are needed: accurate effort, cost, and schedule data; accurate defect and quality data, etc."

6.6 NCSLOC METRIC

Probably the most-used direct measure of software size is to count of the number of lines of code that have been implemented. These were originally called LOC. Then to distinguish them from the executable code produced by a complier, they were called SLOC. With the advent of reuse and commercial off the shelf (COTS), it became important to distinguish the code that had to be developed from that reused, and so the term NCSLOC was adopted. NCSLOC is the size used for staffing and schedule estimating. Note that many actual physical lines in the source code file may be blank or comments and not contain any language statements. When a project adopts NCSLOC for its size metric, counting rules attempt to make the counts consistent. Here is one such a set of rules:

(1) Counting standard: Define logical LOC.

(2) Limit module size: 50 LOC to 1000 LOC.

(3) Code configuration management: Store source and object code for each module as a file. Use a PiDENT (program identifier) to name the module. A good format is **logical_name@type.version**, where type is source, object, or even documentation. The logical name may follow some hierarchical breakdown structure based on the logical view of the software architecture. PiDENT can name more than programs.

(4) Coding standard: Good practice applies a ratio of one logical LOC to one physical line in the file. The coding standard also incorporates format matters like indenting. A quality coding standard makes readable code and provides for a more easily designed counter. Use only one language within a file. When more than one language is used in an environment, separate PiDENTs are used and historical data banks are kept for each language. The version field of the PiDENT can be used to track language.

(5) Use checklists: Rules are enforced by software auditing programs following firm checklists. For example, a standard for counting C code could count each instance of the following as one LOC, but not comments and blank lines: each brace, closing and opening; each executable line; each declaration of a variable or function, including a function header; each for (loop), if (condition), do, return (value), or while (condition); each instance of a compiler directive.

Case Study: The Case of the Bard's Bulge

A metric popular in the 1970s was the ratio of comment lines to LOC. The goal was a ratio of 1, but a project with a 0.5 ratio or higher was considered well documented. Bernstein was once appointed project manger for a project with a ratio of 2. He was duly impressed until he began to read some of the code. There were long quotes from *Hamlet* included in the commentary.

After a quiet meeting with the offending programmer where the project manager made it clear that, although he would not be fired, project policy would henceforth expressly limit the content of comments to relevant software issues. The programmer's dramaturgical tastes were admirable but constituted unhelpful help.

Word spread through the land that the new project manger actually read code! There was a flurry of documentation activity for the next several weeks.

Result: The next time the code was read, the ratio was 0.9, but the commentary was cogent. The exercise on everyone's part revealed that too much in-line commentary obscures the code. Programmers were encouraged to include narratives and design information in preface sections to modules and to use few in-line comments.

It is essential for the manager to look beyond the metric to gain insight and understanding. This technique is sometimes called "management by walking around."

6.6.1 Company Statistics

Lines of code can also be easily applied to company statistics such as productivity (NCSLOC per programmer hour); defect rates (defects per 1000 NCSLOC). NCSLOC can also be used in determining the effectiveness of product reviews and inspections. The problem is that there is little agreement about what to count. A good practice is not to count comments and track one LOC for each carriage return. To emphasize that you are estimating the effort required, do not count LOC of operating systems or platforms in the development estimation. One should also count the LOC in reused components, but use different effort estimation algorithms than for new development. A reason for using LOC is the ease of counting them and sorting them into these categories. But LOC tends to reward the wrong behavior. Crisp, clear, and concise programs are the objective, not lengthy ones.

6.6.2 Reuse

With some extra effort, new modules can be declared reusable. Reuse can cut down on defect counts if care is taken to test them exhaustively, define their interfaces well, and assure compatibility.

MAGIC NUMBER!

Three times the effort is needed to transform a single system module into a reusable component, so know beforehand its likely frequency of reuse.

It takes 1.5 to 2.2 times the effort to write a software module in a way to be a reusable asset for these reasons:

(1) Standard interfaces to the operating system must exist and be followed. For example, kernel changes to UNIX are not acceptable. This reduces flexibility in handling new communication protocols.
(2) Standard approaches to module interfaces must apply universally. Abstract mechanisms, such as self-describing tag-value interface design, can penalize performance.
(3) Application generators need to produce about 25% of the product, especially for user interfaces.

The keeper of a reusable module faces the formidable task of having to know all users when the owner must change it. Take, for example, "diff" in UNIX, the most reused module on Earth. Not many understand how it works, and fewer still try to change it.[5] Here is a fable for our time, told by Doug McIlroy, the AT&T Bell Laboratories inventor, with permission.

The Tale of "Diff": A Cautionary Fable for Developers of Reusable Modules

Once upon a time, there was a mathematical problem of finding the longest subsequence of lines common to two files. "No sweat," thought the developer. A dynamic programming technique that takes time mn and space mn to compare an m-line file to an n-line file would do the trick. But space mn was unacceptable on the small machines of yesteryear. "OK, we'll fly by the seat of our pants," thought our hero. So he read both files until he found a line that disagreed, and then figured he would somehow search forth in both until he got back in accord. *Somehow* was the killer. Suppose the second line in one file agreed with the fourth line ahead in the other and vice versa. How to choose?

Then news came from afar in Princeton that Wizard Hirschberger had seen a way to reduce space mn by a mathematical method to space m, while only doubling the time. "Good deal!" thought our guy. "Now we can afford to run it. It was slow, but it did work and gave an explainable right answer in a clearly defined way."

But the people complained. When they moved a paragraph, it showed up as two changes, a deletion here and an addition there. So our hero made a "diff" that found moves. It was again seat of the pants, but it ran pretty well. Yet, sometimes, an evil occurred. If the people ran it on stuff where the same line occurred in many places, like assembly language or text processing, it discovered lots of deletions and additions that could be explained as moves. Our hero was filled with consternation.

---

[5] Aho, Alfred V. and Ullman, Jeffrey D. *Foundations of Computer Science*, W. H. Freeman, San Francisco, CA, 1992, p. 307.

Then along came a shining knight, Harold Stone, with a dynamic programming technique that reduced the running time from the product to the sum of the file lengths, except in unnatural cases. Now here was something fast enough to use on big files, efficient in space and time, mathematically justifiable as giving a good answer, and experimentally shown to be physiologically useful. "O frabjous day! Calloo, callay!" he chortled in his joy.

But then the people tinkered. Three times they altered output. They added features. They added stars! And the tinkering caused the code to increase and the manual to swell to half again its size. "Well," said our guy. "It is important to know when to stop."

Analyses of reuse of 2954 modules of NASA programs point to the shocking conclusion that to reap the benefits of the extra original effort to make a module reusable, it must be reused virtually unchanged. No change costs 5%; the slightest change drives the cost up to 60%. The clear message is that when you reuse a module, do not modify it. The issues of who pays the differential and who pays for ongoing support remain serious barriers to reuse. Within an organization, however, success is possible. At AT&T, the use of a platform resulted in significant reuse in Network Management Software Systems. To recap, these are the problems with reuse:

(1) We have been unable to systematically reuse software across application domains.
(2) Reuse is successful only when throughput and response time are not overriding concerns.
(3) We have been unable to maintain an asset base of software modules except when they are in C libraries and when they are utility functions.
(4) We have had to maintain a high level of management attention to detail to assure reuse success.
(5) We have been unable to sustain an investment in making application components reusable.
(6) We have been unable to avoid exhaustive retesting when reusing modules.
(7) We have trouble deciding to shift to new technology when we have a library of reusable modules.

6.6.3 Wideband Delphi

As explained previously, Wideband Delphi combines the knowledge of several experts to produce an estimate of project size. It is an iteration of meetings and anonymous estimates and is led by a moderator. Its process goes as follows:

(1) A meeting involving the estimators and the moderator is held to discuss requirements.
(2) Each estimator makes an estimate of the project.

(3) Estimates are anonymously tabulated by the moderator.

(4) Sheets showing the range of estimates are returned to the experts.

The process repeats until the estimates are within an acceptable range. When the process is completed and the estimates have converged, the interval of prediction is the range of all estimates. The confidence level of this estimate range cannot be directly calculated. Its historical performance has been positive, but bias can play a role in Wideband Delphi. It can be time consuming. Nobody can make perfect estimates every time, but estimation is a skill and people can learn to become consistent. To become more accurate over time, an estimator must follow a defined estimation process. Part of this process involves tracking accuracy in a historical database. The size estimate should be an interval with a maximum and a minimum bound. Even having such a historical record, with the wide introduction of the C++ language in the early 1990s, it became apparent that historical data based on C code was no longer insightful.

6.6.4   Disadvantages of NCSLOC

There are real disadvantages to using NCSLOC:

(1) There is no standard for an LOC, and LOC vary from language to language.

(2) It is very difficult to visualize LOC early in the development.

(3) An automatic code counter may not work for all programming styles in the same language.

(4) LOC is a strange term to most people outside the software field, especially customers.

(5) Statistics calculated using NCSLOC could be misleading. Programmers can easily manipulate LOC to enhance their reputations.

Productivity statistics such as "units per person month" and "cost per unit produced" are helpful and common statistics in many fields. For software production, using LOC can make these statistics misleading in a multiple language environment. Table 6.6 shows the costs to implement the same program in two programming languages of significantly different levels.

Using a higher level language reduces the number of NCSLOC and therefore shortens the time needed for coding and testing. Smaller systems are easier to deploy and maintain. Regardless of implementation, the fixed costs of requirements, design, and documentation remain the same. When the total cost for the system is divided by SLOC, the use of the high-level language seems more expensive, because the fixed costs are distributed over fewer NCSLOC. The total cost is lower, and the elapsed time is shorter for the FORTRAN implementation, because the higher level language has a higher expansion factor.

TABLE 6.6. Figures Lie and Liars Figure

Measure	Assembler	FORTRAN
Size—SLOC	10,000	3,000
Function point count	30	30
Requirements (Time in months)	2	2
Design "	3	3
Code "	10	3
Integration and test "	5	3
Documentation "	2	2
Management/support "	3	2
Total Time—months	25	15
Cost per month	$5,000.00	$5,000.00
Total cost	$125,000.00	$75,000.00
Cost per source line	$12.50	$25.00
Source lines per month	400.00	200.00
Cost per function point	$4,166.67	$2,500.00
Function points per month	1.20	2.00

The expansion factor is essentially an independent variable. The benefits of improving the expansion factor can be gained in any application area because it focuses on making the expression of the solution more concise. The expansion factor represents a capital investment in terms of higher level languages and tools to promote a 100 : 1 improvement every 20 years, as shown in Figure 6.6.

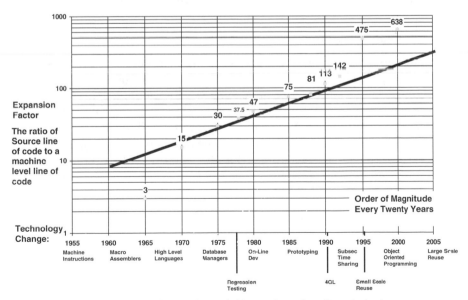

Each date is an estimate of widespread use of a software technology

Figure 6.6. *Expansion factor vs. technology change.*

6.7 PRODUCTION PLANNING

Now with the size of the project estimated, the project manger can plan the development staff and the time needed to develop the project on time and within budget. Most software projects are customized and therefore are labor intensive. Salaries, overhead benefits, computing resources, and tools constitute the most of the project's costs. These factors depend on the number of people assigned to the project. As component-based development and reuse mature, this picture will change. It is essential to project the number of developers from the size estimates using productivity factors peculiar to the problem and the organization.

6.7.1 Productivity

The factors affecting the productivity of an organization are the skill and talent of the staff, the nature of the problem, the relationship with the customer, and the tools and processes used in the development. Spending money on each factor reduces the cost of software development.

Because productivity is linear for small projects, a good project management practice is to break a large project into a collection of small ones. But to make this work, people need to be added to coordinate the activities of the many smaller projects. Well-structured interfaces must be used between the modules so that the components developed from the smaller projects are easy to integrate. System performance reduction of up to 10% can occur, which is a small price to pay for a predictable and orderly development cycle.

6.7.2 Mediating Culture

Bad managers are the biggest cause of software project bankruptcies. Success in large projects requires the creation of a culture, with people at key interface points. Many tools have been developed with the intention of automating processes and eliminating the need for people, which is not sensible in practice. The development staff should not have to learn each new configuration management tool, for instance, that comes down the pike to do their jobs. Rather, the tools should support a separate technical staff whose explicit job it is to build systems, test systems, and get them out the door. The people who define and implement processes are not the same as those who develop the system. The critical limiting resource is top-notch first-line supervisors who can act as lead technical advisors. The goal is to free them from overhead tasks. Management does not have to be in control of every detail. It is more effective to delegate decision making. With dedicated support staff having line responsibility and in-line functions, managers are free to manage by exception.

Another aspect of culture that has proven beneficial in software development is the "Farmers' Market" approach. The idea is to periodically pull together people with specific talents and leave long periods of time for inter-action, which allows a sense of community to develop and collaborative interfacing to occur. The easiest way to accomplish this is within scheduled meetings. This is the story of how Bernstein created this environment.

Biweekly project meetings were scheduled from 8:30 to 3:00, with an agenda prepared in advance. Bernstein deliberately intended that nothing in that agenda extend past 1:30, but kept this intention to himself. The remaining $1^1/_2$ hours were to function as the Farmers' Market where no telephone calls or other meetings could intrude. The uplifting feeling of finishing the agenda "early" gave a subtle message of confidence that the project too could be on time. Regularity and familiarity were important. After the project meetings were successfully held for several months, the local deli that had been deliv-ering the sandwiches for lunch raised their prices, and the administrative assis-tant who handled the arrangements looked for a different deli to deliver the same kind of sandwiches—turkey, tuna, roast beef. But people complained that the project was starting to have troubles. The meetings were somehow not as productive. After one month of vague fears and undefined angst, Bernstein ordered a return to the original deli. Suddenly everything was back to normal, although nobody really knew why.

This could be an important body of research. An anthropological and culi-nary study of software development would be fascinating.

6.7.3 Customer Relations

Projects with teaming relations with customers are twice as productive as those with contractual ones. The most productive organizations build to cost rather than to specification and insist on monthly demonstrations with the customer. For fixed-price contracts, the risk is that customer expectations will exceed the available resources, but it is best to discover this early. Creating close relations with the end user and thereby training the programmers in the problem domain is necessary.

6.7.4 Centralized Support Functions

We recall that project organization is better when the problem or technology is new, but that functional organization is cheaper and more efficient. As part of the decision to centralize functions, special funding must be set aside to accomplish the centralization. Project schedule delays may occur during the transition, and their acceptance is vital to successful centralization. The project senior leadership team must support the centralization and monitor their operations. Even then, constant vigilance will be needed to eliminate redun-dant work. Consider the "Geary Two-Step." Mike Geary, a successful Bell Laboratories project manager, set up centralized functional teams in his 500-person software shop. When he detected project personnel duplicating the functional team's responsibilities, he would immediately and without discussion transfer those doing redundant tasks to the appropriate functional organization. This made the point. Functional organizations have been effective doing the following jobs:

(1) **Technology selection:** Many product teams are in the habit of selecting their technology, which often leads to systems that cannot work together. Components cannot be shared among teams, and basic functions such as human interface, systems administration, and parameterization are duplicated. For example, three related but separate projects can have incompatible human interfaces and their own administration schemes, which allows no opportunity for code sharing. Without being able to share platforms, tools, and assets, duplicate development of similar functions is inevitable. With separate technology selection, every project must employ skilled people devoted to meeting with suppliers, selecting technology, and training new team members on their selected technology.

(2) **Tools:** If every project builds or purchases its own tools, it is difficult to obtain volume discounts from tool suppliers.

(3) **Manufacturing:** This includes trouble tracking, system builds, configuration control, and release packaging. If each team has their own approach to system builds, there are no opportunities for economies of scale. Too often, products in the same product line must work on different physical computers because their installation software is arbitrarily different.

(4) **System Testing:** System test processes and tools should be standardized. Testers are best kept separated from developers so that they may be objective in their evaluations.

(5) **Computer Facilities:** The hidden cost of administering clients and servers spread throughout an organization is high. Volume purchases are difficult to obtain, and computer operators cannot be shared. There can be significant wasted space and duplicate machines. This function should be organized by the physical building occupied, not by project. Standard development environments should be defined. Inadequate desktop tools impact the entire development community and are one root cause of delays in many projects.

(6) **Documentation:** About 25% of effort in program release is documentation. Standard approaches to producing the documentation and to controlling it are mandatory.

(7) **Human Factors Design:** The design of screens, user manuals, performance aids, and system operation is best done by a central organization with people skilled in human behavior. These people are frequently left out of decision making when they are embedded in small projects.

Case Study: The Case of the Well-Shod Management

The Ajax Software Development Company has 1500 people doing technical work. One of its projects has 500 technical people assigned to 22 subprojects located in nine separate facilities across five states. Each subproject team has an average of three people doing configuration, build, and change control work—call this configuration management. That means 66 technical people are not doing the design work for which they were hired. Ms. Ajax, herself an efficient person, is distressed by this situation. After a whirlwind tour across five states, she realizes that centralizing configuration management really requires just two people at each location to handle location-specific needs and eight people at one central location to provide common functions and design the new configuration management process. How does this look on the corporate balance sheet?

Solution: By centralizing, the 66 people now doing configuration management can be reduced to 26 people, i.e., two people at each location and eight people in one centralized location. This would amount to a saving of 40 staff-years, which at a loaded cost of $170K per staff-year results in a $6.8M annual saving. This saving scaled to the three product teams and six integration teams that comprise Ajax yields a $20.4M saving annually just for centralizing configuration management. Ms. Ajax buys herself another pair of Ferragamo shoes on the way home.

6.8 INVESTMENT

So where should you put your bucks? You should invest in gurus and equip them with the best tools. Build prototypes. Team with customers. Reuse components, and employ object-oriented technology. Centralize key functions. But most of all, hire good, experienced managers and support them with a thoughtfully designed organizational structure. Contain investments with good management. Share librarians, function point counters, cost and schedule estimators, human factors experts, and object-oriented design engineers, among others, as roving paladins across projects to save time and money.

Advancing new technology is a tricky business. Professor Ed Richter of the University of Southern California points out that the more technologically competent an organization is, the more difficult it becomes to adopt new technology. Therefore, one subtle way to encourage adoption would be to explore a new tool or process in a prototype, and if it looks promising, try it out on a few projects. With this experience, it could be deployed by suggesting that projects prove it **out** rather than prove it **in**. There is considerable risk in being leading edge adopters, but vast rewards are available to those who meet the challenge.

6.8.1 Cost Estimation Models

Several automated cost estimation models are available. The two most popular are COCOMO and the Software Life-cycle Model (SLIM). The problem with models is that they are **not** normally calibrated to the experience of the organization, which leads to errors in estimations. Unfortunately, these results are often accepted and the ensuing project plan is poorly done. Automated models should not be used in isolation to estimate costs, but they do provide a basis for estimates, schedule planning, and staff planning and permit periodic risk assessment. Models are effective when they are used by experienced estimators and when supported with historical data and previous experience. Models are developed from curve fits to productivity data from many projects. It is important to calibrate the curve fits to the specific problem, the actual development skills, and the available tools. All models need to be calibrated, qualified, and used with good judgment based on experience and measurements.

SLIM is based on Quantitative Software Management's Software Equation derived from the Rayleigh–Norden model. It has been validated with thousands of real, completed projects.[6] The equation is the product of productivity, effort, and schedule:

$$\text{Quantity of Function} = (\text{Productivity})(\text{Effort})(\text{Schedule}).$$

This result means that the product of the time and effort coupled with the productivity of the development organization determines how much function can be delivered. Extensive empirical study of software data has shown that strong nonlinearity exists in software behavior. This is taken into account by the form of the software equation:

$$\text{Size} = (\text{Process Productivity Parameter})\left(\text{Effort}/\text{B}\right)^{1/3} \left(\text{Time}\right)^{4/3},$$

where

- The process productivity parameter is the development productivity of the organization calibrated from historical data.
- Size is the quantity of function created in NCSLOC, function points, objects, or other measures of function.
- Effort is the development staff months required. It includes all categories of labor used on the project.
- B is a complexity adjustment factor. It provides for specialized skills for integration testing, documentation, and management as the size of the system increases.
- Time is the elapsed calendar development time from the start of detailed design until the product is ready to enter into operational service normally with 95% reliability.

[6] All theory behind the model has been published by Prentice Hall in 1992 in the book, *Measures for Excellence: Reliable Software, on Time, Within Budget* by Lawrence H. Putnam and Ware Meyers.

SLIM is applicable to all types and sizes of projects. It computes schedule, effort, cost, staffing for all software development phases, and reliability for the main construction phase. Because the software equation effectively models design intensive processes and is not methodology dependent, SLIM works well with waterfall, spiral, incremental, and prototyping development methodologies. It works with all languages and function points as well as with other sizing metrics. The model clearly shows the inefficiency of rapid staffing. Putnam and Meyers made this seminal contribution showing how sensitive costs are to tight schedules and that there is a limit to just how fast a software product can be built.

6.8.2 COCOMO[7]

The COCOMO cost estimation model is used by thousands of software project managers and is based on a study of hundreds of software projects. COCOMO is an open model, so all details are published, including the following:

(1) The underlying cost estimation equations
(2) Every assumption made in the model (e.g., "the project will enjoy good management")
(3) Every definition (e.g., the precise definition of the product design phase of a project)
(4) The costs included in an estimate are explicitly stated (e.g., project managers are included; secretaries are not)
(5) COCOMO estimates are more objective and repeatable than estimates made by methods relying on proprietary models
(6) COCOMO can be calibrated to reflect any software development environment, to produce more accurate estimates

COCOMO allows you to define a software structure that meets project needs. Initial estimates might be made for a system containing 3K NCSLOC. A second estimate might be more refined as the system really consists of two subsystems with more accurate size estimates for each subsystem. The next estimate continues the process of decomposition and estimation until staff estimates converge from iteration to iteration.

The fundamental calculation in the COCOMO model is the effort equation to estimate the number of staff months required to develop a project. Most other COCOMO results, including the staff estimates for determining requirements and doing maintenance, are derived from this quantity. The effort equation is **Effort in Staff Hours = aNCSLOC^b**, where *a* is the inverse of the productivity of a software shop measured in NCSLOC/1000 staff hours and

---

[7] http://www.softstarsystems.com/overview.htm More details can be found at http://sunset.usc.edu/research/COCOMOII.

the exponent b reflects the diseconomy of scale for different types of projects. Efforts for reused components are counted with a different but similar model. The Bernstein model, explained in the magic number following, provides rough estimates for this productivity depending on the type of software being developed.

 **MAGIC NUMBER!**

In the 1960s, Bernstein needed to estimate the size of the staff that would be needed to develop the SAFEGUARD antimissile missile system. This succinct model resulted.

(1) Limit PiDENT size to 1000 LOC to avoid the nonlinear effects of the diseconomies of scale.

(2) Define a formal PiDENT interface tool and process. Isolate the PiDENT interactions to this interface mechanism.

(3) For code that is close to the architecture of the computer or communications hardware or those that have hard real-time constraints, estimate that a good designer will produce 50 LOC per staff month. This is typical for operating systems, communication protocols, or time-constrained, hard real-time systems.

(4) For code that is transaction-oriented, Web-based, or online, estimate 250 to 500 NCSLOC per staff month.

(5) For code that is processing-intensive, estimate 500 to 1000 NCSLOC per staff month for normal applications (low risk, online).

(6) For reused code, estimate 10,000 NCSLOCs per staff month. Sometimes reusing code that does not provide the exact functionality needed can be achieved by reformatting a module's input and output. This decreases performance but dramatically shortens development time and effort.

(7) A staff month is 126 staff hours of actual project work (or 75% of time clocked). Estimates based on number of staff months avoid variables like inflation and currency exchange rates.

(8) Multiply the staff estimate by 1.1 to account for the infrastructure staff needed for build support, coordination, and communications.

Typical values for a and b in the COCOMO model for various circumstances are as follows:

(1) Embedded, operating system, hard real-time software: $a = 3.6$, $b = 1.2$
(2) Semidetached online transaction software: $a = 3.0$, $b = 1.12$
(3) Application report generation and processing software: $a = 2.4$, $b = 1.05$

The b coefficient reflects the variation in scale for different types of projects:

> $b < 1.0$ means that economies of scale exist (hardware manufacturing and component-based software development)
>
> $b > 1.0$ means that diseconomies of scale exist (software development)
>
> $b = 1.0$ means that a linear relation exists and holds for small software projects or components)

Example: The staff needed to develop 100K NCSLOC for an embedded system is $3.6 \times 1001.2 = 900$ staff-hours.

COCOMO was enhanced so that projects could tune the exponent to their type of software and risk factors. The enhancement, COCOMO II, allows estimators to calibrate the exponent b for their organization and problem domain:

$$\text{Effort} = 2.94\,(1.0)\,(8)^{1.0997} = 28.9$$

where $b = 1.01 + 0.01 + \Sigma SF(j)$, $1.01 \leq b \leq 1.26$ and $SF(j)$ are five scale factors representing risk factors for the project and $EAF(i)$ is 1 of 17 cost drivers.

The COCOMO calculations are based estimates of NCSLOC, with the following parameters:

(1) Only source code DELIVERED as part of the product is included— test drivers and other support software are excluded.
(2) The project designers create source code. Code created by applications generators is excluded.
(3) Declarations are included in NCSLOC.
(4) Comments, COTS, reused, and open source code are not counted as NCSLOC.

The original COCOMO was defined in terms of delivered source instructions, which are similar to NCSLOC. The major difference between delivered source instructions and NCSLOCs is that a single SLOC may include reused code. Note that an "if–then–else" statement could be counted as one LOC, but might be counted as several delivered source instructions, leading to confusion in counting rules.

6.8.2.1 COCOMO and Function Points

Versions of COCOMO that support the use of function points have been available since 1987. COCOMO

II supports the use of either function points or SLOC. In both cases, this is done via "backfiring" tables of SLOC per function point for source languages at different levels. This approach is suspect and must be used with care to get a ballpark estimate. Then the estimates can be refined as the project evolves. To translate function points into NCSLOC for use by COCOMO II, the UFPs are used. The UFP is multiplied by a calibrated conversion factor to get an estimate of the NCSLOC. Typical conversion factors for popular languages are shown in Table 6.7.[8]

TABLE 6.7. COCOMO II UFP Conversion Factors by
Language (http://www.qsm.com/FPGearing.html)

Language	Typical Conversion Factor (SLOC/Function Point)
C	128
C++	53
HTML	53
JAVA and JAVA script	63
Perl	21
UNIX Shell	21
Visual Basic	29
Visual C++	34

Organizations should develop their own conversion factors from their historical project data. These conversion factors are consistent with the expansion factor of languages. The lower the conversion factor, the higher the expansion.

6.8.2.2 Scale Drivers SF(j)   In COCOMO II, some of the most important factors contributing to a project's duration and cost are the Scale Drivers. You set five Scale Drivers to describe your project; these Scale Drivers determine the exponent used in the Effort Equation. The Scale Drivers are as follows:

(1) Precedentedness measures the amount of experience an organization has in the application domain. As new versions of a software product are developed, a software product line emerges. The longer the organization works on the product line, the higher the precedentedness.
(2) Development Flexibility.
(3) Architecture/Risk Resolution.
(4) Team Cohesion.
(5) Process Maturity.

[8] This table is adapted from Boehm, Barry. *Software Cost Estimation with COCOMO II*, Prentice Hall, Englewood Cliffs, NJ. Appendix lists "typical" conversion factors for 46 source languages.

6.8.2.3 Cost Drivers EAF(i) COCOMO II has 17 cost drivers. You assess
your project, development environment, and team to set each cost driver. The
cost drivers are multiplicative factors that determine the effort adjustment
factor (EAF) needed to finish a software project. For example, if your project
will develop software that controls an airplane's flight, you would set the
required software reliability (RELY) cost driver to very high. That rating
corresponds to an effort multiplier of 1.26, which means that your project will
require 26% more effort than a typical software project. COCOMO II defines
each cost driver and the EAF associated with each rating.

6.8.2.4 COCOMO II Effort Equation The COCOMO II model makes its
estimates of required effort in staff months, based primarily on the estimate
of the software project's size: Effort = (2.94) (EAF) $(KSLOC)^b$, where EAF
is derived from the cost drivers and the coefficient b is an exponent derived
from the five scale drivers. Here, 2.94 is derived from calibrating the small
module productivity as 1000 LOC/2.94 = 340 LOC/staff month. We switch to
staff months because for larger projects, it is easier to plan in staff months.

Example: A project with all nominal cost drivers and scale drivers would have
an EAF of 1.00 and coefficient, b, of 1.0997. Assuming it is projected to consist
of 8000 NCSLOCs, COCOMO II estimates that the project requires 28.9 staff
months:

$$\text{Effort} = 2.94 \, (1.0) \, (8)^{1.0997} = 28.9$$

If the project did not have a nominal EAF, but is rated very high for complexity (effort multiplier of 1.34), and low for language and tools experience
(effort multiplier of 1.09), and all other cost drivers are rated to be nominal
(effort multiplier of 1.00), the EAF is the product of 1.34 and 1.09:

$$\text{Effort Adjustment Factor} = \text{EAF} = (1.34)(1.09) = 1.46,$$

$$\text{Effort} = (2.94)(1.46) \quad (8)^{1.0997} = 42.3 \, \text{Person-Months.}$$

6.8.2.5 Scheduling with COCOMO II Once a project is sized in terms of
the number of NCSLOC or function points and the number of staff months
required is computed, the nominal elapsed time in months to develop the
project may be estimated (T_{nominal}). Studies of many projects show that development schedules set at less than $0.75 \, T_{\text{nominal}}$ fail most of the time.

The schedule model is $T_{\text{nominal}} = 2.5 \, (\text{staff months})^{1/3}$ and, once knowing time
and the number of staff, the plot shown in Figure 6.7 may be drawn.

The project manager can now develop a staffing plan by dividing the
number of staff months needed by the nominal time. The staffing plan must
allow for some indoctrination and training time initially and for phasing staff

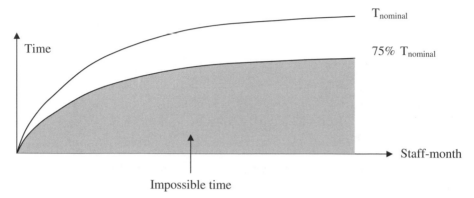

Figure 6.7. Nominal time to project completion. Barry Boehm. Software Engineering Economics, 1982. Reprinted by permission of Pearson Education Inc., Upper Saddle River, NJ.

MAGIC NUMBER!

Barry Boehm points out that "A project cannot be done in less than 75% of theoretical time."

---

onto and off the project in addition to straightforward development. Another staffing consideration, as we have seen in the calculation of Bernstein's model in Section 6.8.2, is that people tend to spend 25% of their work time on non-project activities.

COCOMO II has a slightly different schedule equation. The constant permits a different curve fit. The duration is based on the prediction of the effort equation:

$$\text{Duration} = 3.67 \quad (\text{Effort})^{\text{SE}},$$

where Effort is derived by the COCOMO II effort equation and SE is the schedule equation exponent derived from the five scale drivers.

Example: Substituting 0.3179 for the exponent SE that is calculated from the scale drivers yields an estimate of just over a year, and an average staffing of between three and four people: Duration = 3.67 * $(42.3)^{0.3179}$ = 12.1 months, and then Average staffing = (42.3 Person-Months)/(12.1 Months) = 3.5 people.

6.8.2.6 SCED Cost Driver

The COCOMO cost driver for the required development schedule (SCED) is unique and requires a special explanation. The SCED cost driver is used to account for the observation that a project developed on an accelerated schedule will require more effort than a project developed on its optimum schedule. A SCED rating of very low corresponds to an effort multiplier of 1.43 (in the COCOMO II.2000 model) and means that you intend to finish your project in 75% of the optimum schedule (as determined by a previous COCOMO estimate).

Example: Continuing the example used earlier, but assuming that SCED has a rating of very low, COCOMO produces these estimates:

Duration = (0.75)(12.1 Months) = 9.1 Months,

Effort Adjustment Factor – EAF = (1.34)(1.09)(1.43) = 2.09,

Effort = 2.94 (2.09) $(8)^{1.0997}$ = 60.4 Person Months,

Average project staffing = (60.4 Person-Months)/(9.1 Months) = 6.7 people.

Notice that the calculation of duration is not based directly on the effort (number of staff-months); instead, it is based on the schedule that would have been required for the project assuming it had been developed on the nominal schedule. Remember that the SCED cost driver means "accelerated from the nominal schedule."

The NASA module reuse analyses mentioned in Section 6.6.2 are shown graphically in Figure 6.8. Notice the nonlinear relationship between the amount of change and the cost of making the change.

Example: The software engineer can trade off duration for effort. Let us estimate the staffing needed for a new customer relations management project. Project architecture is client/server with online transactions. About 20% of all modified modules are changed. From Figure 6.8, changing them would cost half of the original development, so a coefficient of 0.5 is used. The reused "as is" modules and the COTS are estimated to require 5% of the cost of original development for transaction systems suing the Bernstein model. The size of the modules and project is shown in SLOC in Table 6.8.

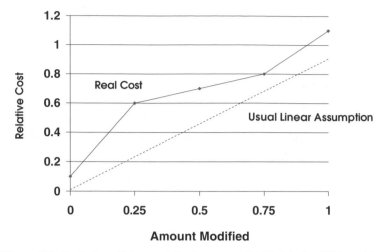

Figure 6.8. *Cost of modifying modules for reuse—NASA data for 2954 modules.*

TABLE 6.8. Example Project Size in SLOC

	New Modules	Modified Modules	Reused "as is"	COTS
Client	25 k	5 k	10 k	0
Server	13 k	15 k	10 k	100 k
Total	38 k	20 k	20 k	100 k

Size = new code + 0.5 (modified modules) +
   0.05 (reused modules + COTS modules) = 54 k SLOC.

Using the likely estimate from Table 6.9, the project requires about 11 people for 20 months. Then the nonproductive time must be included, $(11) \times (1.25)$ is about 14 people, and if we include 1 month for training and orientation and 1 month phase-out, the project needs 14 people for 20 months. Rather than having a flat staffing plan, it is better to bring a few people on early and then add people as you need them.

TABLE 6.9. COCOMO Yield

	Time	Effort
Optimistic estimate	18 months	172 staff months
Likely estimate	20 months	216 staff months
Pessimistic estimate	21 months	270 staff months

6.8.2.7 Recap   Follow these steps to apply an estimation model:

(1) Understand and validate the requirements, and sketch out a first-cut architecture.
(2) Estimate the size of the product.
(3) Estimate the staff-months needed using COCOMO II or SLIM, Wideband Delphi, and Bernstein's model.
(4) Compare the results, and understand significant differences.
(5) Iterate until estimates tend to converge.
(6) Account for expansion provided by Web toolset.

6.8.3 Scheduling Tools—PERT, Gantt

We have decided what is to be done and have planned the order of doing it. Now names must be put to tasks. Plan by using a chart of activities in the form of a network, called a PERT chart. It shows dependencies and elapsed time for each task. For each milestone, keep two dates, one the "schedule" that you own and the other, a "current estimate" that the developer owns. Critical path analysis (CPA) can be used in conjunction with PERT analysis to identify critical tasks in the project. Gantt charts, which are named for their inventor, are bar charts that display the project status and results of PERT in a format that can be readily understood. Planning is not complicated, but it is tedious; that is why the temptation is so strong to avoid it or to do it once and then not keep the plan current.

A project is a set of activities that ends with a specific accomplishment and that has (1) nonroutine tasks, (2) distinct start/finish dates, and (3) resource constraints (time/money/people/equipment). Tasks are activities that must be completed to achieve project goal. Therefore, break a project into tasks and subtasks. Tasks have start and end points, are short relative to the project, and are significant with measurable end points. Use verb–noun form for naming tasks, e.g., "create drawings" or "build prototype." Use action verbs such as "create," "define," and "gather" rather than "will be made." Each task has duration. It is good to estimate a likely, optimistic, and pessimistic duration for each task and then compute an estimate using the PERT approach as

Estimate = (optimistic duration + 4 likely duration + pessimistic duration)/6.

Milestones are important checkpoints or interim goals for a project. They are used to detect scheduling problems early. Name milestones using noun–verb forms, e.g., "test plan due," "computer ordered," or "prototype complete."

6.8.3.1 Work Breakdown Statement   A work breakdown statement (WBS) is a categorized list of tasks with an estimate of resources required to complete the task. A small sample of a WBS appears in Table 6.10.

TABLE 6.10. Work Breakdown Statement

WBS #	Task Description	Est. Staff Hrs	Who	Resources
5	Profile operating system			Target computer
5.1	Design test driver	20	SE, JM	
5.2	Build test driver	15	SE, JM	Frame & brake parts
5.3	Test 3 components	3	SE, JM	Data reduction
5.4	Plot torque vs. speed	2	JM	Excel

6.8.3.2 *Gantt Chart Basics*   Make a big project into lots of small ones. A Gantt chart is a project-planning tool that represents the timing of all tasks required to complete a project. Gantt charts are used by most project managers for all but the most complex projects because they are simple to understand and easy to construct.

In a Gantt chart, each task takes one row. Dates run along the top in increments of days, weeks, or months, depending on the total length of the project. The expected time for each task is represented by a horizontal bar whose left end marks the expected beginning of the task and whose right end marks the expected completion date. Tasks may run sequentially, in parallel or overlapping.

As the project progresses, the chart is updated by filling in the bars to a length proportional to the fraction of work that has been accomplished on the task. This way, one can get a quick reading of project progress by drawing a vertical line through the chart at the current date. Completed tasks lie to the left of the line and are completely filled in. Current tasks cross the line and are behind schedule if their filled-in section is to the left of the line and ahead of schedule if the filled-in section stops to the right of the line. Future tasks lie completely to the right of the line.

In constructing a Gantt chart, keep the tasks to a manageable number (no more than 15 or 20) so that the chart fits on a single page. More complex projects may require subordinate charts that detail the timing of all subtasks that make up one of the main tasks. Have a column with initials that identifies who is responsible for the task.

Often the project has important events that you would like to appear on the project timeline, but that are not tasks. For example, you may wish to highlight when a prototype is complete or the date of a design review. You enter these on a Gantt chart as "milestone" events and mark them with a special symbol, often an upside-down triangle. Decide what resolution to use in the timeline. For projects of 3 months or less, use days, for longer projects use weeks or months, and for very short projects, use hours.

You can create Gantt charts using a project management computer package or Excel. A sample chart made using Microsoft Project, the most widely used scheduling tool, appears in Table 6.11. It is easier to track progress daily using a table of events with name, schedule date, and current estimate. Then the Gantt need be updated only monthly or quarterly.

TABLE 6.11. Sample Gantt Chart

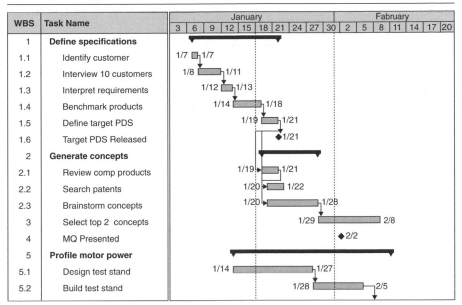

WBS	Task Name	January									February						
		3	6	9	12	15	18	21	24	27	30	2	5	8	11	14	17	20
1	**Define specifications**																
1.1	Identify customer	1/7 ▫ 1/7															
1.2	Interview 10 customers	1/8 ▭ 1/11															
1.3	Interpret requirements	1/12 ▪ 1/13															
1.4	Benchmark products	1/14 ▭ 1/18															
1.5	Define target PDS	1/19 ▭ 1/21															
1.6	Target PDS Released	◆1/21															
2	**Generate concepts**																
2.1	Review comp products	1/19 ▭ 1/21															
2.2	Search patents	1/20 ▭ 1/22															
2.3	Brainstorm concepts	1/20 ▭ 1/28															
3	Select top 2 concepts	1/29 ▭ 2/8															
4	MQ Presented	◆2/2															
5	**Profile motor power**																
5.1	Design test stand	1/14 ▭ 1/27															
5.2	Build test stand	1/28 ▭ 2/5															

6.8.4 Project Manager's Job

A project manager must be responsible for the technical integrity of the system and must have the authority to make tradeoffs among the three main ingredients of project planning, which are like the three sides of a pyramid. These are **resources**, **schedule**, and **features**. If the project as a whole is to retain its shape, your boss or the customer can control any two, but you as the project manager must control the third.

Believe that nobody lies! When you get contradictory reports, bring those involved together and hash it out. People have their own, sometimes different, perceptions of the same situation.

Pay attention to details. Successful software managers track the details and are seen regularly in the thick of things. Do collect appropriate data, but never collect data that you do not use. When things are the worst and nothing is working, the leader is required to show unwarranted optimism.

These points are a "Road Map to Success:"

(1) Start with a small team with broad objectives and build a prototype.

(2) Put the prototype into the field, and use it. Estimate the size of the job. Use function points and an estimation tool such as COCOMO.

(3) After an analysis of the prototype, enlarge the organization from a small team to a large one. If necessary, write detailed requirements and control them.

(4) Using top-down design, partition the project into modules, define and control interfaces, and appoint module owners. Use modern software interface conventions such as object classes, pipes, tag value data, etc.

(5) Reduce complexity in the design with a formal "design minimization" effort. Establish a target of 40% simplification by maximizing reuse, eliminating redundancy, and simplifying algorithms.

(6) Implement designs, using structured programming techniques, only after they have been inspected. Submit tested software, and work practices through an independent manufacturer (or builder) to the quality assurance and integration organization.

(7) Test incrementally. Create a simple working system, and then add sets of changes to gradually increase capability. Do regression tests on each new increment using test cases developed for the previous increment.

(8) Find a friendly operational site where the operators are willing to let developers try out new features before they are formally released.

(9) Have a soak site for new product releases.

(10) Avoid developing a new application on new hardware and/or new operating system software.

(11) Have maintainers share some continuing development responsibility.

6.9 EXAMPLE: APPLY THE PROCESS TO A PROBLEM

We will take a project from the prospectus though first-cut architecture and the resolution of its first major crisis in confronting a business reality. Along the way, we will apply the processes that have been discussed.

6.9.1 Prospectus

A service company currently lacks an online system to allow their clients to access billing information. They recently renovated their company extranet to provide their customers with personalized content. The company needs to aggregate data from various sources including their Microsoft CRM system and QuickBooks Online to provide online invoices and statements. Microsoft CRM stores specific account information, whereas QuickBooks Online houses invoices. The purpose of this new Web system, cleverly called NWS, is to provide a unified programming interface that allows customers to access their account information and invoices without worrying about their underlying details.

The scope of this system is to create a Web service to aggregate accounting information primarily from QuickBooks Online and secondarily from Microsoft CRM. The aggregation of data will be done by interactions among ASP.NET v1.1, Microsoft CRM, and QuickBooks.

NWS supports account inquiries, outstanding invoices, and overdue invoices. Note that this does not include invoices being processed. NWS will support simultaneous access for a minimum of 168 customers and a maximum of 1000 customers with an average of 250.

6.9.2 Measurable Operational Value (MOV)

The present method of operation (PMO) requires a clerk to spend an average of 15 minutes per call for 60 calls per month, or 15 hours/month, handling invoice inquiries. NWS must reduce calls to the clerk by half.

6.9.3 Requirements Specification

There are several assumptions. First, NWS will be written in ASP.NET v1.1. Also, the CRM database will be updated to include information that will help to access invoices, and customer authentication will be done by the CRM administrative module and login.

These assumptions are constrained in certain ways. The system will respond to principle customers only, and they will be permitted to view only their invoice information. NWS will support only Windows 2000 and 2003 advanced server. NWS must comply with these standards: Hungarian notation (The types of variables are encoded into their name; see http://c2.com/cgi/wiki?HungarianNotation), XML document standards for return data, and NUnit testing (see http://www.nunit.org/).

The external interface requirements affect both user and software interfaces. As far as the users are concerned, the invoice interface will look just like what they currently see when they look at their paper invoices. The style of the website will be formatted according to style sheets that are currently being used. This platform-independent application programming interface (API) aggregates data from NWS.

Functional requirements are the same for direct users and for gatekeeper users. Each can view the following:

(1) Single invoices
(2) Outstanding invoices
(3) Overdue invoices
(4) Historical invoices
(5) Next invoice's due date
(6) Add-ons requested from a list that must include core product (license and maintenance), *fund of funds*, directs, benchmarking, private informant, archivist, and analyst (developers, runtime)
(7) Contract terms

Performance requirements demand that the system can handle multiple logins, which means that more than one user should be able to access NWS simultaneously. A user already logged into the system cannot log in again. The invoice request turnaround time should be no longer than 15 seconds, depending on the bandwidth and network used.

System attributes can be described in terms of availability, security, and maintenance effort. The Web service is available 24/7, with scheduled downtime for administrative purposes. The downtime will be scheduled during times when the website will not incur heavy traffic. NWS securely connects to Microsoft CRM and the QuickBooks API using SSL shown in Figure 6.9. Security keys ensure that only authorized customers can make calls to NWS. Concerning ease of maintenance, the software modules code must be loosely coupled, allowing scaling as the customer base grows. The project must be well documented and follow coding conventions. The project must provide a defined normalized interface. The project development will be driven by a combination of prototyping/unit test-driven development through NUnit. The NWS API will be defined using WSDL. Finally, NWS does not modify any existing customer data on either QuickBooks Online or Microsoft CRM.

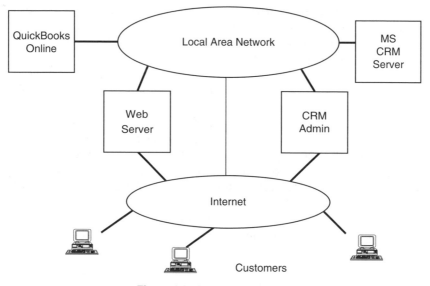

Figure 6.9. First-cut architecture.

Table 6.12 tallies the various elements that are counted for UFPs. For EI and EO, customer access is critical because NWS is a Web service. Customers enter requests as data on a screen and get a screen for every request. A single invoice could be queried by entering a client name, invoice number, or date. The client has the additional option of choosing whether to retrieve an invoice that is historical, outstanding, or overdue. These are four EIs and four EOs. As development proceeds, these may change if new requirements emerge. EQ concerns the fact that NWS must maintain the format of the interface of the current billing system, which can query by customer name, invoice number,

TABLE 6.12. Calculating Unadjusted Function Points for NWS

EIs	4 × 4	16
EOs	4 × 5	20
EQs	3 × 4	12
ILFs	0 × 10	14
EIFs	4 × 7	28
Total UFP		**90**

and date. It will have to deal with the added component of an authentication token to ensure that the customer has permission to access the database. There are three EQs. ILFs are simple internal caches and not counted because they are deemed trivial. EIFs from Figure 6.10 are shown to be CRM, Quick Books, Schematic, and Process/Rules, so there are four.

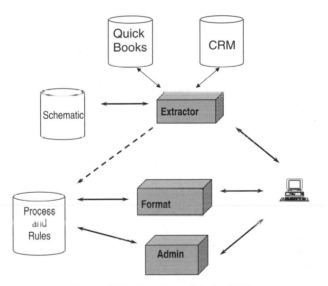

Figure 6.10. *Function points for NWS.*

Table 6.13 shows the degrees of influence ranging on a scale of zero, no influence, to five, strong influence, for each of the 14 general system characteristics.

$$\text{Technical Complexity Factor} = 0.65 + 0.01 \quad * \quad \text{GSC}$$
$$= 0.65 + 0.01 \quad * \quad 29$$
$$= 0.94.$$

$$\text{Function Points} = \text{UFP} \quad * \quad \text{TCF}$$
$$= 90 \times 0.94$$
$$\approx \textbf{85 FPs.}$$

TABLE 6.13. Ranking of General System Characteristics for NWS

General System Characteristics	Degree of Influence	Explanation
Data Communication	5	This has a strong influence because this has to be high because we are constantly communicating with the CRM.
Distributed Data/Processing	2	Data will be distributed between two separate sources, but little processing is needed on data.
Performance Objectives	2	The response time and the throughput are required for this Web service.
Heavily Used Configuration	0	N/A
Transaction Rate	4	The current transaction is extremely critical to the Web service; hence, it has a higher degree of influence.
Online Data Entry	1	Very low operational inputs to software.
End-User Efficiency	3	This application has been designed to improve about 50% efficiency for the clients.
Online Update	0	N/A
Complex Processing	1	It has little mathematical or logical processing.
Reusability	4	This application is being used for many clients; hence, it is given a higher degree of influence.
Conversion/Installation Ease	0	N/A
Operational Ease	3	Simplicity of deploying and operating the Web service.
Multiple Site User	4	This service must maintain integrity when accessed by multiple users.
Facilitate Change	0	N/A
Total Degree of Influence VAF	**29**	

Result of Requirements Specification: The project manager decides to use an incremental development approach with five intermediate prototypes and finds that the customer schedule needs cannot be met. When the Gantt chart in Table 6.14 is developed, however, it is clear that there is trouble. The product

TABLE 6.14. Gantt Chart for NWS

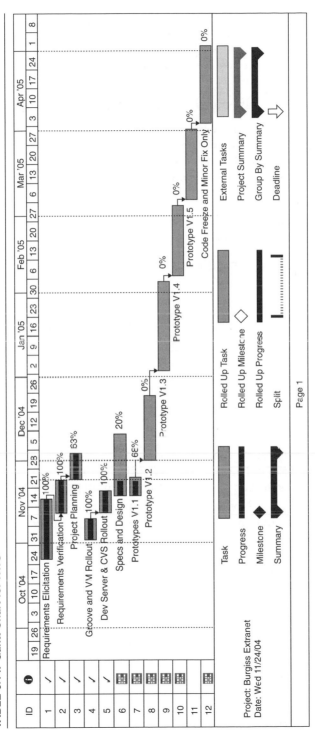

has to be delivered in 15 months, and only 3 developers are available. Notice the aspirations for work in November. Too many tasks were scheduled for the staff available, making the development plan unrealistic. Adjustments can be made to reduce the features, find components to reuse, or hire more staff.

6.9.4 Schedule, Resources, Features—What to Change?

The only option left to the project manager is to drop some features. The simplified quality function deployment (sQFD) approach helps decide which features are expendable. The customer and the developers weigh various requirements as shown in Table 6.15.

TABLE 6.15. sQFD for NWS

System Requirements Features/ Software Functions	Historical Invoices	Outstanding Invoices	Overdue Invoices	Ease of Implementation
Fast Turnaround Time	3	4	5	6
Constant Availability	7	8	8	5
Ease of Use	5	5	5	3
Security	9	9	9	8
Usage	3	6	6	5
Total	27	32	33	

The principle requirements features used as columns in the sQFD for NWS were based on feedback from the customer. They said that NWS must retrieve these three types of invoices. The developers defined the software functions that make up the rows in the sQFD:

(1) Fast Turnaround Time: Turnaround time is the measure of a request to the service and a response (round-trip). Higher priority indicates to us that the system and code must be given attention to optimization.

(2) Constant Availability: The service must maintain high availability while allowing some maintenance time. NWS must be available to respond to customer requests.

(3) Ease of use: Usability is a concern for customers and other developers who will be using the Web service interface. Ease of use should be uniform throughout the feature set so that consistency can be maintained.

(4) Security: Safeguarding customer information is a high priority that must be addressed for all features because NWS accesses and distributes private data.

(5) Usage: The frequency of features use.

Before dropping any feature, a check of the ICED-T analysis is important to consider the overall view of the system as seen by the customer (Table 6.16).

TABLE 6.16. ICED-T Analysis for NWS

	Intuitive	Consistent	Efficient	Durable	Thoughtful
Present Business Process (PMO)	2	4	2	1	1
NWS as an Extranet Future Method of Operation (FMO)	4	5	4	5	5

The ICED-T compares the process in place for invoice retrievals with an NWS-based process. The PMO requires a person to retrieve invoices by manually searching through Quick Books files. Once the invoice is retrieved, it is mailed, e-mailed, or faxed to the customer. NWS allows customers to forego the call and access their invoices. The ICED-T analysis for the PMO is as follows:

(1) Intuitive (I): The business process currently in place is not intuitive. If the current clerk leaves, the replacement would not easily learn the tricks for finding invoices.

(2) Consistent (C): The business process in place is rated at a high consistency level because the same process is always used when an invoice is requested.

(3) Efficient (E): The current process is not efficient because on average 15 minutes is required to retrieve an invoice. Also, once the invoice is retrieved, there is no guarantee that the customer will not call back and request the same invoice again because it was lost in the mail.

(4) Durable (D): The current process is not durable because it relies on one person to retrieve all invoice requests.

(5) Thoughtful (T): The current process is not thoughtful because by retrieving invoices manually, the time required means that despite best efforts, there are long delays.

Based on the first-cut architecture, an ICED-T evaluation of the future method of operation (FMO), i.e., NWS, showed these results:

(1) Intuitive (I): NWS is intuitive because it uses standard inquires and simple formats. If it was not, the customer would disdain the service we have created and would continue to call for invoices.

(2) Consistent (C): NWS is consistent because queries are made against CRM and QuickBooks. Coding standards and documentation standards will also be consistent because developers need to be able to enhance the system.

(3) Efficient (E): NWS must be efficient because it must be able to serve a large number of users and have fast turnaround time for invoice inquiries.

(4) Durable (D): NWS must be durable because it must be essentially available to customers 24/7, excluding any scheduled downtime.

(5) Thoughtful (T): NWS is thoughtful because it speeds the current business. Also, unlike the manual invoice retrieval process, there is no lost time retrieving the same invoice multiple times and tracking paper invoices. The use of the CRM system and the QuickBooks without modification is vital to easy introduction of the system and eliminates database conversions.

6.10 ADDITIONAL PROBLEMS

6.10.1 Your team is developing a system for a small company that sells one-of-a-kind antiques on the Web. The system will contain modules for creating and editing descriptions of items for sale, uploading descriptions to the website's database, taking orders over the Web, validating and processing credit card payments, maintaining the status—for sale, ordered, or shipped—for each item, creating records of ordered items for mailing by the shipping department, and performing accounting activities for tax and other purposes. Completion on the various modules is as follows:

TABLE 6.17. For Problem 6.10.1

Development Task	Percent Complete
Creating and editing descriptions of items for sale	80%
Uploading descriptions to website's database	90%
Taking orders over the Web	75%
Validating and processing credit card payments	65%
Maintaining the status for each item	95%
Creating records of ordered items' shipping	80%
Performing accounting activities	60%

You estimate that you are about 2 months behind schedule. You will have to tell the client, who understands that scheduling software is not a precise science and will probably agree to a 2-month extension if you have data to show. You are meeting with the client soon. You estimate that you can accomplish one of the following by the time of the meeting. For each possibility, state if you would or would not choose it. Support your answer with a reason based on the mantra: *In all cases do the right thing!*

a. Work on all modules to get them, with any luck, to 90% completion.

b. Get the editing and uploading functions 100% complete and working. Leave five modules in their current state of development.

c. Get status maintenance, shipping order, and accounting functions 100% complete. Leave the four other modules at the current state of completion.

d. It does not matter as none of the three alternatives is any better than the others.

6.10.2 A software organization builds four products. The first one takes 40 staff-months in 4 months' elapsed time. The second takes 10 staff-months in 2 months. The third takes 30 staff-months in 10 months. The fourth assigns two people to it for 2 years.

a. What is the average number of people assigned to a project for this organization?

b. What is the standard deviation of the number of people?

c. What is the median time interval for these projects?

d. If all projects together comprised 10,000 LOC and there were 100 LOC per function point in the language chosen, what is the productivity of the organization in function points per staff-month?

e. What is the range of productivity expressed in function points/staff-month?

6.10.3 A software project is estimated to take 12 months to deliver a release with a four-person team. Three staff-months are devoted to project coordination. In an effort to push forward the delivery date, the client insists that an eight-person team be employed. How long, giving a range of a number of months (min, max), would you now estimate the development time? Provide your analysis.

6.10.4 You are the project manager for a software project with the following statistics:

TABLE 6.18. For Problem 6.10.4

Item	Size
Online Application	100K NCSLOC
4 GL Support Software	250K NCSLOC
Test Drivers	50K NCSLOC
Comments	40% of delivered code
Total Effort	1200 staff-months
Coding and Unit Testing	250 staff-months
Management and Administration	20%

Compute the productivity for the project, and estimate the effort and time it will take to complete the project, making sure to qualify your answer.

6.10.5   You work for a firm that develops software, under contract, to firms in a variety of business areas. You are the project manager of a team working on a 9-month project to develop a new marketing system for a large manufacturing firm. Installation of the system is projected to begin in the middle of month 9. React to the following statement. The best time to raise the question of postinstallation maintenance of the new software is just before installation of the new system (explain your position quantitatively).

a. agree strongly

b. agree

c. disagree

d. disagree strongly

6.10.6   You are working for Optimistic Software Inc. The company is doing fairly well, but it has been over budget and past deadline on too many projects in the past few years. The problem would most likely be corrected by hiring:

a. More good programmers

b. More requirements engineers. (A requirements engineer deals with the customer to determine and specify exactly what the software to be developed by Optimistic Software Inc. should do and how well it must perform, in terms of response time, transaction rate, up-time, etc.)

c. More code testers

d. A management consultant

6.10.7   You are working for Superior Software Inc., a software company that is small enough to have software developers deal directly with customers. The Superior Software sales staff has been talking to Delicious Bakery Inc., a large baked-goods company about developing software to automate one of Delicious Bakery's business operations. You have been assigned to be lead software developer on the Delicious Bakery project. When you determine how much work it will be to develop the software, you decide that you will need one or two of your Superior colleagues to work on the project with you. The best thing to do before you begin to write the software is to:

a. Have the Superior Software sales people who brought the work to Superior spec out the details of the software to be developed and give you the specifications.

b. Discuss the details with the sales staff's Delicious Bakery contact.

c. Discuss the details with the supervisor of the Delicious Bakery department that will be using the software.

d. Discuss the details with the supervisor of the Delicious Bakery department that will be using the software and with the clerks who will be using the software.

6.10.8   You are solving a critical software problem at a customer location. The customer has given you everything you need to do the job, including a comfortable office. The customer asks you to implement an additional new, easy-to-implement feature in the module you are working on. React to the following statement. The best thing for you to do is to reciprocate the customer's kindness and implement the feature.

   a. Agree strongly

   b. Agree somewhat

   c. Disagree somewhat

   d. Disagree strongly

6.10.9   Adding competent programmers late in a project when it is in trouble (explain your answer and cite references) . . .

   a. delays project completion.

   b. speeds project completion.

   c. has no effect on project completion.

6.10.10   Which type of error typically takes the greatest amount of time and effort to correct once a piece of software has been released to the customer?

   a. An error in requirements specification

   b. An error in design

   c. An error in implementation

   d. An error in testing

6.10.11   As a software engineer, you use a PERT chart to plan your project. A segment is shown here:

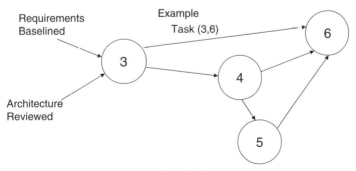

Figure 6.13. For Problem 6.10.11.

TABLE 6.19. For Problem 6.10.11

Task	Description	Time Min. Likely Max.
(3,6)	Staff Project	8 weeks, 12 weeks, 16 weeks
(3,4)	Gather Field Data	1 week, 3 weeks, 5 weeks
(4,5)	Design Scenarios	2 weeks, 4 weeks, 6 weeks
(4,6)	Design Processes	4 weeks, 6 weeks, 8 weeks
(5,6)	Purchase Test Lab equipment	2 weeks, 2 weeks, 2 weeks

(1) Use average times for each task to find the critical path. [Hint: Average time for a task = (Minimum Time + 4 *Likely Time + Maximum Time)/6]

(2) You now have to decide where to invest resources to get your product to market in 8 weeks. Which tasks would you invest in and how would you make the investment?

6.10.12 As a software engineer, you use a PERT chart to plan another project similar to that in 6.9.11. A segment of the PERT chart is shown in 6.10.11.

(1) Use average times for each task, and find the critical path(s).

(2) What is the standard deviation of the critical path? Hint: [standard deviation]^2 = [(upper bound of estimate − lower bound of estimate)/6] and $[1.414]^2 = 2$ and $[1.732]^2 = 3$.

Max Task (3,6) = 12; Min Task (3,6) = 8.

(3) Your manager decides to shift an existing organization from its current work to work on your project, cutting the staffing time of task (3,6) in half. Now what is the critical path(s)?

(4) You now have to decide where to invest resources to get your product to market. Which task would you invest in and why?

6.10.13 Your organization produces five function points per staff-month. You are asked to develop a project with a TCF of 0.9. You size the project in terms of a UFP count of 1000. Qualify your answers. How many people are needed to complete the project if you can fully staff it instantly?

BIBLIOGRAPHY

Albrecht, Allan J. "Software Function, Source Lines of Code, and Development Effort Prediction: A Software Science Validation," *IEEE Transactions on Software Engineering*, Vol. SE-9, No. 6, Nov. 1983, pp. 639–647.

Arthur, Lowell Jay. *Programmer Productivity: Myths, Methods, and Murphology A Guide for Managers, Analysts, and Programmers*, John Wiley and Sons, 1983, pp. 25–27.

Bachman/Function Point Analyst, Product Announcement, Bachman, Inc., 1994.

Bernstein, Lawrence and Lubashevsky, Alex. "Living with Function Points" *AT&T*.

Bernstein, Lawrence and Yuhas, C. M. "Software Investment Strategy," *Engineering Management Journal*, Vol. 7 No. 4, Dec. 1995, pp. 15–21.

Boehm, Barry et al. "Prototyping Versus Specifying: A Multiproject Experiment," *IEEE Transactions on Software Engineering*, May 1984.

Boehm, Barry W., Gray, T. E., and Seewaldt, T. "Prototyping Versus Specifying: A Multiproject Experiment," *IEEE Transactions on Software Engineering*, Vol. SE-10, No. 3, May 1984.

Boehm, Barry. "Software Risk Management, Principles, and Practices," *IEEE Software*, Jan. 1991.

Carleton, Anita D., Park Robert E., and Goethert, Wolfhart B. "The SEI Core Measures: Background Information and Recommendations for Use and Implementation," *CrossTalk*, May 1994.

Desmond, John. "IBM's Workgroup Hides Repository," *Application Development Trends*, April 1994, p. 25.

Dijkstra, E. "The Humble Programmer," 1972 ACM Turing Award Lecture in *Classics in Software Engineering*, 1979.

Fairley, Richard. "Risk Management for Software Projects," *IEEE Software*, May 1994, pp. 57–67.

"Function Points as Asset Reporting to Management," *IFPUG*, 1990.

Garmus, Dave. "Function Point Counting," *Software Development*, Sept. 1993, pp. 67–69.

Humphrey, Watts. *A Discipline for Software Engineering*, Addison-Wesley, Reading, MA, 1995.

Humphrey, Watts. *Managing the Software Process*, Addison-Wesley, Reading, MA, 1989.

International Function Point Users Group.

Jones, T. Capers. "What are Function Points?" *Software Productivity Research*.

Jones, T. Capers. *Applied Software Measurement*, McGraw-Hill, New York, 1991.

Jones, T. Capers. *Programming Productivity*, McGraw-Hill Book, New York, 1986, pp. 83–210.

Kemerer, Chris F. "Reliability of Function Points Measurement," *Communications of the ACM*, Feb. 1993, pp. 85–97.

Lusher, Paul W. "Function Point Analysis for Real Time Weapons Control," *IFPUG Conference Proceedings*, Sept. 1992.

Mills, Harlan. *Software Productivity*, Dorset House Publishing, New York, 1988, pp. 13–18.

Poulin, J. S., Caruso, J. M., and Hancock, D. R. "The Business Case for Software Reuse," *IBM Systems Journal*, Vol. 32, No. 4, 1993, pp. 567–594.

Pressman, Roger. "Hackers in a Decade of Limits," *American Programmer*, Jan. 1994, pp. 7–8.

Samadani, Hamid, et al. "Army Reuse Center Tackles CASE-Based Reuse," *Cross Talk*, May 1994.

Selby, R. "Empirically Analyzing Software Reuse in a Production Environment," in *Software Reuse: Emerging Technology*, W. Tracz (Ed.), IEEE Computer Society Press, New York, 1988, pp. 176–189.

The National Software Council Charter, April 1995.

Tomayko, James E. *Sizing Software*, Carnegie Mellon University, Pittsburgh, PA.

Walston, C. E. and Felix, C. P. "A Method of Programming Measurement and Estimation," *IBM Systems Journal*, No. 1, 1977, pp. 54–60.

Yourdon, Edward Nash. *Classics in Software Engineering*, Yourdon Press, New York, 1979, p. 122.

7

Design for Trustworthiness

Software design usually means a description of the implementation of a software system after it is finished. This "bottom-up" approach can result in working systems, but they are difficult to enhance and it is even more difficult to determine how trustworthy they are. By trustworthy we mean that a software product or component is safe, reliable, and secure. Software design is an important first step, not the final step, when creating trustworthy systems. This chapter provides design techniques and constraints on the software implementation that will lead to making a system trustworthy. The goals of the design process are to create a simple and concise solution. Simplicity improves reliability, and conciseness reduces the time and cost of implementation.

Software system development is often dominated by schedule and cost. Sometimes performance and functional technical requirements become an issue. Rarely has trustworthiness been considered in any but the most critical systems, but this is changing. Society as a whole is beginning to recognize that not only must software designers consider how the software will perform, but also they must account for the consequences of failures. Trustworthiness encompasses this concern.

This issue is so important that it is a fundamental theme taught in all courses in the quantitative software engineering program at Stevens Institute of Technology and in the Graduate School on Trustworthy Software Systems (TrustSoft) at the University of Oldenburg, Germany. Ph.D. fellowships are being offered for the study of trustworthy software; see http://trustsoft.uni-

Trustworthy Systems Through Quantitative Software Engineering,
by Lawrence Bernstein and C. M. Yuhas
Copyright © 2005 IEEE Computer Society

oldenburg.de. Les Hatton, now Professor of Forensic Software Engineering at the University of Kingston in London, developed the study of software forensics to get to the root causes of system failures. Colin Tully has done seminal work analyzing software system failures; his report on the London Ambulance Dispatch System was the basis for the case study in Chapter 3. Professor Sha of the University of Illinois has written eloquently on how simple software leads to reliable software.

The dependency on software systems intensifies the consequences of software failures. The need for trust is gaining industry awareness. Several software vendor consortia plan to develop "Trusted Computing" platforms. These initiatives focus primarily on security, but trustworthiness is a much broader concept. The hope for the software industry rests with people who recognize this responsibility and embrace it.

This chapter departs from the usual approach of software design literature that focuses on describing tools, data layouts, and object classes.[1] Although these issues are important, they are not sufficient to deal with the issue of getting the design right. Everything may be done brilliantly without a thought to high complexity. Complexity is always expensive in terms of staff, time, and reliability. The approach we take is to apply the concept of design simplification to software because it will give you a system that is stable and trustworthy, cheaper and sooner.

7.1   WHY TRUSTWORTHINESS MATTERS

The software industry seems to be exempt from liability suits and from the legal need to practice due diligence. The underlying problem with making systems trustworthy is not technical—it is the legal and business structure of the software market. This tacit exemption slows the adoption of trustworthy technology because every business responds primarily to what the customer demands in order to prosper and conversely to what will damage the business if it is not provided. The state-of-the-**practice** lags the state-of-the-**art** by a wide margin. There are few financial consequences to companies that produce dangerous software, but their survival is at stake for companies that are slow to market. The software industry operates on the caveat emptor principle.

Corporate fraud has stimulated the call for corrective action. The Sarbanes–Oxley Act (SOX) is driving a wider interest in trustworthy software. Over half of Fortune 1000 companies are still using spreadsheets or other manual methods to manage and control commissions and other types of variable pay. These methods are error-prone and raise concerns under SOX. Enterprise incentive management software must enable the financial control cleanup required by SOX, Sections 302 and 404 of which are reprinted in the Bibliography.

---

[1] Van Vliet, Hans. *Software Engineering—Principles and Practices*, 2nd ed., John Wiley and Sons, New York, 2000, ch. 10–12.

Trustworthiness is a holistic property, encompassing security, safety, and reliability. It is not sufficient to address only one or two of these diverse dimensions, nor is it sufficient to simply assemble components that are trustworthy. Integrating the components and understanding how the trustworthiness dimensions interact is a challenge. The increasing complexity and scope of software will make trustworthiness a dominant issue. Microsoft claims to have undertaken a Trustworthy Computing initiative. Bill Gates sent a memo to his entire workforce demanding ". . . company-wide emphasis on developing high-quality code that is available, reliable and secure-even if it comes at the expense of adding new features."[2]

Software **fault tolerance** is at the heart of the building trustworthy software, although it seems a contradiction in terms at first blush. Trustworthy software is stable. It is sufficiently fault-tolerant that it does not crash at minor flaws and will shut down in an orderly way in the face of major trauma. Trustworthy software does what it is supposed to do and can repeat that action time after time, always producing the same kind of output from the same kind of input. The National Institute of Standards and Technology (NIST) defines trustworthiness as "software that can and must be trusted to work dependably in some critical function, and failure to do so may have catastrophic results, such as serious injury, lost of life or property, business failure or breach of security."[3] Some examples include software used in safety systems of nuclear power plants, transportation systems, medical devices, electronic banking, automatic manufacturing, and military systems. To repeat, trustworthy software is software that is appropriately dependable. The architect working with the engineer determines what constitutes appropriateness. A committee of the International Federation for Information Processing, IFIP WG-10.4, defines dependability as, "the trustworthiness of a computing system which allows reliance to be justifiably placed on the service it delivers."[4]

A study sponsored by the NIST in 2001 found that software errors cost the U.S. economy an estimated $59.5 billion annually, or about 0.6% of the gross domestic product. Much effort has been expended in developing methods for reliability, safety, and security analysis, as well as methods to design these systems; yet the "good practice" results of this work are often not used in system development. This chapter integrates these design methods within a trustworthiness framework.

7.2 SOFTWARE RELIABILITY OVERVIEW

The most common reliability model is $R(t) = e^{-\lambda \cdot t}$, where λ is the failure rate. This equation is valid when the failure rate is constant over time and implies

---

[2] *Information Week*, Jan. 21 2002, No. 873, p. 28.
[3] NIST SP 500-204 High Integrity Software Standards and Guidelines, July 1992.
[4] http://www.dependability.org/wg10.4.

a Poisson probability distribution of failures. This assumption is reasonable if we constrain the design of the software, even though faults tend to cluster in a few software components. A constant failure rate was reported in the second issue of the *IEEE Dependability Magazine* based on IBM and Microsoft data.[5] To paraphrase their results, if good change control and attentive corrective maintenance is practiced, 10 months after the third release, the failure rate is a constant.

MAGIC NUMBER!

First, make it work.
Then, make it work right.
Finally, make it work better.

Software execution is sensitive to initial conditions and the external data driving it. What seem to be random failures are actually repeatable. The problem in finding and fixing these problems is the difficulty of doing the detective work needed to discover, first, the particular initial conditions and, second, the data sequences that trigger the fault so it becomes a failure.

In a two-state continuous-time Markov chain, the parameters to be estimated are failure rate λ and repair rate v.

The Mean Time Between Failures (MTTF) = $1/\lambda$.

The Mean Time To Repair (MTTR) = $1/v$.

The steady-state availability is

$$\text{Availability} = \text{MTTF}/(\text{MTTF} + \text{MTTR}) = 1/(1 + \lambda/v).$$

The goal of software testing is to make $R(0) = 1$.

The goal of Software Fault Tolerance is to make Availability = 1.

Professor Sha's model of reliability is based on these observations:

(1) Complexity introduces faults and faults lead to failures. For a given execution time software reliability decreases as complexity increases.

(2) Faults are not equal; some are easy to find and fix and others are not. Faults are not random, but they are sometimes obscure and make failures intermittent.

(3) All budgets have limits, so there is not unlimited time or money to pay for exhaustive testing.

---

[5] Siewiorck, Daniel P., et al. "Reflections on Industry Trends and Experimental Research in Dependibility," *IEEE Transactions on Dependable and Secure Computing*, Vol. 2, No. 2, April/June 2004, p. 120.

Sha chooses the MTTF as equal to E/kC. Then the reliability of the system is $R(t) = e^{-kCt/E}$, where k is a scaling constant, C is complexity, E is the development effort, and t is the continuous execution time for the software. Determining complexity (C) is the challenge in establishing the reliability of a software system. The development effort (E) can be estimated by such tools as Checkpoint, Constructive Cost Model (COCOMO), or the Software Life-Cycle Model tool (SLIM). These estimators give a lower bound to the staff and time needed. Project managers can choose to staff beyond these estimates to improve the reliability of the software. Development effort is a function of the complexity of the software in the models, so average complexity should be used. $R(0) = 1$ because all startup failures are assumed to be removed through classic unit, block, and system testing.

Bernstein extends the equation by adding an effectiveness factor (ε) to the denominator: $R(t) = e^{-kCt/E\varepsilon}$, where ε reflects the investment in software engineering tools, processes, and code expansion that makes the work of one programmer more effective. Let ε be the expansion factor that expresses the ability to solve a program with fewer instructions with a new tool such as a complier.

The longer the software system runs, the lower the reliability and the more likely a fault will be executed to become a failure. Reliability can be improved by limiting the execution time t; by investing in tools, thereby increasing ε; by simplifying the design to reduce C; by increasing the effort E in development to do more inspections or testing than required; or by a combination of these factors.

A software engineer can make tradeoffs among schedule, level of effort, complexity, tools, and execution time by using this equation, so we call it the Unified Equation of Software Engineering. It is reasonable, if unorthodox, to model the software engineering process based on this model. The longer the software executes, the more likely it is to execute a latent fault that soon becomes a failure. A fault is an external human error that becomes incorporated in the software. Failure is a state of no response to external stimuli because a fault executes.

The difference between a fault and a failure can be understood through a concrete example. Suppose a civil engineer decides that a bridge needs to bear no more that 10 tons in the form of any single vehicle. The size and strength of the materials are based on this, as is the design. There is a sign at both ends of the bridge that says "MAX 10 TONS." A truck with a 25-ton load goes onto the bridge and the bridge collapses. The bridge had a fault, the 10-ton limit based on a traffic analysis that the civil engineer could not know was wrong, but the bridge did not fail until the fault was executed.

The λ incorporates the factors a software project manager controls through the development process. By providing better tools (such as higher level languages) to the designer, the reliability of the final product is better. The project manager reduces the complexity of the system by reusing reliable components and properly integrating them, again making it more reliable. Adding staff beyond the minimum staff predicted by models so that effort can be placed on such activities as diabolic testing and system audits is another way to increase trustworthiness. Specific technologies like software rejuvenation can bound software execution to make it less vulnerable to latent faults.

Trustworthiness has the implied quality of "no surprises." Users (end user or developer integrating a component into a system) have good reason to expect to understand the behavior of the software under all anticipated ranges of inputs and environments, which raises questions about how well the operational context and likely evolution of the system are understood. It also implies that to be trustworthy, software probably has to be robust in the face of unexpected uses and evolutionary change, or at the least, if it is fragile, it has to fail in understood ways. Current software is too surprising, and the sources of these surprises are poorly understood. The software engineer must design for transparency and for better characterization of robustness and the expected operational environment.[6] For example, an air traffic control system that occasionally just stops working is clearly less trustworthy than one that stays alive. If another stays alive but occasionally displays hazardous or misleading information, is it more trustworthy than the one that crashes? The first is unreliable, and the second is unsafe. Both are untrustworthy.

7.3 DESIGN REVIEWS

In our industry, there is a lack of expertise, expensive unproven tools, and questionable practices. The focus on design analysis and simplification offers a low-cost way to introduce trustworthy design principles. The most important step any software organization can take is to conduct design reviews before coding for the production system begins.

The introduction of design reviews in software engineering originated at NASA after the tragic fire on January 27, 1967 during the first major dress rehearsal for the first manned Apollo space flight. Gus Grissom, the first person in space flight; Edward White, the first person to walk in space; and Roger Chaffee all died. Although the unmanned Apollo flights continued on schedule, the manned flights were delayed 18 months for design reviews. On July 16, 1969, Neil Armstrong and Buzz Aldrin on Apollo 11 executed the first lunar landing mission. NASA achieved the national goal set by President Kennedy in 1961 to land on the moon and return to Earth safely within the decade of the 1960s. They did it by developing rigorous design methodology and by capturing the support and hopes of the country.

At Bell Laboratories, the Safeguard Anti-Ballistic Missile (ABM) project adopted NASA's reviews that were developed from 1966 to 1976. Management worked hard to make sure that the reviews did not become pro forma. Two levels of management frequently participated in reviews with engineers, and occasionally higher level managers did.

---

[6] http://www.nap.edu/readingroom/books/trust/.

The reviews dealt with critical issues in a nonthreatening way. Those engineers who found serious problems were publicly lauded and financially rewarded. The culture of the project became one of open discussion of problems before they became crises. Hiding problems was frowned on. At first, it was difficult for managers to understand that the reviews were not a forum for evaluating people. Rather, the reviews were a place to define problems and introduce discipline to the process. Some managers never learned this lesson, and their projects suffered. Another problem was that programmers rebelled at reviews conducted by those whom they could not respect. Whenever management tried to enforce a review but did not participate, it led to a waste of time and poor morale.[7]

IBM Federal Systems Division honed the process of identifying action items and periodic project reviews as a means to follow-up on the problems found during reviews. A top-ten list prepared by the project manager was a valuable tool in focusing the project on the most important problems and allowed all project members to understand how these were solved through written responses that were published in the project meeting reports. These reports became the "newspaper" for the project. The process of reporting on design problems and changes in a project newsletter is good. The project manager gains the "power of the press" through these regular reports.

MAGIC NUMBER!

A project with no problems is a project in deep trouble.

7.3.1 Topics for Design Reviews

The modules that make up the system are identified and mapped into executable processes; their interface data structures are defined, and user interfaces and interactions are specified. Before entering the design review, it is essential to have a reasonably complete set of use-case business scenarios available against which designs can be mapped along with the intent of the requirements.

During the review, select the most important processes; describe how they work together and how data and control logic are exchanged among them. Within each process, select the most important modules and describe their data structure and how they work. Pseudo-code, the prototype, or program

---

[7] Crowly, Thomas H. "Safeguard Data Processing System," *Bell System Technical Journal, Special Supplement*, AT&T, 1975, Section VI.

commentary are useful expressions of the design for these reviews. It is sometimes important to describe complex designs several ways.

These topics need to be covered at the design review:

(1) Modules and their interactions

(2) Process structures

(3) Performance budgets

(4) Data structures and flow

(5) Control structures and flow

(6) Interfaces between processes and with humans

(7) Critical modules including reuse and design patterns

(8) Design for testability

(9) Design for maintainability

(10) Design for reliability

(11) Design for simplicity

(12) A new computation of function points

(13) A new computation of sQFD

(14) A new computation of ICED-T

(15) A current Gantt chart based on the project sizing estimates derived from the design

The design review makes the system more reliable because the process aims at removing complexity, thereby reducing the numerator of the exponent in the universal software engineering equation.

MAGIC NUMBER!

The function points calculated after the design review should be at least 20% less than when the requirements were baselined.

7.3.2   Modules, Interfaces, and Components

The architecture gave a view of allocating software functions to subsystems or modules that are relatively self-contained. The product of this effort is a logical block diagram. Each block contains a set of functions that are logically grouped into modules. The modules hide details of their structure from one another. The features, performance, and trustworthiness of each module need to be understood. Then the module can in turn be subdivided into smaller logical modules.

MAGIC NUMBER!

The lowest level module will contain software that implements one to five function points.

Each module will have a design specification, a schedule, and estimates of staff and performance. Modules may be objects consisting of data structure and procedures or methods with states and defined behavior. The modules are tracked throughout the development process. If incremental programming is used or if there are multiple releases, a module vs. release matrix is useful for planning and tracking.

Case Study: The Case of the Personal Transport Pile-Up

Magilla Transporters, Inc. manufactures one model of the Magilla Personal Transporter that they sell directly to customers. Magilla's computer system consists of an order entry subsystem (OESS) and an inventory/order fulfillment subsystem (I/OFSS).

Orders arrive by telephone or snailmail and are entered into the OESS by clerks. The website also enters orders directly into OESS. The OESS's main function is to check the validity of each incoming order, retain a copy of each valid order in its database, and send valid orders to the I/OFSS.

I/OFSS checks whether there are enough Personal Transporters to satisfy an incoming order. If there are not enough Personal Transporters to fulfill the order, the inventory system puts the order in its database as a "back order." Warehouse workers check back orders each day and notify Magilla's Manufacturing Division whenever the backorders start to pile up.

Magilla currently uses Commercial off-the-shelf (COTS) software packages for its OESS and I/OFSS. They are proprietary products, distributed only as an executable; customers do not get the source code. The following are the transactions recognized from terminals or the website by the OESS:

Place New Order
View All Orders
Cancel Order by Order Number

You also have access to the system's main customer/order file. Manual pages detail the transactions and access to the file.

The system was working well and Magilla's sales were increasing nicely when they suddenly got word that Schlepper Shipping, Inc. is going out of business. Mr. Schlepper is retiring to Florida. The U.S. Post Office (USPO) agrees to contract for the shipping, but So-So Software, Inc. has neglected to include the customer name in the file and the USPO will do the shipping only if the customer name is added to the address. Mr. Schlepper was kind enough to ship without customer names, even though it caused some problems (he liked talking to people and working things out). Magilla asked So-So Software to make this small change in the system, but So-So wants far more money than Magilla feels is reasonable.

You are the CIO heading the Magilla IT shop. You are asked to upgrade the system and free Magilla from So-So's control. Your people need to make the changes without modifying So-So's code so as not to void the 5-year service warranty that Magilla bought from So-So. You assign a top-notch team of five people, and after 2 weeks, they produce a prototype of the upgraded system with this "4 + 1" view (Figure 7.1).

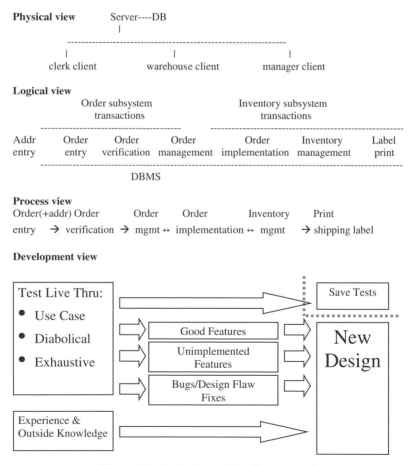

Figure 7.1. *4 + 1 views of Magilla case study.*

Your people have benchmarked the system and are well on their way to meeting Magilla's needs. You have just committed the version for operation in 3 weeks to the CEO and the board of directors showing that the IT shop meets the needs of the business. Then So-So releases a new version of the system to save their contract. So-So insists that all their customers upgrade to the new version, because the older version is no longer supported. The contract allows for such upgrades, and if customers demure, So-So may discontinue support. Your people have developed the simplified quality function deployment (sQFD) in Table 7.1 and ask for a 1-month extension to the schedule to fold in the new So-So feature set. The sQFD shows that So-So's features are fundamental to Magilla's business.

TABLE 7.1. sQFD For So-So's Feature Set

Features/ Functions	Ease of Implementation	So-So Feature Set	Zip code	Search	Shut down	Multiuser
Software Stability	1	10	0	0	0	6
Label Changes	8	3	10	10	10	0
New Inventory Pending	8	5	10	6	1	5
More efficient	4	10	0	0	0	5
TOTAL		28	20	16	11	16

You decide to hold to the committed schedule and hope that because So-So wants to keep the business, they made sure the new release works. Your test team does regression testing, and all goes well. You release the system with great fanfare, and 1 month later, it fails because of a memory leak and a counter overflow. The memory leak failure was a fault in the original So-So code that happened never to be executed previously.

Conclusion: Even if your development shop can produce trustworthy systems on schedule and within budget, there are things out of their control:

(1) Do not trust legacy code.
(2) Do not expect fixes from the supplier if you fire them.
(3) A new module delivery requires exhaustive testing.
(4) Do not compromise your development processes to meet a date.
(5) Never make two changes at once. Minimize risk by relying on your **previously tested** configuration and upgrade the supplier's in a later release.

7.3.3 Interfaces

A single entry and a single exit point make updating interfaces easier (Figure 7.2). The module starts with a text preface explaining its functions, inputs, outputs, and containing change control information. A jump table follows to gain access within the module. All control and all data are passed to the jump table that then transfers execution to the appropriate place in the module dictated by the input parameter. If this transfer is too expensive in execution time, direct transfers and passing data through memory is possible, but this obscures the dependency and makes it more difficult to reduce coupling. The goal of the design is for high cohesion within a module and low coupling between modules.

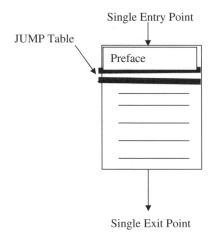

Figure 7.2. *Ideal interface.*

Parnas points out that design can be the assembly of many modules. The modules can be connected together and may have interchangeable parts, but they must be able to be designed, implemented, and tested independently. A software module is a cohesive collection of data and procedures that provides a set of services to other modules. The module provides an interface that allows other modules to use the services the module provides or pass data between modules, where the interface is language for requesting services. For a low-coupled design, add a level of indirection passing data and control parameters through a special interface object class, which makes the system harder to understand but easier to evolve.

In Figure 7.3, let C stand for the module order entry from the Magilla case study, let M stand for order management, and let S stand for inventory management. They all use the same parameters. This requires code in each of the three modules to handle two parameters—six interfaces. We can refactor the interfaces to create a single interface object that C, M, and S use to reduce the code. The added benefit is that the structure of the parameters can be elim-

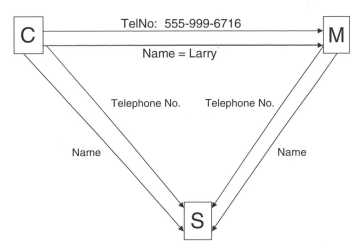

Figure 7.3. *Canonical form.*

inated by using a canonical form so that we avoid the undesired interactions described in Jackson's design methodology.

Now if a change is made to the definition of the parameters between C and M but not S, all modules and use cases require retesting. To avoid affecting S and further decoupling the modules, a tag/value language can be used for parameter passing (Figure 7.4). The tag carries the definition of the parameter, and similar code is added to each module to interpret the parameter's structure.

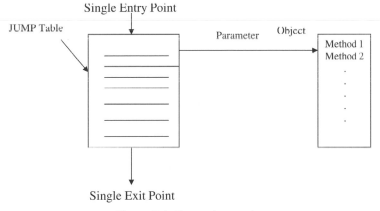

Figure 7.4. *Parameter passing.*

Consider the problem caused when using a method that runs different paths depending on the type of parameter. We create a separate method for each type of parameter as shown in the following example:

```
Set value (String Name, Value){
        If Name.equals ("height")
            Height = value
        if Name.equals ("width")
            Width = value
        if Name.equals ("Anything else")
            Error ("Input should be width or height")
```

If the units change from integers to floating point, all modules will have to change. A better arrangement is

```
            Set height (integer, argument)
                Height = argument
            Set width (floating point, argument)
                Width = argument
```

Now when C and M change, a new data item can be added to the object along with changes to parameter handling code in C and M, but S remains unscathed by the change. This decoupling avoids the cascading problem that makes it so difficult to changes modules and their interfaces.

7.3.4 Software Structure Influences Reliability

Parnas uses structure to mean how a software system is divided into modules and the assumptions that the various modules make about each other. A module is intended to be a unit of work assigned to groups of programmers or individual programmers. If the module is also a component, it can be constructed with no knowledge of the internal structure of other modules.

Parnas explains that **reliable** software need not be **correct** software. "We may consider the system reliable in spite of faults if either (1) the programming errors do not make the system unusable (e.g. format of output, erroneous output which is easily detected and corrected by the user) or (2) the situations in which the errors have an effect do not occur very often, and the situations are not especially likely to occur at moments when the need for the system is very great."[8] If the domain of execution of the software is bounded so that a fault is not executed, the system cannot fail because of that latent fault.

Unreliability occurs when modules are designed on the assumption that nothing will go wrong. The software structure may assume that everything

[8] Parnas, D. L. "The Influence of Software Structure on Reliability," *Proceedings of the International Conference on Reliable Software*, ACM Press, Los Angeles, CA, 1975, http//portal.acm.org/citation.cfm?id=808458.

outside the software behaves correctly; software faults will not be executed. Alternatively, the structure can assume an "all or nothing" approach with no definition of degrees of imperfect behavior. These precautions must be taken to avoid problems:

(1) Specifications for the system and each module must define the desired behavior and what to do when perfect behavior is not obtainable.

(2) Interfaces between the system and its environment and the interfaces between modules require the programs to be suspicious. Specify not only what the interfacing elements should do in the normal case, but also which assumptions should be verified by run-time checks and which actions are required when an error is detected.

(3) Include in the interfaces conventions for informing affected modules about things that have gone wrong elsewhere in the system.

Table 7.2 below shows a possible checklist. It is possible to generate an arbitrarily long checklist of such questions, ending when the risk exposure is acceptable.

TABLE 7.2. Parnas Design Checklist for Reliability

	Event	Does the architecture define:
On interfaces	Communications equipment failures during transmission	a. How will the system be informed? b. How much information about the failure will be supplied? c. How should the system respond?
	Operator error	a. What action should the system take if an operator inputs a message with a priority beyond the operator's privileges? b. How can an operator indicate that an error was made?
Does the system keep message logs?	Secondary storage or storage area network failure	a. What corrective action should the system take if the mass storage device or storage area network loses the logs? b. How fast must messages be recovered from any backup?
Fault Tolerance	Memory error	a. How can the system detect the failure of part of the main memory? b. Does the interface to the memory allocation module allow it to be informed that a part of the memory is malfunctioning and should not be allocated? c. What is the response to a detected deadlock? d. If a program erroneously asks for resources without returning them, how should modules be informed of this problem? How should they react?

A strong module interface language makes it easy to handle designs that deal with problems identified from using the checklist. The interface procedures may share data structures and layers of software services. The Flexible Computer Interface Form (FCIF) and TL/1 are examples of such interface languages.

The principles of modular design separate solution details with horizontal decomposition, letting different parts of the problem be handled by different modules. The interface design provides vertical decomposition as modules call one another. Some key ideas are as follows:

(1) Abstraction that leaves things unlikely to change in the interface and implementation details likely to change are left out of the interface.
(2) Information hiding shields design decisions likely to change from other modules, and each module's implementation is a "secret."
(3) Little languages method makes the interface a language that can solve a family of problems instead of just a single problem.

7.3.5 Components

A component is a module that is independent, with clearly defined small interfaces using a highly expressive interface language. Its implementation details are hidden from other modules, and data structures are accessible only through the interface language. It follows a standard. If two components need to transfer data directly because of performance reasons, they are no longer separate components but may be integrated into one component. Components may evolve without requiring a complete set of system tests, but module changes typically require exhaustive release testing.

MAGIC NUMBER!

Testing takes 40% as much time as development for a software release.

7.3.6 Open&Closed Principle

Software components are open for extension and repair but closed for modification.[9] When a component is opened to make a modification, it becomes a new component. Although the notion of components is more limiting than the generality of object-oriented modules, they are the building blocks for stable

---

[9] http://hjem.get2net.dk/nimrod/tipdesign.htm.

and reliable software design. Components isolate software modules. Components are less likely to be unstable.

A module is open if it is still available for extension by adding new code. For example, it should be possible to add fields to the data structures it contains or new elements to the set of functions it performs. A module is closed if it is available for use by other modules and it has a well-defined, stable description in addition to an interface that follows the principles of information hiding. The source code of such a module is inviolate. The only source code changes permitted are those needed to fix a problem, and even these must be carefully controlled.

For programming languages, a closed module is one that may be compiled and stored in a library for others to use. The C run-time libraries are the best example of such libraries. For an application module, closing a module simply means having it approved by management, adding it to the project's official repository of accepted software items, and recording its interface for the benefit of other designers.

The tension between closed and open creates problems in many development approaches. With inheritance and polymorphism, a class can be closed (in the sense that it is complete and delivers what its interface description promises) and open (because you can specialize it). When new subclasses are introduced, neither the original class nor its clients need to be edited or recompiled. This is the **open&closed principle**. When a single change to a program results in a cascade of changes to dependent modules, that program becomes fragile, rigid, unpredictable, and not reusable. This is bad design. The open&closed principle requires that you design modules that **never change**. When requirements change, you extend the behavior of such modules by adding new code, not by changing old code that already works.

It would seem that the open&closed principle is at odds with itself. The normal way to extend the behavior of a module is to make changes to that module. A module that cannot be changed is normally thought to have a fixed behavior. In C++, it is possible to create abstractions that are fixed and yet represent an unbounded group of possible behaviors. A module can manipulate an abstraction. Such a module can be closed for modification because it depends on an abstraction that is fixed. Yet the behavior of that module can be extended by creating new derivatives of the abstraction. It is by using inheritance that we can create derived classes that conform to the open&closed principle.

7.3.7 The Liskov Substitution Principle

The Liskov Substitution Principle states that pointers or references to a class should be able to use objects of derived classes without knowing it. The importance of this principle is illustrated when one considers the consequences of violating it. If there is a function that does not conform to the Liskov Substitution Principle, then that function uses a pointer or reference to a base class but must know about all derivatives of that base class. Such a function violates the open&closed principle because it must be modified whenever a new derivative of the base class is created and leads to cascading changes.

7.3.8 Comparing Object-Oriented Programming With Componentry

The basic idea in object-oriented programming is that software should be written according to a mental model of the actual or imagined objects it represents. It attempts to create "verbs" and "nouns" that can be used in intuitive ways, ideally by end users as well as by software developers.

Software componentry, by contrast, makes no such assumptions, and instead, it states that software should be developed by gluing prefabricated components together. This process would create a "compile, integrate, and test" software process akin to the "assemble, wire, and test" hardware factories. The definitions of useful components, unlike objects, can be counterintuitive. In general, it discourages anthropomorphism and naming, and it is far more pessimistic about the potential for end-user programming.

It takes significant effort and awareness to write a software component that is effectively reusable. Here is a checklist for a software component:

(1) Does it only send and receive data through formal and normalized interfaces?
(2) Is it fully documented?
(3) Has it been tested for its functions and reliability and has it been put under stress?
(4) Are the test plans and results available?
(5) Does it do robust input validity checking?
(6) Does it pass back useful error messages?
(7) Does it anticipate unforeseen uses?
(8) Is building the component financially viable?

Another way to simplify is to use proven software components. For example, projects that want to build their own file manager would need a compelling performance reason to do so. Projects use commercial database systems to avoid the complexity of building their own. Dave Thomas points out that the 1970s table-driven programming approach is an excellent way to build components.[10]

7.3.9 Politics of Reuse

A good idea lives or dies not solely on the basis of its merit, but also by several factors that surround it. "Politics of reuse" means the acceptance of the idea of standardized parts in terms of the creative culture of programming, the busi-

---

[10] Thomas, Dave. "Design to Accommodate Change," IEEE Software, Vol. 22, No. 3, May/June 2005, pp. 14–16.

ness environment in which it is practiced, and the mathematical theory that supports it. The productivity gains promised by reusing software arc problematical. Executives want to see reuse to be competitive; they tend to think it is a matter of discipline in the programming ranks. Engineers, although historically fond of standardized parts, know that reuse without sound theory and control leads to disaster. Everyone is willing, but the application and rewards remain stubbornly elusive. The specter of using a critical billing subsystem that propagates a poor algorithm still lurks.

Many trends, however, suggest that reuse will become commonplace, even though large-scale reuse of software modules is difficult today. There are some successes with reuse to suggest that some projects are getting shorter development intervals at lower cost. Projects that use LINUX, UNIX, and its C libraries get 20% reuse without extra effort. The goal is to reuse software modules as if they were interchangeable parts of hardware.

One big obstacle is that software revision is difficult without the originator's help because so much code is obscure. Designers must work hard to get the logical organization right at every level. It is even more difficult with object-oriented code because the long-reaching effects of early decisions in bottom-up design demand greater insight than top-down design. Managers do not praise their product's internal clarity. Yet only clear code can be modified.

Preserving clarity through cycles of modification is labor-intensive. During Norman Wilson's 5-year tenure as the primary maintainer of research UNIX, he wrote a negative amount of code. The system became more capable, more maintainable, and more portable. Imagine a major software project subtracting code in the course of adding a feature. A four-fold increase in productivity is projected once 80% reuse is achieved, but that percentage is as yet unrealistic. PORTAL provides a set of billing components that can be reused in network management systems to bill for Internet services.[11] PORTAL designers had the foresight to keep the interfaces clear and simple and limit the size of their object libraries. COTS components can lead the software industry to better system designs.

7.3.9.1 *Qualified Successes* Using network management platforms has resulted in significant reuse in software. Fifty percent reuse became commonplace by 1995 after widespread use of platforms, although in 1985 reuse was the exception. Now, however, only a few situations lend themselves to this kind of success.

First, the financial payoff for reuse comes only after a module is used three times. The investment needed to make a module reusable increases the cost of the first use to no benefit for the sponsoring project. The incremental cost for reusability needs somehow to be borne by future users.

Second, today's software development processes are defective because they treat everything as new development. There is no recognition of or funding

---

[11] Buchultz, Chris. "Elevating the Platform," *Telephony*, April 7, 1997, pp. 32–33.

for module owners in one application area to maintain modules for developers in other areas. The "you use it, you own it" philosophy implicit in most software groups makes a self-sustaining reuse culture impossible. I have an example close to home. My son reused a string package to track his school library's overdue book notices. The index scheme needed to be changed. After 2 weeks of failure, he left the package to compute its own worthless index and added a postprocessor to compute the proper index. This processor added a 20% performance overhead, but there was no way to modify the module reliably and the module owner was nowhere to be found. The system was used cheerfully for years, consuming more computer resources than strictly necessary. When his system was expanded to another library, he was long graduated, so the administrators wisely decided not to tinker. If you ever come across a "Glenwood Library Overdue Notice" from some place other than the Glenwood School, you will know that reuse constraints prevented a name change. The lesson learned is that when you reuse a module, do not modify it. Get the module owner to make it more general, live with it as is, or develop it from scratch.

7.3.9.2 *Conditions Fostering Reuse*   The literature, IBM's experience, and our work shows that the following criteria must be met to create a reusable module that is an asset:

(1) Standard interfaces to the operating system must exist and be followed. For example, kernel changes to UNIX are not acceptable. This reduces flexibility in handling new communication protocols.

(2) Standard approaches to module interfaces must apply universally. Abstract mechanisms, such as self-describing tag-value interface design, can penalize performance.

(3) Application generators need to produce about 25% of the products, especially for user interfaces.

7.3.9.3 *Reuse "As Is"*   Data collected on the reuse of 2954 modules of NASA programs (see Figure 6.8) clearly demands the shocking conclusion that to reap the benefits of the extra original effort to make a module reusable, it must be reused essentially unchanged. No change costs 5%; the slightest change drives the cost up to 60%. Within an organization, however, success is possible.

In the category of currently intractable problems, it has been impossible to systematically reuse software across application domains. There is ongoing work in modeling application domains to capture the relationship between requirements and object types so that selecting these features can reuse software architectures. Also, reuse even in the same application domain is successful only when throughput and response time are not overriding concerns. Finally, it is not yet possible to maintain an asset base of software modules except when they are in packaged libraries and when they are utility functions.

Where reuse is successful, there is a high level of management attention to detail and a willingness to invest in design for reusability. Software configuration management assumes that there is an existing base of software components from which the components of a specific system are chosen, assembled, tested, and distributed to a user. Even then, exhaustive retesting is still required to root out what Jackson called "undesired interactions."

7.4 DESIGN PRINCIPLES

Poor design introduces unnecessary dependencies and makes components more difficult both to understand and to integrate into products. Good design is essential to eliminating barriers to multiuse. Good multiuse design requires good software design, using well-known software design principles as well as newer multiuse principles:

(1) Strong cohesion
(2) Weak coupling
(3) Information hiding
(4) Inheritance
(5) Generalization/abstraction
(6) Separation of concerns
(7) Removal of context

7.4.1 Strong Cohesion

When code is cohesive, each code module contains a well-defined set of related functions and does not contain extraneous functions. Strong cohesion reduces the chance that a multiuse component will contain features that are useless or unwanted by other products. For example, a component that intermingles database access statements with data manipulation functions will not be attractive to a product that uses a different database or no database at all.

Even worse, if the data manipulation algorithms in this component depend on the specific type of database access, the component will be unusable in products that store data in different ways. Highly cohesive code would have isolated database access from data manipulation and cleanly separated the two types of code into two modules. Following the practice of strong cohesion will help you to keep invariant features, such as data manipulation, separate from variant features, such as the type of data storage a product uses.

7.4.2 Weak Coupling

Strong cohesion and weak coupling usually go hand in hand. Weak coupling between modules promotes the independence of each module, so that one module does not require knowledge of another. Weak coupling keeps a multi-use component self-contained and more portable, both at compile time and at run-time.

For instance, highly coupled code is likely to bring extraneous include files and functions into the compile; and it is likely to produce overly large run-time components that will port poorly. High coupling usually means unnecessary and unwanted features, more complex product customization, and a greater possibility of disruptive side effects.

7.4.3   Information Hiding

Information hiding and the use of abstract data types allow a product to access a multiuse component without needing to know how the component represents and handles its internal data. Information hiding is the principle that the internal data and operations of a module should remain hidden from other modules. Modules should communicate with each other only through clearly defined interfaces and only communicate what external modules need to know. Information hiding promotes a clear external interface and enhances the ease of use of the component.

Abstract data types are a special case of information hiding, in which a data structure and the functions to manipulate it are encapsulated within a module. Abstract data types provide an important simplification for the product developer, by hiding the details of data handling in the multiuse component.

Another benefit of information hiding is that the multiuse component and product can maintain independent development cycles, where changes to the internal data and operations of one do not affect the other. Information hiding is an important aspect of object-oriented programming.

7.4.4   Inheritance

Inheritance is another important object-oriented principle. Inheritance is the ability of an object to include characteristics of a parent, or class, object in an object instance. Inheritance lets developers separate general and common characteristics from specialized and variable characteristics. Using the principle of inheritance, a component developer can place commonalities in class objects, and let product developers specify variabilities in individual object subclasses.

7.4.5   Generalization/Abstraction

To generalize or abstract a component is to ensure that the component will handle general, rather than specific, conditions. For example, if a list algorithm has been written specifically for **byte** data, the algorithm could be generalized to handle **short**, **long**, or **double** data as well. In some cases, the algorithm could be generalized even more to handle any type of data.

As another example, suppose that array manipulation depends on hard-coded array boundaries. In almost all cases, you want to generalize this code to accept user-defined array boundaries. However, the range of acceptable user-defined boundaries is determined by the domain analysis.

Generalizing database access functions to handle records of any type or length is a significant step toward creating a multiuse database component. Generalizing these functions to also handle any number of index keys, or to handle keys located at any record offset, would greatly increase the range of use of this database component.

Generalization is the process of removing unnecessary detail and nonessential restrictions from a component. Generalizing a component is limited by the effort required to reengineer the component, and by the range of variability shown in the domain analysis. If the domain analysis indicates that current and future products will use single key data access, it may not make sense to generalize database functions to handle multiple keys.

7.4.6 Separation of Concerns

Separation of concerns is the principle of organizing software so that you need handle only one issue at a time. Separation of concerns is what distinguishes a multiuse component from a single-use, or product-specific, component. Separating concerns lets the component developer see which decisions are integral to the component and which decisions should be deferred to the product developer. The decisions the component developer makes concern the commonalities and range of variability of the domain. The decisions the product developer makes are the selection of the appropriate values for the variabilities and the determination of when to use the values.

Separating concerns will dictate the design of the component by showing what can be fixed in the component and what must be customized. Keeping product development concerns strictly separate from component development concerns is the way in which you help to remove or reduce the dependencies that will prevent multiuse.

7.4.7 Removal of Context

Removal of context is similar to generalization, but it applies to the component interface rather than to the component internals. Context, in this sense, refers to the assumptions the component makes about what is outside of it: services, resources, infrastructure, and hardware platform. Infrastructure includes the operation system and available communication mechanisms. Context also includes assumptions about surrounding components and the messages, or information, they will pass.

An effective way to remove context is to design weak **preconditions** into a component's interface. Preconditions are expectations that a component, or interface function, has about the data that are passed to it or its state when it is called. For example, expecting that an input parameter will always contain valid data is a strong precondition. This precondition requires external components to check the validity of the parameter before they pass it and may make it hard to integrate this component into different products. To weaken this precondition, the component should verify the validity of the input data before continuing.

Expecting a particular order of events is also a strong precondition. For instance, a component may assume that an external component will call its initialization function before any other functions or that a passive component may assume that its caller will call entrance and exit functions for it. To weaken such preconditions, the component can store information about its current state in global flags. For example, an initialization function could set an **INIT** flag that would be checked by all subsequent functions that require initialization.

Removal of context can be a difficult effort. The domain analysis determines which context, and how much of it, should be removed for the component to have multiple uses. The available development resources will certainly influence how much context is actually removed.

7.5 DOCUMENTATION

Documentation promotes multiuse because it improves the product developer's understanding of a component and thus makes the component easier to use in products. Good documentation is particularly essential to multiuse components because of the following:

(1) Many developers may use this component and will need to know its behavior, external interfaces, and required resources.
(2) The component cannot be properly integrated into a product unless the component dependencies are clearly known.
(3) Product developers need to know how to build and test the component within the product's own build and test environment.

In the single-use development process, design documents, code comments, and module or function headers provide the information needed to test and maintain a component. This type of documentation is equally important for the maintenance and test of a multiuse component. However, a multiuse process requires a second type of documentation: the information needed to select, customize, and integrate the multiuse component into products. You can think of this second type of information as customer documentation for the multiuse component's users, the product developers.

To use a component effectively, the product developer needs this information:

(1) The component requirements

(2) The external interface specifications, including visible data types, parameter types, and their order and special constraints, limitations, and assumptions

(3) The prescribed sequence of operations and events

(4) How the component handles exceptions and errors

(5) How the component handles control; is it re-entrant, passive or active, synchronous or asynchronous

(6) The required run-time resources, such as memory, peripheral device, file systems, CPU usage, and other services

(7) The component performance properties and real-time constraints

To review, a well-designed component that has weak coupling, strong cohesion, weak preconditions, and a clear external interface is usually easier to understand than a poorly designed component. Ideally, a product developer does not need to know a great deal about a component to use the component correctly in a product. In particular, the product developer should not need to know the internals of a component to integrate the component into a product.

The format document that can be used to satisfy the above needs contains the following general terms[11]:

(1) Title: This is the name of the system component being specified or described. It must be unique among all system components. This requirement is imposed both by system coordination and by design considerations.

(2) Heading: This contains a variety of entries identifying the person responsible for the design and key descriptors of the component or document. One such descriptor is the type of document that would be Functional Specification, Design Specification, or Design Description.

(3) Purpose: A one- or two-sentence narrative stating the purpose of the component within the system.

(4) Description: An approximately 500-word discourse on the functions the component performs.

(5) Inputs: The data and/or control information a component provides and the name of the component where it goes.

(6) Outputs: The data and/or control information a component provides and the name of the component where it goes.

(7) References: The connectivity information identifying the relation of this block to other blocks in the system as well as references in the lit-

---

[11] The list of terms is derived from Bernstein, L. and Slokowski, F. E. "An information system for the coordination of program design," *Proceedings of 21st National Conference Association for Compution Machinery*, ACM Publication P-66, Thompson Book Company, New York, 1966.

erature. One set of references reflecting the program production structure consists of "uses" and "sends outputs to" and their inverses "used by" and "receives inputs from."

(8) Diagrams or Pseudo-code: Data flow and control charts or pseudo-code describing how the component works internally. For object-oriented programs, class diagrams should be included.

(9) Block Test Plan: An account of how this block will be or was tested as a separate unit. It would include the test procedures and test results necessary to verify the operation of the block.

7.6   DESIGN CONSTRAINTS THAT MAKE SYSTEMS TRUSTWORTHY

Most current software theory focuses on its static behavior by analyzing source listings. There is little theory on its dynamic behavior and its performance under load. Often we do not know what load to expect. Dr. Vinton Cerf, inventor of the Internet, has remarked "applications have no idea what they will need in network resources when they are installed." As a result, we try to avoid serious software problems by overengineering and overtesting.

Software engineers cannot ensure that a small change in software will produce only a small change in system performance. Industry practice is to test and retest every time any change is made in the hope of catching the unforeseen consequences of the tinkering. The April 25, 1994 issue of *Forbes Magazine* pointed out that a three-line change to a 2-million line program caused multiple failures because of a single fault. There is a lesson here. **It is software failures, not faults, that need to be measured.** Design constraints that can help software stability need to be codified before we can hope to deliver reliable performance.

7.6.1   Simplify the Design

Before getting to the design review, a design simplification process eliminates "gold plating" that was identified as one of the top ten risk items for project success. Gold plating is producing software embodying the most complicated interpretation of the requirements, which occurs when designers have limited domain knowledge and do not understand the few places in the design where generalizations are critical, so they generalize everywhere. It is also the consequence of not using prototypes during the requirements phase. For example, in his seven-team experiment cited earlier, Boehm remarked:

> the comparisons of the relative sizes of the products and the relative effort required to develop them produced a striking result: the prototyping teams' products were 40% smaller, on the average, and required 45% less effort to develop, with roughly equivalent performance. The specifying people indicated that it was very easy to over promise and over generalize in their specifications.

For example, when confronted with a request such as, "Some users would like to enter data by rows as well as columns," the developers who relied on specifications would tend to say, "Sure, that's just another sentence in the spec." When confronted with this sort of comment in their prototype review, prototypers had a better feel for the programming implications and tended to say, "We'll put that in if we have time." The 3:1 range in product sizes is remarkable, considering that each team was developing essentially the same product. The main reason for this effect appeared to be that prototyping fostered a higher threshold for incorporating marginally useful features into a software product. The process of prototyping gave software developers a more realistic feel for the amount of effort required to add features to a project, and the lack of a definitive specification meant that prototypers were less locked into a set of promises to deliver capabilities than were the specifiers. In the somewhat rueful words of one of the specifiers, remarking on his team's efforts to fulfill the promises in their ambitious specification, "Words are cheap."[12]

MAGIC NUMBER!

Only 60% of the features in a system are actually used in production.

7.6.2 Software Fault Tolerance

If we cannot avoid a failure, then we must constrain the software design so that the system can recover in an orderly way. Every software process or object class should provide special code that recovers when triggered. A software fault-tolerant library with a watchdog daemon can be built into the system. When the watchdog detects a problem, it launches the recovery code peculiar to the application software. In call processing systems, this usually means dropping the call but not crashing the system. In administrative applications where keeping the database is key, the recovery system may recover a transaction from a backup data file or log the event and rebuild the database from the last checkpoint. Designers are constrained to explicitly define the recovery method for each process and object class using a standard library.

Many highly available and reliable applications are deployed on Microsoft's Windows NT. Transaction processing and process replication technologies make these applications industrial strength and resistant to failures.

---

[12] Boehm, Barry W., Gray, Terence E., and Seewaldt, Thomas. "Prototyping Versus Specifying: A Multiproject Experiment," *IEEE Transactions on Software Engineering*, Vol. SE-10, No. 3, May 1984, pp. 290–301.

Transaction processing is the most widely used technique for fault tolerance among commercial fault-tolerant products. With a transactional processing system, applications usually have a well-defined transaction boundary, such as updating a record or keeping a communication channel operating in the face of bit errors. When a fault occurs, both the client and the server abort the ongoing transaction and roll back to a clean state. This approach was used in the Safeguard ABM system in its "mission mode." Special code was added to each transaction to rationally respond to failures. For example, on a divide by zero abort, the processor would clear tracking data for a target that might have vaporized during atmospheric re-entry.

Process replication allows faster recovery than transactional processing and provides recovery for nontransactional processes. It is ideal for military, avionics, and telecommunication applications that must continually manage or monitor some physical device.

A cold replication assumes there is only one active copy of a fault-tolerant process. The order of priority is when the active copy fails, recover the failed process locally; if the local recovery fails, migrate the process to another machine. This process can be done with a cold, warm, or hot replication design. In warm replication, one or more backup processes run on a network, and the primary process periodically checkpoints its state to its backup processes. Only the primary process can provide services to client applications; the backup process receives only checkpoint messages from the primary process. If the primary process fails, one backup quickly becomes the primary and resumes services. A hot replication scheme monitors all replicas of a fault-tolerant process. When a failure occurs with one server, the failure is masked and the computation continues if there is one server running. No rollbacks are necessary on either the client or the server.

To successfully implement the checkpoint technique, one needs facilities not provided by Windows, these being application monitoring, application failure recovery, application checkpoint/message logging, file replication, Windows events logging/replay, IP packets dispatching, and IP address fail-over.

Avaya (http://www.research.avayalabs.com/project/swift/) offers a reusable library called Software-implemented Fault Tolerance (SwiFT). It is a set of reusable software modules for building reliable, fault-tolerant Windows NT, LINUX, UNIX, and JAVA applications. These modules can either stand alone or be integrated into existing software products to provide fault tolerance. Therefore, SwiFT is designed especially for object, process, and application replications using cold, warm, and hot replication schemes. SwiFT detects hang failures in addition to crash failures. These modules emerged from fundamental Bell Laboratories research in fault-tolerant software pioneered by Bernstein and Kintala.[13]

---

[13] Bernstein, L. and Kintala, C. "Components for Software Fault Tolerance and Rejuvenation," *AT&T Technical Journal*, Vol. 75, No. 2, Mar./Apr. 1996, pp. 29–37.

SwiFT's library modules include:

(1) **Watchd** for process failure detection, recovery, replication manage-ment, and distributed system services. It detects application process fail-ures and machine crashes. This watchdog daemon process can run on either a single machine or on a network and uses an adaptive diagno-sis protocol to detect machine failures so each Watchd pings its neigh-bor Watchd; if its neighbor fails, Watchd pings its next neighbor; and so on. Once Watchd detects a failure with an application program, it will restart the application program automatically. If the client application fails more than the threshold given to Watchd, Watchd will reboot the system and restart the application. It also is used to restart an applica-tion for rejuvenation purposes.

(2) **Winckp** for transparent process checkpointing and mouse/keyboard events logging and replaying.

(3) **Libft** for data checkpointing, communication messages logging, and recovery.

(4) **REPL** for online incremental file replication and disaster recovery.

(5) **One-IP** for IP packets dispatching, fail-over, and rerouting.[14]

7.6.3 Software Rejuvenation

The third constraint is to limit the state space in the execution domain. Today's software runs nonperiodically, which allows internal states to develop chaoti-cally without bound. Software rejuvenation is a new concept that seeks to contain the execution domain by making it periodic. An application is grace-fully terminated and immediately restarted at a known, clean, internal state. Failure is anticipated and avoided. Nonstationary software processes are trans-formed into stationary ones. One way to describe this is rather than running a system for 1 year with all of the mysteries that untried time expanses can harbor, run it only 1 day, 364 times. The software states would be reinitialized each day, process by process, while the system continued to operate. Increas-ing the rejuvenation period reduces the cost of downtime but increases over-head. One system collecting online billing data operated for 2 years with no outages on a rejuvenation interval of 1 week.

A Bell Laboratories experiment showed the benefits of rejuvenation. A 16,000 line C program with notoriously leaky memory failed after 52 itera-tions. Seven lines of rejuvenation code with the period set at 15 iterations were added, and the program ran flawlessly. Rejuvenation does not remove bugs; it merely avoids them with incredibly good effect.

---

[14] For a complete description of these technologies, please refer to Huang, Y. and Kintala, C. M. R. "Software Implemented Fault Tolerance: Technologies and Experience," *Proceedings of 23rd Intl. Symposium on Fault-Tolerant Computing*, Toulouse, France, June 1993, pp. 2–9. *watchd, libft,* and *REPL* are registered trademarks of AT&T Corporation.

This phenomenon was first recognized in the 1970s in the software development for the BISCOM store-and-forward message switching system used by five telephone companies to process customer service requests. The problem then was that hash tables were used to index into a file system. The service requests were different sizes, and the service request numbers followed a structured pattern. The original design tried to maintain the file structures for 30 days or more, which led to many clashes and secondary indices. When service requests were fulfilled, they were deleted. The garbage collection software that tried to reclaim file space was complicated. After months of system aborts, angry customers and frustrated software developers, rejuvenation was born. The system was shut down every night for backup, report generation, and other administrative tasks and the file structure was maintained from shutdown to startup. At startup, the file manger would accept all existing files as new input, recompute the hash tables, and restore the messages. Hash table conflicts became rare. Garbage collection problems were insignificant. The system was more reliable. This added 10 minutes of elapsed time to the startup process and was easily accommodated in the administration procedures. The execution life of the file system was 1 day.

The idea of rejuvenation was applied to Lucent's Billing Data System (BILLDATS) in the 1980s when it was ported to UNIX. There were no reported outages for at least the first 10 years of use at over 50 customer sites. Rejuvenation worked and then was extended to a UNIX library of features. BILLDATS collects billing information from automatic message accounting transmitters situated in or close to switching offices. BILLDATS is the "middleman" in the billing process. The system collects, validates, and adds identification information regarding origination and destination. This information is transmitted directly to the Revenue Accounting Office, which processes the billing information. Some of BILLDATS more interesting features are as follows:

(1) Runs under UNIX
(2) Rejuvenates daily
(3) Can store 12 to 44 million calls
(4) Inserts the switch type and ID onto every call record
(5) Collects data from up to 600 switches

The FAA's Voice Switching Communication System (VSCS) was upgraded in 2003 from UNIX to WinNT. Harris Corporation supplied VSCS. As a result, the Microsoft problem of clock expiration after 49.7 days became an FAA problem that led to a massive failure as described in Section 5.11.2. Harris did not use rejuvenation technology that could have prevented this failure. During VSCS development, the issue of WinNT as an industrial strength, reliable platform raged in the telecommunications software trade press. Even though

Microsoft had upgraded WinNT with clustering technology in a two-node fail-over configuration, industry skeptics argued against the risk of moving away from UNIX.

The Harris website reports:

> The Voice Switching and Control System (VSCS) provides the Federal Aviation Administration (FAA) with a computer-controlled, highly distributed communications and control system to support air traffic management into the 21st century. The Harris-developed VSCS allows air traffic controllers to establish all Air-to-Ground and Ground-to-Ground calls for current and projected traffic volumes. The VSCS has completed design, development, testing, production and installation of the system for all 21 FAA ARTCC locations ... Software design and development, using SEI Level 3 methodologies; test plan development; software testing; data analysis; various legacy systems and tools ... VSCS is based on independent distributed processors and switches, fault-tolerant databases, redundant high-speed bus interconnections, and extensive switching for real-time reconfiguration and redundancy to achieve an operational availability of 0.9999999. Switchovers during fault detection, isolation and resolution are done without breaks in communications, so failures are transparent to the ATC ... Production completed achieved 100% on-time system delivery, installation, test, and acceptance of all 23 systems. [Harris was] contractor of the year [and won an] award from the Human Factors Engineering Society for excellence in human-machine interface design. Customer quote: 'In my association with Harris on the VSCS project, they have shown a dedication towards providing excellence. Their people are professional[s] who reflect pride in their company and their products.[15]

The Microsoft software contained an internal clock designed to shut the system down after 49.7 days to prevent it from becoming overloaded with data. Shutdown is better than allowing an overloaded system to keep running and potentially give controllers wrong information about flights. This strategy was the right one given the design and uncertainty of the traffic load. When we try to run software beyond its specified domain, we often fail in obscure ways. A better strategy would have been to use rejuvenaiton technology weekly and roll over to backup hardware to eliminate the risk of the this fault becoming a failure. Greg Martin, the chief FAA spokesman in Washington, said the failure was not an indication of the reliability of the radio communications system, which he described as "nearly perfect." Harris programmers were operating at, or better than, the state-of-the-practice. They were SEI 3, and apparently the application was robust. The problem is that the software industry is not aware of nor using available tools that would prevent many failures. Even worse, the same problems reoccur because we rarely study software failures with the intention of teaching better methods.

---

[15] http://www.harris.com (and search for VSCS).

7.6.4 Hire Good People and Keep Them

This constraint might have been the first because it is so important, but any software organization can adopt the first three constraints as they set about improving the quality of their staff. Hiring good people is not easy. Every shop claims to have the "very best' people"; obviously, very few actually could.

MAGIC NUMBER!

It takes 16 weeks to bring a new hire onboard: 8 to fill the job, and another 8 to train the person in the ways of the project and the company.

The high correlation between defects in the software product and staff churn is chilling. Defects are highly correlated with personnel practices. Groups with ten or more tasks and people with three or more independent activities tended to introduce more defects into the final product than those that are focused. Large software changes are more error-prone than small ones, with changes of 100 words of memory or more being considered large. Hatton reports that defects grow exponentially with size, which may have some relationship to the average size of human working memory. The high 0.918 correlation between defects and personnel turnover rates is telling. When Boeing improved their work environment and development process, they saw 83% fewer defects, gained a factor of 2.4 in productivity, improved customer satisfaction, and improved employee moral.

7.6.5 Limit the Language Features Used

Most communications software is developed in the C or C++ programming languages. Les Hatton's book, *Safer C*,[16] describes the best way to use C and C++ in mission-critical applications. Hatton advocates constraining the use of the language features to achieve reliable software performance and then goes on to specify instruction by instruction how to do it. He says, "The use of C in safety-related or high integrity systems is not recommended without severe and automatically enforceable constraints. However, if these are present using the formidable tool support (including the extensive C library), the best available evidence suggests that it is then possible to write software of *at least* as high intrinsic quality and consistency as with other commonly used languages." For example, a detailed analysis of source code from 54 projects showed that once in every 29 lines of code, functions are not declared before they are used.

[16] Hatton, Les. Safer C: Developing Software for High Integrity and Safety-critical Systems, McGraw-Hill International, London, 1996.

C is an intermediate language, between high level and machine level. There are dangers when the programmer can drop down to the machine architecture, but with reasonable constraints and limitations on the use of register instructions to those very few key cases dictated by the need to achieve performance goals, C can be used to good effect. The alternative of using a mixture of assembly language and high-level language code brings with it the headaches of managing configurations and integrating modules from different code generators. The power of C can be harnessed to assure that source code is well structured. One important constraint is to use C function prototypes or special object classes for interfaces.

7.6.6 Limit Module Size and Initialize Memory

MAGIC NUMBER!

The optimum module size for the fewest defects is between 100 and 1000 NCSLOC. Smaller modules lead to too many interfaces, and larger ones are too big for the designer to handle. Structural problems creep into large modules.

All memory should be explicitly initialized before it is used. Memory leak detection tools should be used to make sure that a software process does not grab all available memory for itself, leaving none for other processes. This creates gridlock as the system hangs in a wait state because it cannot process any new data.

7.6.7 Check the Design Stability

Software developers know that their systems can exhibit unexpected, strange behavior, including crashes or hangs, when small operational differences are introduced. These are not random events. They may be the result of new data, execution of code in new sequences, or exhaustion of some computer resource such as buffer space, memory, hash function overflow space, or processor time. Fixes and upgrades create their own errors. The fact that the only recourse has been exhaustive retesting limits the growth of software productivity in enhancements to existing systems and modules. Experienced software managers know to ask, "What changed?" when a system that has been performing reliably suddenly and catastrophically fails. Under current methods of software production, systems are conditionally stable only for a particular set of input and a particular configuration.

A software system is stable if a bounded input creates a bounded output. Instabilities develop in the following circumstances:

(1) Computations cannot be completed before new data arrive.
(2) Round-off errors build or buffer usage increases to eventually dominate system performance.
(3) An algorithm embodied in the software is inherently flawed.

Feedback control theory makes it possible to design adaptive software that meets prespecified performance requirements. Design controllability and observability are possible with feedback control. Controllability is a measure of the ability to use a system's external inputs to manipulate its internal state. Observability is a measure of how well internal states can be inferred by knowledge of external outputs. Many real-time systems make control decisions. These decisions are usually made by software and based on feedback from the hardware under its control (termed the plant). Such feedback commonly takes the form of an analog sensor that can be read via an A/D converter. A sample from the sensor may represent position, voltage, temperature, or any other appropriate parameter. Each sample provides the software with additional information upon which to base its control decisions.

7.6.7.1 *Closing the Loop* Systems that use feedback are called closed-loop control systems (Figure 7.5). The feedback is used to make decisions about changes to the control signal that drives the system. An open-loop control system does not have or does not use feedback. A basic closed-loop control system can describe a variety of control systems, including those driving elevators, thermostats, and cruise control.

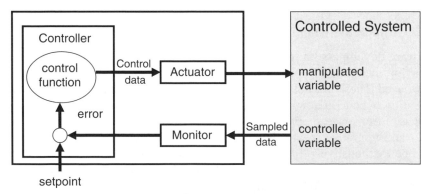

Figure 7.5. *Closed-loop control system.*

7.6.7.2 *Bang Bang Control* How much should the software increase or decrease the drive signal? One option is to just set the drive signal to its minimum value when you want the plant to decrease its activity and to its maximum value when you want the plant to increase its activity. This strategy is called ON–OFF control, and it is how many thermostats work.

ON–OFF control does not work well in all systems. If the thermostat waits until the desired temperature is achieved to turn off the heater, the temperature may overshoot. See Figure 7.6. The same amount of overshoot and ripple is not acceptable when stopping an elevator.

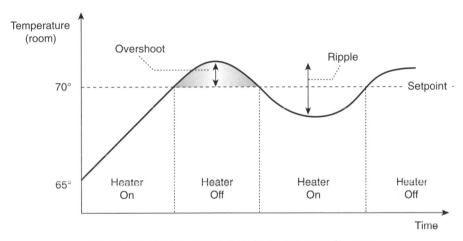

Figure 7.6. *Overshoot and ripple in* ON–OFF *control system.*

Proportional control is the primary alternative to ON–OFF control. If the difference between the current plant output and its desired value (the current error) is large, the software should probably change the drive signal a lot. If the error is small, it should change it only a little. In other words, we always want a change like:

$$y(n+1) = c(y - y(n)),$$

where y is the desired output or setpoint, $y(n)$ is the actual output at sample n, and c is a constant proportional gain set by the system's designer.

If the proportional gain is well chosen, the time the plant takes to reach a new setpoint will be as short as possible, with overshoot (or undershoot) and oscillation minimized. ON–OFF and proportional controls are two basic techniques of closed-loop control.

Consider the open loop system in Figure 7.7, where:

$x(n)$ is a sampled sequence of inputs

$y(n)$ is a sequence of outputs computed by the program

$h(n)$ is the difference equation coded in the software module

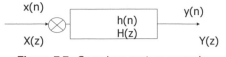

Figure 7.7. *Open-loop system example.*

It may be the moving average difference equation:

$$h(n) = 7/8\ h(n-1) + 1/8\ (n),$$

and the Z transform is

$$Z(\{x(n)\}) = X(z),$$

$$X(z) = \sum x(n)\ z^{-n} \quad \text{for } n = 0 \text{ to } \infty.$$

Consider the closed-loop system in Figure 7.8, where:

$$Y(z) = H(z)\,[X(z) - Y(z)],$$

$$Y(z) + H(z)Y(z) = H(z)\,X(z),$$

$$Y(z) = X(z)\,H(z)/[1 + H(z)],$$

but H(z) cannot equal −1 or the output is infinite for any input!

$$y(n) = Z^{-1}\{Y(z)\}.$$

Figure 7.8. *Closed-loop system example.*

Note that $n \geq 0$ for real casual systems.

As an example, we are asked to implement the following innocent-looking difference equation by the specification:

$$y(n) = 4[y(n-1) - y(n-2)] + x(n-1)$$

or

$$y(n) = 5y(n-1) - 4y(n-2) + x(n-1) - y(n-1).$$

Programming it would not be hard, but is it stable? Take the Z transform and factor out the z^n term:

$$Y(z) = Y(z)[5z^{-1} - 4z^{-2}] + X(Z)z^{-1} - Y(z)z^{-1},$$

$$Y(z)/X(z) = z^{-1}/4z^{-2} - 4z^{-1} + 1.$$

Now find the values for Z when the demoninator is zero.

$$4z^{-2} - 4z^{-1} + 1 = 0,$$

$$z^2 - 4z + 4 = 0,$$

with two roots at z = 2.

Because the roots exceed 1, the system will grow without bound near Z = 2. It is unstable and will lead to an unreliable and unsafe system.[17] The ethical software engineer would not implement this specification as it stands.

This feedback control technique is being used to analyze these software problems:

(1) Web caching QoS
(2) Active queue management in networks
(3) Processor thermal controls
(4) Online data migration in network storage
(5) Real-time embedded networking
(6) Control middleware
(7) Real-time scheduling
(8) Target tracking

We must learn to approximate nonlinear systems with linear ones to use this technique widely. Be aware that modeling mapping control objectives for a system to feedback control loops is challenging.

7.6.8 Bound the Execution Domain

Software needs to perform reasonableness checks on all inputs and outputs. For example, the system should not accept a result of an altitude calculation that claims that an aircraft is at 67 ft off the ground when the plane is warming its engines on the ground. The domain experts specify a range of acceptable values for all inputs and outputs, and the software needs to validate that the values fall within their defined ranges. When they do not, then fault-tolerant software is invoked.

Input validation on all data coming from user fields on an input screen is now common. A good design approach is to have two stages of abstraction. The first allows the human factors designer to arrange the fields to best fit the task. The second allows domain experts to validate the data.

---

[17] The details of this analysis are beyond the scope of this book; see *Feedback Control of Computing Systems*, which is listed in the Bibliography, for an excellent treatment of the subject.

Then data pass through an interface object or structured language to the processing software. The processing programs receive data that are normalized and validated, which isolates the processing programs from the idiosyncratic behavior of the human operator and of the external environment. It reduces the need to change the application to stay in lock step with screen changes. If the resulting system does not provide the required performance because of this indirection, it is best to buy a faster machine. This is a hardware problem, not a software problem. Should this argument fail with the budget manager, then the designer must invent Fast Path processing to bypass the overhead of indirection. The architecture becomes more tightly coupled and therefore more complex, which causes the software to become harder to fix and extend. Fast Path processing is used for just this purpose, to bypass the overhead of indirection, by IBM in their database access system.[18]

Unfortunately designers are not always as careful as IBM was in bounding and qualifying their interface. Here is a case in which a simple index was not bounded. We have the ethical responsibility to teach the **cause** of the failure to our colleagues so that designers can avoid it in the future.

Remember the Comair story in Section 5.11.1. The crew-scheduling application was not written in-house at Comair, but by another large aerospace company—SBS, which is owned by Boeing (http://www.sbsint.com/). This bit of software does not use an external database; it tracks everything itself. It is a dedicated system responsible only for flight crew assignments. Most of Comair's traffic flows through the Midwest, and the central base of operations is in Cincinnati. The Midwest was hit by a major snowstorm during the week in question, which caused many crew reassignments. It seems that the application had a hard limit of crew changes per month. Consider that Comair runs 1100 flights a day and there are usually three crew members on each aircraft. That is a lot of crew changes.[19]

7.6.9 Engineer to Performance Budgets

Understanding the performance implications of a design is critical when deciding if there is a risk of not fitting the application onto the target computing resources or network. Simple estimates of CPU usage and memory occupancy from instruction counts can be helpful. This is a static view of the system performance. A dynamic view, using simple queuing models, is necessary to understand bottlenecks.

Case Study: The Case of Heigh Ho, The I/O!

A distributed system with many servers to handle more than one million requests a day was built but could not handle the load. Forty percent of the

[18] http://publib.boulder.ibm.com/infocenter/dzichelp/index.jsp?topic=/com.ibm.ims9.doc.as/sag12.htm. Explains the use of fast path.
[19] http://www.informationweek.com/shared/printableArticle.jhtml?articleID=56700162.

traffic arrived during the busy hour from 10:00 AM to 11:00 AM. That meant 400,000 transactions arrived in 1 hour, or 400,000 transactions per busy hour/3600 seconds/hour = 111 transactions/busy second.

Each request took on average 25 ms to process, so designers assumed (111 transactions/second) (0.025 seconds/transaction) and planned to use three servers. They did not account for queuing buildup and the need to design for 60% server utilization to avoid unacceptable response times. They actually needed more like five servers (a processing capacity of 2.7 servers at 60% utilization requires 4.5 actual servers).

Simple queuing theory could have told them that.

Conclusion: When sizing an application, consider not only the CPU utilization but also the input/output (I/O) bandwidth and random access memory (RAM) utilization, the end-to-end response time for frequently used transactions, and the number of concurrent users expected during the busy hour.

Transaction instruction counts can be put into a model and calibrated with test data from the prototype and eventually from the production system. The offered load is based on the specified use cases and then on measured traffic. In general, the number of transactions a system can handle is the minimum number of transactions that fit within the CPU cycles, RAM, and I/O of the target computer considering the traffic profiles. In some severe cases, the need to recover every transaction limits the number of transactions to what the backup system can recover. A detailed accounting of RAM occupancy and I/O channel utilization considering potential memory thrashing also gives insight to system capacity. These are **static** views of system capacity.

Studying the growth of queues gives the most important insight into the effects of load on system performance. Queue occupancy dominates system capacity planning, so the idea is to empty queues quickly. However, some transaction schedulers ask for more work even when their queues are almost full in the mistaken belief that they are honoring the requirements specification. The additional processing required to manage the queues under these conditions grows exponentially, and the system slows to a crawl or crashes. A better strategy is to set a higher priority for software processes doing the work than for the processes requesting the work, such as screen handlers, even though this seems to violate the requirements specification.

To understand this effect, assume transaction arrival times and transaction processing times are both random. How could a queue of significant length ever develop? If the arrival times were correlated with the processing times, a queue might be very short, but transaction arrival and processing times are uncorrelated. A cluster of transaction requests with very short interarrival times might well contain many that require long processing times. That is when a queue of significant length would develop. If the mean interarrival time is shorter than the average processing time (T_s), the queue will grow without bound, overflow, and become useless. Another way of expressing this is to introduce a new parameter defining the load (L) or the occupancy of the queue and calculate the average delay (T_{avg}) for a message to pass through a queue.

MAGIC NUMBER!

$T_{avg} = T_s/1-L/100$, where L is the percentage occupancy of the queue.
L = 100(arrival rate/server rate), where rate = 1/time.

Example: A processor sends ten exponentially distributed disk I/Os per second. The average disk service time is 20 ms. Then the disk utilization or load is

> Load = arrival rate/server rate = 10 requests/1 request services/0.02
> seconds × 100 = 20%

The delay in the system is

$$T_{avg} = T_s/1 - L/100$$
$$= 20\,\text{ms}/1 - 0.02 = 25\,\text{ms}.$$

As the queue exceeds a load of two thirds of the capacity, the delay seen by the user as response time becomes unacceptably long.[20]

A promising software engineering process called performance aware software development (PASD) combines requirements specifications with architecture and resource demand budgets. It moves the focus of performance engineering from just predictions to goal setting, tracking, and prediction. The budgets are planning figures created by estimates and measurements. Budgets are planned and analyzed statically and dynamically for resource demands with a validation check using the prototype. Unified Modeling Lange (UML) use cases can drive the process. The use of current estimates tracked along with project budgets for each module works as well here as it does for scheduling.

In PASD, demand budgets are allocated to modules and a performance model verifies the entire budget. The nonfunctional as well as the functional requirements are included in the analysis for operating system, database manager, middleware, the environment, and competing application overheads. Finding bottlenecks indicates budget adjustments.

---

[20] To pursue this analysis, see Wilbur Highleyman's *Performance Analysis of Transaction Processing Systems*, Prentice-Hall, Englewood Cliffs, NJ, 1989.

A budgeting approach to performance applies a "divide and conquer" policy. First, it divides the problem into parts that correspond to module responsibilities and to the work of separate developer groups, and then it estimates the overall performance that will result if all budgets are met. The effects of the execution platform, such as contention, queue, overheads, and latencies are included. The budgeting process adds a layer of procedures and reasoning to the techniques of predictive modeling in software performance engineering. PSAD uses the performance model to set performance goals as well as to predict outcomes with the ability to evaluate design changes and provides a tool for the automatic generation of performance models.

Case Study: Magilla Transporters Redux

Let us return to the case study on Magilla Personal Transporters from Section 7.3.2 and check the transactions against the budgets the developers laid out. First the developers measured the performance of the existing system using an expected mixture, based on the traffic profiles in the requirements specification. They repeated the performance measurement after the upgrade. Table 7.3 contains module processor times using a nominal use case mixture. *Legacy* is the system before upgrading.

TABLE 7.3. Magilla Module Execution Times (MS)

Module	Legacy	Upgraded
New Order	54	51
View Order	12	13
Modify Order	1255	47
Cancel Order	1221	24
Search Customers	1223	26
Delete Customers	1213	22

The developers detected a 1200-ms loop in the legacy system that they bypassed to make a 25-fold reduction in processor utilization. This change impacted four of the six modules and contributed to meeting the customer's desire for a 3-second response time. From this analysis and in discussions with the customer, they set response time performance budgets for each module. Even though not every transaction is less than 3 seconds, the upgraded system meets user needs as confirmed by detailed operator task analysis. Then the developers examined the implication of porting to different operating systems and noted that Linux is more efficient than Windows, with WinXP adding the most overhead (Table 7.4).

7.6.10 Reduce Algorithm Complexity

One way to simplify computations is by making reasoned approximations. This concept is illustrated in the following case study with several examples from

TABLE 7.4. Comparison of Various Operating Systems in Seconds

Module	Budget	Win2k	WinXP	Linux
New Order	2.0	1.74	1.82	1.51
View Order	2.5	2.57	2.71	2.44
Modify Order	4.0	3.11	3.14'	3.06
Cancel Order	2.0	1.92	2.01	1.84
Search Customers	4.0	2.92	2.84	2.71
Delete Customers	5.0	2.84	2.88	2.81

code that all Internet uses invoke hundreds of times a day, automatic repeat request (ARQ).[21]

Case Study: The Case of Get Me to The Host on Time

The transmission control program (TCP) uses an ARQ protocol for flow and error control. TCP divides a message into segments, and the network layer Internet protocol (IP) subdivides the segments into packets. These packets are sent across the Internet and then assembled into segments at the receiver. The receiver returns an acknowledgment message back to the sender. Once the acknowledgment gets to the sender, it clears its buffers so that it can send new segments. When the sender transmits a segment, it sets an RTT that counts down to zero. If the acknowledgment does not get back to the sender before the RTT times out, the sender resends the segment. The schematic of TCP/IP in Figure 7.9 shows how the RTT works.

The problem is to set the RTT timer so that it is long enough to allow segments to travel across the network and the acknowledgment to return, but short enough so that the network is not idle. Too short an RTT leads to many extra retransmissions, and too long an RTT leads to wasted network capacity. If one packet of a segment is lost, TCP resends the entire segment. The Internet architects decided that they had to measure the RTT for each segment and then average the measurements to reduce the effect of the variance of the RTT. For example, if a route changes during a transmission, queues may momentarily delay the message of one router (R). They decided to average the last **ten** measurements to set the RTT countdown clock:

$$\text{Average RTT} = 1/10 \sum_{i=1}^{10} \text{RTT}(i).$$

This equation requires dropping the previous eleventh measurement from a file of RTT measurements, inserting the current measurement, and then

[21] Yao, Yu Dong, Bernstein, Larry, and Yao, Kevin. *Special Topic: Software Engineering Study of the Reliability of Wireless ARQ Protocols*, Technical Report 2003–5, Stevens Institute of Technology, 2003. This is available on the course website.

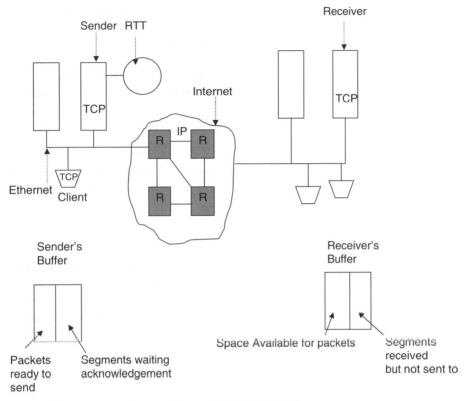

Figure 7.9. *TCP/IP—RTT.*

accessing and adding them. The result is then divided by 10. The RTT clock after the first 11 transmissions would be

$$\text{Average RTT}(11) = 1/10 \sum_{i=1}^{11} \text{RTT}(i).$$

In general for the $j + 1$ transmission:

$$\text{Average RTT}(j+1) = 1/10 \sum_{i=j-9}^{j+1} \text{RTT}(i).$$

The simple idea of averaging becomes a complex software design. The first simplification is to make this approximation using a recursive equation known as a moving-average filter:

$$\text{Average RTT}(j) = 9/10 \ (\text{Average RTT}(j-1)) + 1/10 \ \text{RTT}(j).$$

This equation is a filter with infinite memory, but by the time the eleventh measurement's value affects the result, it has been reduced by $(0.1)(0.9)^{10} = 0.028$. This design simplification eliminates managing a ten-item buffer of measurements and indexing the measurements. It still requires computers to divide by ten. The second simplification is to approximate ten measurements on average by eight because computers naturally deal with powers of two by shifting

$$\text{Average RTT}(j) = 7/8 \quad (\text{Average RTT}(j-1)) + 1/8 \quad \text{RTT}(j).$$

This moving-average equation is used in TCP to compute the setting for the RTT countdown timer. The moving average takes in one new sample and drops the oldest sample each sample period. The moving-average filter reduces random variations in RTT by the square root of 8, or 2.8.

7.6.11   Factor and Refactor

Factoring is the mathematical technique of finding common terms in an equation. Software designers need to look for common requirements, functions, and code throughout software development. "Refactoring" tweaks the factoring concept and applies it to software design. Refactoring defines the software technology aimed at reducing the size of the software by finding and eliminating redundant functions and code and dead-end code. Refactoring is the redesign of software in ways that do not change its functionality. The idea is that the first and second iterations of the software design and implementation stressed understanding the feature, the problem domain, and getting the software to work. Refactoring is left to the third iteration—"make it work better."

Refactoring can be used for small changes to incrementally improve structure. As defined by Martin Fowler:

> Refactoring is a disciplined technique for restructuring an existing body of code, altering its internal structure without changing its external behavior. Its heart is a series of small behavior preserving transformations. Each transformation (called a "refactoring") does little, but a sequence of transformations can produce a significant restructuring. Since each refactoring is small, it's less likely to go wrong. The system is also kept fully working after each small refactoring, reducing the chances that a system can get seriously broken during the restructuring.[22]

Refactoring can also be used to make major changes to a module by indicating it needs to be rewritten, but by keeping its functions and its interfaces constant while changing its internal structure. One approach is "refactoring to patterns" that marries refactoring—the process of improving the design of existing code—with patterns, the classic solutions to recurring design problems. Refactoring to patterns suggests that using patterns to improve an exist-

[22] http://www.refactoring.com.

ing design is better than using patterns early in a new design. In the last case study in Section 7.6.10, we simplified the equations to reduce complexity. Network managers noted that even with averaging, there were too many resends. The network designers needed to compute a variance for RTT and combine it with the average RTT:

$$RTT_{setting} = Average\ RTT + 4\sigma,$$

where 4 gives a reasonable margin and σ is the standard deviation. Taking a standard deviation requires computing a square root, so once again an equation simplification is made to approximate the average standard deviation by an average of the absolute deviation:

$$Average\ Deviation = 1/10 \sum_{i-1}^{10}\ |Average\ RTT(j) - RTT(j)|,$$

and here we can see a pattern. So we create a design pattern

$$Average\ Parameter\ (j) = 7/8\ Average\ Parameter\ (j-1) + 1/8\ Parameter\ (j)$$

and use it for both computing the average and for the deviation by refactoring and eliminating, or not implementing in the first place, the duplicate code for the moving average equation. This pattern was generalized further by making the smoothing constants seven-eighth and one-eighth parameters.

Refactoring was used to great effect in the early 1970s when it was applied to the redesign of a very buggy radar controller. The software was redesigned and reimplemented to make it robust with exactly the same functionality and interfaces. The project was called "Radar Control Maintainability Improvement." The idea was embraced by the customer because of catastrophic problems with the existing code. By not changing the functions or the interfaces, new features in other modules could be integrated without close release coordination with the new radar controller. The radar controller size was reduced from 5355 LOC to 2681 LOC, and the concept of "design for maintainability" was created. The goal of the designers and implementers was to reduce CPU, RAM, and I/O use while delivering a failure-free module. They accomplished their goal.

Allocating as much as 20% of the effort on a new release to improving the maintenance of the system pays large dividends by making the system perform better, avoiding failures induced by undesired interactions between modules, and reducing the time and space constraints on new feature designs. The goal is to reduce the amount of processor time old modules use, the amount of memory they occupy, the amount of I/O they trigger while holding their interfaces fixed. Other modules may be modified or new ones added to provide new features. This strategy naturally leads to reuse within the system. The greatest economic benefit is to reuse software at the application level.

Unfortunately this process is not widely deployed because of the emphasis on new features. A bug-ridden store-and-forward system did use this concept through the 1970s and as a result grew to be extremely reliable. Rather than being tossed out and replaced with the next new thing, it continued to switch messages until 1995, when spare parts could no longer be obtained for the hardware. An unexpected benefit of "design for maintainability" was that new modules and those being upgraded for new features were also more reliable because developers did not face harsh space or time constraints. They could focus on getting their module to work while others concerned themselves with reducing the size of modules that did not contain new features.

MAGIC NUMBER!

Once a system is deployed, 20% of the development effort should be devoted to improving the maintainability of failure-prone modules that do not undergo feature enhancements.

7.7 PROBLEMS

7.7.1 A server is responding to a request from a client. The server has three queues, shown in Figure 7.10 with a "Q." There is an input queue, a disk access queue, and an output queue. The disk queue only accepts one message at a time from input processing. The local area network operates at 10 Mb per second. The sum of all protocol overheads is 100 bytes. The chain of queues in Figure 7.11 models the flow of the transactions.

The slow processor in the server requires 10 ms per instruction, and it takes 800 instructions to process an average input request, 500 instructions to access data from the disk for this request, and 200 instructions to send the result back

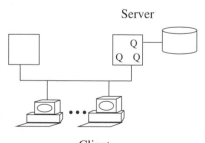

Server

Client

Figure 7.10. Network for Problem 7.7.1.

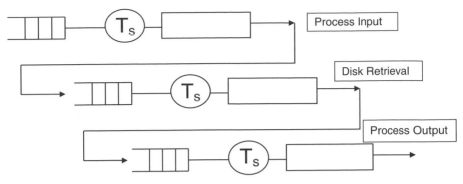

Figure 7.11. Transaction model for Problem 7.7.1.

to the client. The message from client to server contains 1000 bytes and from server to client contains 2000 bytes. If there is no other transaction, what is the response time?

7.7.2 Now the load increases in the client server system in Problem 7.7.1 as three clients try to access the server with the same transaction requests every second. Assume that the messages do not clash. Now what is the response time for a message?

7.7.3 A server sends 1000 byte messages to a client using buffers and acknowledgments. It takes 225.3 ms to process and send the message when there is no other traffic on the line. Each message is uniformly distributed in time. If there are two applications on the server sending messages to the client and the load on the queue for the line is 96.5%, what is the expected response time?

7.7.4 Define coupling and cohesion. What should you strive for when designing any software components in terms of coupling and cohesion (i.e., high or low)?

7.7.5 What is the Parnas information hiding and encapsulation principle?

7.7.6 A company wants to adapt its configuration tracking software, which was previously used to configure its network, to configure connections between computers. A **connection** is used to connect two computers. (A computer can be connected to only one other computer at any given time.) Each of the two computers is attached to a **post** of a cross-connection box, and the two posts are connected with a **jumper**. Figure 7.12 shows a cross-connection box with six posts; a system will consist of multiple cross-connection boxes, and different boxes may have different numbers of posts, half on the left, or west, side, and half on the right, or east, side.

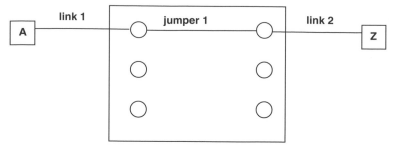

Figure 7.12. *Cross-connection box for Problem 7.7.6.*
Note: The circles inside the cross-connection box are called "posts." In this example, link 1 is used to attach computer A to the top west post of the cross-connection box and link 2 is used to attach computer Z to the top east post of the cross-connection box; jumper 1 is used to establish the connection between A and Z.

The following relevant extracts are from the requirements document:

(1) "There are two major operations, connect (X, Y) and disconnect (X, Y). . . . In the initial state of the system, there are no computers connected through links to posts and there are no jumpers between posts."

(2) "Jumpers may only connect east posts to west posts."

(3) "Because it is hard to close and lock a cross-connection box that contains too many long jumpers, when a connection is being established, the software must choose the east post and west post, from among all available east posts and west posts, in such way that the sum of the lengths of all jumpers is small as possible."

(4) "If a link (to a computer) is attached to a post that has no jumper attached to it, and there are no unattached posts in the box, then the link (and the computer) may be replaced by a new link (and computer) to facilitate the establishment of a new connection."

(5) "If all posts in a cross-connection box are already being used for connections, then a new connection must find another cross-connection box that has available posts or has posts that can be made available. If no such cross-connection box exists, the software will repost the problem to a technician and request human assistance."

As an example of the principle conveyed in requirement **c** above, the configuration of Figure 7.13 would be preferable to that of Figure 7.14.

The project has been running for 6 months and is in deep trouble. Performance of the software is unacceptably slow, and the code is buggy. The former architect had been reporting that his team had 80% of the code complete and there were no known problems.

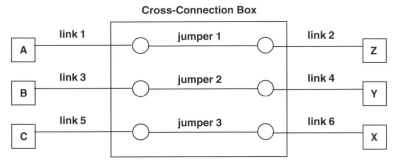

Figure 7.13. *Preferable configuration for Problem 7.7.6.*

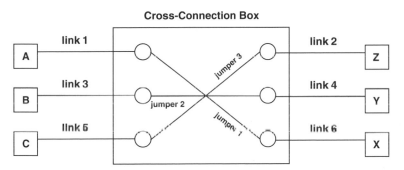

Figure 7.14. *Less desirable configuration for Problem 7.7.6.*

You have been asked to be the new architect. What step(s) do you take?

a. You may ask for a design review.
b. You may ask for performance measurements on the existing code to find the hotspots.
c. You may institute code inspections.
d. You may look on the Web for a new job.

7.7.7 A careful consideration of the data structure in Figure 7.15 leads you to realize that it contains unnecessary information. What information in the data structure is unnecessary and how is it causing a problem?

7.7.8 Given this pseudo-code, extract the algorithm:

procedure connect (X, Y)
begin
  min_available_length = distance between maximally - distant east - west post pair in any Cross - Connection Box

Connection

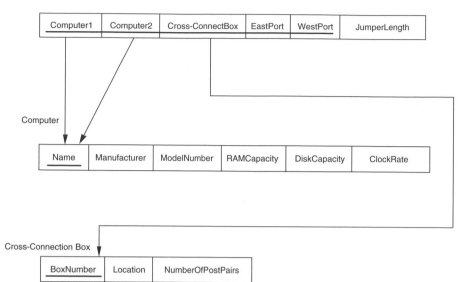

Figure 7.15. *Data structure for Problem 7.7.7.*

```
min_box = 0
min_free_west_post = 0
min_free_east_post = 0
for each i from 1 to number of Cross-Connect Boxes do
for each j from 1 to number of post pairs in Cross-Connect Box i do
  if (west post j in Cross-Connect Box I has no jumper connected)
    for each k from 1 to number of post pairs in Cross-Connect Box i do
     begin
        let d = the length of a jumper from west post j of Cross-Connect
Box i to
        east post k of that box
        if (d < min_available_length)
 end
 begin
  min_available_length = d
  min_box = i
  min_free_west_post = j
  min_free_east_post = k
 end
```

7.7.9 You simplify the design by eliminating the jumper length. Why isn't it necessary to store the jumper length?

7.7.10 Write pseudo-code, in the style of the pseudo-code in Problem 7.7.8, for the simplified version of the algorithm that makes this revelation possible.

BIBLIOGRAPHY

"Trust in Cyberspace" *Committee on Information Systems Trustworthiness*, National Research Council, 1999.

Braude, Eric-, *Software Design From Programming to Architecture*, John Wiley and Sons, New York, 2004.

Finegold, Ed. "Microsoft NT Makes its Move on Telcom IN," *Billing World*, Jan. 1998, pp. 16–19.

Fowler, Martin. *Refactoring: Improving the Design of Existing Code*, Addison Wesley, Reading, MA, 2000.

Hellerstein, Joseph L., Diao, Yixin, Parckh, Sujay, and Tilbury, Dawn. *Feedback Control of Computing Systems*, Wiley-Interscience, New York, 2004.

IEEE Software, Vol. 22, No. 3, May/June 2005. Entire issue devoted to adapting agility.

Liskov, Barbara. "Data Abstraction and Hierarchy," *SIGPLAN Notices*, Vol. 23, No. 5, May 1988.

Man, Fu-Tin. "A Brief History of TL1," *Journal of Network and Systems Management*, Vol. 7, No. 2, June 1, 1999, pp. 143–148.

Meyer, Bertrand. *Object Oriented Software Construction*, Prentice-Hall, Englewood Cliffs, NJ, 1988, p. 23.

Parnas, D. L. "Information Distribution Aspects of Design Methodology," *Proceedings of IFIP Congress*, 1971.

Parnas, D. L. "On the Criteria to be Used in Decomposing Systems into Modules," *Communications of the ACM (Programming Techniques Department)*, Dec. 1972.

Parnas, D. L. "On the Response to Detected Errors i~ Hierarchically Structured Systems," *Technical Report*, Carnegle-Mellon University, 1972.

Parnas, D. L. "Some Conclusions from an Experiment in Software Engineering," *Proceedings of the 1972 FJCC.*

Sha, Lui. "Using Simplicity to Control Complexity," *IEEE Software*, Vol. 18, No. 4, July/Aug. 2001, p. 27.

Shaw, Mary and Garlan, David. *Software Architecture: Perspectives on an Emerging Discipline*, Prentice-Hall, Englewood Cliffs, NJ, 1996.

Siddiqui, Khalid H. and Woodside, C. M. "Performance Aware Software Development (PASD): Using Resource Demand Budgets," *Workshop on Software and Performance Proceedings of the third international workshop on Software and performance Rome, Italy SESSION: Extending Performance Approaches to New Application Domains*, 2000, pp. 275–285.

Trivedi, Kishor, et al. "On the Analysis of Software Rejuvenation Policies," *Compass '97, Proceedings of the 12th Annual Conference on Computer Assurance*, June 16–19, 1997, pp. 88–96.

Sarbanes-Oxley Act of 2002

Phillip Armour, a senior consultant at Corvus International, Inc, in Communications of the ACM June 2005/vol 48, No. 6, (pp 15–17) points out that not only do a company's accounting and financial software systems come under the jurisdiction of Sarbanes-Oxley but also any systems that feed them data. He goes on to suggest that the software that comprise these systems may themselves become assets that must be managed as part of a companies portfolio. With SOX in place there is a need for trustworthy software systems.

Here are relevant sections of the Sarbanes-Oxley Act of 2002 to software engineers:

Title 3 section 302

". . . The signing officers

(A) are responsible for establishing and maintaining internal (financial) controls

(B) have designed such internal controls to ensure that the material information relating to the issuer . . . is made known.

(C) have evaluated the effectiveness of the internal controls . . .

(D) have presented their conclusions about the internal controls."

Section 404: Management Assessment Of Internal Controls.

Requires each annual report of an issuer to contain an "internal control report," which shall:

(1) state the responsibility of management for establishing and maintaining an adequate internal control structure and procedures for financial reporting; and

(2) contain an assessment, as of the end of the issuer's fiscal year, of the effectiveness of the internal control structure and procedures of the issuer—for financial reporting.

Each issuer's auditor shall attest to, and report on, the assessment made by the management of the issuer. An attestation made under this section shall be in accordance with standards for attestation engagements issued or adopted by the Board. An attestation engagement shall not be the subject of a separate engagement.

The language in the report of the Committee which accompanies the bill to explain the legislative intent states, "—the Committee does not intend that the auditor's evaluation be the subject of a separate engagement or the basis for increased charges or fees."

Directs the SEC to require each issuer to disclose whether it has adopted a code of ethics for its senior financial officers and the contents of that code.

Directs the SEC to revise its regulations concerning prompt disclosure on Form 8-K to require immediate disclosure "of any change in, or waiver of," an issuer's code of ethics.

Part 3

Taking the Measure
of the System

8

Identifying and Managing Risk

Software is a risky business. Recall from the previous chapters the spectacular software project failures: the plight of people needing ambulance services in London, aircraft trying to land without radio contact, and NASA probes missing Mars. Software project mangers tend to ignore or minimize risks in their enthusiasm to convince stakeholders to fund or participate in a project. There are great personal rewards for winning project support and little penalty for software project failure. Often a project's first manager is promoted or moved to a new project and is long gone before risks become crises. Neither praise nor blame—and certainly no legal responsibility—devolves back to the original decision maker, but this is commonly accepted business practice. The lack of risk analysis does not lead to a judgment against the vendor whose software project is canceled. If we wish to have the respect and rewards of being professionals, we must accept the responsibility that comes with affecting people's lives.

Software risk management deserves its own chapter because risks transcend the life of projects. The hallmark of successful projects is the ability to identify risks and develop contingency plans to deal with them. Reviews of failed projects typically find that problems would not have become crises if there had been a systematic review of high-risk areas at the start of a project and, more importantly, throughout the life of the project. At the start of each task, circumstances that may prevent the accomplishment of the task, called

Trustworthy Systems Through Quantitative Software Engineering,
by Lawrence Bernstein and C. M. Yuhas
Copyright © 2005 IEEE Computer Society

an event, need to be identified. Every event needs a corresponding risk containment and contingency plan.

8.1   RISK POTENTIAL

A risk is the possibility that an undesirable event in the life of a project can happen. Risks involve uncertainty and loss. Events guaranteed to happen are not risks. Events that do not negatively affect the project are not risks. Proactive risk management is the process of trying to minimize the potential bad effects of events.

Risks can affect the project plan and are therefore **project risks**. They can affect the quality of the product, and these are **technical risks**. They can affect the viability of the product, and these are **business risks**. Calculated risk-taking is vital to gain competitive advantage or to pioneer new technology. Rewards await bold and thoughtful risk-takers; obscurity awaits those who take risks blindly and without fallback, also called contingency, plans. Sarbanes-Oxley (SOX) compliance introduces **legal risks** if the elevator injures someone and the cause is traced to the software.

MAGIC NUMBER!

Boehm's hypothesis: Project risks can be resolved or mitigated by addressing them early.

Example: Suppose a project manager is asked to deliver trustworthy software for new high-performance hardware that will be used to control an elevator. This is already problematical because both hardware and software are untried. Table 8.1 provides some risks the project manager identified and classified once the architecture was in place.

With the risks identified, the project manager can keep the project risks and delegate the technical risks to the architect and the business risks to the product manager. All three must determine the likelihood that risk events will occur and estimate potential loss, but at this stage the risks are too general and need to be decomposed into detailed risk events.

TABLE 8.1. Risk Identification in Early Stages

Risks	Project	Product	Business	Legal
Incomplete and fuzzy requirements	X	X	X	X
Schedule too short	X		X	
Not enough staff	X			X
Morale of key staff is poor	X			
Stakeholders are losing interest			X	
Untrustworthy design		X		X
Feature set is not economically viable			X	
Feature set is too large	X			
Technology is immature		X		
Late planned deliveries of hardware and operating system	X		X	
Sarbanes-Oxley (SOX) compliance				X

8.2 RISK MANAGEMENT PARADIGM

"While we can never predict the future with certainty, we can apply structured risk management practices to peek over the horizon at the traps that might be looming, and take actions to minimize the likelihood or impact of these potential problems."[1] The goal of risk management is to make risk-taking a thoughtful and quantitative process. Both short-term and long-term risks need to be considered. The project manager makes sure that the project can succeed if the risk event happens. If the consequences are too great, then a new strategy is needed. One strategy is the early cancellation of a project so that the software organization can fail small and succeed big on some future project, having established their probity.[2]

The Software Engineering Institute (SEI) Risk Management paradigm is shown in Figure 8.1. The paradigm illustrates a set of functions that are identified as continuous activities through the life of the project.

8.3 FUNCTIONS OF RISK MANAGEMENT

Each risk event is examined periodically and formally discussed at project or subproject meetings. This is an important fixed agenda item for these meetings. Risk assessments are assigned as action items and tracked, and new risks are identified and analyzed. The contingency or containment plan for one risk event may yield another risk throughout the project life cycle. The processes for each step of risk management illustrated in Figure 8.1 are enumerated in Table 8.2.

---

[1] Keil, M., et al. "A Framework for Identifying Software Project Risks," *Communications of the ACM*, 1998, Vol. 41, No. 11, pp. 77–83.
[2] http://www.sei.cmu.edu/programs/sepm/risk/risk.mgmt.overview.html.

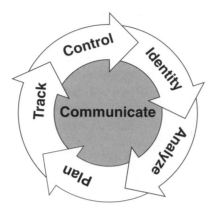

Figure 8.1. SEI risk management paradigm.

TABLE 8.2. Processes for Risk Management Steps

Step	Process Description
Identify	Search for and locate risk events before they become crises. Assign risk analysis to a project member as a tracked action item.
Analyze	Transform risk data into decision-making information. Evaluate risk likelihood, loss, exposure impact, and timeframe; classify risks; and prioritize risks.
Plan	Translate risk information into decisions and actions for containment and contingency and implement those actions.
Track	Monitor risk indicators and actions.
Control	Correct for deviations from the risk management plans.
Communicate	Provide information and feedback internal and external to the project on the risk activities, current risks, and emerging risks. Project meetings, progress report, project meeting minutes, and newsletters are effective tools for this communication.

The sophistication of the risk analysis tools depends on the nature of the system, its complexity, the availability of data, cost and schedule constraints, and trustworthy and performance constraints. Modeling is a powerful tool that can predict outcomes and consequences, as well as analyze the interrelationships of subsystems and components. For example, simulation models can analyze failure modes and the consequences of specific risk events. They can be used to conduct "what if" analyses to make engineering tradeoffs.

8.4 RISK ANALYSIS

In 1988, Barry Boehm provided this list of the top-ten software risk items in his seminal Spiral Model paper:

(1) Personnel shortfalls

(2) Unrealistic schedule and budgets

(3) Developing the wrong software functions

(4) Developing the wrong user interface

(5) Gold plating

(6) Continuing stream of requirements changes

(7) Shortfalls in externally furnished components

(8) Shortfalls in externally performed tasks

(9) Real-time performance shortfalls

(10) Straining computer science capabilities

Since then, he re-examined this list of risks in light of newer agile development methods in his 2004 "Guide to the Perplexed" paper. The risks still hold
true. Additionally, he and Richard Turner identified five project factors that
influence the choice of development methodology: **size**, **complexity**, **dynamism**
of the environment and software function, **personnel**, and **culture**. These
factors have remained remarkably consistent over time.

We saw that product size dominates the estimates for staffing and schedule. Product size also dominates project risk. Large products require more
people, take longer to produce, and are riskier than small ones. The project
manager needs to manage these project risk items: project size, project structure, and selection of project technology. Table 8.3 shows how we define size.

Large and huge projects must be decomposed into medium projects with a
firm architecture, interface discipline, and formal frequent human communications. Highly structured projects that follow an established development
plan are less risky than unstructured projects. The introduction of new technology is always risky.

Based on the risk factors, we can draw Table 8.4 and map the qualitative
risk assessment onto a five-ordinal scale (zero through four). This process
yields a quantitative estimate of the probability of project success, in which
four is likely success and zero is certain failure. Then we map to the range by
dividing by five and rounding appropriately.

TABLE 8.3. Project Size Parameters

Size	Developers	Function Points
Small	fewer than 10	150 or fewer
Medium	10 to 25	150 to 750
Large	25 to 200 developers	750 to 6000
Huge	200	Beyond 6000

TABLE 8.4. Risk Analysis

If Size is	And Structure is	And Technology is	Then the Project Risk is	Probability of project success is
Large	High	Low	Low	0.8
Small	High	Low	Lowest	0.9
Large	High	High	Medium	0.4
Small	High	High	Low-med	0.6
Large	Low	Low	High	0.2
Small	Low	Low	Medium	0.4
Large	Low	High	Highest	0.1
Small	Low	High	High	0.2

8.5 CALCULATING RISK

The probability that a **favorable** event (E) in a task will occur is

$$P(E) = m/n$$

where
P is the probability operator and $0 \leq P \leq 1$.
m = is the total number of favorable events.
n = total events.
Risk = $1 - P(E)$ is the probability that an **unfavorable** event will occur.

Risk exposure is the expected value or loss of the risk event, which is calculated by multiplying the risk probability by the cost of the risk event.

Risk Exposure (RE) = (Risk) (loss expected if risk happens).

Example: Given that there is a 0.5% probability that a latent fault will execute and lead to failure, and that such failure would cost the customer $100,000, then

$$RE = (0.005)(100,000) = \$500.00.$$

To manage this risk, we consider holding a design review. We estimate that the cost for holding this design review in terms of professional time is $100 and that it will halve number of faults and a new risk exposure (NRE) calculation. Should we hold the review?

$$NRE = (0.005/2)(100,000) + (0.9975)(100) = \$350,$$

where the second term is the cost of the review times the probability that the problem will not happen.

Risk reduction leverage (RRL) is calculated as (RE − NRE)/cost of risk reduction. Therefore, in this example,

$$RRL = (500 - 350)/100 \text{ or } 1.5.$$

Although a failure may not be avoided, design reviews tend to reduce their occurrence. Even if the RRL = 0, there may be intangible benefits for improving the product, such as making it easier to install, operate, or enhance. One benefit is preventing the erosion of the software structure. Designing for easy maintenance makes room for new modules and enhancements while relieving developers from the harsh resource constraints of fitting into the target computing environment. This effort reduces the risk of implementing future enhancements.

MAGIC NUMBER!

In practice, it is hard to quantify risk probability precisely. Data having a precision greater than its accuracy invites skepticism and mistrust.

A good practice is to qualify the likelihood of a risk event **not** occurring (because it seems easier for designers to think in terms of success rather than failure). A handbook entitled *Software Risk Abatement*[3] used by the U.S. Air Force offers a reasonable way of qualifying both the probability and the impact of risks. First, the probability of the risk event not occurring is categorized as very low, low, medium, high, or very high. Second, the loss to the project for that risk event is estimated using an ordinal scale and Wideband Delphi to do the mapping. Third, the loss is evaluated as negligible, marginal, critical, or catastrophic. Using the second and third subjective measures, an impact/probability matrix is developed to rank order the risk. The matrix should be unique to the problem domain and development organization.

Here are guidelines for assessing risk impact. The definitions of the impact parameters are from Boehm and the quantitative thresholds in Table 8.5 are based on the authors' experience.

Catastrophic: If the risk event occurs, the mission fails or customers refuse to purchase. If the risk event is a project issue, then the cost or schedule overruns exceed 50% of commitments.

---

[3] http://www.eas.asu.edu/~riskmgmt/intro.html.

TABLE 8.5. Risk Priority Matrix

Impact/Probability	Very High	High	Medium	Low	Very Low
Catastrophic	10	10	6	5	2
Critical	9	9	5	2	0
Marginal	6	5	2	0	0
Negligible	5	2	0	0	0

Critical: If the risk event occurs, the mission might fail or the product might be only a marginal, unprofitable market success. If the risk event is a project issue, then the cost or schedule overruns exceed 30% of commitments.

MAGIC NUMBER!

Reality check: 65% of all software projects suffer **catastrophic** or **critical** risk events.

Marginal: If the risk event occurs, the product may miss a secondary or tertiary objective, or it would yield a return on investment of 10% or less. If the risk event is a project issue, then the cost or schedule overruns exceed 10% of commitments.

Negligible: If the risk event occurs, there would be an inconvenience or non-operational mission impact. Although the early technology adopters would buy the product, the general market would wait for future releases. If the risk event is a project issue, then the cost or schedule overruns exceed 5% of commitments.

Once the analysis is complete, some risks can be chosen and assigned for action. As each is addressed, the next highest priority would be added to the list. The project manager should expect that there would always be action risk studies underway for a medium or large project because, as we have stated several times already, a project with no problems is in deep trouble.

MAGIC NUMBER!

Projects should have ten active risk studies underway, unless they are small projects.

The Constructive Cost Model II (COCOMO II) provides a risk level entry screen for each module and computes risk as the sum of the entries:

$$Total\ risk = schedule\ risk + product\ risk + process\ risk$$
$$+ platform\ risk + reuse\ risk.$$

COCOMO II also provides a heuristic risk assessment capability using the screen in Table 8.6 as input for postarchitecture stage risk assessment.

8.6 USING RISK ASSESSMENT IN PROJECT DEVELOPMENT: THE SPIRAL MODEL

Now that we know some ways to determine the risk and risk exposure for a project and we understand that it is an imprecise science because we are estimating the likelihood of future events, let us examine how we can systematically use these results.

TABLE 8.6. COCOMO II Risk Assessment Capability

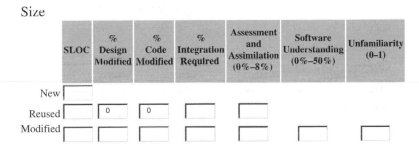

Rate each cost driver below from Very Low (VL) to Extra High (EH). For **HELP** on each cost driver, select its name.

	Very Low (VL)	Low (L)	Nominal (N)	High (H)	Very High (VH)	Extra High (EH)
Scale Drivers						
Precedentedness	○ VL	○ L	◉ N	○ H	○ VH	○ XH
Development Flexibility	○ VL	○ L	◉ N	○ H	○ VH	○ XH
Architecture/Risk Resolution	○ VL	○ L	◉ N	○ H	○ VH	○ XH
Team Cohesion	○ VL	○ L	◉ N	○ H	○ VH	○ XH

TABLE 8.6. (Continued)

	Very Low (VL)	Low (L)	Nominal (N)	High (H)	Very High (VH)	Extra High (EH)
Process Maturity	○ VL	○ L	◉ N	○ H	○ VH	○ XH

Product Attributes

	Very Low (VL)	Low (L)	Nominal (N)	High (H)	Very High (VH)	Extra High (EH)
Required Reliability	○ VL	○ L	◉ N	○ H	○ VH	
Database Size		○ L	◉ N	○ H	○ VH	
Product Complexity	○ VL	○ L	◉ N	○ H	○ VH	○ EH
Required Reuse		○ L	◉ N	○ H	○ VH	○ EH
Documentation	○ VL	○ L	◉ N	○ H	○ VH	

Platform Attributes

	Very Low (VL)	Low (L)	Nominal (N)	High (H)	Very High (VH)	Extra High (EH)
Execution Time Constraint			◉ N	○ H	○ VH	○ EH
Main Storage Constraint			◉ N	○ H	○ VH	○ EH
Platform Volatility		○ L	◉ N	○ H	○ VH	

Personnel Attributes

	Very Low (VL)	Low (L)	Nominal (N)	High (H)	Very High (VH)	Extra High (EH)
Analyst Capability	○ VL	○ L	◉ N	○ H	○ VH	
Programmer Capability	○ VL	○ L	◉ N	○ H	○ VH	
Personnel Continuity	○ VL	○ L	◉ N	○ H	○ VH	
Applications Experience	○ VL	○ L	◉ N	○ H	○ VH	
Platform Experience	○ VL	○ L	◉ N	○ H	○ VH	
Language and Toolset Experience	○ VL	○ L	◉ N	○ H	○ VH	

Project Attributes

	Very Low (VL)	Low (L)	Nominal (N)	High (H)	Very High (VH)	Extra High (EH)
Use of Software Tools	○ VL	○ L	◉ N	○ H	○ VH	
Multisite Development	○ VL	○ L	◉ N	○ H	○ VH	○ XH
Required Development Schedul e	○ VL	○ L	◉ N	○ H	○ VH	

Submit | Reset

Boehm's Spiral Model proposed a risk-driven software development process. The idea was to identify risk, build prototypes, and evolve software reliability. As originally envisioned, the iterations were typically 6 months to 2 years long. Each stage is a normal development project producing a super-set of the prior stage, which will be a subset of the final system. Planning for each successive stage is structured to exploit the experiences of the former stages and to reduce risk factors in the current and future iterations. Although numerous Spiral projects have succeeded splendidly, the Spiral approach has not achieved universal acceptance and has not always produced the results its proponents predict. This model was not the first to discuss incremental design, but it was the first model to explain why iteration matters.

Each development cycle starts with a design goal and list of risk events and ends with a risk assessment and a stakeholders' review of the progress thus far. Analysis and engineering efforts are applied to each phase of the project, with an eye toward the end goal of the project.

For a typical application development, you might build a minimal set of fea-tures, without the the user interface. Once there is a usable application, devel-opers add feature sets in increments that correspond to each cycle of the Sprial. Within each cycle there is a mini-Waterfall development and a collec-tion of risk action items. Features are added cycle-by-cycle until the deliver-able product is complete.

Typically there will be feature sets left for future releases of the product as the project manager trades off features to meet schedule commitments. A good process is for the project manager to define two sets of features for each release: those that are commitments and those that are goals. The difference between the sum of goals and commitments and commitments alone is the project manager's safety margin. The commitments need to consitutue an eco-nomically viable software product.

Using the Spiral Model schedule, and cost estimates are accurate because a risk analysis explicitly addresses budget and schedule problems. The esti-mates get more realistic as work progresses because the ongoing analysis uses the most current project information. The spiral method copes well with the inevitable changes that face software developers.

Software engineers sometimes become bored and restless with protracted design. The Spiral Model allows coding for the prototype earlier than in a document-driven method. It may be just experimental code to try new algo-riothms or to understand performance complexity. This aspect of the Spiral Model deals with the problem of retaining and attracting top-notch people to the project. Using the Spiral Model becomes a risk containment step in itself.

The Sprial Model is ill suited to small and moderate hard-drivng, schedule-focused projects where there is an experienced team in place. When time-to-market is the overriding concern, project managers define lean feature sets and use agile methods.

The Spiral Model is effective in addressing such challenges as rapid devel-opment, commercial off-the-shelf (COTS) software integration, new technologies, and product line management. However, some organizations have experienced difficulties with Spiral development because of overly relaxed controls as compared with document-driven approaches, poorly estimated risks, existing sequential development policies, inflexible financing mechanisms, ingrained cultures, and confusion about what Spiral development is and how to apply it.

Some of the critical success factors for Spiral development are as follows:

(1) Schedules cannot be overly compressed.

(2) Risks must be managed.

(3) Stakeholders must be involved.

(4) The technology must be ready. Combining research with technology adoption and shakedown can be part of a spiral cycle, but adding product development inhibits thoughtful risk assessment. Prototype demonstrations must be in an operationally relevant environment before proceeding to the next cycle.

(5) Requirements must be flexible. Consider an information query and analysis system. The contract was written to require a 1-second maximum response time, which turned out, after 2000 pages of design and documentation were written, to cost $100 million. At that point, a prototype, which would have been created sooner had the requirement been more flexible, showed that a 4-second response time was acceptable and would cost one third as much.

(6) The culture must be supportive. "Buyer, user, and vendor are a team. There is an attitude of partnership, trust and cooperation. There is a presumption of trustworthiness for reputable commercial organizations. Purchase decisions are heavily influenced by personal relationships."[4]

(7) A significant inhibitor is that stakeholders are wary of taking a delivery that only partially satisfies requirements, even though this is their usual software product experience. Retraining at a rapid pace is difficult to tolerate. Good spiral project managers balance training time with the time the release will be used when grouping features into sets.

In one company, field fault densities per 100,000 new or changed thousands source lines of code (NCSLOCS) declined by 62% over 3 years using the Spiral Model, this in an organization already having attained Capability Maturity Model® Level 5 status. This is charted in Figure 8.2, where it is worth noting the industry average of 500 defects per 100K NCSLOC and where the industry best in class lies.

---

[4] http://www.sei.cmu.edu/cbs/spiral2000/february2000/BoehmSR.html.

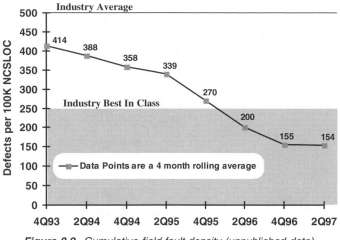

Figure 8.2. Cumulative field fault density (unpublished data).

8.7 CONTAINING RISKS

Having the right people and meeting schedules are the most frequently occurring risks to software projects. We will examine the risk containment steps that the project manager can take. Let us return to the risks listed in Table 8.1 in the first section and discuss how to contain each one:

(1) Incomplete and fuzzy requirements
(2) Schedule too short
(3) Not enough staff
(4) Morale of key staff is poor
(5) Stakeholders are losing interest
(6) Untrustworthy design
(7) Feature set is not economically viable
(8) Feature set is too large
(9) Technology is immature
(10) Late planned deliveries of hardware and operating system

8.7.1 Incomplete and Fuzzy Requirements

Different stakeholders in a software development project have their own agenda that often conflicts with the objectives of another stakeholder. For instance, users may require a robust, user-friendly system with many functions that can support their tasks, whereas development team members hope to encounter interesting technical challenges. These differing expectations create fundamental conflicts when simultaneously approached, resulting in unclear or misunderstood requirements.

It may be time consuming and difficult to collect and record all of the required details from all prospective users, resulting in the project team not knowing enough about what is required to complete the project successfully. This may lead to developing a system that cannot be used, mainly because a proper systems analysis to develop a complete and accurate set of requirements has not been performed. Often developers and analysts think of additional capabilities or changes, gold plating, which they think would make the system better and more attractive in their view. These deviations may result in unsatisfied users and unnecessary costs.

Boehm found that a continuous stream of requirement changes is a significant risk. As the users' needs change, so do the requirements of the project. The system will drive changes to business practices that in turn will dictate changes in the requirement. One risk containment approach is to freeze a set of features and a delivery date, but a frozen design does not accommodate changes in business practices. With a frozen design, the developer has little flexibility to change the specifications. Continuous and uncontrolled changes in requirements, however, will inevitably lead to a delay in the project schedule. The software engineer balances these needs.

8.7.2 Schedule Too Short

Yourdon describes the consequences of impossible deadlines and relentless rush, "The key point is to recognize and understand your own motivations at the beginning of a death march project, so that you can make a rational decision to join the team or look elsewhere for your next job. Since many of these projects are initiated during periods of great corporate stress and emotion, rational decisions are not as easy to make as you might think; it's all too easy to be swept away by the emotions of your fellow colleagues or your manager."

Obviously for any important system, other things being equal, the sooner it can be delivered the better. Sometimes circumstances dictate an absolute deadline, like Mother's Day or Y2K. Often some arbitrary deadline, often motivated by political considerations or personal ambition, is proposed, accepted without proper estimating or planning to establish its viability, and then becomes a fixed part of the landscape for managers and developers alike, to be defended at all costs. Where there is a client–contractor relationship, contractors are all too willing to collude with their clients' delusions. Even as the deadline gets nearer and common sense would seem to dictate that it is increasingly unachievable, there is no review and no attempt to change either the deadline or the solution. Shortcuts are taken, and essential processes (such as testing, reviews, problem resolution, and training) are ignored in the rush to complete essential technical tasks. Senior managers rarely take action to prevent this; on the contrary, they are often the prime sources of pressure.

╔══╗

MAGIC NUMBER!

Sixty percent of all projects suffer from compressed schedules.

╚══╝

8.7.3 Not Enough Staff

Product managers, executives, and customers are not impressed with a project manager's strident claims of not enough people to do the job. They want to see analysis supported by credible data. To make matters worse, the various estimating processes can yield different staffing estimates by as much as 50% and there is a highly nonlinear relationship between staffing and schedule time, based on the Rayleigh curve.[5]

Example: Consider a 310 function point project with a second generation lan guage that expands to 107 instructions per function point.[6] The software life-cycle model tool (SLIM) yields an estimate of 144 staff-months of effort. With eight people assigned to the project, a linear extrapolation will indicate that 18 months are needed, but SLIM shows that only 15 months are required. If the schedule is relaxed to 21 months, then four people are needed. If the fully loaded cost of a developer, including salary, benefits, and general and administrative costs is $70/hour or $12,000 per month, the conventional schedule will cost with linear extrapolation: (18 months)(8 developers/month)($12,000) = $172,800. Similar calculations show results for the nominal schedule and the relaxed schedule in Table 8.7.

TABLE 8.7. Staffing vs. Schedule Time

	Developers	Schedule (Months)	Cost ($12k/SM)
Conventional Linear Extrapolation	8	18	172,800
Nominal Schedule	8	15	144,000
Relaxed Schedule	4	21	100,800

[5] Putnam, Lawrence H. and Myers, Ware. *Industrial Strength Software: Effective Management Using Measurement*, IEEE Computer Society Press, Piscataway, NJ, 1997, Ch. 18 for discussion of SLIM and Rayleigh curve.
[6] http://www.spr.com/products/programming.shtm.

Considering that most project cost estimates are low by a factor of 2 or 3, these costs estimates, and remember that is all they are, are reasonably close. The SLIM tool exaggerates the effects of compressing schedules, but the point is valid and within reasonable estimating bounds. Without this analysis, the cost estimates become a matter of opinion. Bosses tend to trust their own opinions unless they are given the facts.

In an atmosphere of internal or external pressure to cut or control costs, cost reduction becomes the single-minded goal of the boss. Low development cost is deemed essential to gaining project approval or the prime criterion in bid selection. Just as there is resistance to changing deadlines, there is often a natural reluctance to cancel projects with runaway costs. Investment already made in the project feeds the escalation cycle and results in throwing more money after bad, rather than a re-evaluation of the return on continuing investment.

8.7.4 Morale of Key Staff Is Poor

Experienced project managers understand that containing risks is an effective way of keeping the morale of the staff high. Project managers who do not actively manage risks before they become crises rely on heroic efforts to keep the project on track, which burns out the staff and lowers morale. Developers will tend to stay to complete the current feature set and then leave the project when it is released.

Studies of risk management show that as the number of projects managed increases, the risk factors "unrealistic schedules and budgets" and "misunderstanding the requirements" occur less often. Managers can learn. No similar conclusions are possible for the other risk factors. Middle managers need to nurture the development of project mangers with formal training and education in software project management skills. Assigning novice project managers to small subprojects is a good first step. These might be leadership in developing a feature set requiring the coordinated work of two to four people. This builds confidence and esteem from colleagues. A proven record of accomplishment of project success is the best recommendation for a project manager. Having active project managers participate in reviews of other projects is effective in giving the project manager insight without having to suffer "trial by error" learning. It also encourages technology transfer between projects.

Software developers need to feel that they are growing in their field. They fear becoming obsolete and like to try new approaches and new technology. By providing life-long education and discretionary money for exploration, executives will manage this morale risk. These personal goals and values contrast with those of the executive. Once people are comfortable that they are being paid fairly and are satisfied with their standard of living, then different reward systems seem to motivate people in different jobs:

(1) CEOs seek compensation.

(2) Managers seek promotions.

(3) Salesmen seek commissions.

(4) Administrators seek appreciation.

(5) Software developers seek opportunities to tinker.

8.7.4.1 *Agile Methods* Agile methods are a risk containment process for the restless programmer. Agile methods encourage collaboration with people they respect and with whom they can grow.

Microsoft Program Manager David Anderson started as a game developer in the 1980s; he was involved in emerging agile techniques such as pair programming and short lead times. He later went on to help develop feature-driven development and comments:

> Agile is really catching on all over the company, within product groups and the internal IT organization. We're seeing . . . experiments with test-driven development and program managers running Scrum-like 30-day sprints and daily stand-up meetings. There's a growing community of agile believers . . . program managers at Microsoft don't have direct reports, so they don't manage programmers – development managers do that. However, both program managers and development managers need to be technical. It's all about respect. Developers need to respect the technical ability of their leader. Without respect, you cannot lead; and without leadership, software projects tend to fail . . . I'm not a believer in measuring individuals by their code production. Developing software is a team sport; it requires interaction and mutual support across the team. It's knowledge work and is best done in an environment of knowledge sharing. When you reward people for individual effort relative to their peers, you encourage them to hoard knowledge rather than share it. The manager should be measured by the productivity of the team, not the individual team members for their individual efforts . . . I reward people to learn and share. It's behavior compatible with team success . . . People won't follow unless they see and understand where they're going, and see confidence and resilience in their leadership . . . strong management is essential. Management must be prepared to instill and enforce discipline. Discipline in software development is what delivers high-quality, low-defect code.[7]

Philippe Kruchten, the inventor of the "4 + 1" architecture model, points out that the agile process "sweet spot" is for small teams of 10 to 15 developers who are colocated and communicate verbally as opposed to with documents. The customer representative on site is domain literate and empowered to make decisions. The projects have short life cycles of weeks or months (not years), and they use powerful development tools including automated rapid development, frequent (usually daily) builds, and automated test drivers and regression test suites.

[7] http://click.sd.email-publisher.com/maac2NEabc3WmbdnjEbb/.

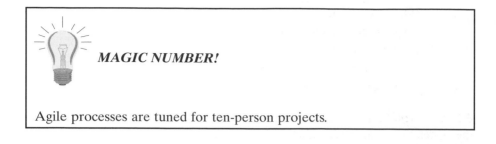

MAGIC NUMBER!

Agile processes are tuned for ten-person projects.

8.7.4.2   *Best for Small and Medium Applications*   Agile methods seem to work best for small- and medium-sized business applications rather than for high-performance embedded and real-time systems. New developments rather than maintenance projects are well suited to the agile methods. But maintenance, high performance, and large 200-staff projects are not going away. These large teams are geographically distributed, have few development tools, and an empowered customer is never present; they rely on documents for communication and strive to minimize changes. With a component-based architecture, a large project can be broken into a collection of medium projects and then decamped again into small projects. The architecture relies on a strong interface language that restricts how components exchange data and control; this constraint may be relaxed by skilled gurus, but it is inadvisable to do so. Then agile methods can be happily used to build the small components, and then their source code is transferred to the manufacturing team.

The manufacturers build a system following the instructions of the integration team. The components are recompiled and then linked, loaded, and regression tested. The integration team then performs functional tests based on use cases, reliability, and stress tests. If even more trustworthiness is needed, the system can be handed to a specialized team of diabolic testers. The integration team verifies that the system is ready for release. Even after release they may continue to test the release certifying the ability of the release to handle anticipated customer demands as the release is deployed. In this scheme, developers are related to agile method-based teams to build components. Then the realization for the software system becomes an integration process. Various software foundries build software components using agile methods. They feed their source code to carefully controlled libraries, and the technical integration team gives build instructions to the software manufactures who compile the source, load it into a system test machine, link the components, and run regression tests. Then the integration team tests the system to make sure it is ready for release. This **Compile, Link, and Test** metaphor for building software systems requires substantial support and emphasis on non-coding activities.

MAGIC NUMBER!

Five percent of a large project's staff is needed for communication among small agile teams, preparing system-wide documentation and packaging software for release.

8.7.5 Stakeholders Are Losing Interest

Users become more involved when there is a steering committee in place and they are informed of the impact of scope changes. They need to be welcome at all project meetings and have access to project information. The project manager who builds trust with the stakeholders increases the productivity of the organization and is more apt to build products that will be bought and used. The steering committee's goal is to stabilize requirements and specifications and to select feature sets proposed by the project manager.

When all stakeholders from customer to user to developer to supplier identify themselves as a member of the project before they identify their organization or role, the project manager will know that the stakeholders are not losing interest. It is a warning sign of trouble when stakeholders consistently miss steering meetings or send ineffective delegates. The risk containment action is to visit the stakeholder one-on-one and face-to-face to discuss their concerns. If this is impossible, then the project manager needs to find new stakeholders. Experienced project managers sometimes "fire a customer." Project managers need to report to their bosses and project team members the results of their periodic and frequent meetings with their customers. Another risk containment strategy is for the project manager to visit the users' workstations and see how the system is operating. On-site observations build confidence in the customer's staff that you care about them.

8.7.6 Untrustworthy Design

Requirements creep can subvert assumptions that underpin the architecture. New requirements need to be carefully controlled. Loose talk by developers quickly leads to commitments in the minds of customers. Although it is important to encourage open and complete communication between developers and users, it is just as important to be clear that only the project manager can make project commitments. Do everything to ensure common understanding of requirements among stakeholders.

Reuse can be a key issue. Systematic and well-managed reuse of elements of previous systems/solutions can bring great benefits, but without proper understanding and analysis, they can be high risk. Wrong decisions on technology infrastructure can have massively damaging effects. Distributed computing rather than large computers requires middleware and complex programming to share workloads, which adds risk to overcommitted software activities.

8.7.7 Feature Set Is Not Economically Viable

The risk of developing the wrong software functions and of doing the features wrong is reduced when the project is divided into separately controlled subprojects and requirements specifications are stabilized.

8.7.8 Feature Set Is Too Large

This is known as the Big Bang implementation. The attempt to leapfrog to a system that delivers the expected functionality and benefits in a single-shot implementation is fraught with risk. With complex systems, phased implementation of each phase delivers some useful functionality and builds on what already exists. This offers a controlled approach to dealing with risk. The Spiral Model offers one way to contain this risk. The overall effort can be assessed based on results to date, and it becomes easier to spot trouble earlier and to adjust overall effort if necessary. This approach also gives users a flavor of what the system can do for them, can generate enthusiasm and support, and can reduce resistance. On system cutover from a legacy process or system, a tried and true fallback system provides risk containment. Of course, the necessary cutover procedures with staff trained in their use are always important, but it is even more so when the Big Bang is attempted.

8.7.9 Technology Is Immature

Blind optimism that novel technology solutions are achievable is contagious and dangerous. Developers by their nature tend to innate technological optimism, and this is not always counterbalanced by management realism. Management is often technically obsolete. High levels of system complexity, ambition, and innovation are not recognized, and necessary steps to manage them are not taken. Many projects fail because they seem to be always adopting the latest and greatest before they capitalize on their last investment. Tool suppliers know to sell their new products to the developers and let them champion the tool to their management.

The prospect of enormous benefits and the splendor of technical achievement mask the scale of the challenge and the risks of failure. Experience with smaller simpler systems, or in other domains, makes software people believe that they are qualified to take a leap of faith. The required knowledge for attempting such a breakthrough in technology does not exist, and the need to extend budgets and schedules to allow for research and experiment to acquire that knowledge is critical.

How can project managers choose technologies? Refusing all technology changes leads to obsolescence. Need, expertise, and experience influence a technology choice. To manage the risk, the project manager assigns specific resources to explore the technology, then tries it in a few isolated cases in the environment of the project, and finally trains the full staff to adopt the chosen technology.

Case Study: The Case of Trouble in Paradise

At Paradise Software, C++ is de rigueur, but lately there has been trouble in Paradise. Many field problems have been traced to pointer arithmetic errors. The new kid proposes shifting to JAVA. Some developers like the idea because they can learn a new language and programming environment. It will make them more attractive should they ever need to find a new job, not that they are eager to leave Paradise.

The project manager is old and battle-scarred. He lost 6 months of production from every staff member when they converted from C to C++ 10 years ago. After 18 months the loss was recovered, but it was a difficult 18 months. True, his software shop did gain a reputation for world-class, low-defect, on-time software afterward. JAVA will probably yield higher productivity eventually, but not immediately.

The project manager reflects with pain on the earlier transition and sighs. He knows JAVA produces better code, but he wonders if it yields acceptable application performance and if the tool base is stable. Is this the right time to switch from an old technology to a new one? He decides to hedge his bets this time around.

The project manager agrees to set up a pilot program of no more than three people for no longer than 6 months. Their job is to qualify, quantify, and formally report the performance impact of the new language and the quality of the support tools. In addition, the project manager does his homework researching the experience of other projects with JAVA and finds this amazing graph, Figure 8.3.

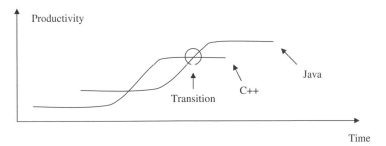

Figure 8.3. *Productivity vs. learning curve re C++, JAVA.*

Conclusion: The pilot program reports are satisfactory, and the project manger sets up and pays for trials with training and technology experts assigned to work in the trials. Once the trials are complete, a decision for project-wide deployment may be reached. If at any point the risk of adopting the new technology is too great, the technology can be dropped. The new kid thinks Paradise is a pretty good place to work. They listen.

MAGIC NUMBER!

One pilot plus three trials equals informed decisions.

8.7.10   Late Planned Deliveries of Hardware and Operating System

Alerts to potential problems may come from a variety of sources: past experience, warnings from knowledgeable sources, feedback from reviews, jeopardy reports, observation of events, or just plain common sense. Deafness to such alerts may afflict any stakeholder group including executives, customers, product management, project management, and developers. When those capable of sounding the alert observe that deafness or punishment is the usual outcome, then the alert will be sounded less frequently.

Dysfunctional relationships among stakeholder groups can develop. These key stakeholder groups may include executives, middle managers, developers, the project sponsors, or the system users. Agile methods and the WinWin Spiral Model demand that all stakeholder groups be integrated into the development process. Everyone needs an effective voice to express both their needs and their knowledge. Poor intergroup communication increases risk, and success relies on establishing stakeholder ownership and commitment. Examples of dysfunctional relationships between groups include:

(1) "Range Chicken," a concept that originated during missile tests and carries over to enterprises that require the cooperation of several independent organizations. As launch time or due dates draw near, organizations having problems delay reporting their problem in the hope that they will find a fix before they must confess to not being ready. They do not want to be blamed for delays.

(2) Unwillingness of executives to understand issues, get involved and committed, organize for the systems effort, and undertake properly informed decision making.

(3) Resistance of middle management to relate concurrent problems or changes within the enterprise and to understand and deal with their

interactions. For example, computer systems cannot automate chaotic processes.

(4) Unreasonable pressure by customers or senior management on development schedules.

(5) Lack of attention to staff concerns of both developers and users exacerbated by overspending of scarce resources on glossy brochures, management consultants, and corporate image, or by perceptions that it is lying to the public. Several systems have failed when union workers perceived that the objective of the system was to eliminate their jobs. They made sure it did not work. People want software systems that enhance their positions, not replace them.

(6) A climate of fear, blame, and low morale among developers, vendors, or users.

(7) A culture of strong internal politics, improper relationships, and vested interests among customer agents, developers, or suppliers.

8.8 MANAGE THE COST RISK TO AVOID OUTSOURCING

Although project teams are effective in determining customer needs and satisfying them, they are not efficient in their use of resources. There is much duplication between teams in the areas of tool selection, technology evaluation, process design, software manufacturing, computer administration for both clients and servers, and in setting up and operating system test environments.

MAGIC NUMBER!

Up to 20% of the budget for large multiproject organizations is wasted in redundant activities or lost because they do not receive volume discounts for hardware or software COTS tools and components.[8]

Software shops can gain the efficiency they need to be competitive and avoid the outsourcing risk by forming some functional departments to serve across all projects. Introducing centralized functional departments often fails, so it must be done with great care and middle management buy-in. Choosing the tasks to centralize and full commitment by the entire leadership team are

[8] Internal Bell Laboratories study of a 2000-person, 150-project software shop led by Bernstein.

vital. On the other hand, centralized departments too often become bureaucratic and lose the sense that their mission is to serve the projects. To manage this risk, rotate middle and first-line managers through the functional organization periodically.

MAGIC NUMBER!

Rotate managers in functional organizations to project organizations every 2 to 3 years. Staying longer tends to make the functional organization less responsive to the current needs of the projects. Fresh managers update the centralized activities.

8.8.1   Technology Selection

Centralized functional organizations are more effective at choosing technology because uncontrolled diversity often leads to systems that cannot work together. Components cannot be shared among teams, and basic functions such as systems and network management are duplicated. Even worse, any resemblance among systems administration for different product lines is purely coincidental. Without being able to share the platform rules, tools, and assets, it is näive to think that application areas can be shared. Each project loses skilled people to meeting with suppliers, selecting technology, and training new team members on their selected technology.

8.8.2   Tools

When every project team does this, it duplicates the efforts of the others. It is difficult to obtain leveraged purchases on favorable terms from tool suppliers when each team buys for themselves.

8.8.3   Software Manufacturing

A duplication of effort to control changes and build releases across projects without adherence to cross-project standards leads to difficult system integration. Often products must work on different physical computers from the same manufacturer and with the same configuration because the software executables are arbitrarily different. Each team has its own approach to system builds, and there are no opportunities for economies of scale This increases testing costs as well as cost to the customer. Software manufacturing activities include trouble tracking, system builds, configuration control, and release packaging.

Centralize these functions, and include a trained set of program administrators whose job is to adhere to standard processes so that the programmers learn to trust the professional software builders.

8.8.4 Integration, Reliability, and Stress Testing

This area should come under centralized functional management, and the system testers should be placed on loan to product teams for specific tasks. System test processes and tools should be standardized. Subject matter experts need to remain with the project teams, but software testing technologists and their tools may be centralized. The new concept of software component foundry and "Compile, Link, and Test" software factory is an effective way to gain economies of scale, in which component is a technical definition constraining the characteristics of a software module.

8.8.5 Computer Facilities

The administration of the client and server computers spread throughout the organization is a hidden expense. Volume purchases are difficult to make, and systems administrators with the knack of keeping the computers operating are not shared. There is significant wasted space and duplicate machines. Inadequate desktop tools can impact the entire development community and were one root cause of delays in several projects.

8.8.6 Human Interaction Design and Documentation

Almost 25% of the total staff is devoted to ease of use and user documentation. Standard approaches to doing the design, producing, and controlling the documents can be centralized. Skilled human performance engineers and technical writers can be loaned to projects as needed, which improves their morale because they are not lost in a program design organization and have a path for career growth.

All six of these functions can be separated from the project teams and managed in a single integrated support department. This matrix organization works when funding for their funding is not within each project team. The centralized team has its own budget with usage-based charge-backs to the project teams. Cost under-recoveries reduce profits for all projects inversely proportional to their use of the centralized activities, and over-recoveries increase project profits based on their use of centralized activities. They are a cost center; the project teams are the profit center.

This centralization would not only improve productivity but also would reduce time to market and improve quality. Many project teams cannot make incremental builds. They always deliver their whole product package to the customer. This is costly to both the projects and the customers. It is a major customer dissatisfaction as they expect products from the same software shop to "look and feel" the same, share file storage and networks, and have a common system administration. The centralized team may in turn sell their services and tools outside the organization, but only through a project established for that purpose.

This approach is the foundation for establishing a climate for reuse that leads to a significant increase in productivity. The essence of the these standards is to define and implement a set of engineering rules that make it possible to practically integrate products into customer-specified solutions through reuse and commonality of processes, development methodology, and tools. The engineering rules encompass four categories: software architecture and platform; environment and tools; integrated product offers, and documentation, including sales-ware.

Case Study: The Case of the Perpetual Pendulum

A classic management problem is how to determine the best structure for an organization that must be nimble, yet at the same time stable enough to get the work done. Change renews and invigorates, so long as it does not happen too often. This risk management technique prevents the ossification of a company. Remember *The Case of the Well-Shod Management* in Chapter 6; this is the next episode.

The manager found that 20% more savings were possible by adhering to engineering rules. This amounts to a saving of 40 people $\times$ 0.20 = 8 people or another $1.3 million annually. This leads to a 50% cost reduction.

Arriving back at corporate headquarters, the manager delivers this good news. The Executive Council has been infected with "outsourcing fever" ever since their CIO attended a 2-day seminar. Not only do they applaud the news, but they leap to send every last employee out the door by outsourcing everything.

The manager pauses to reflect that successful outsourcing by a company requires dedicated company project managers and software engineers, special testing, travel, communications, and equipment costs.

Conclusion: This letter to the Executive Council by the project manager successfully argued against outsourcing this project. The project is still staffed domestically today.

To: Vice President, Operations Support Systems Business Unit

There is no need to outsource to gain competitive advantage. Our development team is in place, is skilled, and has gained extensive problem domain knowledge. There is significant opportunity to further improve our productivity and quality while reducing time-to-market. Introducing centralized functional organizations is a vital part of this effort. Action is being taken to obtain an immediate 10% elimination of redundant effort, which is expected to grow to 20% in 3 years. Specific areas that will to be addressed include:

(1) Engineering rules conformity

(2) Reuse

(3) Platform and library use across projects

(4) Use of a software fault-tolerant library to reduce testing efforts and produce a better production product

(5) Software project management training

(6) Move to "buy instead of build" culture and create a "link, compile and test" software shop

(7) Migrate to JAVA and JAVA platforms

(8) Set a 40% design simplification goal

(9) Reward developers for writing less code per feature

Yours truly,
The Project Manager

8.9 SOFTWARE PROJECT MANAGEMENT AUDITS

Management malpractice is a serious risk to project success. When a software project is in trouble, a software project audit can help. Audits are for the project manager and not for higher management. The audit team needs to gain the trust of the software developers. Audits should be a regular action taken early in the development process before implementation begins. McDonald writes that with this approach, "The audit became relatively painless for the project team; it is likely to cause a much more positive change in the software development environment. . . ."

Software project management audits address the risk of management malpractice and pressure the project leaders to create a realistic project plan early in the development cycle. Audits crisply identify the highest project risks and estimate their probability of failure.

The audit is requested by the project manager. McDonald recommends, and we agree, that the best " time for conducting a project management audit is during the definition phase of a project, shortly after the business case or contract has been baselined, a solid project plan has been developed, the architecture has been baselined and at least some of the detailed requirements have been developed." But an audit can be useful anytime. A software project management audit includes a review of the business case, the development plan, the architecture, and the requirements specification. If a prototype is available, the audit team examines it also. They visit the development team in their workplace and at their desks. They observe activity in the test laboratories. Fundamental to the audit is one-on-one interviews with a cross section of the project team by an independent set of experienced managers who have managed similar projects.

The audit produces feedback only to the project team; they may in turn comment on it and forward it to their executives or customers as they see fit. It is their intellectual property.

Audits have contributed to project success when the project manager embraces them and uses the results constructively. The project manager and the development team members get the most benefit when they view the auditors as fellow developers interested in their success, not as part of an inquisition.

8.10 RUNNING AN AUDIT

Before an audit takes place, the project leaders spend time learning about the project and creating their measurable operational value and development plan. The project manager and the audit team leader jointly clarify the scope and the objectives of the audit and schedule it. It is not a surprise visit by an outside set of professional auditors. The project manager helps the audit team leader recruit audit team members and communicates audit findings with follow-up actions to the entire project team.

The audit team leader is an experienced software project manager who has previously participated in audits and will choose three or four other audit team members, who are skilled project managers. The audit team leader structures a detailed time schedule for the audit and a questionnaire. The project manager approves these.

McDonald reports the results of 21 audits of medium- to large-scale software projects. He was on each audit team. As predicted by Boehm, project schedule and requirements management issues were the most frequently cited risks.

8.11 RISKS WITH RISK MANAGEMENT

All software engineering processes have advantages and disadvantages. Risk management is no exception. The project manager reaches a balance between control and productivity so that the development staff can be effective and efficient. Risk management is a worthwhile process, but it can intimidate an organization when risks are "overestimated." Then too many resources may be diverted to contingency planning and containment steps and too much money may be spent on the most vocal risk identifier's pet part of the project. Experienced project managers are needed to contain this risk. When software shops approach schedule deadlines, a nervous tension close to panic is observed. Managers seek delays identifying all possible risks. The project managers use the top-ten problem list to manage these risks and judge the state of the project by examining the nature of the problems. The mantra at this late stage switches from "What's the problem?" to "Plan on Success." This requires delicate and experienced judgment at a critical phase. On one project, the reports of problems reached such a crescendo that the customer suggested that the project be delayed. The project manager cautioned not to revise the project plan until after the next critical milestone. Then, if necessary, have a critical schedule review. In addition, minor adjustments were made in staff assignments setting up a task force of testers and developers to help in component testing. Happily the dates were made, and there was no need for the review. Keeping firm in times of project turmoil is essential, but not easy.

Risks may be dismissed and their impact underestimated, which gives the stakeholders a false sense of security. This risk can be contained by the use of project audits. Software shops that underestimate risks become victims of reactive crisis management. Blame must be avoided when a project gets into this state. Public recognition and appreciation for those identifying problems is necessary to establish the open and trusting project environment needed to deal with crises.

Choosing projects that minimize all risk can lead to dull projects and drive away the gurus. These projects are typically less profitable. Risk management can be expensive and, as with all processes, needs to be managed to make sure it is finding real problems, inspiring quality solutions, closing risk items, and not breaking the bank.

8.12 PROBLEMS

8.12.1 Given that there is a 0.1% probability that a latent software fault will execute and lead to failure, and if a failure occurs the customer would lose $100,000, what is the RE?

8.12.2 To manage the risk found in Problem 8.12.1, we consider a holding a formal design review. How much can the project manager afford to spend on the design review and break even? (Hint: Break even means the RE without design reviews equals the RE with design reviews.)

8.12.3 List four principle requirements risks as defined by Boehm in the development of software products.

8.12.4 You are the project manager for a customer resource management system. Your sales force tells you that the architecture impacts their ability to sell your software product. Here is the prospectus:

Department stores, software companies, and utility companies all have call centers that handle customer complaints. Your primary customer employs 1000 agents. Call center managers have the authority to hire and fire agents and can purchase incidental equipment for the operation of the center. Purchases of more than $100,000 require corporate approval including a review by the CIO. The CIO is charged with reducing information technology costs and the number of suppliers. Typically an agent uses a predefined script to capture the customer's problem. Once the problem is defined, it is resolved or handed off to a second-tier expert. The agents must strictly follow the script that can resolve 50% of the problems. For example, if a customer claims that they have already paid a bill, the agent asks for the invoice number and checks the accounting database. If the customer's payment has been recorded in the time since the bill was mailed, the agent cancels the bill; if this is a first customer complaint and the bill is less than $10, the agent forgives the charge. The system must be generally available in 9 months.

An existing customer for your software company badly needs such a system to automate these business tasks. They want to purchase the system in 6 months. This customer has had serious problems with another system they recently bought from your company, and their CEO has formally complained to your CEO about late delivery, "obvious" bugs, and poor support.

For the CRM system, your staff of five developers prototype a new speaker-independent voice recognition system, using JAVA, and find that customers prefer the clarity and patience of the computer to that of many agents. Reliable and consistently friendly agents that exercise good judgment are hard to find and train at the wages companies are willing to pay. An agent is paid $30,000 yearly, and the overhead is twice the salary.

Based on the prototype, you size the project at 50 function points. Desktop computers equipped with voice recognition equipment, communication hardware, and platform software costs $10,000. These computers can replace one agent.

Server computers can share the new speaker-independent voice recognition equipment, and communications hardware and platform software costs $120,000. Each server can replace 300 agents, which results in a cost of $4000 per agent.

Financial times are hard, and your likely first customer, the CIO, is insisting that new systems yield a 2-month or less break-even time where the cost of money is not considered because interest rates are 1% annually. The cost of developing the software is $800,000. This is true for either the server or the desktop solution.

Identify the top-ten risk events that you need to put on the agenda for the next CRM project meeting:

8.12.5 You are asked to build a system that is priced to yield a profit of 10% of the cost of the system in 3 years if it is successfully deployed. Use a constant interest rate of 5%. (Hint: To discount the cash flow, compute today's value of future money by using this formula:

$$\mathbf{NPV} = CF/(1+IR)^n,$$

where
NPV = Net present value
CF = Cash flow
IR = Interest rate (3%, for example)
n = Number of years

a. What is your return on investment in the third year?

b. The schedule is known to be tight, and the nominal schedule is estimated to be 44 months. A schedule with 95% confidence is estimated to be 60 months. Estimate the probability that the system will be delivered on the 3-year schedule if all delays are assumed to be uniformly distributed.

c. What is the expected profitability of the system?

8.12.6 Recall the case study about Ajax Transporters, Inc., which manufactures exactly one size of one model of one product, the Ajax Personal Transporter, in Chapter 7.

You work for Amber Consulting, Inc., and your group at Amber has just been given the job of making the change to Ajax's system, but without changing the COTS product currently in use. You are required to keep the COTS subsystems current.

Define five risks for this project, and calculate a risk exposure for each. State your estimate of risk likelihood and risk cost.

8.12.7 You are the project manager for a large transaction system with access to a large database. You estimate that the development will take 3 years, and you propose to provide annual releases. You estimate that you will need 40 to 60 people per year, and you request a budget for 55 people. Your boss challenges the accuracy of your estimates. You respond that they are accurate to about +20%. He reduces your budget request by 11 people. What is your response?

a. Accept the change and try harder.

b. Look for a new job.

c. Point out that just as you may have estimated high, you may have estimated low and that you might be overbudget by 11 people.

BIBLIOGRAPHY

Addison, Tom and Vallabh, Seema. "Controlling Software Project Risks—an Empirical Study of Methods used by Experienced Project Managers," *Proceedings of SAICSIT*, 2002.

Department of the Air Force, Software Technology Support Center. "Guidelines for Successful Acquisition and Management of Software Intensive Systems: Weapon Systems, Command and Control Systems," *Management Information Systems*, Vol. 1, Version 1.1, Department of the Air Force, Software Technology Support Center, Salt Lake City, UT, 1995.

Asaravala, Amit. "Managing at Microsoft," *SD PEOPLE & PROJECTS*, Jan. 2005.

Bernstein, L. "Software Project Management Audits," *Journal of Systems and Software*, Vol. 2, 1981, pp. 281–287.

Boehm, Barry. *Software Engineering Economics*, Prentice-Hall, Englewood Cliffs, NJ, 1981, Chs. 19 and 20.

Boehm, Barry. "A Spiral Model of Software Development and Enhancement," *IEEE Computer*, May 1988, pp. 61–72.

Boehm, Barry. *Software Risk Management*, IEEE Computer Society Press, New York, 1989.

Boehm, B. and Ross, R. "Theory-W Software Project Management Principles and Examples," *IEEE Transactions on Software Engineering*, Vol. 15, 1989, pp. 902–916.

Boehm, Barry W. "Software Risk Management: Principles and Practices." *IEEE Software*, Vol. 8, Jan. 1991, pp. 32–41.

Boehm, Barry, et al. *Software Cost Estimation with COCOMO II*, Prentice-Hall, Englewood Cliffs, NJ, 2000, p. 403.

Buckle, J. K. *Managing Software Projects*, American Elsevier, New York, 1977.

Endres, Albert and Rombach, Dieter. *A Handbook of Software and Systems Engineering—Empirical Observations, Laws and Theorems*, Pearson Addison Wesley, Reading, MA, 2003, p. 201.

Keil, M., et al. "A Framework for Identifying Software Project Risks, *Communications of the ACM*, Vol. 41, 1998, pp. 77–83.

McDonald, James. "Software project management audits—update and experience report," *The Journal of Systems and Software*, Vol. 64, 2002, pp. 247–255.

Putnam, Lawrence H. and Myers, Ware. *Industrial Strength Software: Effective Management Using Measurement*, IEEE Computer Society Press, New York, 1997, Ch. 18 for discussion of SLIM and Rayleigh curve.

Yourdon, Edward Nash. *Death March: The Complete Software Developer's Guide to Surviving 'Mission Impossible' Projects*, Prentice-Hall, Englewood, Cliffs, NJ, 1997.

9

Human Factors in Software Engineering

The study of human factors ranges across a continuum from the philosophical meaning of the nature of work to the details of optimal screen design. The product and process aspects of this study greatly influence the acceptance of the product by the user and the cost of development. The details of human factor design for end users have received the most attention, perhaps because of the work of pioneers like Henry Dreyfuss at Bell Laboratories whose elegant design of everyday things enriches our lives, Alan Kay who made computers comprehensible to nonprogrammers, and Steve Jobs whose iPod was the hot 2004 product.

9.1 A CLICK IN THE RIGHT DIRECTION

Apple's iPod is handy, and its ease of use makes it a best seller. It is upgraded to have the same touch-sensitive Apple Click Wheel that debuted on the *iPod mini*. With it you can easily select play lists, scroll through thousands of songs, and start the music playing. Just a single click is all you need.[1]

Human factors specialists do more than design friendly icons, however. They bring two important kinds of knowledge to bear on systems development: first, human abilities and limitations and second, empirical methods for

---

[1] http://www.apple.com/ipod/.

Trustworthy Systems Through Quantitative Software Engineering,
by Lawrence Bernstein and C. M. Yuhas
Copyright © 2005 IEEE Computer Society

309

collecting and interpreting data from people. They define criteria for ease of use, ease of learning, and user acceptance in measurable terms. New technology demands much thought about the role of the tool. The distress and aversion many people manifest toward computerization is perfectly rational in the presence of ill-conceived design. Figure 9.1 shows some poor design; while driving toward West Street in New York City, we faced this daunting decision as we approached the intersection. It became clear eventually that there was

Figure 9.1. *So many signs, so little clarity.*

a second street. Too many of our systems confuse the operator without providing an opportunity for clarification.

The story of software development is as uniquely American as the westward expansion. It is rough and tumble, driven by a get-it-done attitude. It is studded with heroic figures who make brilliant leaps into new territory. Its products have amazed and astonished the population at large and created a mystique of invincibility. Only a moment ago have its predecessors, the lone gunslinger, the paladin troubleshooter, and the flashy but inefficient Pony Express, come under some civilizing rule. It has been the place to be for the last three decades, and this is just the beginning. Every kid in an earlier time watched Westerns; now they plug into the Internet. The reason is simple. Creating and using the magic stuff called software is emotionally engaging, difficult, and wildly exciting.

At the risk of belaboring the Wild West analogy, we might say that the Mark Twain of programming is Fred Brooks. He wrote *The Mythical Man-Month* 20 years ago and recently reissued it with updates. He is a clear-eyed, astringent observer of both strengths and foibles in programming. He says, "A clean, elegant programming product must present to each of its users a coherent mental model of the application, of strategies for doing the application, and of the user-interface tactics to be used in specifying actions and parameters. The conceptual integrity of the product, as perceived by the user, is the most important factor in ease of use . . . managing large programming projects is qualitatively different from managing small ones, just because of the number of minds involved. Deliberate and even heroic, management actions are necessary to achieve coherence."

There are elements of coming full circle back to the much-maligned intractable individualist in the concepts for the future. The cottage industry mentality used to be the bane of team programming, but prototyping calls for a small team with a coherent view. Boehm's Spiral Model starts with a kernel of an idea that expands. The Internet is the ultimately diversified large system made from small parts. This brings attention back to the guru or master programmer, which is an issue for software project managers. Quality theory presumes low variances in productivity, but, in fact, several studies have found wide variance in individual performance.

One benefit of this circling back to an emphasis on the individual or small group might be in the area of ethics. A large project with hundreds of peer workers belongs to nobody. A large project conceived by a few has an owner, someone who is ultimately answerable for choices. Here are examples of what results from a lack of ownership that should be dear to taxpayers' hearts.

The U.S. Army stopped the development of a system that was supposed to replace 3700 older systems by the year 2002. After $158 million and 3 years of effort, the new system was far behind schedule and well over budget. The method for choosing the developer encouraged low bidding to get the contract, and then throwing money at a slipping schedule. The Army failed in having specified no way to know if the project was on track. The developer failed in not knowing the scope of the problem better than the customer. Both failed in that nobody was ultimately responsible. Appointing a project manager, splitting projects into pieces for which individuals are responsible, and enforcing risk management could produce a more logical approach.

The second example is worse because it is life threatening. The Department of Energy (DOE) keeps a record of every ounce of plutonium, enriched uranium, and other highly radioactive materials created, transported, or sold in the United States, which amounts to several hundred tons. The tracking system was obsolete, and the DOE contracted for a replacement. When Congress asked the General Accounting Office (GAO) to check up on the project a year later, the GAO reported that the developer had started programming without adequately analyzing the problem, the user needs, or the final cost of operation. Furthermore, the developer could provide no specifications, no test results, and no status reports. The GAO recommended canceling the project because "the history of software development is littered with systems that failed under similar circumstances." Nevertheless, the DOE switched over to the new system without ever requiring that the software pass any acceptance tests. Clearly there are ethical issues on the part of all three organizations, but individuals, not organizations, practice ethics.

9.2 MANAGING THINGS, MANAGING PEOPLE

It is important to distinguish between the management of things, like data, and people. Say the word *manager* and most people will think of a Peter Drucker clone, that is, an intermediary between the executive and people who actually perform physical work. Drucker's idea was that managers would benevolently pursue the interests of society. Given the turmoil in many large companies and the resonance that Dilbert cartoons have with many people, it would seem that this idea did not work out well, and some major change is happening. Perhaps the ground swell is coming from the barely perceived impression that computers should augment workers, not substitute for them. Knowledge that is freely available flattens office hierarchies and increases the total amount of work it is possible to achieve. A Drucker-type manager need no longer exist when the computer does that job better and faster as, for example, in Customer Relations Management (CRM).

MAGIC NUMBER!

There is a 10:1 difference in productivity among software shops.

The best performers tend to be in the same organizations. They migrate to work environments where they can be most productive and help each other grow. Private offices and large workspaces are essential to having a productive organization. IBM studies of software developers led them to build their Santa Teresa facility with the goal of 100 square feet of dedicated space per worker, 30 square feet of work surface per person, and noise protection with enclosed offices for half the staff, each accommodating only one or two people.

These guidelines were first adopted at Bell Laboratories, when they built their Holmdel facility in 1962. They made no distinction between developers and researchers. Invention and innovation thrived. Saving money on space is a false economy,[2] and the ubiquitous open cubicle is unsuitable for chickens, not to mention thinking humans.

9.2.1 Knowledge Workers

So what job must be done? It is the job of considered judgment, creative ideas, and efficient problem resolution. Better, faster, more intelligent technology actually serves to minimize the less desirable hostile tendencies in human nature and nurture the more collegial tendencies.

Shoshana Zuboff[3] foresaw the changing nature of work two decades ago. A powerful new technology fundamentally reorganizes the infrastructure of the work world, especially in the distribution of knowledge in the workplace. Information technology renders events and processes visible and knowable in a way that must be shared and interpreted by workers who exercise judgment. The human factors problem is to design sufficient feedback into computer systems to allow people to function effectively. Zuboff remarks, "The psychological discomfort that gives rise to doubt reflects the loss of an immediate knowledge for which there is as yet no replacement. Knowledge had depended in large measure upon the body and its experience of concrete cues. Now the operator feels both personally diminished and weakened by a loss of crucial contextual information. A new sense of certainty depends first upon clarifying the referential function of the data. Deductions are not read off the face of appearances; they are not transparent features of the terminal screen. Rather, they depend upon understanding, and understanding can be developed only from a solid intellective skill base that recognizes what icons are supposed to represent and that has invented mechanisms for validating that they really do carry such force."[4]

9.2.2 Collaborative Management

As software becomes more sophisticated, problems, when they occur, will be complex. Guru software developers gravitate to managers who encourage the

---

[2] DeMarco, Tom and Lister, Timothy. *Peopleware-Productive Projects and Teams*. 2nd ed., Dorset House, New York, 1999, p. 53.

[3] Zuboff, Shoshana. *In the Age of the Smart Machine*, Basic Books, New York, 1988.

[4] Zuboff, *Ibid.*, pp. 83–84.

spirit of hypothesis generation, testing, and "playful" manipulation that is above all a collegial one. To software developers, new software technology is exciting. The more technical leadership shown by software managers, the higher the productivity of the organization.

End users do not want a computer that will steal their jobs; they want a computer that will enhance personal status. Computerization broadens and expands the available work, but how acceptable this kind of problem-solving, decision-making work is to people who have no experience or preparation for it will be the staff management challenge.

The overall quality of the body of work depends on the totality of individual judgments. Military historians understand that the outcome of a war depends on the cumulative effect of many individual decisions, each made in the heat of battle, in a split second, based on some subset of the whole truth. Decisions that looked good at the time can turn out later to have been not so good. The only tool to minimize the bad collective decision is widely distributed relevant and accurate data in an easily recognizable form. It is a liberating idea that wars, history, economies, businesses, and software projects are not deterministic, that things do not have to turn out in only one particular way, and that choices might be different if bits of data were presented more clearly to a wider audience. If information technology improves a work environment by giving a larger and clearer view of the truth of a situation, better individual decisions can be made in moments of crisis. Individual and group judgments can improve. This style of management is worth cultivating in a rapidly changing world for which there is not much of a template.

Individual designers move quickly between the concrete and the abstract. They work in the problem domain and the solution domain at the same time. The role of the human in the system is not always obvious, and too often developers leave it to users to make up for automation shortfalls. These are called "workarounds" and are an indication of design flaws. Top-down may be a good way to describe how a system works once it is built, but collaborative, interactive efforts are used to come up with the design. The prototype gives the designers the opportunity to evaluate designs. They are especially useful for evolving the human interface design.

Examples of people dealing with the unknown and unpredictable are the FAA, the former Bell System, and NASA human factors specialists. NASA teams preparing for early space missions developed specific techniques of group interaction that fostered optimal group problem solving. It was a collegial style that involved much exchange and repetition of information for maximum clarity. It also involved practice in simulated situations and much hypothesizing of alternatives. These specialists made sure that human capabilities and limitations were properly reflected in the system requirements. The astounding success of the early missions and commercial flight safety demonstrates the value of human factors applications.

Human factors are relevant to meeting system performance and functional requirements:

(1) Human performance (e.g., human capabilities and limitations, workload, function allocation, error rates, hardware and software design, decision aids, environmental constraints, and team versus individual performance)

(2) Training (e.g., length of training, training effectiveness, retraining, training devices and facilities, and embedded training)

(3) Staffing (e.g., staffing levels, team composition, and organizational structure)

(4) Personnel selection (e.g., minimum skill levels, special skills, and experience levels)

(5) Safety and health aspects (e.g., hazardous materials or conditions)

One example of a human capability, time perception, can be shown to affect the functional requirements of a software design. Table 9.1 shows time perception across various tasks and media.

TABLE 9.1. Time Perceptions Across Media

Human Perception	Transaction Time	Application	Preferred Physical Architecture
instantaneous	Less than 1/3 second	Software Development	Personal computer or workstation
fast	Between 1/3 and 1 second	Simple query	Client/server
pause	Between 1 and 5 seconds	Complex query and application launch	Thin client
wait	Greater than 5 seconds	Action Request	Background Batch

Transaction interactions should be without a perceived wait, and the standard deviation of all transactions should be less than 50% of the mean.

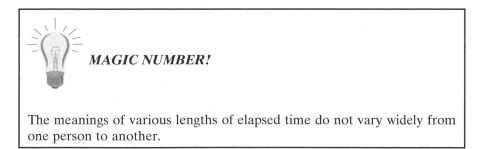

MAGIC NUMBER!

The meanings of various lengths of elapsed time do not vary widely from one person to another.

The human factors specialists on a requirements engineering team provide the support for the integration of human factors engineering throughout the development of a software system. They find problems that might otherwise go undetected for their obscurity, complexity, or elaborate interrelationships. The human performance considerations are developed for staffing levels, operator and maintainer skills, training strategies, human–computer interface, human engineering design features, safety and health issues, and workload and operational performance considerations in procedures and other human–system interfaces.

9.3 FAA RATIONALE FOR HUMAN FACTORS DESIGN

The FAA recognizes that growth in air traffic means imminent overload of the air traffic control system and its controllers. The retirement of a large percentage of the current controllers in the next 10 years with not nearly enough new controllers in training to replace them exacerbates the situation. There are practical limits to adding more controllers, so the place to look for improvement is in technological changes. To evaluate competing solutions, it will be important to identify requirements important in supporting human performance and to determine system performance criteria necessary to enhance human problem solving and effective decision making. Risks associated with system and human reliability become increasingly important as automation begins to greatly expand the potential to support problem detection and error management. Systems that consider human factors pay off in improved acquisition decisions, reduced training and maintenance costs, fewer human errors and improved safety, higher probability of system success, and improved user acceptance. The FAA considers it highly unlikely that an effective air traffic control system can be developed without applying systematic human factors analysis. The FAA takes seriously Glib's advice, "Don't try to correct poor software design with good documentation."[5]

To date, the FAA's experience has been that consideration of human factors issues and their mitigation in project development and deployment has varied in cost from approximately $1 million for a small project to $100 million for the Voice Switching and Communication System (VSCS). In these projects, human factors considerations were an integral part of the design process and in no way delayed the project schedules.

In addition, there is a projected $175 million outlay for the Standard Terminal Arrival Route System (STARS). STARS started as a commercial off-the-shelf (COTS) effort, but later it was discovered that human factors issues required an extension in project implementation by 2 years. Clearly, says the FAA, the required effort to address human factors issues and its costs will depend on how complex the system is, how much it will directly impact day-to-day operations, and the skill required by the workforce to learn the new

[5] Glib, Tom and Weinberg, Gerald M. *Humanized Input Techniques for Reliable Keyed Input*, Winthrop, Cambridge MA, 1977, p. 62.

system. Complexity impacts the level of skills required, which is directly related to the issue of usability. The greater the usability, the lower the cost.[6]

The FAA on some level understands what needs to be done and is aware of the science that must be addressed to accomplish trustworthy systems. However, as the following case study shows, "there's many a slip 'twixt cup and lip'."

Case Study: "Ground Control, Speak Up! I Can't Hear You!"

Paul Cox of the FAA Seattle Center describes this case.

> 'I'm an air traffic controller. . . . To do their job, air traffic controllers need one thing above all: They need the ability to communicate with the aircraft they're controlling.
>
> The VSCS puts all of our communications into one spot including air-to-ground, ground-to-ground calls to other facilities and calls within our own facility. It's a purely digital system; all the incoming feeds are converted to bits and bytes and switched through a series of servers and such until they're turned back into analog and put into the controller's ear through a headset.
>
> The VSCS system was designed and built by Harris Corporation, but their contract ran out some time ago. The FAA, coming to the end of the contract, decided to go a much less expensive route and replace all the servers with Dell boxes and their own programming.
>
> In theory, there's nothing wrong with this; perform the required maintenance, and there's no problem. But the system does have design flaws. The system needs to be reset about once a month—or more specifically, once every 30 days or so. There's a risk right there; "once a month" probably means "once every 30 or so days", not "once in a calendar month" which could leave an interval as long as nearly 60 days in between resets . . .
>
> Now, there's a backup system for VSCS. It's called VTABS, and is basically a reduced-capability server that normally runs the VSCS system on the air traffic control simulator that's used to train students. The VTABS system . . . cannot run the entire control room on all of the frequencies that the control center has, so it's a hassle to go to VTABS.
>
> Whenever the reset on VSCS is done, you have to run on VTABS for a while, which usually means it's done on graveyard shifts to reduce the impact on live traffic. The downside to this is that the VTABS system also doesn't get a full workout. So the next risk pops up: the backup system wasn't fully checked out . . . when air traffic control needs it, it might not work.
>
> Sure enough, that happened. When VSCS died, LA Center switched to VTAB and it also didn't work right. Big trouble, now.

---

[6] http://fast.faa.gov/human/htm/specialtopic.htm.

Finally, the FAA . . . a while back removed a last-ditch backup system called EARS. EARS was . . . a hard-wired, all-analog system that only provided the most crucial thing: air-to-ground communications. EARS . . . had a big advantage over VSCS or VTABS. If the power died for, say, 20 seconds, as soon as the power was back on EARS would work with no . . . startup time. VSCS takes up to 45 minutes to completely start up, and VTABS has a significant delay in startup time as well.

The LA failure was both ridiculous and scary. It's ridiculous [because] the fact that the system is designed to shut itself down is silly . . . [In effect] the system crashes to protect itself from crashing. When suddenly you can't talk to the airplanes, you don't much care whether it's an intentional shutdown or an accidental buggy shutdown. Therefore, the designers might as well remove this intentional design . . . It's ridiculous that the first backup system didn't work right simply because people did not test it properly.

And it's scary to think that this could've happened in an even busier airport than LA. For example, the morning crush of traffic in New York or Boston . . . has more traffic packed into less airspace than out west in LA.[7]

Conclusion: These steps could have prevented the human factors problems from becoming a crisis:

(1) Software rejuvenation libraries could have been used to prevent a shutdown and thereby eliminate the human restart task, which makes the system more reliable.
(2) Understand that "once a month" actually means "once every 30 days," and ensure that a critical job is done, on time, and correctly.
(3) Have a tested backup system that can actually do the job.

The FAA had the knowledge to do the job properly, but it was not communicated to the people who actually took over the work on VSCS when the Harris Corporation contract ran out. The FAA management did not actually require that a human factors specialist be part of the in-house team, which was a grave error.

Another common design failure is not attending to features needed by system administrators. They have responsibilities for diverse tasks:

(1) Training
(2) Configuring the computer to run the software
(3) Defining network requirements
(4) Setting up data files
(5) Maintaining adequate response time
(6) Trouble shooting

[7] http://www.interesting-people.org/archives/interesting-people/200409/msg00284.html.

9.4   REACH OUT AND TOUCH SOMETHING

Humans make mental maps through tangible input to our senses. We want to see, hear, touch, feel, and to a lesser extent, smell the environment to make logical order of it and draw conclusions. Purely intellectual understanding is a level removed and therefore slower to translate to action. The efficient software system activates as many senses as possible to provide input to the human for decision making.

9.4.1   Maddening Counterintuitive Cues

Too many operating systems are counterintuitive as we recall from the case study in Chapter 5, *The Case for Minding Your Mother*. Everyone has a favorite example of this. Why do you edit the header in the view menu and not the edit window in Word? Linux is not easy for the naïve user either. Difficult software installations frustrate users. At first, there were two ways to install software on Linux: building from source or installing from using a packaging system. Each had its faults: Average users cannot or will not install from source; packaging systems are fragmented without easily downloadable packages. Today, wizards make the task less daunting. Latex is a lovely language that requires initiation into a cult of users who hand the knowledge out to chosen initiates. There is no Latex in the ". . . for Dummies" series of self-help books. The list is endless.

9.4.2   GUI

The graphical user interface (GUI) is a particularly apt style of interaction because of the possibility of a flexible approach to the organization of tasks through multiple windows and graphics.[8] The human capacity to perceive patterns is enormous, and GUIs try to capitalize on it by promoting visualization. To understand a problem with visualization, a person must collect data and have some intuition about data interaction.

9.4.3   Customer Care and Web Agents[9]

Customer Care modules integrate the customer contact function in CRM systems. They provide interfaces for agents or customers to access ordering,

---

[8] Cunningham, James P., Blewett, C. Douglas, and Anderson, J. Scott. "Graphical Interfaces for Network Operations and Management," User Interface Design and Development Issue, *AT&T Technical Journal*, Vol. 72, No. 3, May/June 1993, pp. 57–66.
[9] Krulwick, Bruce. "Automating the Internet: Agents as User Surrogates," *IEEE Internet Computing*, July/Aug. 1997, pp. 34–38.
   Huhns, Michael N. and Singh, Munindar P. "Workflow Agents," *IEEE Internet Computing*, July/Aug. 1998, pp. 994–996.

billing, and shipping data. CRM platforms interface with many systems to reduce the number of screens a user must handle. Software encapsulates business process knowledge in executable form. Expert systems capture the decision-making processes concerning customer credit worthiness, combinations of services, and appliances. With object-oriented design and distributed object modules connecting information sources, databases can be updated online, and groups of people can work more easily together. The growing complexity and the need for mass customization place enormous demands on the architecture of the system. Many companies provide CRM access via the Web. The Web provides easy, standard access to multiple servers via a protocol call Hypertext Markup Language (HTML). If the customer has a computer, an Internet service provider, a Web browser, and some Internet literacy, he or she can place orders.

Access brings dangers, constraints, and obligations along with convenience. Rather than allow all users access everywhere, software agents[10] have been developed to handle transactions. An agent is software that is proactive, personalized to the user, and adapted to a specific function. It allows indirect management of the customer's foray into the company's database in that the agent selects and assembles data for the particular customer and oversees any changes the customer makes. Web applications rely on workflow agents, which take a set of tasks and develop an appropriate workflow.[11] Firewalls[12] must be built at two levels, protocol and application, to deter hackers. Another consideration is that the Web allows one session per transaction, a constraint that must be accommodated by leaving information in the user's computer as "cookies" to pass user data between transactions.

9.5   SYSTEM EFFECTIVENESS IN HUMAN FACTORS TERMS

Effective systems appropriately assign to the computer those tasks that computers do best and to humans those tasks that humans do best. Determining which is which requires prototyping, user-centered design, user testing, iterative design, usability-based enhancements, and usability testing laboratories, all under the aegis of human factors specialists.

9.5.1   What to Look for in COTS

System operation should be tolerant of the user's skill and experience. A minimal amount of documentation and training should be required. A system

---

[10] Krulwick, Bruce. "Automating the Internet: Agents as User Surrogates," *IEEE Internet Computing*, July/Aug. 1997, pp. 34–38.

[11] Huhns, Michael N. and Singh, Munindar P. "Workflow Agents," *IEEE Internet Computing*, July/Aug. 1998, pp. 994–996.

[12] Amoroso, Edward and Sharp, Ronald. *PCWEEK Intranet and Internet Firewall Strategies*, Ziff-Davis Press, Macmillan Computer Publishing, Emeryville, CA, 1996.

should not be idiosyncratic and should be tolerant of missing or noisy data. The system should have an error strategy that detects errors at the earliest possible point in system processing. The user should not be required to repeat information, which the system already has; this is the minimal input principle.

These criteria seem self-evident, but they are difficult to satisfy. For example, among widely used software for lay people is Microsoft's Word for Windows, which has been through several iterations; yet its use still requires knowledge of programming folklore and the purchase of a 2-in thick manual. Unless human factors specialists are involved in the earliest stages of design specification, the difficulty of programming causes these major criteria to be sacrificed. Table 9.2 summarizes the usability principles to which a buyer should demand any software or system product adhere.

TABLE 9.2. Software Usability Principles

Principle	Explanation
Simplicity	Promote clarity and visual simplicity using: (1) Subtractive design—reduce clutter by eliminating unneeded icons, pictures, and text. (2) Visual hierarchy—through task analysis, understand users' tasks and establish a hierarchy of them. Give important tasks special visual prominence. Relative position and contrast in color and size can be used, but be sensitive to partial color blindness and stay away from red on blue.[a]
Speak the users' language	Use familiar words, data labels, and concepts. Present information in a natural and logical order in the user's context. The use of concepts and techniques that users already understand from their real-world experiences allows them to get started quickly and make progress immediately.
Be consistent	Indicate similar concepts through identical terminology and graphics. Adhere to uniform conventions for layout, formatting, typefaces, and labels.
Minimize what users must remember	Rely on recognition, not recall. Do not force user to remember information across documents. Rely on human factor specialists to determine appropriate levels of memory demand based on context and user skill.
Design for flexibility and efficiency	Accommodate a range of user sophistication and diverse user goals. Allow redundant ways of doing tasks. Provide drop-down menus, function keys, and command lines for the same function.
Design aesthetic and minimalist graphics	Create visually pleasing, efficient displays that capitalize on known human capabilities in pattern recognition and color differentiation.
Satisfaction	Create a feeling of progress and achievement. Reflect the results of actions immediately; any delay intrudes on users' tasks and erodes confidence in the system.
Recognize the power of chunking	The capacity of human short-term memory is small, but it can be amplified by grouping subsets of information around keywords, by completing single thoughts in one document, and by keeping tasks short but information-rich.

TABLE 9.2. Continued

Principle	Explanation
Predictability	Let users easily determine the action that should be taken with an object, such objects usually mimic real-world objects.
Screen Layout	Design screen layouts that map to each user motif and let the user customize it. Do not eliminate extra space just to save space. Use white space to provide visual "breathing room."
Naturalness	Build on users' prior knowledge. Users should not have to learn new things to perform familiar tasks.
Structure progressive levels of detail	Organize information hierarchically, with more general information appearing before more specific detail. Allow the user to stop when sufficient information is received.
Navigation	Allow user to determine the current position in the program structure. Make it easy to jump among related tasks. Make it easy to return to an initial state.
Safety	Keep the user out of trouble. Users should be protected from making errors. The burden of keeping the user out of trouble rests on the designer. The interface should provide visual cues, reminders, lists of choices, and other aids. Make the help helpful. Test the help with naïve users.

[a] http://www-306.ibm.com/ibm/easy/eou_ext.nsf/publish/6.

9.5.2 Simple Guidelines for Managing Development

If the system or software will be developed, not purchased, the opportunity exists to do it correctly in human factors terms from the start. The following are some simple guidelines a manager can consider to allow the process to occur. But the overarching principle is that human factors work requires specialists. Design does not happen based on programmers' intuition, managers' instincts, or luck. Systems that are difficult to use are an ongoing expensive exercise in programming arrogance and are unworthy of computer design professionals.

Hire human factors professionals. A large body of research in human perception, measurement, and user-centered design can be practically applied. Integrate the human factors specialist into the design team. If there is a human factors department in your organization, view it as a resource to support the specialist devoted to your design team, not as a marketing frill to mention in a sales brochure.

Expect the human factors specialist to test the product on specific, measurable criteria for usability and to develop testing scenarios. Such criteria include rate of human error, time to learn specific functions, speed of task performance, subjective user satisfaction, and human retention of functions over time. Expect to devote resources to prototype trials, field trials, and user surveys.

Explicitly assign resources to address usability. Test laboratory time, and space must be allotted for evaluating prototypes and system releases based on human factors criteria.

Do not relegate the human factors specialist to the publications department. Although good graphic design of supporting documentation is a part of system usability, the major contribution of the human factors specialist is identifying software usability problems and working with programmers to arrive at functional solutions.

Support technology transfer for human factors specialists as you would for any other member of the design and development teams.

9.6 HOW MUCH SHOULD THE SYSTEM DO?

One of the most difficult design tasks is to anticipate the ultimate uses of a system. It seems that users will happily manipulate a simple system to provide outcomes that were not conceived by its designers (in the law, this is a loophole), but they expect that if it can do some tough analysis, it should be able to do it all. Zuboff identified this as a "trough of disillusionment," which hints at a certain anthropomorphizing of the machine. Users want it to communicate and "think" like a human being.

Review the design to discover opportunities for user error and confusion. Users should never have to rely on their memory for something the system already knows, such as previous settings, file names, and other interface details. If the information is in the system in any form, the system should provide it. Once data are entered into any computer, they should be automatically retrievable, with appropriate safeguards, by any systems.

MAGIC NUMBER!

Never force data to be entered twice.

Two-way human/computer communication is sometimes needed to clarify or confirm requests, or to remedy a problem. In the past, many interfaces have made communication one-way, computer-to-user. Communications should be interactive and as rich in presentation and interaction capabilities as the rest of the interface. It should present relevant information, provide access to related information and help, and allow users to make task-specific decisions to continue. Implement a "did you mean?" feature. Observe patterns of use, automatically encapsulate the pattern, and offer it to the user. Support alternative interaction techniques. Allow users to choose the method of interaction that is most appropriate to their situation. Interfaces that are flexible in this way can accommodate a wide range of user skills, physical abilities, interactions, and usage environments. Table 9.3 shows some steps for gathering insight.

TABLE 9.3. Steps for Extracting Insights From Data

Define the problem	Set objectives and data required
Data access	Retrieve the data.
Data scrubbing	Assure consistency and accuracy of data.
Data mining	Extract information.
Data presentation	Show results in a form that eases decision making.
Business impact	State the impact and value of the discovery on specific business processes.
Indecisive Findings	Discover changes from earlier operational state. Ask with intense perseverance, "What's changed" until the change is found.

Floods of data are useful only when transformed into knowledge. Visualization and Expert System are the best techniques to understanding massive amounts of data that are often largely ignored because of lack of time or analysis tools. Data visualization exploits the sophisticated visual acuity humans have for pattern detection by using color, position, and texture to display encoded data on a graphics workstation. There are design guidelines for building information-rich visualizations of business data. Visualizations work best if they are task-oriented, domain-specific, and colorful; they must also have high information density controlled by interactive filters, linking to other views, and animation. Figure 9.2 perfectly illustrates the concept with a graphic display of overloaded telephone lines.

Figure 9.2 shows the visualization of traffic on AT&T's Long Distance network minutes after an earthquake in Los Angeles. With one glance, you can see long-distance calls overloading trunks, which caused the network management systems to automatically limit calls to the West Coast and avoid a network crash. The picture also shows a problem between Harrisburg, Pennsylvania and Kansas that the network managers would have missed in the deluge of data stimulated by the earthquake. Manual steps were taken to reroute this traffic away from the earthquake-induced overloads as the software kept the network functioning in the face of loads that exceeded all verification tests.

9.6.1 Screen Icon Design

Most icons consist of a pictorial image surrounded by a shape with a distinct border. Some also include a text label. Each component is critical to effective design. The picture should be an effective metaphor, providing an analogy that the user infers the behavior of the system. Using different background shapes behind a pictorial image is effective for warning and information icons.

MAJOR U.S. CITIES

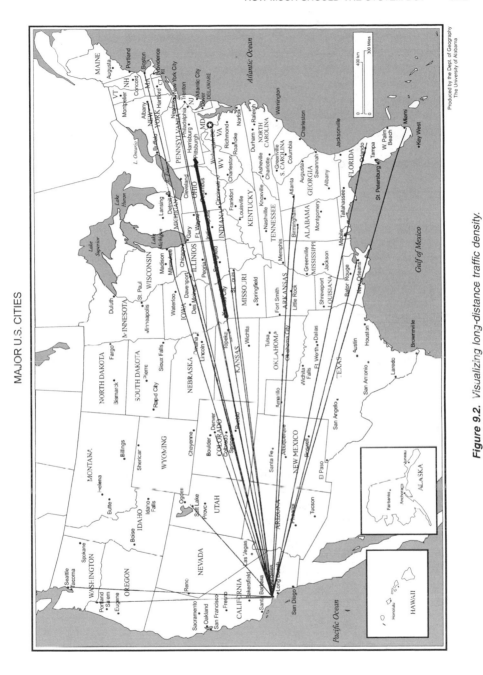

Figure 9.2. Visualizing long-distance traffic density.

Produced by the Dept. of Geography
The University of Alabama

Although shape coding is not used frequently for computer icons, it can be an effective method of increasing the amount of information conveyed to the user without increasing the number of overall icons.

Coding conventions such as color and flashing are components of an icon used as the users interact with it. Color acts as an enhancer in search tasks and identification tasks and improves recognition performance and allows for faster and more accurate responses.[13]

9.6.2 Short- and Long-Term Memory

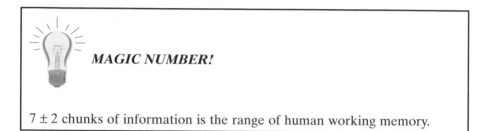

MAGIC NUMBER!

7 ± 2 chunks of information is the range of human working memory.

This magic number is well used, but is it valid? Ben Shneiderman writes, "Miller identified the limited capabilities people have for absorbing information. People can rapidly recognize approximately 7 chunks of information at a time [this value was contested by later researchers, but serves as a good estimate].[14] Bob Bailey reports that "... in the early 1970s, investigators began broadening their view of short-term memory to a more useful one that became known as "working memory." The current concept of working memory describes a memory system that does more than just temporarily store small amounts of information."[15] We conclude that 7 ± 2 is still a good design rule for making system easy to use, but less is more.

Miller, who wrote the paper defining 7 ± 2, also wrote "The span of absolute judgment and the span of immediate memory impose severe limitations on the amount of information that we are able to receive, process, and remember. By organizing the stimulus input simultaneously into several dimensions and successively into a sequence or chunks, we manage to break (or at least stretch) this informational bottleneck ... the concepts and measures provided by the theory of information provide a quantitative way of getting at some of these questions. The theory provides us with a yardstick for calibrating our stimulus materials and for measuring the performance of our subjects. ..."[16]

---

[13] http://hf.tc.faa.gov/technotes/dot-faa-ct-tn02-12.pdf.

[14] Shneiderman, Ben and Plaisant, Catherine. *Designing The User Interface*, 4th ed. Pearson Addison-Wesley, Reading, MA, 2005, ch. 11, also p. 459.

[15] http://www.humanfactors.com/downloads/sep00.asp.

[16] http://www.well.com/user/smalin/miller.htm.

The World Wide Web has made it possible for consumers to access computers. Some studies of interactions are available, and those that are recurring will become guidelines. The data are still too raw to be considered design rules. Nevertheless, these findings give insight to Web application design in 2005. Ease of use, trustworthiness, and a low perceived degree of risk increases purchases through the Web, and satisfied customers are more loyal to websites than to brick-and-mortar stores. Consumer product sites that invest in good writers and artists who produce dynamic graphics increase the willingness to purchase online, enhance site loyalty, and even improve consumers' attitudes about company stores.

Rapid blast messages are more likely to be noticed and noticed faster than ticker messaging or slowly fading messages, but the content of ticker alerts is remembered better than rapid blast or slowly fading messages.

Conventional blue-colored links are the most frequently used. Customers have learned to use them, and so they are most recognizable for navigation and are easier to click than black ones, even though black ones have higher visual contrast and are easier to see. Keyboard shortcuts are significantly faster and more accurate than mouse clicks. Despite having practiced using a mouse, nearly all users prefer using keyboard shortcuts.[17]

9.7 EMERGING TECHNOLOGY

The ability of computers to detect and interpret human body gestures decouples people from input devices. This opens the possibility of new applications where an input device can be cumbersome. Teaching the computer to understand American Sign Language, augmented with standard keyboard function key gestures, will allow widespread use of a new generic interface with computers using gestures of the human body, typically hand movements.

In gesture recognition technology, a camera reads the movements of the human body and communicates the data to a computer that uses the gestures as input to control applications. For example, a doctor or emergency medical technician signals "open EKG" to see a plot of the patient's heartbeat during a medical procedure when the gesture is fed through a computer.

Gesture recognition helps the physically impaired to interact with computers, such as interpreting sign language. The technology changes the way all users interact with computers by eliminating input devices such as joysticks, touch pads, mice, and keyboards. This allows the unencumbered body to give signals to the computer through gestures such as finger pointing. Gesture recognition does not require the user to wear any special equipment or attach any devices to the body. A camera instead of sensors attached to a device reads the gestures of the body. Gesture recognition technology also can be used to read nods, expressions, and eye movements.[18]

---

[17] http://www.humanfactors.com/downloads/dec04.asp.
[18] http://homepages.inf.ed.ac.uk/rbf/CVonline/LOCAL_COPIES/COHEN/gesture_overview.html.

Case Study: The Case of Higgins vs. Hoover

Congress raised concerns in 2002 about the development of a new system the FBI was developing. For this case study, we will allow the project manager, Sherry Higgins, to speak for herself. Read her testimony carefully for trustworthy concepts. Then read the *New York Times* news article that follows it, dated 3 years later.

Testimony of Sherry Higgins, Project Management Executive for the Office of the Director, FBI

Before the Senate Judiciary Subcommittee on Administrative Oversight and the Courts

July 16, 2002

"FBI Infrastructure"

Good morning. I'm Sherry Higgins, the FBI's Project Management Executive for the Office of the Director. I have been asked to talk to you about how the FBI is fixing old problems and building a collaborative information infrastructure to better support our mission. I have also been asked to share with you some personal perspectives on how the FBI differs from the private sector in developing our computing infrastructure. . . .

The FBI's problems with information technology didn't occur over night and they won't be fixed over night either. That is because it is more important to get it right and know that we have the systems and capabilities that precisely fit our mission as well as cure past problems.

The first major step in this direction is our Trilogy Program. The Trilogy Program was designed as a 36-month effort to enhance our effectiveness through technologies that facilitate better organization, access and analysis of information.

The overall direction of the Trilogy Program is to provide all FBI offices with improved network communications, a common and current set of office automation tools, and **easy-to-use**, re-engineered, web-based applications. . . .

The Information Presentation Component relies primarily on commercial-off-the shelf (COTS) hardware and software products that provide a modern desktop environment and connectivity, thus facilitating employees' ability to input, retrieve, manipulate and present information in text, image, audio and video formats. The Information Presentation Component is replacing our antiquated computer workstations, providing an updated e-mail capability, and includes simple things like additional printers and scanners that increase productivity. **This component is nearing completion . . .**

The User Application Component is replacement of user applications that will enhance our ability to access, organize and analyze information. Specifically, the Trilogy Program will migrate five investigative applications into a "Virtual Case File" (VCF), to provide **user-friendly**, web browser access to mission critical information. A web-based interface will enable our users to have a graphical interface with investigative information. It will eliminate the cumbersome aspects of our current system; greatly enhance our collaborative environment . . .

Under the FBI's old legacy investigative information system, the Automated Case Support (ACS), users navigate with the function keys instead of the point and click method common to web based applications. Simple tasks, such as storing an electronic version of a document today, require a user to perform twelve separate functions, in a "green screen" environment. That will soon change with Trilogy. Automated workflow will allow for a streamlined process to complete tasking. Storing a document for the record will occur with a click of the mouse button. This will make investigative and intelligence information immediately available to all personnel with appropriate security.

Enhanced ad hoc reporting, online information sharing and state-of-the-art analytical tools will permit those conducting investigations and analyzing data to easily organize and filter events and trends. Representatives from our field offices who are defining the VCF user needs are also challenging current FBI business practices to improving workflow and to ensure that archaic business rules are not automated.

Multimedia functionality will allow for the storage of information in its original form. Under the old system, agents cannot store non-compatible forms of digital evidence in an electronic format, instead having to describe the evidence and indicate where the evidence is stored in a control room. Multimedia functionality will facilitate electronic storage of digital evidence and media to the investigative case file, allowing access to the information from the desktop . . .

The User Application development is now planned in two increments . . . Release One has a targeted completion date of **December 2003**. This release will allow different types of users, such as agents, analysts, and supervisors, to access information from a "dashboard" that is **specific to their individual needs** . . .

The VCF Team is currently using an industry-standard process called Joint Application Development (JAD) planning, to define and prioritize the users' operational requirements. By joining the application developers with the users (agents, analyst, and support personnel), applications will be built that will reflect the items needed by these individuals to perform their jobs. This approach differs from the old way of doing business: figuring out how to do your job with the tools you already have. JAD is not a rebuild of the old system. It has brought users, designers, future systems operators together to develop applications that are operationally sound and maintainable. JAD sessions started at the end of January this year and are expected to conclude next week. Additional JAD sessions will take place as part of the process for VCF Release Two.

As with any automation project, a number of risks must be managed to a have a successful Trilogy Program deployment. The top three are all related to our aggressive deployment schedule. I believe all are manageable . . .

Our aggressive schedule also leaves little time for . . . preparations in support of the deployed infrastructure . . .

Interoperability with legacy applications is another risk area. There is currently a lack of documentation in place that captures the old legacy system functions and operations. Therefore, the UAC team is still identifying new interfaces and modifications to existing interfaces. Our schedule allocation for engineering and testing may not be adequate for successful integration infrastructure deployment with the current applications and servers. To mitigate this risk, the test team is also prioritizing these test requirements and developing a common understanding of system acceptance test coverage, conditions and criteria.

Once we catch up to a standard PC environment, the future looks very positive. We are planning for a technology refreshment program (TRP) which will replace Trilogy network and workstation hardware, network data storage, server hardware, and embedded software on a periodic basis to prevent system performance degradation and rising O&M costs due to obsolescence. The TRP also envisions the incorporation of new technology as it becomes available in the private sector and the study of emerging technologies to evaluate potential future uses and benefits and to better anticipate future resource needs. In essence, a viable infrastructure technology refreshment plan is essential to maintain the benefits of the Trilogy investment, the efficiency and capabilities of FBI investigative support systems and to better plan and budget for out year expenditures.

I have been asked to provide my personal perspective on what I have changed since reporting to the FBI this March, and how the FBI contrasts with my experience in the private sector.

Before my arrival at the FBI, the Trilogy Program was overly focused on achieving an accelerated schedule. Although the Trilogy Program will still be brought in ahead of its original schedule, we have begun allowing for more test time to ensure we deliver a quality product to the field. Industry best practices recommend "building in quality", instead of "inspecting it in". Using quality standards and compliance up front will allow us to identify and prevent mistakes that would require expensive fixes later on down the line.

Effective communications within and without the Trilogy Program is also essential to our success. I am in the process of developing a Trilogy Communications Plan that will promote effective communications across our business enterprise, so that valuable development information is not retained in pockets.

I am also developing an integrated master schedule for the Trilogy Program, which will reflect the program's critical path, dependencies and integration tasks between our three components. We will constantly review this schedule to capitalize on efficiencies and schedule improvement opportunities.

One of the striking differences between the private sector and the FBI is the Bureau's lack of a dedicated corps of acquisition specialists with which to plan, develop and manage large projects. The FBI has many talented people with some of these requisite skills; we have pockets of expertise in program management disciplines, such as financial analysis, budgeting, contract management and system engineering, residing in different divisions. However, the FBI has operated for too long without an organization responsible for proper development business practices, which would ensure that FBI systems under development are responsive to our users' requirements.

Private industry and most government agencies recognize the advantages of instituting a project management executive with a project management office to manage complex, expensive, high-risk development efforts. According to the Gartner Group, "enterprises utilizing a project office to manage the growing complexity involved with creating or acquiring—and then implementing and managing—these applications have a distinct advantage over those that do not." Perhaps the most frustrating experience I have had since coming to the FBI from private industry is trying to work information technology issues that cut across the FBI's organization. "Stove piped" communications internal to the FBI prevents information and communications flow that is required to be responsive to our users and oversight. Successful project development and implementation at the FBI requires constant and accurate communications across our entire business enterprise.

To make this a reality, I have recommended, and Director Mueller has approved of the establishment of an Office of Programs Management. This office will develop, manage, and deploy high-priority, complex and high-risk projects of high dollar value, to successfully support the FBI's operational mission. The office will have a staff of subject matter experts in key program management functions, matrixed to development project managers. These project managers will be "loaned" from their sponsoring divisions to the Office of Program Management during the development of the project, from the concept phase until the project is ready to be transitioned to operations.

In addition, the Office of Program Management will be charged with using repeatable processes for these efforts; in other words, we will implement a business approach to our large acquisition efforts, by instituting core program management disciplines from a project's concept phase until it is transitioned to operations and maintenance. We will train a skilled corps of FBI PM subject matter experts, and advise the FBI Director on program management and acquisition-planning related organizational issues, proposals, and strategies.

Because of its user/management orientation, the Office of Program Management will be in a position to make the most informed recommendations concerning trade-offs between performance, schedule, and costs of projects, to determine the best course for return on the FBI's investment in IT. This office will also gauge the impacts of delays of delivered functionality for the field divisions and headquarters, and develop budget justifications for the acquisition of required resources to support approved systems projects.

In summary, Trilogy gives the FBI workable standards and a base it can build upon. Trilogy is being built to allow for interchanges with different systems, internal and external, so that the historical problem of "not putting the pieces together" is no longer an issue. Trilogy will provide the resources and tools the FBI needs to support investigations and the critical building blocks for future improvements. The Trilogy Program is focused on getting these critical resources to our Special Agents and field support personnel as quickly as possible.[19]

New York Times, January 14, 2005
F.B.I. May Scrap Vital Overhaul of Its Outdated Computer System (reprinted with permission of The New York Times Company)
By Eric Lichtblau

WASHINGTON, Jan. 13—The Federal Bureau of Investigation is on the verge of scrapping a $170 million computer overhaul that is considered critical to the campaign against terrorism but has been riddled with technical and planning problems, F.B.I. officials said on Thursday.

In a last-ditch effort to save the program, the bureau has hired a research firm at a cost of $2 million to evaluate the mounting problems in creating a "paperless" work system and to determine whether any parts of the project can be salvaged, officials said. One idea under strong consideration is for the bureau to use [commercial] off-the-shelf software instead of the expensive customized features it has unsuccessfully sought to develop.

The development is a major setback for the F.B.I. in a decade-long struggle to escape a paper-driven culture and replace antiquated computer systems that have hobbled counter terrorism and criminal investigations . . .

"It's immensely disappointing to learn of this type of failure," Lee H. Hamilton, the vice chairman of the Sept. 11 commission, said in an interview. "The F.B.I. cannot share information and manage their cases effectively without a top-flight computer system, and we on the commission got assurances again and again from the F.B.I. that they were getting on top of this problem. It's very, very disappointing to see that they're not."

While other intelligence agencies like the C.I.A. and the National Security Agency developed sophisticated and secure computer systems long ago, the bureau has been much maligned for years for its failure to develop a modern system. Members of Congress have joked that their grandchildren could send e-mail messages and search databases more easily than F.B.I. investigators could.

Among other problems, officials blame technical and financial missteps, a rapid turnover among the bureau's information-technology personnel, difficulties in developing a system that is both secure and accessible to investigators, and, perhaps most critically, a resistance among some veteran agents who favor pens and pads over computers.

"I am frustrated by the delays," Mr. Mueller said Thursday in Birmingham, Ala., according to The Associated Press. "I am frustrated that we do not have on every agent's desk the capability of a modern case-management system."

The bureau said that it had made some significant inroads in the last few years in overhauling its computer capabilities, with the installation of 30,000 new desktop computers and the development of a secure, high-speed network.

[19] http://www.fbi.gov/congress/congress02/higgins071602.htm.

But the F.B.I.'s "virtual case file" system, the last in a three-part computer upgrade totaling more than half a billion dollars, has proved the most difficult. The system was designed to give the bureau's nearly 12,000 agents around the country instant access to F.B.I. databases, allowing speedier investigations and better integration of information both within the bureau and with other intelligence agencies that must coordinate national security matters.

But the project is over budget and behind schedule, and F.B.I. officials acknowledged on Thursday that they were uncertain whether it would ever be completed. Only about 10 percent of the project, delivered by the Science Applications International Corporation of San Diego, is now in use, officials said.

A draft report from the Justice Department's inspector general, first reported last month by the industry publication Government Computer News and again on Thursday by The Los Angeles Times, concluded that the case file system as now designed and conceived would not work and could not be put into use.

A senior F.B.I. official, who gave reporters a formal briefing on the issue on Thursday on the condition of not being named, was not willing to go that far but acknowledged "a number of deficiencies" and frustrations in the project and said, "The application, the way it's built now, is under evaluation . . ."

Problems with the "virtual" case file project have been well documented for many months, but the acknowledgement Thursday from the F.B.I. offered the clearest indication yet that the system may be headed for extinction.

As it stands now, the bureau's counter terrorism files are largely online, but investigators often may not have immediate access to data from other parts of the bureau. So, for instance, an agent may not be immediately aware of information from an investigation into credit-card fraud that could be relevant to a terrorism case. In addition, the bulk of the internal reports and documents produced at the bureau must still be printed, signed and scanned by hand into computer format each day, officials said.

"I did not get what I envisioned" from the project, the senior official acknowledged. But he said the F.B.I. today had a better understanding of its computer needs and limitations as a result of the effort." The lesson we have learned from this $170 million is invaluable," he said . . . after a series of failed computer projects at the F.B.I. dating back to the mid-1990's, many members of Congress say they are hesitant to give the bureau more money without clearer assurances of success.

Lawmakers have asked the Government Accountability Office, the investigative arm of Congress, to conduct an inquiry into failings in the bureau's computer systems . . . Mr. Leahy said lawmakers had pushed the bureau for "realistic assessments" of the Virtual Case File's performance, amid increasingly glum reports in the news media and in government about its chances for success.

"As recently as last May, the F.B.I. was still claiming that V.C.F. would be completed by the end of 2004, and that it would at last give the F.B.I. the 'cutting-edge technology' it needs," the senator said.

"The F.B.I. needs to stop hiding its problems and begin confronting them early on," he said, adding, "Bringing the F.B.I.'s information technology into the 21st century should not be rocket science."[20]

Conclusion: As late as July 2004 the FBI claimed that the job would be done and would help their agents. But influential agents resisted the system—notice the January 2005 comment on using paper and pen as a preference—and the focus is on the geeky details rather than on VCF usability. Then a review showed that the system was in trouble and various areas were playing "range chicken." A detailed problem list was not provided in July and contingency plans were not in place. Notice there is no mention in the *New York Times* article of Sherry Higgins standing up to take personal responsibility as project manager. She seems to be gone. It would seem, because of the extreme resistance to the new system throughout the Bureau, that there was no strong human factors presence on the design team. Perhaps, if no funds were available for human factors analysis, they could instead have afforded an exorcist to purge the ghost of J. Edgar Hoover and break the old cult of the lone individual, fighting for freedom.

9.8 APPLYING THE PRINCIPLES TO DEVELOPERS

People who like to solve problems, try new tools, and tinker are attracted to the software industry. They like the excitement of interacting with the computer. They like to see their programs work. They discuss clever solutions endlessly and are happy to debug a program that eluded others. Programmers like to learn and grow; they need change.

Programmers want to document, comment, and have a controlled development process—it is just that they are ill suited to repeatedly do the necessary detailed clerical work if bosses do not provide the tools or support staff.

MAGIC NUMBER!

Programming is hours of frustration interspersed with moments of ecstasy.

Agile methods institutionalize the work habits of the highly skilled programmer. They allow for experimentation and revision. They demand flexibil-

---

[20] Copyright 2005 *The New York Times Company*. Reprinted with permission.

ity and loose work structure. The focus of these methods is meeting schedules. Agile methods are schedule-driven in comparison with the Spiral risk-driven, incremental feature package-driven, and Waterfall document-driven approaches to software development. The difference between them is how bureaucratic they are in achieving the planning and control needed to assure product quality. Agile methods trust the developers to honor the control and deliver features when required. Programmers like these agile methods because they put the burden on them, not on management or a control group to do the right thing. The problem is that many developers need more structure to their lives than agile methods provide. Nevertheless, agile methods attract the best and can be used on small teams to great effect. The accomplished project manager knows how to integrate the products of these loosely controlled teams into a tightly controlled system. The development first-line and middle managers must be technically competent for this to work. They need to make sure that the developers are solving the right problem, and they need to leave it to others to provide the structure that makes sure the project comes together in the right way.

Agile methods build a spirit of competence and pride. This is the core of human factors design.

In the turbulent world of business and technology, scrupulously following a plan can have dire consequences, even if it is executed faithfully. However carefully a plan is crafted, it becomes dangerous if it blinds you to change. Successful projects rarely delivered what was planned at project inception; yet they succeeded because the development team was agile enough to respond repeatedly to external changes.

Contract negotiation, whether through an internal project charter or external legal contract, is not a bad practice, just an insufficient one. Contracts and project charters may provide some boundary conditions within which the parties can work, but only through ongoing collaboration can a development team hope to understand and deliver what the client really needs.

Welcoming changing requirements, even late in development, lets agile processes harness change. Turbulence—in both business and technology—causes change, which can be viewed either as a threat to be guarded against or as an opportunity. Rather than resist change, the agile approach strives to accommodate it as easily and efficiently as possible, while maintaining an awareness of its consequences. Although most people agree that feedback is important, they often ignore the fact that the result of accepted feedback is change.

"Tacit knowledge cannot be transferred by getting it out of people's heads and onto paper," writes Dixon. "Tacit knowledge can be transferred by moving the people who have the knowledge around. The reason is that tacit knowledge is not only the facts but the relationships among the facts—that is, how people might combine certain facts to deal with a specific situation."[21] So the

---

[21] Dixon, Nancy. *Common Knowledge*, Harvard Business School Press, Cambridge, MA, 2000.

distinction between agile and document-centric methodologies is not one of no documentation versus extensive documentation; rather, it is a differing concept of the blend of documentation and conversation required to elicit understanding.

Agility relies on people who are alert and creative and who can maintain that alertness and creativity for the full length of a software development project. Sustainable development means finding a working pace of 50 to 60 hours a week that the team can sustain over time and remain healthy. Successful professionals neither expect nor experience 35-hour workweeks.

MAGIC NUMBER!

"Ninety percent of success is showing up." Woody Allen

Continuous attention to technical excellence and good design enhances agility. Although agile development is similar to rapid prototyping's speed and flexibility, there is a big difference in technical structure. Agile approaches emphasize quality of design. Agile processes assume and encourage acceptance of feature changes while the code is being written. Design cannot be a purely up-front activity to be completed before implementation. Every iteration requires design work.

"Simple, clear purpose and principles give rise to complex, intelligent behavior," says Dee Hock, former CEO of Visa International. "Complex rules and regulations give rise to simple, stupid behavior." No methodology can ever address the complexity of a modern software project. Giving people a simple set of rules and encouraging their creativity will produce far better outcomes than imposing complex, rigid regulations. To be challenged is to be uncomfortable. Managers tell their people that they believe in challenge and they can expect to change jobs when they master their current jobs. They explain that with this opportunity for growth, they have the obligation to help if there is trouble in their former jobs that their successors cannot solve. So, rotate developers' assignments. Software people should not be doing the same thing for more than 3 years.

9.9 THE BELL LABORATORIES PHILOSOPHY

Many wonder at the accomplishments of Bell Laboratories, its Noble Prize winners, its inventions and its innovations. Dealing with people issues were vital to the past success of Bell Laboratories. There was a sense of mission, stability of direction, constancy of purpose and closeness to customers in the daily work life with a sense of a first-rate professional community.

Developers at Bell Laboratories could impact their destiny, and there were stressful but meaningful management mechanisms to couple diverse organizations. There were common reviews, centralized support staffs, and a company-wide problem escalation procedure. After some horrific experiences of losing entire organizations, management realized that it was better to move the work to the people than the people to the work. This meant transferring projects between organizations. The stress came when managers fought losing some of their people and responsibility. The goal was to establish a synergy between personal goals and company needs.

The future quality of a company depends on the quality of new hires. Bell Laboratories attracted excellent college graduates by offering them a free graduate education. It was a sort of signing bonus. It involved a high-energy recruiting process that occupied line managers with visiting universities and interviewing candidates. During hectic hiring periods, line managers might spend 6 or more hours a week for 3 to 4 months interviewing. Choosing future employees was the responsibility of the best people because the executives of that time understood that people never hire anyone better than themselves— they simply cannot recognize the value before their eyes. Specific measures taken to maintain the Bell Laboratories technical excellence were equally important and were recognized, preserved, and enhanced. When these policies changed, the Bell Laboratories culture degraded and lost its competitive edge.

These overriding values at Bell Laboratories fostered the respect of the individual and individual excellence, but the individuals worked on teams. These teams were empowered to let the core value be brought to bear on complex projects. These were the core values, as shown in Table 9.4

TABLE 9.4. Bell Laboratories' Core Values

Enhancing the reputation of individual departments and their professional work environment.
Insisting on high-quality technical supervision.
Providing quality education, training, and personal development.
Having first-class reward systems benchmarked, including merit pay, compensation, promotion, and technical recognition.
Providing an opportunity to rise by excelling in function.
Fostering mechanisms for intergroup learning such a project management and architecture reviews.
Having a critical mass of highly skilled people in needed technologies.
Having stimulating coworkers available for informal discussions; an important role of Bell Laboratories researchers was visiting development shops. Often the brightest developers spent a year working with the researchers.
Insisting on challenging work, full utilization of capabilities, and access to needed information.

9.10 SO YOU WANT TO BE A MANAGER

Here are the approved and expected ethical responsibilities of the software manager; we need say no more:

Software engineering managers and leaders shall subscribe to and promote an ethical approach to the management of software development and maintenance. In particular, those managing or leading software engineers shall, as appropriate:

1. Ensure good management for any project on which they work, including effective procedures for promotion of quality and reduction of risk.
2. Ensure that software engineers are informed of standards before being held to them.
3. Ensure that software engineers know the employer's policies and procedures for protecting passwords, files and information that is confidential to the employer or confidential to others.
4. Assign work only after taking into account appropriate contributions of education and experience tempered with a desire to further that education and experience.
5. Ensure realistic quantitative estimates of cost, scheduling, personnel, quality and outcomes on any project on which they work or propose to work, and provide an uncertainty assessment of these estimates.
6. Attract potential software engineers only by full and accurate description of the conditions of employment.
7. Offer fair and just remuneration.
8. Not prevent someone from taking a position for which that person is suitably qualified, without cause.
9. Ensure that there is a fair agreement concerning ownership of any software, processes, research, writing, or other intellectual property to which a software engineer has contributed.
10. Provide for due process in hearing charges of violation of an employer's policy or of this Code.
11. Not ask a software engineer to do anything inconsistent with this Code.
12. Not punish anyone for expressing ethical concerns about a project.[22]

9.11 PROBLEMS

9.11.1

a. A software shop is concerned with the productivity of its developers, so they do a time study. They survey 22 software people for a typical 40-hour workweek. The results are shown in Table 9.5.

---

[22] This code was developed by the ACM/IEEE-CS Joint Task Force on Software Engineering Ethics and Professional Practices (SEEPP): Executive Committee: Donald Gotterbarn (Chair).

TABLE 9.5. How Developers Keep Busy for Problem 9.11.1a

Activity	Hours Spent
Nonproject Meetings	3.0
Field Support Problems	3.0
Planning Meetings	3.0
Administrative chores	0.5
Equipment Problems	0.25
Junk Mail	1.0
Customer Interaction	0.0
Training	0.0
*Testing	8
*Documenting	5
*Analysis	4
*Design	4
*Coding	7.25
Idle	1.0

*Task contributes to productivity.

The 22 people surveyed work on transaction-based systems. They use the document-focused Waterfall Model for development. The organization averages two function points per staff-month and wants to increase productivity to three function points per staff-month. The tasks without asterisks are overhead.

You use Table 9.6 describing software productivity increases in terms of the expansion factor defined as the ratio of the number of lines of executable code obtained from the number of lines of source code.[23]

What management policies changes would you try? Support your answers quantitatively.

b. An analysis of the time spent is shown in Table 9.7.

A simple solution is to increase the time on the project by

$$28.25 \text{ project hours}/ \times 50\% = 14.125 \text{ hours.}$$

What do you think?

c. What process changes would you try?

d. What product changes would you try?

e. What project management changes would you try?

9.11.2 You are asked to become the project manager for a project in deep trouble, but they report no development problems. The schema for the software is defined in Figure 9.3. When you review the design, you find one module

---

[23] Bernstein, Lawrence and Yuhas, C. M. "Software Investment Strategy," *Engineering Management Journal*, Vol. 7, No. 4, Dec. 1995, p. 20.

TABLE 9.6. Expansion Factor for Problem 9.11.1a

Improved Technology: Current Technology	Expansion Factor
Macro Assembler: Machine Instruction	3 : 1
FORTRAN / COBOL: MACRO Assembler	5 : 1
Database Mgmt: File Manager	2 : 1
Regression Testing: Big Bang Testing	1.25 : 1
Online: Batch Development	1.25 : 1
Prototyping: Waterfall (Top-Down Design)	1.6 : 1
AGL: In-line Reports	1.08 : 1
Subsecond Time Sharing: Online Dev	1.4 : 1
Reuse UNIX™ Libraries: No Reuse	1.35 : 1
Object-Oriented: Procedure Programing	3 : 1
Large Scale Reuse: Small-Scale Reuse	1.5 : 1

TABLE 9.7. Activity Analysis for Problem 9.11.1b

Activity	Hours Spent	Time Spent on Development
Nonproject Meetings	3.0	0
Field Problems	3.0	0
Meetings	3.0	0
Administrative Chores	0.5	0
Equipment Problems	0.25	0
Junk Mail	1.0	0
Customer Interaction	0.0	0
Training	0.0	0
Testing	8	8
Documenting	5	5
Analysis	4	4
Design	4	4
Coding	7.25	7.25
Idle	1.0	0
Total	40	28.25

with a data structure that does not map the physical problem well. As a result, there are many thousands of lines code written to manipulate the data structure to perform the need functions.

Physical Problem: In the cross-connect box shown in Figure 9.3, the software is to assign connections to links so that the length of the jumpers is minimized. In this diagram, the jumper is the largest it can be. The software is expected to move A's connection down or Z's connection up.

You find that to fit within the constraints imposed by the customer, a hierarchical data model is used. The database schema is shown in Figure 9.4.

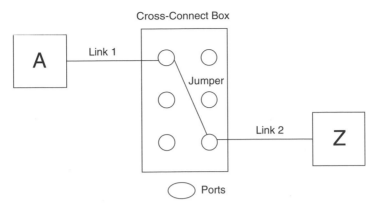

Figure 9.3. *Cross-connect box for Problem 9.11.2.*

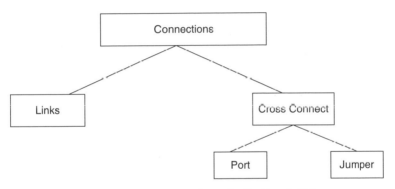

Figure 9.4. *Database schema for Problem 9.11.2.*

a. List three problems you might expect to find.

b. List five steps you might take to improve morale and productivity.

9.11.3 You are developing a system in which code will be written in C++ with mySQL for the database access. As usual your schedule is tight. Marketing needs to have the product released in 6 months. Three people report to you. They are skilled in C++, but not in mySQL. You estimate that there are six staff-months of C++ work and four staff-months of mySQL work needed to get the product to system testing. Your staff has a record of being 50% effective when they first use a new technology. System testing estimates that 1 month is required for testing and release packaging. You cannot hire any more people, so you have decided to send all three to 1 week of mySQL training.

Explain the advantages and disadvantages of each strategy and your best estimate, assuming there are no task dependencies, on how long it will take to get the product released. Which is the best software engineering strategy?

a. Do the C++ first and then send the three people for mySQL training.

b. Send the three to mySQL training after they have done about half of the C++ and Perl coding. History shows they lose a week of work when they are interrupted.

c. Send the three to mySQL training before doing any C++ work.

9.11.4 You are eager to improve the long-term productivity of the group of developers you are managing so you:

a. ask them to work overtime.

b. provide them with new tools.

c. manage them more closely.

d. measure their workload and typical day.

9.11.5 You are asked to produce a program on a tight schedule. Your boss tells you what functions are needed. You are free to use the tools of your choice. To meet the schedule you:

a. begin coding immediately.

b. meet with the user.

c. research other solutions.

d. design the interfaces.

9.11.6 How does the human engineering coupled with prototyping reduce the effort and time needed to build the system?

BIBLIOGRAPHY

Arthur, Lowell Jay. *Programmer Productivity: Myths, Methods, and Murphology A Guide for Managers, Analysts, and Programmers*, John Wiley and Sons, New York, 1983, pp. 25–27.

Bailey, Robert. *Human Performance Engineering A Guide for System Designers*, Prentice-Hall, Englewood Cliffs, NJ 1982.

Bernstein, L. "Software Project Management Audits," *The Journal of Systems and Software*, Vol. 2, No. 4, Dec. 1981, pp. 281–287.

Bernstein, L. and Yuhas, C. M. *Basic Understanding of Telecommunications Networks: Copper to Sand to Glass to Air*, Kluwer Academic Publishing, New York, 2000.

Bernstein, Lawrence and Yuhas, C. M. "Software Investment Strategy," *Engineering Management Journal*, Vol. 7, No. 4, Dec. 1995, pp. 15–21.

Boehm, Barry W. "Software Engineering," *Classics in Software Engineering*, Yourdin Press, New York, 1979, p. 325.

Boehm, Barry W., Gray, T. E., and Seewaldt, T. "Prototyping Versus Specifying: A Multiproject Experiment," *IEEE Transactions on Software Engineering*, Vol. SE-10, No. 3, May 1984.

Brooks, Frederick P., Jr. *The Mythical Man-Month: Essays on Software Engineering Anniversary Edition*, Addison-Wesley, New York, 1995.

Chen, Stephen. "From Software Art to Software Engineering," *Engineering Management Journal*, Vol. 7, No. 4, Dec. 1995, pp. 23–27.

Cunningham, James P., Blewett, C. Douglas, and Anderson, J. Scott. "Graphical Interfaces for Network Operations and Management," User Interface Design and Development Issue, *AT&T Technical Journal*, Vol. 72, No. 3, May/June 1993, pp. 57–66.

DeMarco, Tom and Lister, Timothy. *Peopleware-Productive Projects and Teams*, 2nd ed. Dorset House, New York, 1999.

Fogg, J. (Ed.). "Persuasive Technologies," *Communications of the ACM*, Vol. 42, No. 5, May 1999.

Glib, Tom and Weinberg, Gerald M. *Humanized Input Techniques for Reliable Keyed Input*, Winthrop Publishing, Cambridge, MA, 1977.

Miller, G. A. "The Magical Number Seven, Plus or Minus Two: Some Limits on Our Capacity for Processing Information," *The Psychological Review*, 1956, pp. 81–97.

Pascale, Richard Tanner. "Zen and the Art of Management," *Harvard Business Review*, March–April 1978, pp. 153–162.

Shneiderman, Ben and Plaisant, Catherine. *Designing The User Interface*, 4th ed. Pearson Addison-Wesley, Reading, MA, 2005, ch. 11 and p. 459.

Vredenburg, Karel. "Increasing Ease of Use," *Communications of the ACM*, Vol. 42, No. 5, May 1999, pp. 67–69.

10

Implementation Details

We include here those important implementation details that are not usually addressed in software engineering. Van Vliet's excellent book on traditional software issues[1] can be used in conjunction with this book. Some topics are from the early days of computer science, but as Brooks wrote in *No Silver Bullet*, "There is no single development, in either technology or management technique, which by itself promises even one order-of-magnitude improvement within a decade in productivity, in reliability, in simplicity".[2] Many good processes and tools speed implementation and reduce defects. The software engineer's job is to select those appropriate to the problem. Our software friends love to make bold statements, and here is ours:

MAGIC NUMBER!

No method, process, or technology is best, current, or universally practiced.

---

[1] Van Vliet, Hans. *Software Engineering: Principles and Practice*, 2nd ed. John Wiley and Sons, New York, 2000.
[2] Brooks, Frederick P. *The Mythical Man-Month*, anniversary edition, Addison-Wesley Longman, Reading, MA, 1995, p. 179.

Trustworthy Systems Through Quantitative Software Engineering,
by Lawrence Bernstein and C. M. Yuhas
Copyright © 2005 IEEE Computer Society

Too many managers spend too much time looking for a silver bullet that will end software crises, when engineers know that the approach chosen to solve a problem depends on the problem and the problem solver.[3] Engineers understand many different processes and have the critical judgment to know when and, more importantly, when not to use them. There are so many good software implementation processes and technologies that they fill a six-course graduate program in Quantitative Software Engineering at Stevens Institute of Technology.[4]

There are some implementation details that every accomplished software engineer should know. These are topics we selected for emphasis or because they are misunderstood, ignored, unfamiliar, or emerging.

(1) Structured programming

(2) RUP and UML

(3) Coding styles

(4) Code reviews

(5) Attacks

(6) Open source

10.1   STRUCTURED PROGRAMMING

Structured programming has been with us since the 1970s. It is a foundation for building trustworthy systems. The fundamental principle of structured programming is that at all times and under all circumstances, programmers must keep the program within their intellectual grasp. The ideas of structured programming are lost to many younger software engineers.

MAGIC NUMBER!

Structured programs are prime proper programs that can be separately complied and are no smaller than 50 SLOC or larger than 1000 SLOC.

---

[3] Brooks, Frederick P. "No Silver Bullet: Essence and Accidents of Software Engineering," *Milestones in Software Evolution*, edited by Paul W. Oman and Ted G. Lewis, IEEE Computer Society Press, Los Alamitos, CA, 1990, pp. 293–300.

[4] http://www.cs.stevens.edu/Programs/Grad_Master_Science.shtml.

Early work at IBM by Rick Linger, Harlan Mills, and B. Witt found that reliable systems were more likely if they were constructed from prime proper programs. A **prime** program is a software module with one entry and one exit point. A **proper** program has a path from the entry to the exit through every node of the program, where a node is a segment of code that implements only one of these operations:

(1) Assignment and calculation
(2) If_then_else
(3) Do_while,

A compound or traditional program is structured if it is functionally equivalent to a set of proper programs plus a counter. The seminal paper explaining the need for such structure is Dijkstra's "**GoTo** Statement Considered Harmful," from which the following excerpt is taken.

> For a number of years I have been familiar with the observation that the quality of programmers is a decreasing function of the density of **GoTo** statements in the programs they produce. More recently I discovered why the use of the **GoTo** statement has such disastrous effects, and I became convinced that the **GoTo** statement should be abolished from all "higher level" programming languages (i.e. everything except, perhaps, plain machine code) . . . Our intellectual powers are rather geared to master static relations and that our powers to visualize processes evolving in time are relatively poorly developed. For that reason we should do . . . our utmost to shorten the conceptual gap between the static program and the dynamic process, to make the correspondence between the program (spread out in text space) and the process (spread out in time) as trivial as possible.[5]

Dijkstra's insight supported Mills' early work on structured programming design constraints in the metaphor of the 1960s when Mills' idea was being attacked. Although **GoTo**'s have disappeared in modern programming languages, the need for structured programs has not. This lesson frequently falls through the cracks in our rush to teach the latest technology. Software engineers are not taught the failures of unstructured programming of the past. Dijkstra's provocative warning jolts us so that we avoid the trap of producing unmaintainable, unstructured code in object class methods or in procedural programs.

10.2 RATIONAL UNIFIED PROCESS AND UNIFIED MODELING LANGUAGE

The Rational unified process (RUP) is a framework that incorporates many good software practices suitable for a wide class of software developments.

---

[5] http://www.acm.org/classics/oct95/.

RUP solves many problems endemic to software development. Its unique contribution is that it is architecture-driven and provides the 4 + 1 view of software architecture that is the foundation for creating comprehensive software products. Philippe Kruchten explains that RUP consolidates processes

> . . . into a form suitable for a wide range of projects and organization. In particular, it covers six practices:

(1) Develop software iteratively,
(2) Manage requirements,
(3) Use component-based architecture,
(4) Visually model software,
(5) Continuously verify software quality,
(6) Control changes to software.[6]

RUP includes the powerful Unified Modeling Language (UML). This diagramming language allows developers to visualize and document models of software systems. It is targeted for object-oriented systems but is useful for all systems, especially online transaction ones. UML is not a development method. UML is an industry standard for graphically describing software products.

UML consists of diagrams that model different aspects of a software product. A subset of these diagrams coupled with the 4 + 1 architecture views are a reasonable way to start using UML. As designers become more familiar with the UML approach, they can use other diagrams to visualize and design their product.[7] This startup set of diagrams is the following:

(1) **4 + 1 architecture views** show a logical, physical, process, and development diagram of the system.
(2) **Use case diagrams** show users of the system and the business scenarios of how they will use the system.
(3) **Class diagrams** show the object classes and their interrelationships. For procedural programs, this will be the hierarchy of components and subcomponents, called the work breakdown structure in configuration management.
(4) **Sequence diagrams** show the method calls made by one object to another on a time-based chart. It is an easy-to-follow view of the flow of messages through a software system.

[6] Kruchten, Philippe. *The Rational Unifies Process—An Introduction*, 2nd ed. Addison-Wesley, Reading, MA, 2000.
[7] http://www-306.ibm.com/software/rational/uml/.
http://www.informit.com/articles/article.asp?p=347699&seqNum=3tpo.

Case Study: The Case of the Pokey JiffyLOOP

Prospectus: Telephone companies have dreamt of integrating data about how the network is **constructed** and how it is **used**. Making this dream a reality has eluded them for 30 years. The benefits of such integration are widely known. The introduction of high bandwidth connections for WWW access makes such integration even more important. An integrated engineering/provisioning system is needed to replace legacy systems and to allow the telephone companies to offer new copper-based mid-band technology without suffering the cost penalty of special service processing.

Today an inefficient array of stand-alone systems connects and disconnects customers, installs new equipment, and adds new services to existing customers. Entrenched organizations stand in the way of the introduction of technology that threatens to disenfranchise them. The tools and systems for network managers are hard to use and are not integrated, but once learned they are hard to abandon. Any provisioning system, regardless of its sophistication, is the intellectual descendant of the shoebox full of 3×5 cards that Alexander Graham Bell used to keep track of all the details of the logical network when he first strung wires in Boston. He kept track of the physical equipment with standard engineering drawings. A single computerized data model is the foundation for a new integrated engineering/provisioning system.

MOV: JiffyLOOP almost eliminates the craft time required to provision a special service line by making data easily accessible and, even more importantly, accurate. Table 10.1 illustrates the expected savings.

TABLE 10.1. Functional Area/Savings With JiffyLOOP

Functional Area	Savings/ Assigned Line
Two-wire special (installation time reduction)	$2.43
Four-wire special (installation time reduction)	$4.79
Automated line rearrangements	$3.00
Automated equipment rearrangements	$0.75
Calculating Engineering Characteristics	$0.53
Routine work order generation	$1.45
Elimination of engineer	$10.16
TOTAL	**$23.11**

Requirements Specification: JiffyLOOP is the system designed to enhance the existing engineering, construction, and provisioning process. Specifically, JiffyLOOP will perform the following functions:

- Electrical designs to assure customer service
- Automated equipment rearrangement as a transaction for five or fewer related changes

- Automated equipment rearrangement running in background for more than five related changes
- Repository of the result of electrical designs
- Automated update of legacy systems
- Plant location drawings using satellite data
- Online inquiries based on address and telephone number

Four existing products are integrated to meet these requirements. Table 10.2 names each product and states its role.

TABLE 10.2. Product/Functionality for JiffyLOOP

Product	Functionality
PRIS	• Automates design and engineering • Rearranges equipment • Posts changes to drawings
Mediation & Admin.	• Legacy interfaces • JiffyLOOP system administration
DB-Able	• Stores logical, physical, and graphical data • Map generation
LDB	• Provides drawing and plotting tools • GIS • Windows GUI • Translates graphics

A JiffyLOOP logical view, physical view, UML use case, a class diagram, and sequence chart demonstrate the visualization power of UML. A complete and detailed architecture description is beyond the scope of this case study.

Logical View: Figure 10.1 is a component diagram of the system showing its parts and their relationships. As functions are assigned to subcomponents, the diagram will be decomposed and eventually become a UML chart called a collaborative diagram. Designers use these charts to understand the coupling between subsystems.

Physical View: Figure 10.2 is the physical view for JiffyLOOP. It shows the hardware and operating systems compatible with all component systems. There are many possible client/server configurations. The physical view limits customer selections to a subset. Customers whose IT shops do not support any of this subset can easily see that they cannot use JiffyLOOP.

UML Case Diagram: Figure 10.3 is a high-level use case diagram showing the business flows for a customer requesting service. In this case, the needed equipment is not in place, so instructions go to a constructions crew to rearrange existing equipment and install necessary equipment.

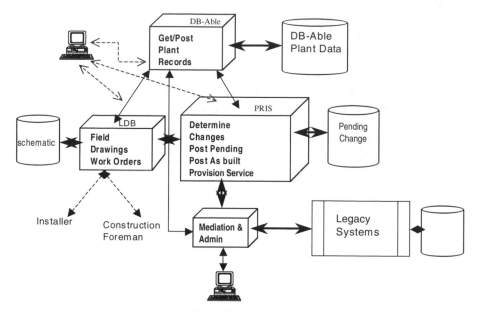

Figure 10.1. *JiffyLOOP logical view.*

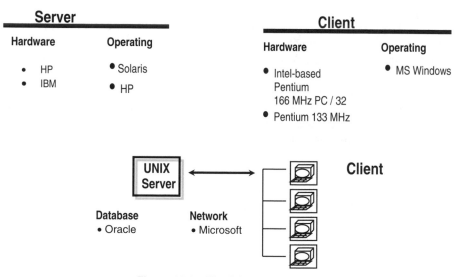

Figure 10.2. *JiffyLOOP physical view.*

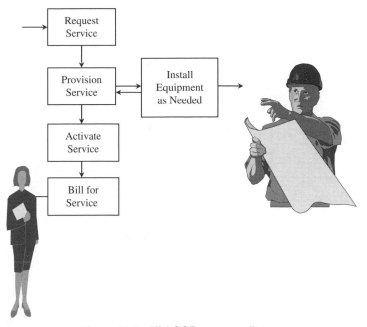

Figure 10.3. *JiffyLOOP use case diagram.*

Class Diagram: It is surprising how difficult it is to create an object class for familiar things. Consider the simple idea of a telephone number that is fundamental to the design of JiffyLOOP data structures and algorithms. If you know my telephone number is 555-999-1111 and dial just that, it is unlikely that my phone will ring. If you are calling from your office, you might need to dial 9 first. In New Jersey, you would need to dial 1 before the ten-digit number.

Here is a simple diagram for a class called telephone number. Consider a North American phone number 555-999-1111. The first three digits, 555, is the area code that informs the geographic location of the telephone. The second three digits, 999, inform the local switch in the neighborhood central office and link to the proper interoffice trunk for routing a call. The last four digits, 1111, point to the individual termination on the local switch attached to the line connected to the telephone. Figure 10.4 shows the information so far.

This telephone number class is still incomplete:

(1) It does not allow calls from North America to Europe, you need to prefix an "11" to a country code.

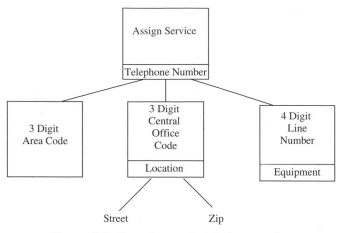

Figure 10.4. *Class diagram for telephone number.*

(2) It does not anticipate ten-digit dialing in New Jersey.

(3) It does not anticipate calls originating from telephones attached to a PBX that require a prefix of "9," "8," or even "7."

(4) It does not anticipate the special numbers "0" for operator, "411" for information, "611" for repair services, or "911" for emergency services.

Such a seemingly simple concept can become a complex class structure. Figure 10.5 shows the sequence diagram for this wire change.

Conclusion: By tracing this case history, you see the usefulness of the 4 + 1 views and the UML diagrams. They give you insight to how the system will work and into how difficult it will be to build and extend it before any code is written. Design changes can be made in this fluid state to simplify the system so that it is more likely to be delivered on time and within budget. Visualizing the interfaces identifies dependencies, potential bottlenecks, and risk exposures. Any bottlenecks or potential deadlocks will be apparent. The design objective is to transform the details of the JiffyLOOP features from the real world to the computer world.[8]

Notice DB-Able's complex interfaces in the JiffyLOOP logical view. A race condition between different interdependent transactions could develop that will impact the system performance. This problem also occurs in the sequence diagram. Redesign is needed. The JiffyLOOP project never produced a product because the stakeholders could not afford the necessary redesign.

---

[8] Bernstein, L. "Get the Design Right!" *IEEE Software*, Sept. 1993, pp. 61–63.

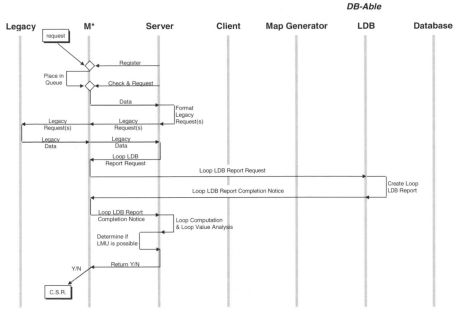

Figure 10.5. *Sequence diagram for complex class structure.*

10.3   MEASURING COMPLEXITY

We have urged you to keep problems simple. The challenge to software engineers is how to measure complexity to tell where simplification is needed. Complexity is an area of software metrics that is focused on direct measurement of software structures. Complexity measures are used to predict the effort and time it will take to build a software product and its reliability and maintainability. Complexity measures help control the development process in a software project. During design, they point to tightly coupled modules. During implementation, they identify the modules most in need of formal code inspections. During maintenance, they provide detailed information about software modules to help pinpoint areas of potential instability.

Software complexity is a function of each of the following:

(1) The type of application, characterized as real-time, online, or report generation. Table 10.3 contains definitions for each type of software.

(2) The nature of the computations performed including the precision of the calculations.

(3) The component's size, measured in function points.

(4) The cohesion of the component. Cohesion is a measure of the mutual affinity of subcomponents within a module.

(5) The coupling within and the coupling between components. Coupling measures the component's external references and dependencies.

(6) The steps needed to assure a component's correctness.

(7) The component's trustworthiness separately and when integrated into a system.

(8) The program control flow.

TABLE 10.3. Defining the Type of Software

Type	Characteristics	Examples
Real-time	(1) Key tasks must be executed by a hard deadline or the system will become unstable. (2) Software must be aware of the details of the hardware operation. The most difficult are the "don't care" states. (3) Generating bit stings to test, configure, or control hardware.	Operating Systems, communication drivers, disk controllers, hardware diagnostics, and embedded software that must deal with all states of the hardware. Games, avionics, and automotive control and military systems are typical real-time systems
Online transactions applications	Multiple transactions are run concurrently. Fast response time is important. Database and transaction recovery is required. Virus protection and GUIs are needed.	Customer Relationship Management, Enterprise Resource Planning, Customer Care, network management, provisioning, and order-entry systems are typical online systems. Database inquiry systems are also typical of this type.
Report generation, analysis, and script programming	These programs run in the background. They can be computationally intensive.	Scientific programs such as those written in FORTRAN or business programs are typical of this type. Most software libraries fall into this category. Examples: fulfillment and off-line inventory management software.

Lui Sha's work relates simplicity to high reliability. His view is that effort to simplify designs and implementation assures the correctness of a component and greatly influences software product reliability. He advocates designs that eliminate singularities in the execution of the component.[9]

---

[9] Sha, Lui, "Using Simplicity to Control Complexity," *IEEE Software*, Vol. 18, No. 4, July/Aug. 2001, p. 25.

Another set of metrics is based on the structure of the program. The most widely used is McCabe's Cyclomatic Metric[10] that measures the number of independent control paths within a program. This metric looks for loops and effectively finds components that are orders of magnitude more complex than others. Trustworthy system design demands that these components be redesigned because reliability increases by reducing complexity. Software tools to measure a program's cyclomatic complexity are commercially available at www.mccabe.com, which states this definition:

> The McCabe Cyclomatic complexity measure is versatile and widely used. It is based purely on the decision structure of the code; it is uniformly applicable across projects and languages and is completely insensitive to cosmetic changes in code. Many studies have established its correlation with errors, so it can be used to predict reliability. More significantly, studies have shown that the risk of errors jumps for functions with a cyclomatic complexity over 10, so there's a validated threshold for reliability screening. Also, this assessment can be performed incrementally during development and can even be estimated from a detailed design.

> For an individual software module, the programmer can easily calculate cyclomatic complexity manually by counting the decision constructs in the code. This allows continuous control during implementation. It is completely independent of text formatting and nearly independent of programming language.[11]

Figure 10.6 shows the control flow graph of a simple software module. Figure 10.7 shows a complex, moderate-risk software module. Figure 10.8 shows an extremely complex, high-risk module. The software functions represented in Figures 10.6, 10.7, and 10.8 have cyclomatic complexity measures of 7, 16, and 22, respectively.

Cyclomatic complexity can be specialized to measure **essential complexity** that finds the amount of a program's unstructured decision logic. Unstructured code, typically caused by using Dijkstra's harmful **GoTo** statements or in modern programming languages by breaking out of loops, is error prone and hard to understand. Such unstructured control logic cannot be decomposed, understood, and modified by itself. **Essential complexity** can measure maintenance risk exposure with a threshold value of four. Cyclomatic complexity increases gradually when code is added during maintenance. **Essential complexity** can increase dramatically by the addition of a single software patch. The patched code is then risky code. Using **essential complexity** to screen modules after each modification during maintenance can manage this risk. Although Figures 10.7 and 10.8 both have high cyclomatic complexity, Figure 10.8 has high essential complexity and thus carries a significantly higher maintenance risk.[12]

---

[10] See Van Vliet, as cited in footnote 1, p. 308.
[11] http://www.mccabe.com.
[12] http://www.stsc.hill.af.mil/crosstalk/1994/12/xt94d12b.asp.

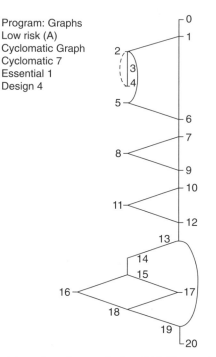

Program: Graphs
Low risk (A)
Cyclomatic Graph
Cyclomatic 7
Essential 1
Design 4

Figure 10.6. *Simple module cyclomatic complexity of 7 (with permission of McCabe Inc).*

MAGIC NUMBER!

The goal of design simplification is to reduce complexity, measured by the number of function points that must be implemented. Eliminate 40% of those counted at the start of the architecture phase by eliminating generality and using the technologies of reuse, refactoring, equation simplification, and reducing the cyclomatic signature of the pseudo-code of a component.

Once the architecture is synthesized, coupling and cohesion measurements begin for each view of the system and within the components. If pseudo-code is used as part of the design, cyclomatic measures can be taken. Then developers can make their measurements as code is produced. This process gives the programmer direct and objective feedback about the module. The test group measures the complexity of every component with every release. Frequent measurements prevent complexity from creeping into the software structure as it evolves.

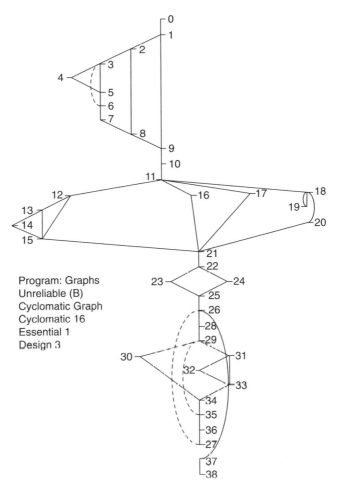

Program: Graphs
Unreliable (B)
Cyclomatic Graph
Cyclomatic 16
Essential 1
Design 3

Figure 10.7. Moderate-risk cyclomatic complexity of 16.

MAGIC NUMBER!

Code inspection and redesign are required for every component with a cyclomatic complexity greater than ten times the median of all components or with an essential complexity greater than five times the median.

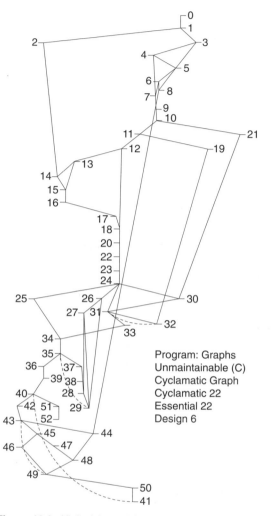

Figure 10.8. *High-risk module cyclomatic complexity 22.*

The form shown in Figure 10.9 is one of many ways to estimate complexity at all development stages. The measures are tracked throughout the life cycle of a software product to observe trends and justify work needed to keep the product simple. Wideband Delphi[13] is used to map qualitative judgments into an ordinal range of 1 to 5.

---

[13] Boehm, Barry. *Software Engineering Economics*, Prentice-Hall, Englewood Cliffs, NJ, 1981, pp. 335–336.

Project or Component Name: _____
Development Stage: _____
Project type: real-time, online transaction or background
Software Engineer_____
(Circle one)
Date_____

Metric for Complexity (1 is simple and 5 is complex)

Factor	Points	Score
Problem Domain • All algorithms and calculations are simple. • Most algorithms and calculations are simple. • Most algorithms and calculations are moderately complex. • Some algorithms and calculations are difficult. • Many algorithms and calculations are difficult.	1 2 3 4 5	
Architecture Complexity • Code ported from one known environment to another. Application does not change more than 5%. • Architecture follows an existing pattern. Process design is straightforward. No complex hardware/software interfaces. • Architecture created from scratch. Process design is straightforward. No complex hardware/software interfaces. • Architecture created from scratch. Process design is complex. Complex hardware/software interfaces exist, but they are well defined and unchanging. • Architecture created from scratch. Process design is complex. Complex hardware/software interfaces are ill defined and changing.	1 2 3 4 5	
Data Structure Design • Simple well-defined and unchanging data structures. Shallow inheritance in class structures. No object classes have inheritance greater than 3. • Several data element types with straightforward relationships. Less than 5 object classes have inheritance greater than 3. • Multiple data files, complex data relationships, many libraries, large object library. No more than 10% of the object classes have inheritance greater than three. The number of object classes is less than 1% of the function points • Complex data elements, parameter passing module-to-module, complex data relationships, and many object classes have inheritance greater than three. A large but stable number of object classes. • Complex data elements, parameter passing module-to-module, complex data relationships, and many object classes have inheritance greater than three. A large and growing number of object classes. No attempt to normalize data between modules.	1 2 3 4 5	

Figure 10.9. *Measuring software complexity.*

Code Design		
• Nonprocedural code (4GL, generated code, screen skeletons). High cohesion. Programs inspected. Module size constrained between 50 and 500 SLOCs	1	
• Program skeletons or patterns used. Programs inspected. Module size constrained between 50 and 500 SLOCs. Reused modules. Commercial object libraries relied on. Coupling/cohesion ratio < 2.	2	
• Well-structured, small modules. Object class methods well focused and generalized. Modules with single entry and exit points. Programs reviewed.	3	
• Complex but known structure randomly sized modules. Some complex object classes. Error paths unknown. Coupling/cohesion ratio ≥ 2.	4	
• Code structure unknown, randomly sized modules, complex object classes, and error paths unknown. Coupling/cohesion ratio ≥ 2.	5	
Total Score		
Complexity		

Complexity = (Total score / 4) x (Type Factor), where
Type Factor = 10 for real-time or high-performance software
5 for online transaction software
1 for background software

Figure 10.9. *Continued*

10.4 CODING STYLES

"Coding skill is just one small part of writing correct programs. The majority of the task is . . . problem definition, algorithm design and data structure selection," wrote Jon Bentley.[14] A coding style that leads to correct and maintainable code emphasizes putting a straightforward mapping of the program and data structures to the problem structure. Efficient and cryptic code with multiple levels of indirection might be fun to write, but it is difficult to fix and enhance.

Tweaking a component with the smallest possible change on the theory, "If it ain't broke, don't fix it," is counterproductive. Code degrades with any change, so effort must be made to leave it better structured than you found it.

10.4.1 Data Structures

Any software system is just one interpretation of the reality of the problem it is solving. Both data structure clashes with the problem and careless use of data structures are principle causes of unacceptable throughput and response time.

---

[14] Bentley, Jon. *Programming Pearls*, 2nd ed. Addison-Wesley, Reading, MA, p. 33.

One problem associated with database systems is the lingering death associated with corrupted databases. Unfortunately, the program that first discovers the corruption is usually the victim and not the perpetrator. Two tedious processes then ensue. First, the result must be corrected, and then the cause must be found and fixed. Finding such problems is difficult because the perpetrator is long gone and leaves few clues. These coding styles can mitigate against corruption:

(1) Put in early alarm systems to detect some problems as they occur, and try to contain them; for example, validity check all records as they are received.
(2) Reduce potential problems by consolidating database access routines that handle inverted files and capture files needed for transaction recovery.
(3) When something does not work that worked before, find "what's changed." Be relentless in searching for the change because there lies the problem.
(4) The coding style for the component interfaces will determine how easy it is to test and enhance a system. Inspect the levels of indirection in data references to make sure they are needed. Root out extraneous levels of indirection in component interfaces.

MAGIC NUMBER!

You can change all of the interfaces some of the time,
You can change some of the functions all of the time,
But you cannot change all of the functions and all of the interfaces at the same time.

With apologies to Abraham Lincoln

Decouple conversion system databases from application system databases by using application system transactions to initialize the database. Otherwise, unnatural coupling and constraints of freezing the database design prematurely seep into the development program. This simplifies the code and prevents design interactions aimed at eliminating performance bottlenecks and potential deadlocks.

Example: The problem is to create data structures about employees that contain name and number of dependents. There are two options:

Option 1 Explicitly code an employee's name and number of dependents in one object class:

```
Class Person
  Attributes: Last_Name; First_Name; Number_of_Depen-
dents;
  end
  Data Definition:
    Yuhas = Person.new;
    YuhasFirstName= "Chris";
    YuhasLastName= "Yuhas";
    YuhasNumberofDependents= "1";
  Print
YuhasFirstName, "/b" YuhasLastName, "has b" YuhasNum-
berofDependent, "dependents"
```

This approach yields clear and understandable code, but if the Human Resources people need to add another attribute, the code must change. This code is awkward to enhance.

Option 2 Carefully use a level of indirection, makeing the code difficult to understand but easy to enhance.

```
  Class Person
  Attributes:  data table
  define initialization ( ); // this is a vital step
too often ignored;
  end
definition for entry
  Yuhas =Person.Name
  Yuhas.data["FirstName"] = "Chris"
  Yuhas.data["LastName"]  = "Yuhas"
  Yuhas.data["NumberofDependents"] = 1;
  Print
  Yuhas.datatable["FirstName"],"/b"
  Yuhas.datatable["LastName"], "has /b"
  Yuhas.datatable["NumberofDependents"], "dependents"
```

A new attribute can be added to the definition of *entry* and change the print statement. However, there is not a clean mapping from the statement of the problem to the coding of the solution, and it is not easily understandable.

So, which coding style is correct? As usual, the correct software engineering response is "It depends." The second approach is preferred if many changes are expected because making the changes will be easier. When there are many complex classes, the first option makes for straightforward reading and understanding.

10.4.2 Team Coding

Programmers need a consistent coding style and process when there are many programmers building a system. Quality cannot be tested in; quality must be designed in.

10.4.2.1 *Testers' Right of Refusal*

The programmer finds and fixes all possible defects before delivering code to the test team. The test team is the arbiter of the "all possible" standard and has the right of refusal because it is expensive for the test team to find defects. If disagreements arise between the test team and the programmers, the manager reviews and adjudicates. This invokes the management technique called **management by exception**.

10.4.2.2 *Program Standard*

Programmers use a written standard:

(1) Naming convention for variable.
(2) Agreement between comments and code.
(3) Commenting conventions. Comments state the intent of a set of instructions and not what they do. Extensive prefaces are the best way to document the algorithms in the code.[15]

MAGIC NUMBER!

When Lines of Comments exceed Lines of Code, code is hard to read.

10.4.2.3 *Wild Transfers*

Programmers must explicitly prevent wild transfers.

(1) Check every entry and exit transfer.
(2) Bound the inputs and the outputs.
(3) Unconstrained pointers can result from poor array bounds that lead to memory leaks.

10.4.2.4 *Initialization*

Programmers must initialize memory, data, pointers, and arrays before they are used.

10.4.2.5 *Subscripts*

Programmers must check code subscripts to keep the program bounded. Consider an array x of i: X[i].

---

[15] http://ei.cs.vt.edu/~cs2604/Standards/Standards.html.

i is defined as $4 \leq i \leq 6$. How many elements are there in the list, two or three? There are three, but too often programmers subtract four from six and forget to add one, which leads to an error. The recommended approach is to define the lower bound as "less than or equals" and the upper bound as "less than" in all cases. Here i is $4 \leq i < 7$; then it is clear that the number of elements is the difference 3. Not following this standard often leads to the common **off-by-one error**.[16]

10.4.2.6   *Loops Terminate*   Make sure that every loop terminates. In fact, make sure that all programs and methods are structured.

10.4.2.7   *Review the Code*

10.4.3   Code Reading

Everybody on the team is involved in this technique. Code is distributed so everyone has somebody else's code to read. Then a team meets to discuss their findings. This process improves the coding ability of the group. Vic Basili has pioneered and promulgated code-reading techniques. He and Richard Selby report, "At NASA/CSC, code reading was more cost effective than functional and structural testing, but there was no significant difference between functional and structural testing. Code reading found 3.3 faults per hour on the average while each of the testing techniques found 1.8 faults on the average."[17] Code reading is difficult, tedious, and important. Even gurus extend and receive this courtesy.

10.4.4   Code Review

The programmer who wrote the code tends to find the most bugs by testing for syntax errors, logic errors, and incompleteness errors. User requirements specifications and coding standards are applied as checks. Code reviews are part of the team programming of the agile methods. A two-person team writes tests, fixes problems, and then jointly reviews the code. This approach speeds development.

10.4.5   Code Inspections

Code inspections are a formal process with teams of two to five code inspectors. The module owner is not part of the initial inspection team. A code inspection is held to improve code and not to evaluate developers. Formal code inspections are a six-step process:[18]

10.4.5.1   *Prepare*   To get ready for the inspection, print separate hardcopies of the source code for each inspector. The hardcopy should contain a count of the NCSLOC.

---

[16] http://cm.bell-labs.com/cm/cs/tpop/warstory.html.
[17] http://www.cs.umd.edu/~mvz/mswe609/book/chapter4.pdf.
[18] http://www.sei.cmu.edu/str/descriptions/inspections_body.html.

10.4.5.2 Scope   The module owner spends 20 to 40 minutes explaining the general layout of the code to the inspectors. The inspectors are not allowed to ask questions; the code is supposed to be self-explanatory.

10.4.5.3 Individual Inspections   Each inspector uses a project coding standard checklist and inspects 80 to 120 NCSLOC per hour.

MAGIC NUMBER!

One person can inspect no more than 125 NCSLOC/hr.

10.4.5.4 Code Inspection Session   All code inspectors for the code at issue attend the meeting. Managers are not present. An experienced mediator chairs the code inspection sessions, which lasts no more than 2 hours.

10.4.5.5 Follow-Up   The defects list is submitted to the programmer for rework. Suggestions can include such avenues as changing code, adding or deleting comments, or restructuring to effect solutions. Inspection meetings are for problem finding, not for problem solving. It is the moderator's responsibility to see that all defects are satisfactorily reworked afterward by the programmer.

10.4.5.6 Record Keeping   Objectively track success in detecting and correcting defects. Count the number of defects and categorize them by type. Eliminate both the perception and the reality that the inspections will be used to evaluate developers.

10.5 A MUST READ FOR TRUSTWORTHY SOFTWARE ENGINEERS

Les Hatton maintains that the best way to use C and C++ in mission-critical applications is to constrain the use of language features to achieve reliable software performance. He gives specific instruction-by-instruction guidance for the constraints. His theme is "The use of C in safety-related or high integrity systems is not recommended without severe and automatically enforceable constraints. However, if these are present using the formidable tool support (including the extensive C library), the best available evidence suggests that it is then possible to write software of *at least* as high intrinsic quality and consistency as with other commonly used languages."[19] We applaud his instruction-by-instruction analysis of the C language. Hatton restricts safety to "freedom from danger or risks" and reliability to "of sound and consistent character or quality."

10.6 CODING FOR PARALLELISM

We start with an example to illustrate the problem. Consider a process with two threads

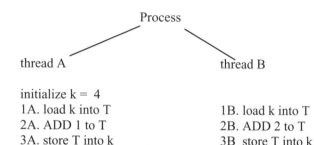

initialize k = 4
1A. load k into T
2A. ADD 1 to T
3A. store T into k

1B. load k into T
2B. ADD 2 to T
3B store T into k

What is the value of k?

(a) k is 7 if thread A is executed before thread B.
(b) k is 5 if thread B is executed first.
(c) k is 5, 6, or 7 if the two threads are run in parallel.

The value of k depends on the particular order of the instructions executed in thread A and thread B.

This simple example demonstrates that synchronization is required between merely two threads. As the number of threads increases, the number of execution steps increases exponentially and synchronization problems become intractable unless steps are taken to be able to trace the execution flow of the program, the number of threads are minimized, the threads are carefully identified, and the threads can be directed to run sequentially.

10.7 THREATS

Trustworthy systems are secure systems, but from the beginning of computing there have been malicious tricksters who try to violate them. As early as the

[19] See Hatton, Les. *Safer C: Developing Software for High-Integrity and Safety Critical Systems,* McGraw-Hill, New York, 1997, p. ix.

1970s there were traps surreptitiously inserted into the kernel of operating systems that deleted users' files.

The possibilities are myriad. Pointers can be corrupted, so JAVA hides pointers from programmers. Service denial attacks take advantages of a design flaw in the Internet TCP/IP protocol standards that allow flooding input buffers. Hackers can send large numbers of message segments during startup. It is well known that many functions provided by the standard C library are unsafe and the C programming language does not automatically perform bounds-checks on arrays and pointer references. Poor programming practices such as assuming input data are valid or misusing pointers permit security breaches.

Recently more general buffer overflows and SQL injection attacks have allowed hackers entry to software systems. These two threats are mentioned to give the software developer insight into the need for design and coding constraints that thwart attacks, even if the cost is performance degradation.

The symptoms of a buffer overflow are an unexpectedly large amount of data written to the buffer, thus overflowing it and overwriting the memory immediately after the end of the buffer. The overflow injects additional code into an unsuspecting process and then hijacks control of that process to execute the injected code. The hijacking of control is usually accomplished by overwriting return addresses on the process stack or by overwriting function pointers in the process memory. Therefore, buffer overflow vulnerabilities in process stacks are a security threat. A hacker can use a static buffer overrum to execute damaging code. One way to detect and thwart such attacks is to check the size of the data strings being loaded into a buffer against the size of the buffer. This approach requires all programmers to know the potential threat and take preventive steps. Legacy systems are a particular problem because it is unreasonable to expect that their programmers were sensitive to these buffer concerns. A software engineering preventive measure adds code to intercept all calls to library functions. The substitute version implements the original library functions with the added advantage that any buffer overflows are contained within the current stack frame at an overhead of no more than 15%.

A threat similar to a buffer overflow is SQL injection. SQL is the standard Structured Query Language (SQL) for accessing and manipulating databases. The threat occurs when data tailored for mischief is included in a database query as a simple string at be added at the end of a legitimate query. It is a simple matter to create a string where anything is possible: deleting data, adding data, and even executing arbitrary harmful code. This is a threat to the database if the application has unlimited data privileges. Preventing SQL attacks requires inspecting user input for suspicious substrings and unexpected SQL query requests and query encodings. When a Web server allows multiple encoding schemes in its input arguments, it is possible to encode attacks and bypass checks. Preventing SQL injection attacks requires the coding discipline to use only stored procedures and not to return SQL database error messages to end users.

SQL injection and buffer overflows are subsets of vulnerability to invalid user input. The idea is to convince the application to run code that was not intended. If an application is creating SQL strings näively on the fly and then running them, it is child's play for a hacker to gain entry and be evil. This nasty bit of warped creativity is called a worm.[20] Preventing SQL injection attacks requires coding discipline to use only stored procedures and to not return SQL database error messages to end users.

As an example, the Computer Emergency Readiness Team (CERT) reported in 2003:

> ... self-propagating malicious code that exploits vulnerability in the Resolution Service of Microsoft SQL Server 2000 and Microsoft Desktop Engine (MSDE) 2000. This worm is being referred to as the SQLSlammer, W32. Slammer, and Sapphire worm. The propagation of this malicious code has caused varied levels of network degradation across the Internet and the compromise of vulnerable machines.[21]

Then again in 2005, CERT reported a new worm known as "Santy" that compromises Web servers with hypertext preprocessing (PHP) enabled and running certain bulletin board software. It is believed that this worm is exploiting ... a lack of input validation ... that may allow a remote attacker to execute arbitrary commands on a vulnerable server. The problem occurs because phpBB bulletin board software does not scan incoming Internet Uniform Resource Locators (URLs) for malicious content ..."[22]

10.8   OPEN-SOURCE SOFTWARE

Open-source software development practices are giving rise to a new view of how complex software systems can be constructed, deployed, and evolved. Open software development does not adhere to the traditional software engineering life-cycle models or to prescriptive standards. It relies on the contributions of geographically dispersed developers. The Internet is used to communicate and collaborate. The availability of source code is a necessary condition for an open-source project, but it is not sufficient. The Open Source Initiative insists that such software be distributed freely, that the source code be readily available to all, and that developers are free to create derived works.[23] Developers can obtain significant open-source tools and components for their projects.

The developers who contribute to an open-source project are always users of the software. But all users need not be developers. Cristina Gacek and Budi

---

[20] http://www.unixwiz.net/techtips/sql-injection.html.
[21] http://www.cert.org/advisories/CA-2003-04.html.
[22] http://www.us-cert.gov/current/current_activity.html#Santy.
[23] http://opensource.org/docs/def_print.php.

Arief examined the motivations for this approach and found that meritocracy and a sense of community encourage participants. They also profit from using open-source software to solve their problems, packaging and selling the derived software and working on a common platform.[24]

Open-source software projects tend to be small, less than 20 developers. They have no contractual deadlines, and they rely on the users to test.[25] This harkens back to the early days of software development when developers "threw programs over the wall" and let the users find the problems. The key to their success and to open-source is small teams of gurus, clever design, solid problem understanding, and rapid bug fixing. Open-source users must take steps to prevent unexpected source changes from causing working software to crash.

This entire course is about what happens when small projects grow up.

10.9 PROBLEMS

10.9.1 A sorting program was written to sort members in a health club. There are 446 members; an ID number was assigned to each member. Members belonging to the same family have the same ID number. The sorting program is required to sort the members based on ID numbers into ascending order. Members with the same ID numbers must be kept in the same order as they were entered.

System testers were informed that there was a known problem in the sorting program. Testers were asked to work around this problem during testing.

```
# bubble-bubble sort v(1) ... v(n) increasing
    void doSort( int n, int v[][])
    {
        int i,j,k;
        for (i = n; i > 1; i = i-1)
        {   for (j=1; j<i; j = j+1)
            {
                if ( v[j][0] > v[j+1][0] )
                { k              = v[j][0];     // swap key
                  v[j][0]    = v[j+1][0];
                  v[j+1][0] = k;

                  k              = v[j][1];     // swap data
                  v[j][1]    = v[j+1][1];
```

---

[24] Gacek, Cristina and Arief, Budi. "The Many Meanings of Open Source," *IEEE Software Developing with Open Source Software*, www.computer.org/software, Jan./Feb. 2004, pp. 34–40.
[25] *Op. cit.*

```
        v[j+1][1] = k;
    }


}
}
```

(1) Inspect the code to find two bugs.
(2) What boundary conditions need to be checked to ensure correct operation?
(3) How would you stress test the sorting program?
(4) How would you test to ensure it meet the requirements? If it did not meet the requirements, please explain. Please show test cases.

BIBLIOGRAPHY

Basili, Victor R. and Salwa, K. Abd-El-Hafiz. *A Knowledge-Based Approach to Program Understanding*, Kluwer Academic Publishers, New York, July 1995.

Bentley, Jon. *Programming Pearls*, 2nd ed. Addison-Wesley, Reading, MA, 1999.

Bernstein, L. "Get the Design Right!" *IEEE Software*, Sept. 1993, pp. 61–63.

Bernstein, L. "Software Fault Tolerance Forestalls Crashes: To Err is Human; To Forgive Is Fault Tolerant," *Advances in Computers*, Elsevier Science, 2003, pp. 239–285.

Blaha, Michael and Rumbaugh, James. *Object-Oriented Modeling and Design with UML™*, 2nd ed. Pearson Prentice-Hall, Englewood Cliffs, NJ, 2005.

Boehm, Barry. *Software Engineering Economics*, Prentice-Hall, Englewood Cliffs, NJ, 1981.

Brooks, Frederick. "No Silver Bullet-Essence and Accidents of Software Engineering," *IEEE Computer*, Vol. 20, No. 4, pp. 10–19, 1989.

CrossTalk Open Source Software—Sharing From a Well of Ideas, *4*, Vol. 18, No. 1, Jan. 2005.

Hatton, Les. *Safer C: Developing Software for High-Integrity and Safety-Critical Systems*, The McGraw-Hill International Series in Software Engineering, New York, 1997.

IEEE Software Developing with Open Source Software, www.computer.org/software, Jan./Feb. 2004, pp. 34–40.

Kernighan Brian W. and Plauger P. J. *The Elements of Programming Style*, McGraw-Hill, New York, 1974.

Koenig, Andrew. *C Traps and Pitfalls*, Addison-Wesley, Reading, MA, 1989.

Kruchten, Philippe. *The Rational Unifies Process—An Introduction*, 2nd ed. Addison-Wesley, Reading, MA, 2000.

Leveson, Nancy G. *Safeware System Safety and Computers*, Addison-Wesley, Reading, MA, 1995.

Lewis, Ted G. and Oman, Paul W. *Milestones in Software Evolution*, IEEE Computer Society Press, Los Alamitos, CA, 1990.

Linger, R. C., Mills, H. D., and Witt, B. I. *Structured Programming: Theory and Practice*, Addison-Wesley, Reading, MA, 1979.

Martin, Robert C. *Agile Software Development Principles, Patterns, and Practices*, Prentice-Hall, Englewood Cliffs, NJ, 2003.

Sha, Lui. "Using Simplicity to Control complexity," *IEEE Software*, Vol. 18, No. 4, July/Aug. 2001.

11

Testing and Configuration Management

Software is our lifeblood and the source of profound advances, but no one can deny that much of it is error-prone and likely to become more so with increasing complexity. Useful software is the abstraction of a problem and its solution, conditionally stable for the operational range that has been tested. That definition has spawned thousands of viewgraphs and millions of words, but still the stuff hangs and crashes. It may be obvious, but not trivial, to restate that **untested systems will not work**.

Today testing is an art, whether it is the fine, meticulous art of debugging or the broader-brush scenario testing. The tools already exist for moving test design theory from an art form to the scientific role of integration and quality assurance. What problems to look for, how to count them, and the most desirable graphic footprint of the test team's work are still open questions.

Dijkstra voices the frustration of system testers when he remarks that "testing can show the presence of bugs, **but not their absence**." The number of tests needed for a finite state machine depends on the number of states. The length of the test trajectory depends on the memory of the system. Then there is the whole question of software dynamics. At some point, it becomes impractical to do further testing, so we had best learn to choose our tests wisely for maximum effect.

Each of these various ideas about testing has merit. A testing definition would have to include the following:

Trustworthy Systems Through Quantitative Software Engineering,
by Lawrence Bernstein and C. M. Yuhas
Copyright © 2005 IEEE Computer Society

(1) Exercising a system to see that it does what it should do and does not do what it should not.

(2) Looking for areas of misconception or misinterpretation rather than for random individual bugs.

(3) Validation across a spectrum of values such as content, function, stress, performance, reliability, stability, and ease of use.

11.1 THE PRICE OF QUALITY

Testing consumes the most computer resources of all development phases. At this point, the static testing of the earlier phases gives way to dynamic testing. Dynamic testing has five parts: unit testing, integration testing, system testing, reliability testing, and stress testing.

11.1.1 Unit Testing

Each module is tested individually with data chosen by examining its source code. The details of the program internals are critical, so unit testing (or "white-box" testing) is performed most efficiently by its owner. The data are chosen to ensure that each branch of the program is executed. Additional stress is applied by introducing data outside the specified data range with at least one point well beyond the range and one point at or near the boundary condition. The module should operate as specified. It is good practice to keep test data and test results with the module's source code.

As programs become complex, there can be too many branches to test. The test data should then be selected by examining scenarios of the expected system use and by considering potential failure modes. Again, it is imperative to test within the specified data range, outside the range, and at the boundary. Unit testing also applies to purchased components, whose source code structure and comments should be inspected.

11.1.2 Integration Testing

Several modules are run concurrently in a string based on a use case defined during the requirements phase. Because a logical sequence may require the presence of modules that are still in development, dummy programs called "stubs" can be used to generate calls to the string being tested or to accept and check its results. As those missing modules become available in the project library, the stubs are replaced and string testing continues.

11.1.3 System Testing

Hardware and software are integrated and challenged to determine if the requirements are satisfied during system testing. The test cases presented to the system are those that were developed in parallel with the program design, using data from the system requirements and scenarios based on the expected use of the system. Because this is a "black-box" process in that the code is not examined, the system test is best done by an independent group. Because the documentation is delivered along with the hardware and software, it is also reviewed during the system test. Robust testing is a form of system testing that mathematically minimizes the number of tests that is required to exhaustively cover combinations of configuration or parameter changes.

11.1.4 Reliability Testing

Software is run repeatedly with the same test cases to find timing problems and smoke out the undesired consequences of changes. Regression testing is a form of reliaibility testing. The C++ complier has more than 3000 self-contained tests that are run weekly. Built into the regression test is the ability to determine if a test ran correctly.

11.1.5 Stress Testing

Software is stressed by offering more than the maximum anticipated loads, by offering no load at all, and by offering the appropriate load in a very short time frame. Software is also stressed by running it longer than the specified run times. Systems fail when arrays or files run out of allotted space or the physical capacities of tapes, disks, or buffers are exceeded. Short-term buffer capacities may be exceeded, or temporary arrays may overflow. This type of failure can be a problem in real-time data acquisition and control systems or in batch systems that must turn around in a fixed time. Special reliability tests are based on expected operational scenarios.

11.2 ROBUST TESTING

Robust testing is a way to move the art to science and is a technique aimed primarily at system testing. Using it can reduce the number of test cases by an order of magnitude and yet achieve the same confidence in the release.

Robust testing means exercising robust requirement specifications in a scientific way. Orthogonal arrays allow testing across a dynamic range. An orthogonal array is a matrix of carefully selected values. When an orthogonal array is used to select test data, each row represents one test case. Each column represents one parameter. The resulting set of tests is capable of detecting all faults resulting from one or a combination of two parameters.

11.2.1 Robust Design

Robust testing uses robust design, also called the Taguchi method. It minimizes the effects of variations, without controlling the cause itself. The methodology can be applied to software tests to eliminate overlap. When it was applied at

Bell Laboratories to a system that did cross-country network monitoring, the results were compelling. The robust software test design exercise was run after the software had passed the conventional tests for that time. Robust testing identified new design-related faults:

(1) There was no message to an operator on link failure.
(2) The system did not switch back to a primary link after link restart.
(3) A process could hang on link disable.

These finds are impressive for a system that was certified for field use by a prestigious organization.

11.2.2 Prototypes

Prototypes continue to play a vital rule in efficient system development, both in determining robust system requirements and in testing. This experience is from one Bell Laboratories project, a network management system:

> TRANSVU introduces a high resolution, multi-window, mouse-controlled user interface. Before TRANSVU, its users were accustomed to working largely from a printer which printed alarms as they were detected. To understand the impact of this major change, a prototype simulated the TRANSVU version of the existing system with a modified database and 24 hours of actual alarm data. The user prototype interaction was very similar to, but not the same as, the one ultimately used. Demonstrations were given at five locations to approximately 100 users of the soon to-be-replaced system and reports were written to document their reactions. The results demonstrated full user understanding of the new features, with most appreciating its advantages. The users also saw the demonstrations as valuable training, and they freely offered suggestions for improvements (literally hundreds)—many of which found their way into the actual design.
>
> As TRANSVU was being developed, portions of the prototype code were implemented as a testing driver. Alarms were "pumped in" TRANSVU to be tested with actual alarm data before being deployed. This was also very effective in finding problems.

Prototypes invite the customer's input in describing the environment in which the system will operate and the priorities of activities. Software must match customer expectations, both explicit and implicit, of accomplishing some objective in a larger business activity. Both these expectations and the system functions can become somewhat elastic. Moving from prototype into production code requires assurance testing. Expert users can be involved in custom testing in the lab and in acceptance testing in their own environment.

11.2.3 Identify Expected Results

The idea of pregenerating expected results, storing the results in files with the test input and then automatically comparing the results of the tested software with the stored results was used in Safeguard. The system prototype is used to generate the test results for comparison in software testing. This idea can move testing from intuitive detective work to scientific analysis.

11.2.4 Orthogonal Array Test Sets (OATS)

Consider the example in Table 11.1 of testing the function "command," which has four possible arguments, A, B, C, D, each with three possible values. The total number of combinations is 81, but with orthogonal array testing, only nine cases are needed. The properties of such testing are as follows:

(1) Balanced coverage of all pair-wise combinations
(2) Fewer test cases than the one-factor-at-a-time method
(3) Detection and identification of all single-mode failures
(4) Detection of all double-mode failures and, in many cases, identification of the specific double-mode failure

TABLE 11.1. Orthogonal Array-Based Tests[1,2]

Test Case	Command			
	A	B	C	D
1	A1	B1	C1	D1
2	A1	B2	C2	D2
3	A1	B3	C3	D3
4	A2	B1	C1	D1
5	A2	B2	C2	D2
6	A2	B3	C3	D3
7	A3	B1	C1	D1
8	A3	B2	C2	D2
9	A3	B3	C3	D3

11.3 TESTING TECHNIQUES

One approach in minimizing the number of test cases that some organizations use is to test the most common, or important, configuration and then vary one or more parameters for the next test configuration and then test that. The concern is to test for possible bad interactions between parameters. That basic fault model is the foundation for using the OATS technique:

(1) Interactions and integrations are a major source of defects.
(2) Most defects are not a result of complex interactions such as, "When the background is blue and the font is Arial and the layout has menus

---

[1] Our test parameters at three levels each: total number of combinations = 81.
[2] Use L_9 orthogonal array to assure pair-wise compatibility of the test program.

on the right and the images are large and it's a Thursday, then the tables don't line up properly."

(3) Most defects originate from simple pair-wise interactions such as, "When the font is Arial and the menus are on the right, the tables don't line up properly."

With so many possible combinations of components or settings, it is easy to miss one. Randomly selecting values to create all pair-wise combinations is bound to create inefficient test sets and test sets with random, senseless distribution of values. The following testing techniques elaborate on this basic fault model.

11.3.1 One-Factor-at-a-Time

This method varies one factor at a time and would require more than the minimum number of tests, but this makes it easier to identify the defective parameter. However, this technique does not expect to encounter any bad interactions between the given parameters because it does not attempt to cover all pairs of parameters. It finds only what Phadke[3] calls single-mode faults.

11.3.2 Exhaustive

For any nontrivial system, this will not be possible. Even if all test configurations were tested, which would find nearly every bad interaction between the given parameters, there will be many more tests with varying circumstances that could be conceived that could take a lifetime and more to conduct.

11.3.3 Deductive Analytical Method

This method attempts to cover all important paths in the code. Any testing strategy should be augmented by some of this type of testing. In fact, this is one type of testing that developers should conduct on their new components before integration testing.

11.3.4 Random/Intuitive Method

This is the most common method used by independent test organizations. This method can be effective at finding defects, but the level of coverage is often questionable.

11.3.5 Orthogonal Array-Based Method

This method finds all double-mode faults that are two parameters conflicting with each other. An example of a double-mode fault is one parameter over-

---

[3] Phadke, M. S., *Quality Engineering Using Robust Design*, Prentice Hall, Englewood Cliffs, NJ 1989.

shadowing another, inhibiting required processing of that other parameter. It is not easy to create nontrivial orthogonal arrays (OAs) that have more than three factors. The difficulty of determining the array limits the technique's use. See aetgweb.argreenhouse.com/brochure./shtml.

Some automated tools that produce sets of tests covering all pairs of parameters do not try to minimize the number of tests. It is a difficult, discrete mathematics problem to create OAs. These tools may come fairly close to a minimum set, but if you can save having to run even one more test, you want to find that minimal set. Some expensive tools can compute OAs, or all pair combinations, resulting in a minimal set of tests for all reasonable numbers of factors and options. Augmented tools eliminate absurd tests.

The OATS manual technique produces a smaller set of tests that exercise all pair-wise combinations of parameters. OATS is simple and straightforward and includes the following steps:

(1) Decide the number of factors to test.
(2) Decide which options to test for each factor.
(3) Find a suitable OA with the smallest number of runs to cover all factors and options.
(4) Map the factors and options onto the array.
(5) Choose values for any options that are not needed (call them leftovers) from the valid remaining options, and delete any columns (factors) that are not needed. A given test situation may not need all factors or all options that a particular OA provides.
(6) Transcribe the runs into test cases, adding additional combinations as needed.

The selection of which OA to use can pose a challenge. The good news is that you do not generally need to compute a new OA for many test situations. If there is not a specific OA for your test situation, you can use one that is similar, delete extra factors (columns), and choose values for the extra options consistent with your test situation. In other words, the real work in creating the arrays has already been done. It takes only a few minutes to apply the array to a specific test situation.

11.3.6 Defect Analysis

Some researchers suggest defect analysis after the completion of system testing to determine the root causes of failure to find faults during the system test. This kind of analysis could help set guidelines for initial turnover to the test team and improve the test team's record of accomplishment. An interesting result of defect analysis is that few faults are the result of tester oversight. Using only system requirements and customer documentation would not expose all problems that turn up in the field.

11.4 CASE STUDY: THE CASE OF THE IMPOSSIBLE OVERTIME[4]

Your manager assigns you a new testing project. "I want you to take over the system integration testing of TCS. We've got three weeks to get it out the door and we're concerned about the integration of all the Web-TCS components."

The Web time charging system (TCS) must run on standard Brand X and Brand Y **central processing units** (CPUs) and the company's current **operating systems** (OSs): Win 98, Win NT, Win 2000, and Win XP. Each platform must support these **browsers**: Microsoft Internet Explorer Version 5.5 and 6.0 and Netscape Version 7.0.

Your manager continues, "And I don't have to remind you about what that last delivered bug cost us."

The Web TCS has two operational **network modes**: internal intranet and modem remote. Employees can log their time in both modes. Various default parameters are established depending on the user's type of **employee classification**, including salaried, hourly, part-time, or contractor. These parameters include default shift, available paid holidays, and so on. Also, the user can set the **time increment** in minutes to 6, 10, 15, 30, or 60.

These features and parameters will be combined into various test configurations, however, one key question is what is the most effective, smallest set of test configurations that will find most parameter interaction defects?

The test group has already defined 15 test cases. Test cases for Login include:

Successful logins on first attempt

Successful logins after one failed attempt

Unsuccessful logins after three failed attempts

Twelve similar test case were defined.

Management has expressed concern about integration defects delivered in recent releases. Any seriously defective interactions between features and various user-assigned and system configuration parameters could prove fatal to the Web TCS upgrade effort and the future of your group (as your boss just emphasized). At any rate, you need to test each parameter paired with every other parameter to be sure that there are no incompatibilities.

"What is the most effective, smallest set of test configurations that find most serious parameter interaction defects?" Notice the qualification "most serious defects." No amount of testing can find all defects. Effective testing techniques can lead to increased confidence and to fewer delivered defects and happier customers, but there are no absolutes.

There are six test parameters with their associated options. To test all combinations of these parameters, $2 \times 4 \times 3 \times 2 \times 4 \times 5$ or 960 test configurations

[4] With permission, Daich, Gregory T. "New Spreadsheet Tool Helps Determine Minimal Set of Test Parameters Combinations," *CrossTalk*, Aug. 2003, http://www.stsc.hill.af.mil/crosstalk/2003/08/.

are needed. Because each test configuration requires 15 system-level test cases, the result is a total of $960 \times 15 = 14{,}400$ test cases that must be executed. It is impossible to execute all 14,400 test cases in 3 weeks. It takes about 3 hours to execute the 15 test cases for each configuration, including setup and reporting. There are about 6 hours per day of productive test execution time, not counting unpaid overtime that you hope to minimize, which gives you 90 hours or 30 test configurations that you have time to perform. Looks like you need 2850 hours of overtime! Is there hope? Can you test all important combinations of parameters in less than 30 test configurations?

TABLE 11.2. Test Parameters for TCS Case Study

A	B	C	D	E	F
CPU	OS	Browser	Network	Type of Employee	Time Increment
Brand Y	NT	IE 6.0	Modem	Salaried	6
Brand X	98	IE 5.5	Internal	Hourly	10
—	2000	NS 7.0	—	Part-Time	15
—	XP	—	—	Contractor	30
—	—	—	—	—	60

The time increment factor has five options, and the OS factor has four options. Thus, we know that there must be at least $5 \times 4 = 20$ runs to cover all combinations of those two options. The trick is to cover all other pair combinations in those 20 runs.

Conclusion: Fortunately, as you agonize at your desk, your eye falls on your August 2003 copy of *Cross Talk* where Gregory Daich explains a tool to determine a minimal set of test parameter combinations. You create a set of 20 test configurations. You have time to run 15 test cases in each of the 20 test configurations within the schedule. The number of test runs is reduced from 960 to less than 30, and there is life after testing.

11.5   COOPERATIVE TESTING

Cooperative testing evolved in several large projects from necessity, which is done among departments outside the test group by any designer who must touch another's software module. This testing is low-profile, friendly and intermodule, with no configuration control. It fosters cooperation among subsystem designers using test beds that may have been provided by the system testers. This approach eliminates problems before they see the harsh glare of the test team's searchlight. This is helpful, but only at the far "art" end of the art-to-science continuum of testing techniques.

Figure 11.1 is typical of the plans of a large system. This is the actual plan of Bellcore's Facilities Assignment and Control System (FACS) in the early

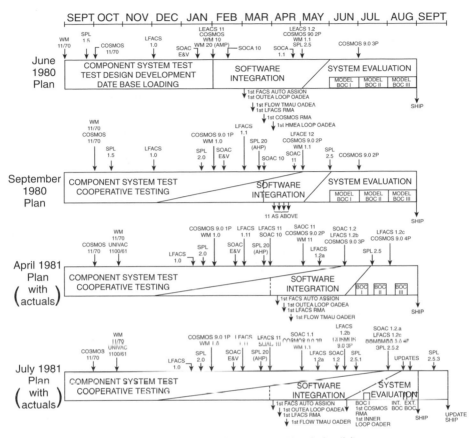

Figure 11.1. Diagram fails to reflect level of activity.

1980s. The details of this plan are unimportant; the point is to show that even this level of complexity does not properly represent the activity. Notice the plan shows neatly defined and cleanly boxed cutoff points.

In real life, testing had to proceed in parallel with incremental releases being given to the test teams when they were ready. Several different types of testing were needed: component function, component performance, system compatibility, system assurance, and system performance. The Spiral Model of software development is more realistic about the way projects actually work, but it relies heavily on having a way to assess the risk in moving to the next levels of development or enhancement.

Currit[5] suggests that debugging is not the correct focus of test activity, because no matter how many errors are removed, neither does one know how many remain nor does the customer care. **The critical measure of quality is**

---

[5] Currit, P. A., Dyer, M., and Mills, "Certifying the reliability of software," *IEEE Transactions on Software Engineering*, Vol. SE-12, No. 1, Jan. 1986, pp. 3–11.

how long the system will run before it fails and the operational impact when it does fail. As in the FACS example, product development is considered a sequence of executable product increments that can be tested as they mature. An approach that gives the odds for staying alive obviously has more meaning to a customer.

Test cases reflecting statistical samples of user operations start with external risk and work backward to module exposure to provide software failures that relate to the operating environment. All else is anecdotal and irrelevant. Instead of randomly testing a system until the likelihood of failure is judged small enough for release, you can test systems until the magnitude of the operational risk of failure no longer justifies the cost of testing.

MAGIC NUMBER!

Statistical testing uncovers failures by a factor of 30 to 1 over random searches. Failure-free execution intervals are the goal.

11.6 GRAPHIC FOOTPRINT

A system that is successfully tested will show a characteristic graphic "footprint" of tests passed. It is not the even, linear progression that is so intuitively satisfying and seems to show steady progress up to a goal. If the number of test cases, planned and started, were plotted against time, a straight linear progression would actually show that there were problems between modules and they were not of sufficiently good quality to use to start integration. There will always be latent integration problems. These are the only ones that should be left for the test team to find. When this is the case, several tests will fail because of a common cause and will be passed with the introduction of a common fix. The test completion curve will look like a series of step functions with rapid progress being made each time an integration problem is found, as in Figure 11.2. If progress is linear, the test team is finding bugs within modules that should be left to the developer to find and fix.

Successful systems leave the footprint in Figure 11.3. It looks like a human skills acquisition graph, with plateaus during which competence is acquired followed by sudden jumps in capability. Statistical failure analysis each phase in software development pinpoints the largest areas that are most likely to be defective. Bugs are not evenly distributed, but instead tend to cluster in specific parts of a system. Eliminating clusters is economical and efficient. Additionally, clustering information can be used to position tests in areas that are likely sites of residual defects. The quality of a functional area is too low when

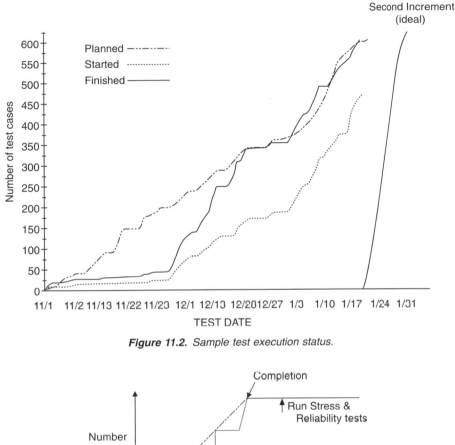

Figure 11.2. Sample test execution status.

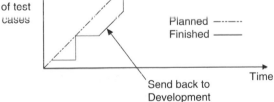

Figure 11.3. Generic test footprint.

the initial test pass rate is too low. It is then appropriate to stop and examine a functional decomposition of the defective area and redesign what is most likely a large design hole. When successful testing gives a linear footprint, it is time to stop testing and return the modules to the individual designers so that system testers are not reduced to debugging.

The ideal slope for the test team is vertical; the worst-case slope is horizontal—nothing works. The slope is limited by the rate of finding and fixing problems. Testing must eventually stop at the point where sufficient stability is achieved for the field, but all systems carry errors. Poor systems have linear progression slopes in the field also, just as they did in the test laboratory, because the test teams were engaged in bug-by-bug detective work. Successful systems show step functions in the field and are generally satisfactory to their users.

11.7 TESTING STRATEGY

It is helpful to have separate system integration and test groups to make sure that the developers do not fool themselves into thinking that the system works or that some situation is too unlikely to deserve its own test case. The test team assures that the system can be duplicated and delivered.

Certainly it is preferable to design reliability into systems, rather than test it in, but testing can move from randomly and ineffectively poking around to truly ensuring that a system performs as expected. The following practices must be observed.

11.7.1 Test Incrementally

Package functions into increments, and validate functions into prototypes. Once the function increment is implemented in the production system, repeat the tests used in the prototype. Compare the results of the tests, and completely account for all differences in the results.

11.7.2 Test Under No-Load

This elementary and easy reliability test is useful for transaction and real-time systems. It induces faults such as memory leaks to trigger failures. The idea is to launch the system and not to enter input. Let it run for ten times the rejuvenation interval, called the "reliability interval." If the system has no such interval, designers must add one. This test can then be enhanced to input one transaction and check its result after the system runs for the reliability interval. The next enhancement is to input one of every possible transaction with expected data and then at the boundary conditions.

11.7.3 Test Under Expected-Load

Use the traffic profile expected during the busy hour to run a series of expected use cases. This is the conventional functional testing effort.

11.7.4 Test Under Heavy-Load

This volume stress test drives the system to its specified maximum traffic. The input is the expected traffic profiles and dispersions around the desired operating point. Make sure to check the test results for validity and physical appearance (e.g., do all charts, tables, lists, etc. fit properly). People do not always look at the output from stress tests when they run into high numbers, but simply running without hanging or crashing does not constitute success.

11.7.5 Test Under Overload

Stress testing is not complete until the points where the system breaks are found. Design margins are the difference between the breaking point and the operating point. This test case is generated by defining a set of transactions and running the set every second, then doubling the set every second for the next test, and doubling again for every subsequent test until the system fails. The selection of the test transactions is varied to stress different parts of the system.

11.7.6 Reject Insufficiently Tested Code

Spend more time testing stability and performance than features. Demand that the developers thoroughly test the features and reject increments that show signs of insufficient testing. The criteria for acceptance and continued testing by the test team are that the developers find and fix all bugs within the limits of their ability to reproduce the system environment. The test team is the judge of their limits. Have a "friendly" user site where developers and testers can do some feature testing before the software is released.

11.7.7 Diabolic Testing

Exercise use case combinations over a range of normal and extreme conditions with test cases defined using the OA analysis. Use data you do not expect the program to see for diabolic testing.

11.7.8 Reliability Tests

Use reliability tests to estimate the number of faults in the rejuvenation interval of the system.

11.7.9 Footprint

Look for the characteristic "stepped footprint" of tests passed to indicate fruitful testing of requirements, remembering that linear footprints indicate most likely the presence of a large design hole.

11.7.10 Regression Tests

Regression testing means to use the same test cases against each release of the system, building a larger set with each release as new features are added. Use regression testing to execute all previous test cases whenever there is a new release. Some tests will be expected to fail because of known system changes. Any unexpected result demands a full investigation.

MAGIC NUMBER!

Testing efforts consume 50% of development time and 20% of project costs. Regression testing halves the time and costs.

11.8 SOFTWARE HOT SPOTS

The distribution of defects in the software is not homogeneous. Defects tend to concentrate in particular areas of the software that are driven by a range of differences in the component complexity, developer's skill, and the coupling of the software architecture. Some components will have far more changes than others. These areas may yield more productive testing.

Figure 11.4 is a *SeeSoft* display showing code coverage for a program executing its regression tests. The color of each line is determined by the number of times that it executed. The colors range from red ("hot spots") to deep blue (for code executed only once). There are two special colors: The black lines are nonexecutable lines of code such as variable declarations and comments, and the gray lines are nonexecuted (not covered) lines. The figure shows that generating regression tests with high coverage is difficult.[6] The display is reproduced here in shades of gray, but it appears in full color in the original publication cited in the footnote.

Criteria need to be developed for the allocation of limited resources while managing risk. One criterion will be the relative rate of change of the code.

Case Study: The Case of the New Kid's Test Kit

You are asked to program a new Automatic Repeat Request (ARQ) algorithm for a wireless communication protocol. Your boss assumes you know all about ARQ, because that is why you were hired. You research the algorithm and create the use cases in Figure 11.5.

---

[6] Eick, S. G. "Graphically Displaying Text," *Journal of Computing Graphical Statistics*, Vol. 3, No. 2, 1994, pp. 127–142.

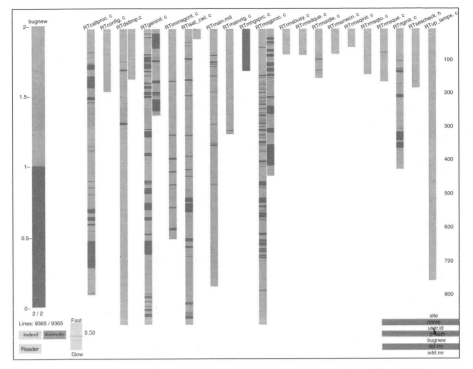

Figure 11.4. ScoSoft display of code execution. (with permission of S. G. Eick)

You create this logical view in pseudo-code for the **sender** side:

1. Generate data messages
   a. Each message is a 20-byte-long string.
   b. Generate the number of messages specified for the test case.
2. Encapsulate message into frames
   a. Use the high-level data link control format under a certain format.
   b. Create a sequence number, acknowledgment number (ACK), checksum, and a message string, and insert them in their proper place in the frame.
3. Control the window
   a. Create a window of a specified number of frames.
   b. Send frames in the window.
   c. When the first n frames are acknowledged, delete them from the window and add n + 1 to the message frame start pointer. The new end point will be pointer + WindowSize. No other condition can cause the window to change.

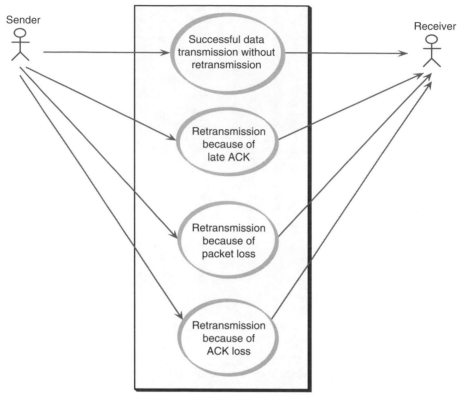

Figure 11.5. ARQ use cases.

4. Timer control
   a. Create a countdown timer for the sending window.
   b. Reset the time for each acknowledgment and sent frame. If the timer counts down to zero, it means that earliest frame has been sent and not acknowledged in the allotted time.
   c. If the timer reaches zero, the sender resends the earliest frame in its window.
   d. No timer limit is set to quit the program when the same frame has been resent many times.

Transmission simulation:

(1) Simulate data transmission from sender to receiver.
(2) Simulate nominal and delayed frame transmission times.

(3) Simulate frame loss during transmission.

(4) Simulate ACK transmission from receiver to sender.

Receiver side window control:

(1) When the receiver gets the specified number of correct frames (WindowSize), it transfers them to its application.

(2) Otherwise, the receiver should just wait.

(3) Receiver sends an ACK to the sender when an error-free frame is received.

(4) Using the sequence number, the receiver determines if the frame is a duplicate. It discards duplicate frames that have been already correctly received. This can happen when the acknowledgment is late getting back to the sender and the sender sends a copy of the original frame. The engineering tradeoff is setting the countdown timer is long times leave the link idle and lower throughput, but short times keep the link busy and increase throughput with duplicate frames.

(5) Discards any frames it detects that are corrupted.

(6) Reassembles messages from frames and sends them to the network layer.

Development view:

(1) MS Visual C++ 6.0

(2) Windows 2000 Professional

(3) PC PIII 866, 512 MB RAM

Physical view:

(1) Windows NT 4.0 with SP6a

(2) PC PIII 866, 128MB RAM

One sequence chart for the architecture is shown in Figure 11.6.

In the sender, the processes A_output sends the frames and A-input receives the ACKs. In the receiver, the processes B_input receives the frames and B_output sends the ACKs.

Test cases:

All tests were executed under the fixed window size of 8. The number of frames in the message varied from 0 to 100 with the probability of a lost or corrupted frame varying from 0% to 100%. Here are two bugs uncovered in testing:

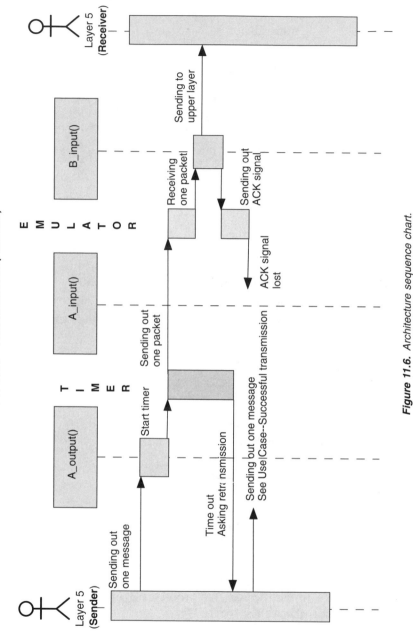

Figure 11.6. Architecture sequence chart.

1. In the functional tests of 100 frames to a message, a variable used for window control that points to the next frame to send exceeded the window size. This led to sending the wrong frames. During the tests, this bug never crashed or hung the program.

2. Under the stress of 100% lost or corrupted frames, a memory leak hung the system. The memory leak fault is present whenever the ARQ system runs but does not cause a failure except under the most stressful conditions. If the system was used in production, a gradually increasing amount of memory would have been used. Other programs running in the same memory space might have intermittently run out of memory and failed through no fault of their own because of ARQ's insatiable thirst for memory. The fault becomes coupled from one program to another and the failure seems random, even though it is perfectly predictable. The stress tests were effective in detecting the fault so that a potential system failure could be avoided.

Conclusion: The next step was to use software rejuvenation without fixing the bug in the code, by employing the fault tolerance library. The test cases were repeated. At the situation with 100% loss rate, the program performed correctly. It never stopped sending messages. The memory usage was bounded. The memory leak failure was avoided. Even with a stressful 98% frame loss rate, 100 frames were successfully transmitted. Figure 11.7 shows the result of the testing.

You write your results for your boss, who is duly impressed with his new hire. Your future looks bright.

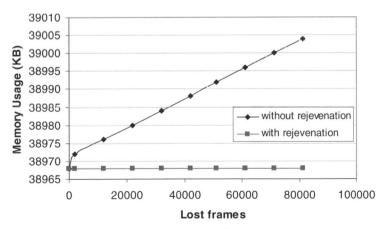

Figure 11.7. *Perfect test results with software rejuvenation.*

11.9 SOFTWARE MANUFACTURING DEFINED

Our objective is to create a software system, package it, deliver it to one or more customer sites, and keep it working. Organizing software development along the lines of using gurus with the aid of librarians and production coders is a notion calculated to improve innovation and productivity within the concept of programming as an art. This may be well and good for the "create" part of the objective, but who shall handle the remainder? Clerks are traditionally concerned with keeping established information orderly. The key word is "established." A new software release is not a piece of established software because it is not working, and it will undergo many changes once it is passed from the developers to the testers. The software manufacturers sit between these groups and at a minimum perform these coordination, production, and configuration management tasks:

(1) Accept individual components from designers

(2) Update and maintain source code files

(3) Check the software static structure of for compliance with format and documentation standards

(4) Compile to produce official executables

(5) Build systems for use by test team

(6) Install on test machines

(7) Create a library of user documents

(8) Track problem reports

(9) Track changes

(10) Document the configuration of each system build

(11) Configure the software for user groups

(12) Reproduce software for each site

(13) Ship software to sites with inventory lists

Concurrently, someone must worry about purchasing computers, issuing management reports, and all other activities that keep the production wheels oiled. Even a cursory glance at these tasks suggests that these activities can impede the actual design function if not done properly; yet they are too complex for clerical levels. The process of building software and controlling it demands a technician with some software training. Skills in shell languages, database control, and machine scheduling are needed. Additionally, to develop tracking, testing, and report production subsystems, system analysis skills are necessary. Finally, volume production and quality control demand an assembly-line, product-oriented frame of reference, with emphasis on scrupulous adherence to procedures and inventory control.

A professional software manufacturing group helps developers get the product to market by performing these tasks:

(1) Freeing developers to concentrate on software development

(2) Giving confidence to the developers that they are working with a common base

(3) Allowing many development groups work on the same products in parallel

(4) Providing tools that allow concurrent maintenance of old releases while testing and shipping new releases

(5) Channeling product changes and eliminating inclusion of unknown changes in the delivered product

(6) Reporting data that provide management and developers with insight into the product and the problems it is facing

(7) Running analysis programs on the source code to find troubled components that are too big or too complex

(8) Gathering productivity, process, quality, and cost statistics that measures the processes with continuous coverage through a centralized pool of resources

(9) Managing communications about problem reports, defects, and change implementation.

11.10 CONFIGURATION MANAGEMENT

Configuration management is a systematic process that controls and tracks all changes to a software product over its lifetime. Managing the flux in projects results in improved quality. Knowing the answer to the "what changed" question is the first step in problem solving. Rather than constraining your team, these controls free team members to focus on the job they do best: bringing your product to market in a timely, cost-effective manner. The software manufacturers perform the configuration management functions that maintain the current project information while enforcing the change management process. With good software manufacturing in place, you can get answers to these questions:

(1) **Requests for Change**   What changes were requested, and by whom? How important is the change, and what is the deadline? If the change will fix a bug, where and how was the bug introduced?

(2) **Implemented Changes**   What changes have been accepted? What product areas—user interface, database, and training—are affected by the change? Which release will contain each change, and what system components were modified?

(3) **Staff Assignments**   Who is responsible for making, testing, and approving the change? How much work is yet to be done for the next release?

(4) **Communication among Workgroups** Who is notified when a change request is made? How are developers assigned to implement a change? How do testers know what to test and when? What changes will be delivered to the customer, and which ones will be held until the next build?

(5) **Quality and Process Metrics** Are problems detected at the expected rate? Is the product ready for delivery? What are the root causes of bugs in the product, and which areas are most error prone? What level of quality is really being delivered to the customer?"[7]

The software manufacturing tasks occur at two points in the software production cycle. First, software manufacturing builds the releases for the test team. Then at the completion of integration and test, software manufacturing does the tasks concerned with preparing and shipping the system. Software manufacturing tasks are shown in Figure 11.8.

When we consider the functions that must be performed in creating and delivering a software system, the issue is fraught with difficulty. Those necessary functions of configuration management documentation, change control, and actual software production tend to be viewed by designers and managers as lesser work. These functions are often relegated to clerks who are ill suited to perform them, or they are done haphazardly at the expense of the design work and the customer, or they are not done at all.

Work tasks that get the product out the door and keep it working efficiently require a unique organization and a different mental set from design processes. Organizing and staffing for the production of deliverable software-based systems can leverage assembly-line techniques. Although these production activities are common to most projects, software manufacturing is defined here as an inline, rather than as a support, task that requires special skills.

Once software manufacturing has a firm grip on its raw materials, this group can help with testing. Testers can select from this database according to their test schedules and be supplied with test data and various configurations. The software used to produce the test data may be under the control of the software manufacturers and operated by them. The testers' ability to be selective in the matter of system builds frees the design programmers from being tied to a test schedule. Because software manufacturing tracks and releases each unit and update, designers may turn over whatever they have available whenever they have it, regardless of test order, thereby avoiding that insidious disease, file rot. The software manufacturing group can maintain and run regression tests after each major milestone.

One special help to testing is a subgroup within software manufacturing, called the quality improvement team (QIT). When the testers identify a particular hot spot during their testing, they refer it to QIT who generates a schematic drawing from MAKE files of module relationships, as in Figure 11.9.

---

[7] http://www.att.com/spt/cms.html.

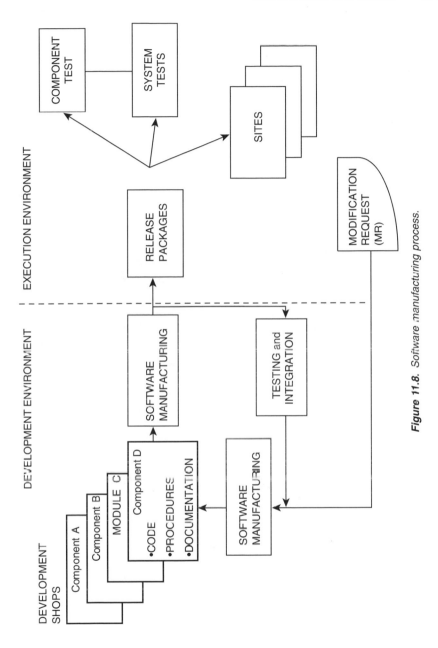

Figure 11.8. Software manufacturing process.

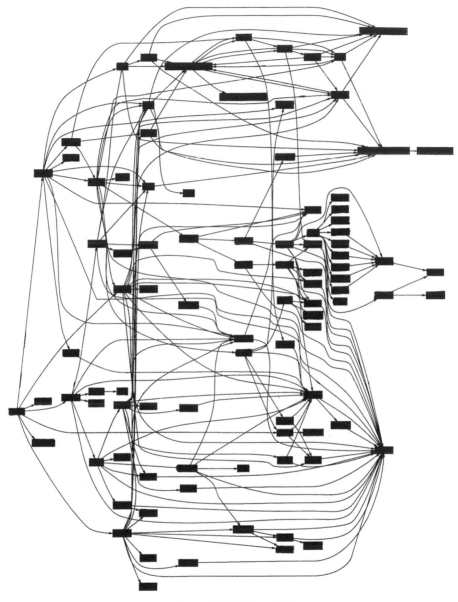

Figure 11.9. Before QIT.

Software manufacturing sends this picture back to the design team who created the modules for their consideration. When the designers have simplified the interactions, QIT generates another schematic. Often it looks considerably better, as in Figure 11.10.

It might help to consider the organization of software manufacturing in the familiar schema of hardware manufacturing, where there are line functions

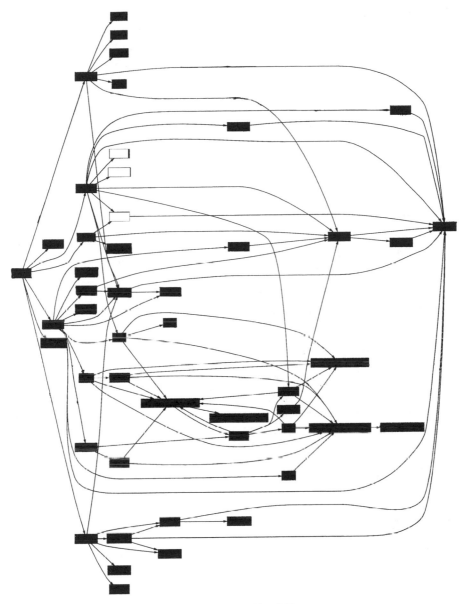

Figure 11.10. *After QIT.*

for day-to-day production and staff functions for monitoring the general well-being of the product. The software manufacturing line functions can now be recognized as those tasks we had earlier identified as necessary in getting from the source code to the product.

The project management must make software manufacturing and configuration management an honest profession by committing a respectable amount of resources and attention to it. Software manufacturing provides a process that is generic to the software development effort. Its introduction leads to systematizing the production of software, making software development people more productive, and therefore to better managed software efforts. This approach differs significantly from a cottage industry approach that relies on developers to perform all functions equally well.

The ultimate release document contains these features:

(1) Highlights feature content

(2) Describes corrections to problems and lists problem reports closed

(3) Specifies the machine and support software

(4) Specifies limitations or deficiencies

(5) Installation instructions

(6) Specifies commercial off-the-shelf required

(7) Specifies training

(8) Lists component

(9) Data conversion instructions

(10) Product configuration lists for each site

11.11   OUTSOURCING

Outsourcing is changing the software industry. Companies have moved from developing and maintaining their systems to buying them from third parties. The split of Lucent Technologies from AT&T in 1996 was the ultimate expression of this policy. With outsourcing comes the challenge of evaluating just how well vendor systems work before making a purchase decision and then controlling changes once they deliver. Strong project management and change control are essential ingredients to successful outsourcing.

11.11.1   Test Models

One company met this challenge with an innovative use of an automated test design and coding tool, which was used for building an object-oriented model of the outsourced system. The model was based on the specifications contained in their Request for Proposal and from system descriptions provided by the supplier. Engineers used this model to first map the functions they wanted against the system description and then against the system itself. This assured them that the contracted functions were present and that they could understand how the new software fit into their business environment. This approach showed how giving modeling tools to the customer allowed system engineers to head off unintended consequences well before the system is even developed.

The model of the service node gave the customer engineers insight into the dynamics of the complex system of systems that made up their business flows. Use cases were developed along with an architectural description and placed under configuration control. With the model, the systems engineers studied the unique call flow for every variation of the business flow. For example, their customers can use 1 of 12 languages to interact with their website. Manual evaluation of the interaction of language selection based on the object libraries with its many variations would have been a huge task without the model and supporting evaluation tools. In traditional manual methods, the system engineers would study the system specifications and then develop a test case to verify that the system worked as expected. Finding the error paths is always a challenge. Typically many review meetings are needed among the system engineers and then with the vendor's technical people to ferret out the potential incompatibilities. With this approach, serious problems are often overlooked, which at best show up in system testing and at worst are found by the paying customers.

The model-based test creation method permits the early involvement of the test organization in the development process and is a powerful tool for facilitating communication between customer and supplier engineers. For example, the customers may use several different database technologies in their business flow. To install one particular new feature, a database of customers was needed that contained administrative data and their service requests. The database initialization process was modeled, such that the database records were automatically generated from the model. Once the testers saw the strength of the model, they adopted it as their test case database repository. Consequently, the model of the databases was used both for populating the component databases in the target system as well as serving as the input data for the test creation process. Expected results from the model were kept and later compared with the results from running the test cases against the production system. When there were differences, analysts would compare the flow in the model with the flow in the service offering and find the problem. This moved debugging from detective work to analysis. Problems were found in the object libraries, component systems, the model, and even the system design.

The model assures all features are present, not just the headliners. Once the software product is installed in the evaluation laboratories, the model produces test suites for automatic test drivers. These tests verify that that the system performs as expected.

The test scripts from the model resulted in high coverage rates for feature testing. Testers are pressed for time and do not have the resources for exhaustive load testing and reliability testing. While testers focus on full load testing, they often do not have the time to run no-load tests. These tests set up one or two simple transactions and then let the system idle, waiting for new work. With the model, setting up such a script was easy to do and pointed to reliability problems in the software system. It was clear from the data that the offered load was triggering reliability problems and there was no argument that this traffic was unrealistic. A long-term benefit is that once the system is installed, the model may be used for regression testing.

11.11.2 Faster Iteration

Faster software development depends on speeding the iteration, not its elimination. Penalizing the innate iterative aspect of human thinking will result in lower productivity, because it will delay the discovery of a significant number of defects. The role of testing during most development phases should not be underestimated as a means of speeding the iterations.

11.11.3 Meaningful Test Process Metrics

Meaningful metrics drive the process to lower cost and higher quality. These metrics drive the process to identify defects earlier and in larger numbers:

a. Ratio of number of defects found during development to number of defects found during 1 year of field deployment
b. Number of hours to find a defect by testing
c. Percentage of tests discovering no defects

11.12 PROBLEMS

11.12.1 Let us return to the same sorting problem we saw in Chapter 10. A sorting program was written to sort members in a health club. There are 446 members; an ID number was assigned to each member. Members belonging to the same family have the same ID number. The sorting program is required to sort the members based on ID numbers into ascending order. Members with the same ID numbers must be kept in the same order as they were entered.

System testers were informed that there was a known problem in the sorting program. Testers were asked to work around this problem during testing.

```
# bubble - bubble sort v(1) . . . v(n) increasing

  void doSort( int n, int v[][])
  {
    int i,j,k;
    for (i = n; i > 1; i = i - 1)
    { for (j = 1; j < i; j = j + 1)
      {
        if ( v[j][0] > v[j+1][0] )
          { k       = v[j][0];   // swap key
```

```
v[j][0]   = v[j+1][0];
v[j+1][0] = k;

k         = v[j][1];   // swap data
v[j][1]   = v[j+1][1];
v[j+1][1] = k;
}


      }
    }
  }
```

(1) What are quantitative boundary conditions that must be checked to ensure correct operation?

(2) State three qualitative boundary conditions that may impact performance and availability and should be checked.

(3) How would you stress test the sorting program?

(4) Show test cases to demonstrate that the program does not meet the requirements.

11.12.2 You use an inception, elaboration, implementation/testing, deployment model for software development. You are the project manager of a team working on a project to develop a new marketing system for a large manufacturing firm. The best time to discuss the question of post-installation maintenance of the new software is:

a. at the start of the inception phase.

b. at the end of the elaboration phase.

c. at or near the end of the deployment stage.

d. it does not make any difference.

11.12.3 You are developing a transaction processing software system for a large international bank. The system will receive transactions 24/7. Research has indicated that the average daily transaction rate, with 95% probability, will be about 240,000 transactions per day. You are constructing a test plan for the system. The project manager feels it safe to test the system for performance at up to 40,000 transactions per hour, i.e., for four times the expected transaction rate. At a project meeting, this point is discussed. Do you:

a. agree strongly.

b. agree.

c. disagree.

d. disagree strongly.

11.12.4 You are the project manager for a software product. You have staffed an independent test team. The test team has defined and executed 2000 tests. All but two have been run successfully. You check the test plans and test cases and convince yourself that the 2000 tests cover the expected operational domain of the software product. The product ship date is 2 weeks away. There are severe financial penalties for missing the date and rewards for shipping early. You would:

    a. increase the testing staff by transferring experienced testers from other projects to discover why two test cases failed.

    b. ship the software immediately and continue testing because all of the functionality defined by the requirements works.

    c. delay shipment to isolate the problem.

    d. increase the testing effort by teaming the product developers with the testers even though it will jeopardize the delivery of the next release of your company's most profitable product.

11.12.5 You have two releases of the system in the hands of four customers. Each customer wants their own changes but does not want to be burdened with the changes of the other customers. Your budget is tight, so you:

    a. insist that there is one release for all and that the customers must upgrade and accept all changes.

    b. adopt a versioning configuration management system.

    c. break the system into four systems and customize each.

    d. refer the problem to the product manager for a business analysis of the best strategy.

11.12.6 Your program has worked for several months and all the users are pleased with it. Suddenly it crashes, so you:

    a. blame the user for not being properly trained.

    b. seek program dumps and begin debugging.

    c. determine what changed in the run that crashed.

    d. look for a new job.

BIBLIOGRAPHY

"Open Source Software: Sharing From a Well of Ideas," *CrossTalk*, 2005 Vol. 18, No. 1. Entire issue is devoted to aspects of Open Source.

Bernstein, Lawrence and Yuhas, C. M. "Software Manufacturing" *UNIX Review*, Vol. 7, No. 7, July 1989, pp. 38–45.

Binder, Robert V. Testing Object-Oriented Systems: Models, Patterns, and Tools, Addison-Wesly, Reading, MA, 2000.

Culbertson, Robert, et al. *Rapid Testing, Software Quality Institute Series*, Prentice-Hall, Englewood Cliffs, NJ, 2002.

Currit, P. A., Dyer, M., and Mills, "Certifying the reliability of software," *IEEE Transactions on Software Engineering*, Vol. SE-12, No. 1, Jan. 1986, pp. 3–11.

Gacek, Cristina and Arief, Budi. "The Many Meanings of Open Source," *IEEE Software*, Jan./Feb. 2004, pp. 34–48.

Humphrey, W. S., Snyder, T. R., and Willis, R. R. "Software Process Improvement at Hughes Aircraft," *IEEE Software*, July 1991, pp. 11–23.

Kulak, Daryl and Guiney, Eamonn. *Use Cases-Requirements in Context*, 2nd ed. Addison-Wesley, Reading, MA, 2004.

Kusumoto, S., Matsumoto, K., Kikuno, T., and Torii, K. "Approaches to Improving Effectiveness of Review Activities in Technical Review Process," *International Software Quality Exchange '92 Conference Proceedings*, Juran Institute Inc., 1992, pp. 7B1–7B16.

Lam, John. "Painless SCM," *Software Development*, Vol. 12, No. 12, Dec. 2004, pp. 23–26.

Leon-Garcia, Alberto and Widjaja, Indra. *Communications Networks—Fundamental Concepts and Key Architectures*, 2nd ed., McGraw Hill, New York, 2004, Sections 5.2 and 5.4.

Levendel, Y. "Improving Quality With a Manufacturing Process," *IEEE Software*, March 1991, pp. 13–25.

McFarlane, M. L. and Sutton, A. *Structured, Automatic Testing: A Hard Slog*, Cadence Design Systems, Santa Clara, CA, Dec. 22, 1989.

Perry, William. *Effective Methods for Software Testing*, 2nd ed. John Wiley and Sons, New York, 2000.

Phadke, M. S. *Quality Engineering Using Robust Design*, Prentice-Hall, Englewood Cliffs, NJ, 1989, pp. 5–6.

Phadke, Madhav S. "Planning Efficient Software Tests," *CrossTalk*, Oct. 1997.

Proceedings of the 2nd International Workshop on Software Configuration Management, ACM SIGSOFT, Vol. 17, No. 7, Nov. 1989, ACM Order NO. 594891, IEEE Order No. 2014.

Sherer, S. A. "A Cost Effective Approach to Testing," *IEEE Software*, March 1991, pp. 34–40.

Staknis, M. E. "Software Quality Assurance Through Prototyping and Automated Testing," *Information and Software Technology*, Vol. 32, No. 1, Jan./Feb. 1990, pp. 26–33.

Whittaker, James A. *How to Break Software: A Practical Guide to Testing*, Addison-Wesley, Reading, MA, 2003.

Yoshida, T. "Attaining Higher Quality in Software Development—Evaluation in Practice," *Fujitsu Science Technical Journal*, Vol. 21, July 1985, pp. 305–316.

12

The Final Project:
By Students, For Students

The objective of this course of study is to educate the people who will provide the scalability, robustness, and reliability needed to manage tomorrow's heterogeneous systems. The techniques provide insights to people, processes, projects, and products from leading thinkers[1] in software issues and our experience. Our goal is to excite the next crop of thinkers to produce trustworthy software on time and within budget.

12.1 HOW TO MAKE THE COURSE WORK FOR YOU

We describe how to close the gap between great expectations and realistic projects. These processes have been used successfully for industrial projects at Bell Laboratories and Telcordia. The processes also work for teaching undergraduate and graduate students the principles of software engineering while they develop a real project for a legitimate customer. Students report that the experience helps them get jobs and advance quickly. They telescope what takes most people years of on-the-job learning into a two-semester project-based course. They are supported by the ideas of the best practitioners of software engineering technology from around the world.

---

[1] The preceding 11 chapters each cite references to major authors in the specific area under discussion. The most relevant books on each topic were selected for reference.

Students work on projects sponsored by companies, government agencies, and academic departments. Projects range from managing patient records on flash memory devices sponsored by FujiPhotoFilm USA, Inc. to speeding software that predicts tides in New York Bay, to Web-based order entry systems, to games, to an administrative tracking tool for the FAA, to a new client/server tool for students to use to schedule classes, and to an online E-banking project, which is presented in this chapter.

The project work demonstrates the power of "just-in-time" teaching. The students learn how to build a software product as they develop it. Text material meets students' need for help as the project moves though its development cycles.

Sponsoring organizations are also happy with the experience. They try ideas with little risk and work with students before hiring them. Sometimes they get software that they can use directly or use as a basis for future work. The students produce almost 5 staff-months of work in teams of seven to ten students. The size of the teams is chosen to give students an understanding of human dynamics in large groups. Other classes demand individual work. Here they experience the challenges of dealing with communication, coordination, motivation, and planning problems on technical, risky product development with firm due dates to real customers. If they miss the delivery date, they miss graduation.

Sponsors gain 5 staff-months of student time on a project of their choosing. Companies may declare a project proprietary, and students sign nondisclosure agreements. Companies have free access to and complete control of any intellectual property that emerges from the project. The students build what the sponsor wants, and the software engineering instructor defines how the work is done following material from this book. Most projects come from professional contacts and from companies that students have worked with, especially during their internships. On-campus projects emerge from opportunities students identify from their campus jobs and activities. Some projects originate from the fertile imagination of the instructor or the students. Students select the project they work on, and sponsors compete for student attention. There is no fee to the sponsor. As a suggestion for a format for a call for projects, the following is used by the author to explain the objectives and responsibilities on both sides.

12.2 SAMPLE CALL FOR PROJECTS

Subject: Requirements for a Stevens Institute of Technology senior class project.

Objective: All Stevens Institute of Technology computer science students must complete a software project to fulfill the requirements for their B.S.

Overview: Students are divided into seven to ten-person teams after they complete a 5-week short project that prepares them for understanding and applying good software engineering practices. They are organized into project teams, conduct weekly project meetings, and write project progress reports weekly, conduct in-class requirements reviews, architecture and design reviews, code and test reviews, and final product demonstrations. These reviews are formal presentations and are accompanied by written project development plan updates.

The project starts on or about October 15 and is completed by May 1. Given student schedules and vacations, about 5 staff-months of effort are available.

Project sponsors from industry and government are needed so that students can face real-world project problems such as:

(1) Managing creeping requirements
(2) Avoiding compressed schedules
(3) Understanding customer needs and desires
(4) Dealing with missing or late dependencies
(5) Facing changing and unavailable sponsors

Sponsor: A project sponsor is the face of the customer. The sponsor defines "what" the project will do. The instructor defines "how" the students will do it. The sponsor is expected to:

(1) Define the project with a project prospectus of one to two pages.
(2) Meet with the project team at least once a month.
(3) Create a good working relationship, including telephone and e-mail access, with the student project manager.
(4) Agree to the written requirements, and negotiate changes with the student project manager.
(5) Attend the final product review.
(6) Provide any special equipment or software needed for the project in a timely fashion as mutually agreed to and documented in the project development plan.

Sponsors are invited to attend all project meeting and reviews. Attending the reviews is encouraged, but not mandatory. Sometimes sponsors attend the early project meetings regularly to make sure there are no misunderstandings. These meetings are held during weekly class meetings. Progress reports and project plan updates are shared with the project sponsor who may read and comment on them.

To maximize the educational experience, all students on all projects have access to all project information except that clearly identified as proprietary.

Sponsors are encouraged to invite students to their workplace.

Sponsors may ask students to respect their proprietary information. Sponsors own any intellectual property emerging from the students' work. Sponsors can restrict access to their private information.

The instructors will not contribute to the design or functionality of the project. This intellectual work is left to the students and their sponsor.

There is no fee for sponsoring a project. Sponsors are encouraged to hire students who fit in their organizations.

Prospectus Outline:

Name of project:

Name of sponsor and organization:

Contact information for sponsor

Project value: (25 words or less)

Project description: (500 words or less)

Project constraints: Outline the technology required, special equipment needs, or software needs. Specify any algorithms, database, or execution project needs.

Project directions: (50 words or less) Explain how this project fits with other organization projects either as part of a product line or as part of automating operational or management processes or in any other way.

12.3   A REAL STUDENT PROJECT

With the permission of the technical sponsor and the team who produced this project, we offer the following development plan exactly as submitted by the students. The team members subsequently entered the architecture phase of their project. They have generously provided the development plan as an opportunity to view a sample result of this course of study. It is provided by students, for students.

Pocket Banking Development Plan Revision 2 1/27/2005

By John Fajardo, John-Paul Kosmyna, Nathan Olcott, Brijesh Patel, Robert Volk, Seung-Ho Won, and Giuseppe Zappia

Contents

X   Schedule Time
XI   Demonstration Plan
XII Product Testing Plan

By Jonathan C. Fajardo

We chose the online pocket banking project. The ultimate goal of this project is to write a program that will enable a pocket PC to do online banking. It should mimic the online banking that can be done from a computer and have the basic banking functions. To ensure luxury and convenience to the end user, everything will be done through vocal commands. The program will use a regular browser on a pocket PC that is SALT enabled for voice recognition.

SALT stands for speech application language tags. It is multimodal so various modes of input can be used (such as speech or keyboard). It works by extending the existing markup languages like HTML. SALT is meant to be embedded into other applications, which makes it flexible and platform independent. It also is compact because it can use functions that already exist in the hosting language.

This project was chosen because it will help us to learn many new things. We get to understand how banking systems work and learn about SALT. Writing this program for a pocket PC offers everyone a faster and easier way to do online banking.

I. Project Overview

II. MOV
By Seung-Ho Won and Nathan Olcott

Our product is designed to be fast, efficient, and portable. We will show that our product is much more efficient than both in-person banking and telephone banking. Although online banking is capable of doing more, our software is slightly more efficient because we are using voice navigation, and less options means the ability to navigate faster.

Times different services are accessible
Our product operates 24 hours a day by telephone, and most transactions are available 24 hours a day on the Internet and during banking hours in person.

The time to complete an everyday transaction
Our product—2 minutes (using voice navigation and inputs tool); Telephone— 5 minutes (calling the bank in person); Internet—3 minutes (using online banking tool); In person—10–15 minutes (meeting the bank in person).

Number of possible transactions completed in 1 day:
Our product: 720 (24 hr × 60 min/2 min = 720 transactions); Telephone: 288 (24 hr × 60 min/5 min = 288 transactions); Internet: 480 (24 hr × 60 min/3 min = 480 transactions); In person: 96 (8 hr × 60 min/15 min = 32 transactions)

Notice that our product is projected to be 33% more productive than normal online banking and 1800% more productive than in person. This 33% may seem like a small fraction, but for someone who is constantly on the move and wants to perform simple banking tasks, this 33% can add up to a lot of saved time over a long period.

III. Management Structure
By Brijesh Patel and Nathan Olcott

We have seven people in our team. Every member has been assigned a role on the project. The assigned roles to team member are subject to change as a contingency plan in urgent situations as the project progresses.

Developers
John-Paul Kosmyna—Senior Developer [Grammar Developer]
Brijesh Patel—Developer, [Project Manager]
Robert Volk—Developer, [Architect, Code Auditor, Interface Designer]
Giuseppe Zappia—Developer, [Server Admin, UI Developer]

Testers
Nathan Olcott—Senior Tester [Senior Documenter]
Jon Fajardo—Tester
Seung-Ho Won—Tester

Documenter
Nathan Olcott—Senior Documenter [Senior Tester]

Team meets once a week and at other times as necessary. Although we have defined roles among our group, and those people are ultimately responsible for their jobs, we find it beneficial to have group input at certain points of our project, especially in regard to requirements. Because we were not given any requirements by our sponsor, it was up to us to create our requirements. Having the entire team give their input on requirements and development made for better and more realistic requirements. Also, although the architect has the final say in the product architecture, it is beneficial to have many members debate the architecture, leading to a well-developed architecture.

IV. Functional and Nonfunctional Requirements with Quantitative Analysis
By Nathan Olcott

Functional Requirements
Users must Login/Logout
Be able to view all bank accounts

User maintenance
Help Screen
Ability to transfer funds between accounts, and schedule those transfers
Users should navigate via speech

Nonfunctional Requirements
Intuitive interface
Reliable system performance
Runs on pocket PC with SALT-enabled browser
Must scale bank's current and future user base

Quantitative Functional Requirements
Users must Login/Logout. The process must take no more than 3 seconds.*
   All accounts that are viewed on the main screen must be displayed in no more than 5 seconds.*

When the user changes anything under the user maintenance screen, all changes must be updated in the database in no more than 30 seconds.

The main help screen must load in under 3 seconds.*
   Any transfers made between accounts must be changed in the database within 20 seconds.

Speech navigation must be 15% faster than using a stylus to perform actions on the system.**
   All speech navigation must bring up the appropriate data with 97% accuracy, and the command must be interpreted by SALT in no more than 3 seconds.

Quantitative Nonfunctional Requirements
System must be available 23 hours a day, 365 days a year, with 1 hour of down-time for backup and maintenance.

The database must support 10,000 customers with an average of five accounts per customer and have the ability to grow to double that capacity.

*All time bounds are assuming a wireless connection using IEEE Std 802.11 b with a minimum connection speed of 5.5 MB/second.

**This references the average time to write a command using a stylus versus saying the desired word.

V. Gantt Chart
By John-Paul Kosmyna, Nathan Olcott, and Brijesh Patel

Revision 1
SALT menu implementation Database setup Basic text-based GUI Banking Framework Help Framework Grammar Development Deployment

Revision 2
SALT input implementation Finalize Database functionality Finalize grammars Basic banking functions QA Deployment

Revision 3
Complete SALT implementation Complete GUI Complete Help Complete banking functionality Production Deployment

VI. 4 + 1 Architecture
By Robert Volk

Process View
Pocket banking uses only three processes to process all requests and transactions. This is to reduce complexity in data locking methods and create a simpler application, which is much easier to develop. The most processor-intensive functions are divided into separate processes, namely, the pocket banking application, speech recognition application, and SQL database, so performance will not be hindered.

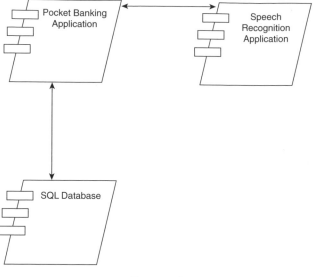

a. Process view.

Logical View

The logical view displays the primary classes used to create the pocket banking and speech recognition applications. The pocket banking classes are derived from the main tables in the database. Each database table translates into two classes, one to represent multiple rows and one to represent a singular row. Creating classes in this way leads to naming conventions across the classes, database tables, and methods. The speech recognition application contains only two classes, Grammar Reader, which parses the XML grammar file, and Speech Recognition, which interprets the incoming voice data stream and compares it with the grammar through the grammar reader class.

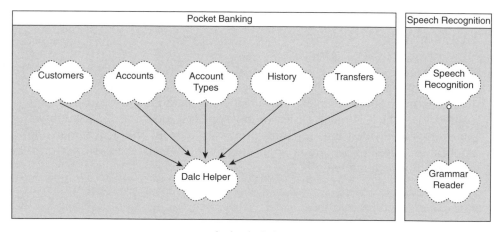

b. Logical view.

Physical View

The pocket banking software runs on two servers for increased performance. The speech recognition application requires a dedicated server because of the large processing overhead required for interpreting speech. The pocket banking application and SQL database run on a separate server. The pocket banking application sends requests and commands to the SQL database, and the database responds with record sets containing the requested data. The pocket banking application forwards the incoming speech data stream to the speech recognition application and that application sends back the plain-text interpretation of that speech based on a predefined grammar.

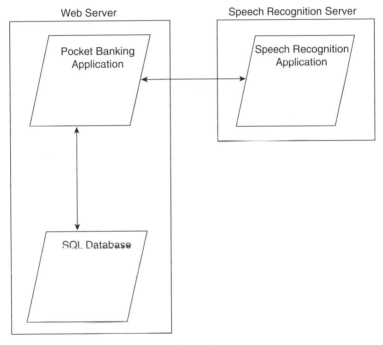

c. Physical view.

Development View

The development view shows all of the modules in the applications that the developers will program separately. The main pocket banking application is divided into three tiers, namely the presentation layer, for rendering the Web pages, the business layer, for encapsulating transaction logic, and the data layer for communicating with the database. The speech recognition application has two classes to develop independently, and the SQL database has two modules to develop separately, the stored procedures and the table schemas.

Pocket Banking Application

Speech Recognition Application

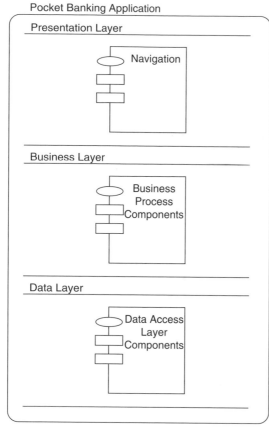

SQL Database

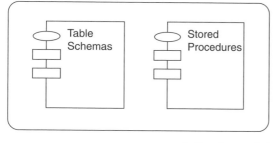

d. *Development view.*

VII. UML Diagrams
By Robert Volk

Application Layers UML Object Diagram
This diagram shows an overview of the logical separation of the application, called layers. The arrows represent the flow of method calls from one layer to

another. The presentation layer can only call methods from the business or the data access layer. The business layer can only call methods from the data access layer. No calls may be made upward in the layers, for instance, from the data access layer to the presentation layer.

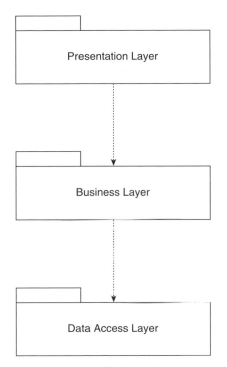

a. Layers UML object diagram.

Presentation Layer UML Object Diagram

The presentation layer renders data returned from the business and data access layers to HTML. Process components, such as CustomerProcess and UIProcess control redirection from one Web page to another for the user.

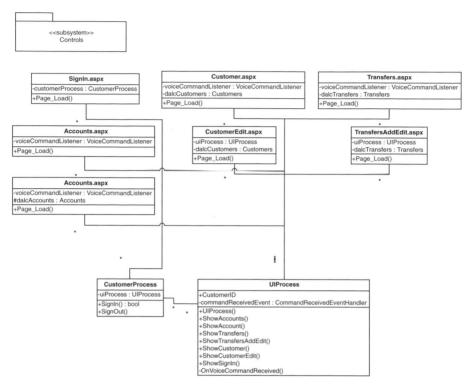

b. *Presentation layer UML object diagram.*

Controls Subsystem UML Object Diagram

The controls in this subsystem encapsulate frequently used presentation items, such as the menu for the website, defined in Header.ascx, and any disclaimers at the bottom, defined in Footer.ascx.

d. *Controls subsystem UML object diagram.*

Business Layer UML Object Diagram

The business layer contains two types of objects: business entities and business components. Business entities are in-memory documents containing selective data from the database. They are not strongly defined in classes; rather, they are represented with DataReader and DataSet classes, which are built into ADO.NET.

Business components contain the business logic of the application. While a user is on a website, he or she has the option to give a voice command to perform some task. The VoiceCommandListener component listens for these commands to come in from the speech application through a process that runs continuously while the user is on a page. When the process receives a command, it raises an event for a class in the presentation layer to interpret. The Md5Hash component uses the one-way MD5 hash to encrypt the customer's pin number. Only the encrypted pin is stored in the database for increased security.

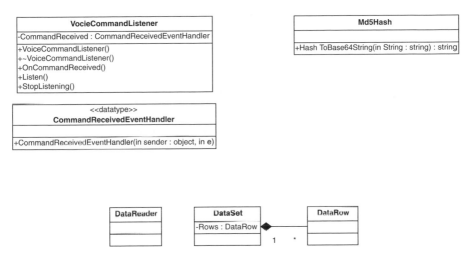

d. Business layer UML object diagram.

Data Access Layer UML Object Diagram

The components of the data access layer interact with the database and return business entities to the caller. Each class contains methods to create, read, update, and delete (CRUD) data. The one exception is the history component, because history should never change. The DalcHelper component contains all connection logic and information to the database. All components inherit this class, so they have access to all of its public and protected methods. The CRUD methods all call stored procedures in the database, which return, where applicable, only the data required.

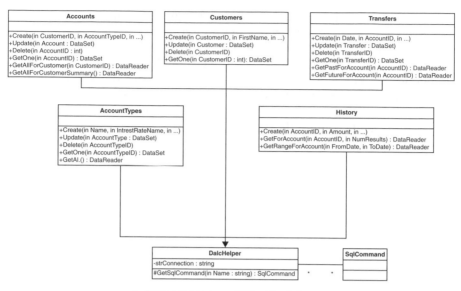

e. Data access layer UML object diagram.

Sign-In UML Sequence Diagram

The sign-in sequence shows the physical interaction between components. A user signs in through the SignIn.aspx Web page. That page calls SignIn () from a customerProcess object. That object hashes the pin and compares it with the pin in the database, retrieved from dalcCustomers. If the hashed pins match, customerProcess calls ShowAccounts () from uiProcess and redirects the customer to the Accounts.aspx page. If the pins do not match, the user is redirected back to the SignIn.aspx page.

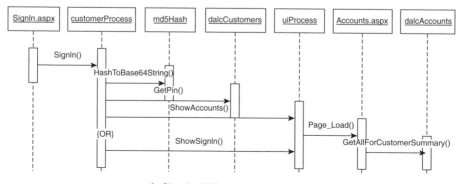

f. Sign-in UML sequence diagram.

Application Sequence Diagram

This sequence diagram shows selected parts of the overall application process. The top half of the sequence shows how different pages are loaded in the system. The bottom half shows how the VoiceCommandListener handles incoming voice commands, as described in the Business Layer UML Object Diagram section.

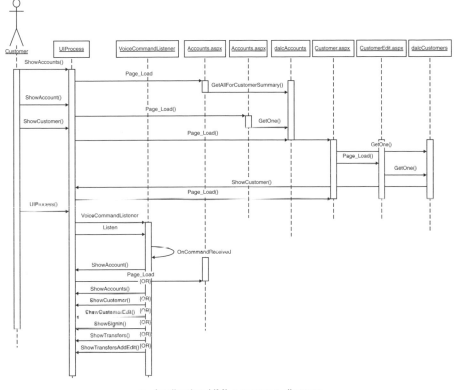

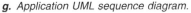

g. *Application UML sequence diagram.*

UML Use Case Diagram

This use case diagram shows the interaction of a customer and the pocket banking application and the various activities a customer can do with it. The customer can sign on or off, view accounts and details on that account including history, manage transfers, and manage their customer data.

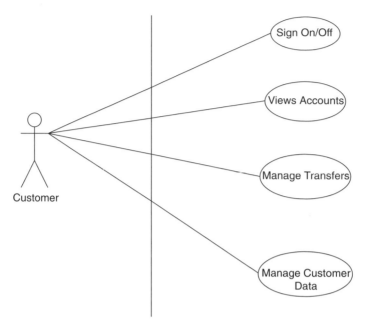

h. UML case diagram.

VIII. Function Point Analysis
By John-Paul Kosmyna and Brijesh Patel

Function Points

	Simple	Average	Complex
Input Types (I)	3	0	0
Output Types (O)	0	0	0
Inquiry Types (E)	5	0	0
Logical Input Files (L)	0	0	0
Interfaces (F)	4	0	0

Unadjusted Function Points

Input Types (I)	$(3 \times 3) + 0 + 0$	9
Output Types (O)	$0 + 0 + 0$	0
Inquiry Types (E)	$(5 \times 3) + 0 + 0$	15
Logical Input Files (L)	$0 + 0 + 0$	0
Interfaces (F)	$(5 \times 4) + 0 + 0$	20
Total Unadjusted Function Points		44

Degree of Influence

Data Communications	5
Distributed Functions	3
Performance	2
Heavily Used Configuration	4
Transaction Rate	4
Online Data Entry	3
End-User Efficiency	5
Online Update	0
Complex Processing	1
Reusability	1
Installation Ease	0
Operational Ease	5
Multiple Sites	0
Facilitate Change	1
Total Degree of Influence	30

Technical complexity factor = 0.65 + (0.01)DI.
TCF = 0.65 + 0.01(30).
TCF = 0.95.
Function points = Unadjusted function point × Total complexity factor.
Function points = 44 × 0.95.
Function points = 41.8.

IX. COCOMO
By John-Paul Kosmyna and Brijesh Patel

The COCOMO function is used for cost estimation. It uses two constants dependent on the category the project falls into and the kilo-lines of code (KLOC) in the project. We estimated the number of lines of code used in our project by using our function point analysis. The number of lines of code per function point is 53 (Applied Software Measurement, Capers Jones McGraw Hill, 1996). By using this information, we come up with the total lines of code needed by our project.

Total lines of code = 41.8 function points × 53 lines per

function point Total lines of code – 2215.4.
KLOC therefore equals 2.22.

$$E = bKLOC^c.$$

This project falls into the semidetached category. In a project falling into this category, the team may show a mixture of experienced and inexperienced people and the project may be fairly large, although not excessively large. We feel this is the best description of our team and project.

The basic COCOMO parameters for a semidetached project are $b = 3.0$ and $c = 1.12$ $E = 3.0$ $(2.22)^{1.12}$ $E = 7.328$ staff-months.

As students, the time we spend on a project is limited to the class time and free time we have. We estimate this as 10 hours per week per student as opposed to a 40-hour week for a professional in the field. Because we are students, we make the assumption of 1 student-month = 4 staff-months; therefore, our project will take 29.02 student-months. Student-months = 4×7.328 = 29.02.

Our team has a total of seven team members using the COCOMO estimation. This project will take our team 4.2 months. Following our grant chart, this proves the project can be completed in the time allotted.

$$29.2 \text{ student-months}/7 \text{ students} = 4.2 \text{ months}.$$

X. ICED-T
By John-Paul Kosmyna, Giuseppe Zappia, and Robert Volk

	Phone	Online	Pocket PC	In Person
Intuitive	2	3	4	5
Consistent	4	4	4	3
Efficient	3	4	5	2
Durable	4	4	4	1
Thoughtful	2	3	4	5

ICED-T

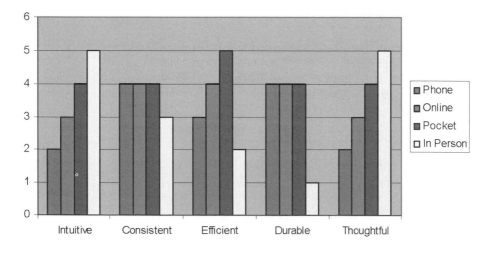

Intuitive—Although not being able to overpower the convenience of having a teller in front of you, our interface will prove to be more efficient than the telephone and normal online counterparts.

Consistency—Consistency will be identical to normal online banking, because they are the same. Using computers to do this task ensures greater consistency than having a person do these tasks.

Efficient—This project will far surpass the efficiency of having a person, telephone, or even a normal online solution. Adding the voice component is an integral part in allowing customers to get as much done as they can in as little time as possible.

Durability—Durability is consistent with online and phone systems, but far greater than having a teller.

Thoughtful—Although not being able to be as thoughtful as having a person present, the voice component will prove to be much more thoughtful than conventional online banking.

XI. Schedule Time
By Brijesh Patel

Although the COCOMO method says that we only need 7.32 staff-months for the development job, but as we are students, our calculated estimate is 29 student-months. In our group, we have seven students, so the actual estimate for the development job is 4.2 student-months. Our time period estimates that we have total 4.4 student-months. We estimate that our project can finish on time. This time estimate could be changed if required to finish up the project a month earlier.

Task	Start date	End Date	Current Est.	Days
Planning	10/27/04	11/09/04		9
Requirements	11/10/04	11/24/04		11
Architecture	01/10/05	01/24/05		11
Database Development	01/14/05	01/26/05		9
Grammar XML	01/10/05	01/24/05		11
Design UI Web Page Flow Chart	01/10/05	01/24/05		11
Coding Revision V1.0	01/25/05	02/14/05		15
Testing	02/15/05	03/02/05		12
Debugging	02/15/05	03/02/05		12
Code Revision V1.2	03/03/05	03/22/05		15
Testing	03/23/05	03/31/05		7
Debugging	03/23/05	03/31/05		7
Code (Final) Revision V1.3	04/01/05	04/14/05		10
Testing	04/15/05	04/25/05		7
Debugging	04/15/05	04/25/05		7
Documentaion	09/15/04	03/30/05		129

XII. Demonstration Plan
By Nathan Olcott and Robert Volk

Our product needs to run on a pocket PC, but because of lack of funds, to demonstrate the product, we will be using a pocket PC emulator running on a laptop with a 1-GHz processor, 256 MB or RAM, and Windows XP service pack 2. Although the computer has much better specifications than a pocket PC, which only has a 400-MHz processor and 64 MB of RAM, the demonstration will still be accurate because the emulator also emulates the speed and RAM of the pocket PC. Provided below are screenshots of the program running on a pocket PC emulator.

XIII. Product Testing
By Nathan Olcott, Seung-Ho Won, and J. P. Kosmyna

Our product will be thoroughly tested using regression testing and unit testing. Some other types of testing that will be performed include functional testing, integration testing, and stress testing. Below is a comprehensive plan to test the result of our code using the pocket PC running a SALT-enabled browser to run our Web application.

Regression Testing
Regression testing assures that features already implemented in previous versions of our software work in all current versions. Test cases run on the first version must run and pass on any subsequent version.

Unit Testing
Various use cases will be executed to ensure that all aspects of the functional requirements are met. This set of use cases will include both realistic and unrealistic scenarios to test the system's ability to detect and handle errors. Parameters will be passed to individual functions, and results will be checked for correctness. We will be using the NUnit test tool for unit testing of C# code.

Functional Testing
Being the type of testing where a developer (usually the one who wrote the code) proves that a code module (the "unit") meets its requirements, the main purpose of this test would be the validity of the result of XML and HTML codes. Units that can be broken up for testing are the individual XML, HTML, as well as the individual tables of the database (SQL server). XML and HTML take in two kinds of inputs: user input and database queries. Each XML document will be considered a unit, and it will be tested independently using valid and invalid inputs. Each table of the database will be considered a separate unit as well and will be verified to accept only valid inputs.

Integrating Testing
A type of testing in which software and/or hardware components are combined and tested to confirm that they interact according to their requirements, we will check the connection of the pocket PC to our web server, web server and SQL server, vice versa, pocket PC to speech server, and speech server to web server, and test that it is working on its maximum capability.

Stress Testing
Because stress testing is aimed at investigating the behavior of software or hardware equipment in unusual operating conditions, it will be tested with realistic and unrealistic scenarios. The production version will be moved to a hosting facility environment for testing.

Hardware required:

- Pocket PCs
- Windows 2003 Server
- IIS Web Server
- Speech Server
- SQL Server

Software required:

- Visual Studio.NET (Version 2003)
- Visual Studio Framework Version 1.1
- Database (SQL Server)
- Version Control Software
- Speech Server
- SALT Enabled Browser

Pocket PC Emulator _ □ X

pocket banking

ACCOUNTS | PAYMENTS & TRANSFERS | ACCOUNT SERVICING | HELP | SIGN OFF

Account Details & Activity

DETAILS   Select an account... ▾

Checking: xxxxx222

	$12,000.00	on deposit
	$12,000.00	available now
Total:	$12,000.00	

◀ Menu   ◀ Account Summary   View More History ▶

ACTIVITY   Sort Order: Select a sort order.. ▾

Date	Description	Amount	End-of-Day Balance
10-31	CASH WITHDRAWL	-$100.00	$12,000.00
10-29	DEBIT CARD PURCHASE SHADY RECORD STORE	-$10.00	$12,100.00
10-28	DEPOSIT	$5,010.00	$12,110.00
10-27	CASH WITHDRAWL	-$500.00	$7,100.00
10-26	DEPOSIT	$1000.00	$7,600.00
10-25	DEBIT CARD PURCHASE	-$100.00	$6,600.00
10-24	DEBIT CARD PURCHASE	-$50.00	$6,700.00
10-23	DEBIT CARD PURCHASE	-$1000.00	$6,750.00
10-22	CASH WITHDRAWL	-$500.00	$7,750.00
10-21	DEPOSIT	$4000.00	$7,250.00
10-18	CASH WITHDRAWL	-$500.00	$3,250.00

Pocket PC Emulator

pocket banking

ACCOUNTS | PAYMENTS & TRANSFERS | ACCOUNT SERVICING | HELP | SIGN OFF

Payments & Transfers

Make a Transfer

Say 'From Account' then the from account name. Then say 'To Account' and the to account name.

From Account   Select an account...

To Account   Select an account...

◀ Menu   Cancel   Next ▶

Transfers Between Linked Accounts

- Set up a Recurring Transfer
- See, Change or Cancel Future Transfers
- See Past Transfers

12.4 THE REST OF THE STORY

Even with this preparation, things go wrong. These is no sQFD, so when problems arose, the team was not able to nimbly discard functions. When two of the seven students slacked off, the team could not compensate for their lost work. The project was incomplete and buggy at the end of the semester. The end-product earned less than an A, which was half the grade; the other half of the grade was for the process used. The students commented that staffing was inadequate and they would have preferred to have 10 people. This project brought home to the students the truth of the maxim, "Even the best processes, tools and technology cannot make up for poor project management."

12.5 OUR HOPE

We want to encourage outstanding people to produce trustworthy products by working with discipline and care for the future of their product. Both the software industry and its customers must insist, at minimum, on this basic code of behavior.

A software architect and a project manager are identified by name for each project; both attest that the software is fit for use.

They analyze software project risks and document their findings.

They make sure that user interfaces are intuitive and easy to use, that "help" is helpful, that private information is protected and that the software is safe for humans.

They understand the larger environment of the specific problem and will educate the customer, if need be, to the appropriate solution.

They follow formal, documented software development processes.

They respect property, copyright, patent and privacy rights.

They publicly advocate ethical behavior.

Index

Trustworthy Systems Through Quantitative Software Engineering,
by Lawrence Bernstein and C. M. Yuhas
Copyright © 2005 IEEE Computer Society